CW01184236

Davenport

I. John Davenport MP. A portrait
in oils by John Philip RA *c.*1840.
(Courtesy Major David Davenport)

Davenport

China, Earthenware, Glass

Terence A. Lockett and
Geoffrey A. Godden

BARRIE & JENKINS
LONDON

First published in Great Britain in 1989 by
Barrie & Jenkins Ltd
289 Westbourne Grove, London W11 2QA

Copyright © Terence Lockett and Geoffrey Godden 1989

All rights reserved. No parts of this publication may be
reproduced, stored in a retrieval system, or transmitted
in any form or by any means, electronic, mechanical,
photocopying, recording or otherwise, without prior
permission in writing from the publisher.

British Library Cataloguing in Publication Data

Lockett, Terence A. (Terence Anthony), *1931–*
 Davenport: china, earthenware, glass.
 1. Pottery. Porcelain. Staffordshire pottery.
 Staffordshire porcelain. Staffordshire pottery &
 porcelain. Davenport pottery. Davenport porcelain.
 Davenport pottery & porcelain.
 I. Title II. Godden, Geoffrey A. (Geoffrey Arthur),
 1929–
 738.2′09424′63

 ISBN 0-7126-2002-8

Typeset by SX Composing Ltd, Rayleigh, Essex

Printed and bound in Great Britain by
Richard Clay Ltd, Bungay, Suffolk

Contents

Acknowledgements	6
Introduction	7
Part One: The Family and Factory	9
1 John Davenport 1765–c.1810	10
2 The Davenport Family	19
3 Politics and Country Life	26
4 Warehouses, Agencies, and Exports	31
5 John Davenport – The Later Years	41
6 William Davenport & Co., 1835–69	51
7 Henry Davenport and Davenports Ltd, 1869–87	63
Part Two: Earthenwares and Stonewares	71
8 The Earthenware and Stoneware Marks	72
9 Creamware and Pearlware	76
10 Coloured-body Earthenware	92
11 Black Basalt	97
12 Caneware and Terracotta	101
Caneware	101
Terracotta	106
13 White Felspathic Stoneware	110
14 Stone China	114
15 Transfer Printed Wares	122
Transfer printing	125
Underglaze blue printed patterns	135
Multicoloured printed wares and flown blue	165
16 Miscellaneous and Later Earthenwares	176
Part Three: The Porcelains	199
17 The Early Davenport Porcelains	200
18 Porcelain Marks	209
19 The Teawares	212
20 Dessert Wares	233
21 Dinner Services	256
22 Useful Wares	259
23 Ornamental Objects	263
24 Painters and Gilders	272
Part Four: Davenport Glass	281
Appendix: The Registered Shapes and Patterns 1849–1886	293
Sources and Bibliography	296
Index	299

Acknowledgements

It is a truism that without the generous help of many people, collectors, curators, photographers, and fellow researchers and enthusiasts, books such as this would never be written. The list of those whom we wish to thank is long, but were we to try to include every single person who has ever written to either of us giving a snippet of information or sending a photograph of a treasured or problem pot, the list would be enormous. There are others who were acknowledged in 1972 in *Davenport Pottery & Porcelain* whose names we have not repeated in this list. We do hope we have not omitted on this occasion anyone whose help we should have acknowledged, and at the same time we send our thanks to all those who have corresponded with us over the years. Even if not acknowledged individually your contribution has not been forgotten. Similarly, we are grateful to those who have supplied information or photographs, but for various reasons wish to remain anonymous.

Our chief thanks for supplying us with documentary references and assistance with the history of the factory goes to Ronald B. Brown and Rodney Hampson, both of whom most generously placed their own research files at our disposal. We are also grateful to Major David Davenport for kind permission to study the family documents, and to use the painting of John Davenport as our Frontispiece. In this aspect of the work we have enjoyed complete co-operation from Christine Fyfe and Margaret Morris in the University of Keele Library; from the staffs of the Hereford and Stafford County libraries, and in particular from Arnold Mountford CBE, formerly Director of the City Museum and Art Gallery, Stoke-on-Trent, and the present members of the Ceramic Department, Pat Halfpenny, the Keeper, and her colleagues Kathy Niblett and Deborah Skinner who have directed Davenport material our way over many years. Similarly, Gaye Blake Roberts, Lynn Miller and Sharon Gater of the Wedgwood Museum, Barlaston have been ever helpful.

We should particularly like to thank Sir Geoffrey de Bellaigue, Surveyor of the Queen's Works of Art, and Mrs Julia Harland for information about the various Royal services, especially that for William IV which is illustrated by Gracious permission of Her Majesty the Queen.

It would be difficult to overestimate the help we have received over the years from Miss Diana Darlington and we are especially grateful to her, to Mr Jack Hacking and Mrs Trixie Iwass for giving us the freedom of their collections to illustrate this book and for hundreds of hours of thought-provoking discussion on Davenport matters. Mr Alan Cleaver and Bevis and Ann Walters have similarly given us free access to their collections, the illustrations from which have been most important for the book.

The illustrations have been prepared for us with professional thoroughness and care by Roy Chatburn of Darwen, Derek Evans of Hereford, Walter Gardiner Photography of Worthing, Chris Halton of Messrs Phillips, Geoffrey Taylor of Hazel Grove, and Stephen Yates of Rossendale. Additionally, we have used photographs taken by photographers at Messrs Asprey's, Messrs Christie's, Messrs Phillips, Messrs Sotheby & Co., Messrs Sotheby's West Sussex, Messrs Henry Spencer & Sons Retford; the Liverpool Museum, the Los Angeles County Museum, the Royal Ontario Museum, Spode Museum Collection Trust, City Museum & Art Gallery Stoke-on-Trent, and the Victoria and Albert Museum.

We have been especially pleased to receive information from a number of correspondents overseas. These include staff at the Boston Museum of Fine Arts, Mrs Leslie Bowman of the Los Angeles County Museum, Mrs Elizabeth Collard of Ottawa, Mrs Nancy Dickenson of Riverside, Connecticut, Mr George L. Miller of Colonial Williamsburg, Mr Edward Monsson of Los Angeles, Mr Alan Powell of Ottawa, Janice Queener-Shaw of the Edward Dean Museum of Decorative Arts, Cherry Valley, California, and staff at the Smithsonian Institution, Washington.

We end these very sincere thanks with a note to those who have supplied us with information, reported wares to us, or kindly allowed us to illustrate pieces from their stock or private collections. To all our thanks. Mrs Elizabeth Adams, Mrs Pauline Agius, Mrs Audrey Atterbury, Miss Stella Beddoe of the Brighton Museum, Mr Harold Blakey, Mr Merrick Bousefield, Mr H. Gilbert Bradley, Mr W. Broad, Mr and Mrs R. Chambers, Mr E. H. Chandler, Mr F. Cherry, Mrs Clarke, Mr L. A. Compton, Mr Robert Copeland, Dr Alwyn and Mrs Angela Cox, Mr John Cushion, Mr John Davenport, Mr W. A. Davenport, Mrs G. Finney, the late Stanley W. Fisher, Mr and Mrs J. K. des Fontaines, the late Rupert Gentle, Messrs Geoffrey Godden, chinaman, Messrs Godden of Worthing Ltd, Messrs David Golding, Messrs Jill Gosling, Messrs Graham & Oxley, Mr Jonathan Gray, the late Nancy Gunson, the late Reginald G. Haggar, Jeanette Hayhurst, Mr Martin Hutton, Mrs Margaret Ironside, His Hon. Judge Christopher James, Mrs Muriel Jones, Mr Patrick Latham, Messrs John Leslie Antiques, Mrs J. Magness, Mr Philip Miller, Mrs W. S. Manor, Mrs Jennifer Moody, Ms Rene Nicholls, Mr & Mrs R. Peers, Mr John A. Potter, Mrs Betty Reed, Mr C. Rhead, Mr L. Richmond, Mrs Jean Sewell, Mr D. Sherborn, Mr and Mrs Anthony Thomas, Messrs J. & E. Vandekar, and Arthur Wood & Sons Ltd.

May we reiterate our thanks to the many hundreds of people whose names do not appear above, but who have all helped in one way or another to make this book possible.

Finally, and most important of all, are our wives, Isabel and Jean who have tolerated our preoccupation with 'the book' with their usual cheerfulness – and we can't even promise we will never write another one!

Introduction

It is now seventeen years since the first and only book on the Davenport factory was published. *Davenport Pottery & Porcelain 1794–1887*, moreover, was written to a formula with a tightly controlled number of words and illustrations. In some respects it has stood the test of time reasonably well, in others it is seriously in need of updating. It was always the intention of the author, Terence Lockett, to write a larger and improved version when time permitted. In the meantime, as the bibliography indicates, there have been several articles published, an Exhibition has been held at Blackburn, and a week-long Summer School held at the University of Keele. These have all provided the opportunity to add more details to the history of the factory, and to describe and illustrate new shapes, forms and decorations of wares which have been discovered with remarkable consistency in the years since 1972.

By the mid 1980s so much new material was available that the time seemed appropriate to begin the task of preparing a new and fuller study. By happy chance Geoffrey Godden was approached by our publishers about the possibility of a book on Davenport, which was generously and immediately discussed jointly, with what we hope is a most fruitful outcome of a very pleasant co-authorship. No prizes will be awarded for those who claim on stylistic – or any other grounds – to be able to tell 't'other from which'!

We wish to stress that this is a completely new book. It is not a repetition of the 1972 work in any manner. Indeed we have gone out of our way to provide new illustrations wherever possible, and to use documentary material that was either unpublished or had only appeared in journals with a limited circulation. Thus on both the history and on the wares there is a wealth of new material in this book, including a full chapter on the glasswares which were totally omitted from the earlier book. There is a much expanded and more detailed treatment of both the early porcelain wares and of the early earthenwares and stonewares. We have also made a special study of the blue printed and multicoloured printed wares of the period 1794–c.1844. The list of patterns published here for the first time cannot be definitive and new examples will undoubtedly emerge in the years ahead. Equally certainly there will be modifications to the views expressed on some of the other wares, especially on the early porcelains and on the marking of the earliest of the earthenwares. But this is as it should be. We hope that collectors and curators will make exciting new discoveries and either publish their findings themselves or let us or other interested parties know about them.

The Davenport concern was one of the most important in the nineteenth century. It was one of the leading quartet of potteries, along with Minton, Spode/Copeland, and, despite fluctuating fortunes, the inevitable Wedgwood. Davenport's export trade was probably as large as any in the industry. Moreover, the story of both factory and family – which is a fascinating one – can be told using contemporary documents which we hope will enable the reader to see the people as well as the pots.

To avoid any confusion with the earlier publication we have used as our title the style which the firm itself adopted on its billheads for many years. For nearly a century the Davenport family at their factories at Longport in Staffordshire were highly successful, and alone amongst English potters were able to claim truthfully that they were 'Manufacturer to Their Majesties' of 'China, Earthenware and Glass.'

February 1989

Terence A. Lockett
Geoffrey A. Godden

Part One :
The Family and Factory

1   John Davenport 1765–c.1810

John Davenport was born on 29 September 1765 in a small house in Derby Street, Leek, in Staffordshire. He died over eighty-three years later in his country home of Westwood, near Leek on 12 December 1848. In the years between, he had founded a business which was known throughout the world, had received the patronage of his sovereign, had been a Member of Parliament or as he expressed it, elected 'to the highest honour obtainable to an English commoner,' and made a very considerable fortune. His story is a fascinating one, not exactly the classical rags to riches epic, but considering that his father died when John was only six, and that his success was gained in an industry with which his family had no previous connection, it is certainly a remarkable achievement.

    John Sleigh (see Sources and Bibliography for details) traces a family pedigree back to 1585, and it would seem that the family were of yeoman stock. In the Foxley Papers there is a document which lists various deeds in which the name of Davenport occurs and we can read of a Richard Davenport who in 1739 is described as 'Late High Sheriff of the County of Staffordshire'. There is a Jonathan Davenport a farmer of Buglawton, John Davenport 'a gentleman' of Leek, and James Davenport a baker in Leek in the 1770s: a family then of the Staffordshire and Derbyshire area with many and varied branches.

    After the death of his father, Jonathan Davenport, John is said to have been removed from school and sent to work. This may be the case, but his level of education as revealed in future years would lead one to suspect this story. It is also alleged that whilst working for Lucas Brothers, button and silk twist manufacturers, the firm went bankrupt, and John's mother Elizabeth lost her 'small fortune' in the enterprise. It is then recorded that John went to Newcastle to work in the bank of Mr Kinnersley where he remained until 1785, when at the age of twenty, having completed his articles, he was offered a post by Thomas Wolfe the well-known pottery manufacturer of Stoke. As with so many of the incidents in the early life of John Davenport, we are heavily reliant for any information on the writings of Ward, Sleigh, and Jewitt, supplemented by occasional references, usually published after his death, in the *Staffordshire Advertiser* or the *Pottery Gazette*. Thus it appears that Wolfe employed Davenport firstly as agent or manager in his Dublin warehouse and then from 1786 at Liverpool, where Wolfe had a considerable export business which is said to have been further developed in both America and India by the young Davenport. It is also recorded that in 1788 he went to France where he spent a year on the firm's business and thereafter became a fluent French speaker, and possibly acquired some knowledge of French porcelain manufacturing methods. There is good evidence that at some point around 1788 Wolfe took Davenport into partnership in the management of his dockside warehouses in Liverpool (*Pottery Gazette*, Fancy Trades Supplement, 1 March 1893).

    In Gore's Directory for 1790, there is an entry listing John Davenport as 'Staffordshire Merchant' of 46 Hurst Street. So it would appear that by this time the twenty-five-year-old felt he had sufficient experience to launch out as an independent dealer in pottery, as well as remaining a partner of Wolfe's. It has been stated on a number of occasions that Davenport became a partner of Wolfe's in the Islington China Manufactory. This statement was made by Reginald Haggar in his *Masons of Lane Delph* (1952) and by myself in my 1972 Davenport book. Detailed research by John Murray on both Wolfe and Pennington has revealed that the Islington China factory was in the occupation of Mrs Jane Pennington until November 1794 and that Wolfe did not take over here until 20 October 1795. My fellow author Geoffrey Godden in a private research paper has summarized the position and it seems clear that John Davenport was not concerned with the porcelain enterprise, which traded as Wolfe & Co. His relationship with Wolfe is admirably summed up in the two notices which announce the dissolution of their Liverpool partnership. *The London Gazette* No. 13713 of 14 October 1794 carries the following notice:

Liverpool. Sept. 23rd 1794
The partnership late carried on in Liverpool by Messrs Thomas Wolfe and John Davenport, Dealers in earthenware under the name or firm of Thomas Wolfe & Company, is this day dissolved by mutual consent. All persons indebted to the said concern are desired to pay their respective Debts to Mr. William Pownall of Liverpool, who is duly authorised to receive the same.
Thomas Wolfe. John Davenport. William Pownall.

It seems clear from this notice that the partners were 'Dealers in Earthenware', and that their partnership did not include the manufacture of either earthenware or porcelain.

However, just two days later, the following notice was published in the *Liverpool General Advertiser* (25 September 1794):

Staffordshire Warehouse.
The partnership concern heretofore carried on by Thomas Wolfe & Co. in Liverpool, in the Manufacturing and selling of earthenware and glass and conducted by the said John Davenport, being now dissolved by mutual consent, John Davenport begs leave to inform the public in general that he continues on his own account to carry on the business of Manufacturing and Selling Earthenware and glasses, in his warehouse on the south side of the old dock lately occupied by Mr. Joseph Leay, where the orders of his friends and the public will be attended to and executed with punctuality and despatch.

It is perhaps a little disconcerting to read that John Davenport continues 'to carry on the business of Manufacturing and Selling Earthenware and glasses'. However, it should be remembered that many dealers styled themselves manufacturers at this time, and there is no evidence whatsoever that John Davenport was at this date manufacturing either earthenware or glass, either alone or in association with a partner. Thus Geoffrey Godden seems totally vindicated in his belief that Davenport's business activities in Liverpool were entirely confined to dealing and not manufacturing.

Clearly, by 1794, John Davenport was experienced in the marketing and selling of earthenware, porcelain, and glass. He had been in the trade for nearly ten years associated with a major manufacturer, about whom alas, we know all too little. This wide experience in Ireland, France, and Liverpool no doubt gave him the confidence to take the next step from being simply a merchant to becoming a manufacturer of his own wares. In 1794 when he purchased the Unicorn pottery in Longport he was in his thirtieth year, but, as far as we can judge, had no direct experience of manufacture. In this respect he differed greatly from many of his celebrated contemporaries who came from families with a long background of employment in the pottery industry. The mere names are redolent of the dynasties of the Stoke-on-Trent area: Spode, Wedgwood, Adams, even Minton. Into this distinguised company there entered a man who, as far as we can ascertain, had never thrown a pot in his life, nor worked a single day on a pot bank. It is worth emphasizing this aspect of the career of John Davenport. He was first and foremost a businessman, not a potter, indeed it is probably wrong to call him a master potter as I did in another publication. He was a merchant or dealer who must have felt that he could make more money from being involved in both the production and distribution of the wares. In this, as time was to prove, he was surely correct.

The pottery which he purchased in 1794 stood on the banks of the canal at Longport and had been erected in 1773 as premises for the potter John Brindley, the brother of the canal engineer James. The map of the area (Plate 1) though dated 1832 still gives a good idea of the site and shows its relationship to future acquisitions by the

Davenports. We can only assume, there is no documentary evidence either way, that this was a going concern, and the workers were retained and production of wares continued. What precisely these were is again unknown, but creamwares, pearlwares, and blue printed wares being the staple of the pottery trade, we must assume that such items formed the bulk of the production of Unicorn Bank. Davenport is said to have extended the works and Plate 2 shows the factory entrance as it was before demolition in the early 1960s. As can be seen, it is a three-storied building with central arch and pointed niche and projecting bays. It would seem to be this building which was added by John Davenport in the early years of his ownership, as well, possibly, as other workshops. To the left of the main entrance stood the house which he was to occupy for several years, illustrated in Plate 3. This was Longport House, which it is said had originally been built by Brindley. As with many such dwellings in the area in the eighteenth century, the bottle oven is virtually in the back garden, if indeed there was any such luxury as a back garden.

It is perhaps appropriate at this point to indicate that parts of Unicorn Bank still stand at the time of writing, and can easily be viewed by going north-west from Trubshaw Cross to the area between Davenport Street and the canal, and then walking along the canal bank at the back of the works as the entire Keele University Ceramic Summer

1. Map of Longport in 1832. From T. Hargreaves, 'Map of the Staffordshire Potteries & Newcastle-under-Lyme' (1832, p. 19).

2. Façade of the Unicorn Bank Works *c.*1960 just prior to demolition.

3. Longport House *c.*1960, just prior to demolition.

12 · The Family and Factory

4. A rather forlorn relic of the main factory just prior to final demolition. (Courtesy J. K. des Fontaines, taken August 1968)

5. Canal-side remains of Unicorn Bank c.1968. (Courtesy J. K. des Fontaines)

6. Entrance to Arthur Wood & Son's factory showing some of the surviving buildings from the Davenport Unicorn Bank site. (Author's photograph, 1987)

School did in August 1987 – all 140 of them. Other sites associated with Davenport still stand and these will be mentioned in the appropriate place in the text. Plate 4 shows the last remnant of the central building just before demolition, and in Plate 5 the derelict canal-side workshops can be seen. However, a substantial portion of the factory still remains in the occupation of Arthur Wood & Sons and Plate 6 shows the present main entrance to their works, of which some of the buildings certainly formed a part of the pottery when it was occupied by the Davenport factory. The chimney can clearly be seen on the large panorama of the works in 1888, still retained in the boardroom of Woods and reproduced here as Plate 7. As indicated, other portions of this part of the factory can be seen from the canal bank which runs along the back of the factory. There are alas, no

13 · The Family and Factory

bottle ovens left standing from this section of the pottery, though some impression of them can be gained from an illustration in D. M. Palliser, *The Staffordshire Landscape* (1976).

It is fascinating to be able still to visit the site which John Davenport bought in 1794 to begin an enterprise which was to last for almost a century. Though nowhere nearly as impressive as it was even thirty years ago, this site and the adjacent properties which the Davenports were eventually to occupy give a substance and an immediacy to the pots we treasure in our cabinets. A pilgrimage is strongly recommended to all collectors of Davenport.

In the year following his move to Longport John Davenport married at Whitmore on 8 December. His bride was Diana Smart Ward, daughter of Michael Ward of Newcastle and reputedly she brought with her a substantial sum of money. Details of their family and the part they played in the business are given later (pp. 19–25). As yet no document has come to light indicating the extent of the fortune Miss Ward brought with her, but there is no doubt that Davenport prospered in the early years of his new business venture as a pottery manufacturer. We are fortunate that there has survived in the Foxley Papers at the Hereford County Record office a Private Ledger of John Davenport (Foxley Papers S 47). From it we learn that he entered a co-partnership with his cousin James Davenport on 1 January 1797. On that day the value of the 'Premises, Stock & balance of debts' was £10,011 0s 9d. To modern ears this may not seem a very great amount, but when his workers were earning only about £1 or 25s a week, this would represent in modern money something of the order of between £750,000 to a million pounds. No mean sum of money for a manufacturer who had been in business only three years or so. That these had been years of success seems very evident, and that success was to continue as all the surviving evidence clearly indicates.

Though he was not to know it, John Davenport had begun his career as a manufacturer at a somewhat inauspicious time. Britain was to be at war with France for most of the first twenty-five years of his venture. For a manufacturer who was especially anxious to expand his overseas markets this must have been somewhat frustrating, but his business acumen and the skill of those he employed seem to have made light of the difficulties. There was the immediate impact of the war in that during the invasion 'scare' of 1803, *Major* Davenport raised four companies of the Volunteer Corps each of eighty rank and file troops. As Ward states, 'this gallant corps Mr Davenport brought into a high state of discipline.' The property which he and his volunteers were defending in 1803 was a greater one than it had been six years earlier when he and James Davenport entered their partnership, for in 1801 on a site adjacent to the potworks he erected a Glass Works. An outline of this side of his activities is given later. It was certainly a bold venture, for though the selling of pottery and glass frequently went hand in hand, as they still do,

7. Photographic panorama of the factory in 1888. The now demolished central portion can be seen on the left and to its left Longport House. This panorama was reproduced in an article entitled 'Davenport Site Re-assembled' recording the acquisition of the Unicorn Works by Arthur Wood & Son in *Pottery Gazette and Glass Trade Review*, May 1959. (Courtesy Arthur Wood & Son)

there was no other manufacturer in the Potteries, or indeed elsewhere in Great Britain, who combined the manufacture of the two wares, least of all on the same site.

Critical for the success of the glass works was the financial support of his old patron Thomas Kinnersley, the Newcastle banker, and the technical expertise of Edward Grafton, a Stourbridge glass maker. The three formed a partnership and traded as Davenport, Kinnersley and Grafton. The bringing of Grafton to manage the glass works was a typical move by Davenport. He seems throughout his career to have been prepared to extend the range of his activities by employing talented specialists. In 1800, a year before the glass works was opened, another specialist was taken on in the pottery who also was to work in the glass department. This was Thomas Lakin.

Detailed research on the life and work of Thomas Lakin has been carried out by Harold Blakey and published in the *Journal of the Northern Ceramic Society* 5, 1984. His involvement with Davenport seems to have lasted for about ten years, from *c*.1800 until sometime in 1810. The precise nature of his function at Davenports is rather obscure. He was certainly a man of importance to the enterprise as he occupied a house and offices with an insurance value of £400. He was never a partner in either the glass or pottery business, but in a handbill advertising his *Receipts* published posthumously by his widow in 1824 we read that he was thirty years in industry 'a considerable proportion of this period as principal manager of the extensive China and Earthenware Manufactory of John Davenport'. However, when the booklet appeared the preface stressed Lakin's glass making activities, noting that 'several windows of exquisite workmanship were executed by him for some of the first noblemen of the kingdom.' He was a First Lieutenant and later a Captain in Davenport's Longport Volunteers. Research principally by Ronald Brown has indicated that Lakin's glass work was supplied to the Duke of Devonshire, the Marquess of Stafford, the Earl of Uxbridge, and Earl Grosvenor (*Journal of the Glass Association* 1, 1985). His pottery activities are less easy to pin down. He certainly appears to have had a very detailed and scientific approach to glaze and enamel colours for pottery decoration, and in certain areas, for example the chalcedony body and glazes (see pp. 92–6) there are marked similarities between the products of Davenport in the years when Lakin was in a managerial position and those of his own pottery after 1810 when he became an independent potter. We can never prove the point entirely, but there is good circumstantial evidence that Thomas Lakin had a strong influence on the decoration and design of Davenport pottery and porcelain, as well as upon the glass ware, in the decade when he was employed at Longport. So far no evidence has been produced to account for his departure in 1810.

With the opening of the glass works and the employment of Lakin and Grafton, John and James Davenport were well set for a decade of prosperity. Some indication of the extent of this prosperity can be gleaned from the Private Ledger mentioned earlier. It gives us a more personal and intimate indication of the lifestyle of John Davenport at this particularly successful period of his career. An entry headed 'Furniture and Books' indicates that on 1 January 1797 these were valued at £400; ten years later on 1 July 1807 he valued them at £1609 14s 3d. This, of course, in an era of minimal inflation. He 'P'd Bourne for Painting at House' £17 17s 6d on 9 December 1807, and on the same day paid 16s 3d for new potatoes. At Christmas that year he showed a generosity with which he was not always credited. He gave £2 2s 0d to the Militia (for seasonal celebration perhaps?), he 'gave old Graham' £1 0s 0d on the same day, and on New Year's Day 1808 the bell-ringer was given 2s 6d, as was 'a poor woman'. But these are paltry sums compared with the purchase on 19 March 1806 of Grand Junction Canal shares to the value of £1418 2s 6d and Rochdale Canal shares totalling £945 3s 6d in the period 2 April 1806 to 9 August 1810. Even his newspaper bill paid on 20 July 1808 amounted to £4 3s 6d. He records that in the period 28 July 1807 to 4 August 1808 he spent the following sums in total: 'House', £19 17s 6d, 'House Extras', £74 10s 4d, 'Cloath'g', £146 17s 10d (his tailor was a Mr Hulme), 'Incid.', £93 4s 6d, 'Furniture' £68 3s 3d. Some of the 'Incid.' and

'Extras' over the years make interesting reading. He notes in 'Sundries owing to my private account', J & R Riley '3 dinner tickets on china biscuit £1 2s 6d' (1803); 'Thomas Lakin, 2 pr blankets £1 4s 6d' (1803); 'Edward Grafton 1 looking glass £3 13s 6d' (Oct. 1802); 'Payments to Longport Volunteers for p. cake (?) £2 17s 0d' (Oct. 1807); 'Piano forte & instructions £62 4s 8d' (24 Nov. 1809). In 1809 he pays 'Walker for spirits £17 0s 0d' and 'Smith, books £14 3s 5d'. There are many more fascinating items of this kind such as the telescope purchased for £3 3s 0d on 21 June 1807 or the soda water at just 1s 9d. Bearing in mind the necessary multiplication factor it is easy to see that John Davenport lead an affluent life at this period. He calculates with an accuracy that would put most modern accountants to shame that in the three and a half years from July 1807 to December 1810 'House expenses' were £3983 0s 7d. A modern equivalent would be in the region of £100,000 a year. I think many of us would settle for that!

The source of this wealth was not exclusively the pottery and the glass manufactories. There are no surviving accounts from either for this period to indicate just how successful they were, and how much they contributed to the overall income of John Davenport. But it must not be forgotten that he ran a very successful warehouse business in Liverpool in which, as far as we can tell, it was not only his own wares which were sold (see p. 31). By 1807 there was also a London showroom. Thomas Byerley writing back to Josiah Wedgwood II at Etruria reports that 'Davenport has taken the Shakespeare gallery for an exhibition of his glass, E'ware and China,' and adds that 'I am not at all frightened of this' (E. Meteyard, *A Group of Englishmen*, 1871, p. 338).

Nor was it just the manufactories and the showrooms. The private ledger shows John Davenport investing as we have already seen in canals (incidentally he received a dividend of £202 10s 0d on his Grand Junction shares in October 1810). He also purchased property on a considerable scale. In 1804 he added the Cliff Bank pottery in Stoke to his holdings, which according to the Foxley papers was leased to the Executors of James Smith for £108 per annum in 1805. The lessee was William Adams. In 1806 he purchased four fields and Parrs Croft together with 16 acres for £735. He had land in Wolverhampton, property in Manchester and Wolstanton, and a half share in woodland at Breadstone in Gloucestershire. This alone produced a payment of £973 in March 1809. These may not represent his entire holdings by any means, they are a sample culled from some of the available records. There may be many more details awaiting the diligent researcher with a taste for the jargon of 'hereditaments', 'appurtenances', and the like. For example there are references to the 'Beeches Taw house' estate and 'the cottages'. Suffice to say that with his usual thoroughness John Davenport summarized his position by reckoning that from 25 March 1806 to 19 June 1809 his costs for the purchases of property were £3247 4s 0d. Once more something in the region of £100,000 per annum in modern currency was being invested in property – this of course quite distinct from his canal investments and his shares in coal mining and other activities.

Surely the most eloquent testimony to the standing and repute of John Davenport within the industry at this time is provided by the visit to 'Messrs Davenport's Manufactory of Ornamental Pottery and China Wares, and Messrs Kinnersley, Davenport and Graftons Glass Works at Longport' by His Royal Highness the Prince of Wales and his brother the Duke of Clarence in September 1806. The future George IV and his brother the future William IV had been staying at Trentham Park with the Marquess of Stafford, and as is the custom of royalty had visited some of the important enterprises in the locality. Just three potteries were visited, those of Spode, Wedgwood, and the pottery and glass works of John Davenport. This must have been a proud occasion for a man who had been a manufacturer for only a dozen years, and a glass maker for a mere five. The report from the *Staffordshire Advertiser* for 20 September 1806 is quoted later (p. 200) and full details of 'a collection of the most beautiful and highly finished specimens' ordered from both the glass works and the Pottery are given in the appropriate chapters on the wares. It is perhaps worth noting at this point that the royal order of 1806 is the first direct evidence of the kind of wares that Davenport was making. As will be seen in subsequent sections it has not been easy to identify and date the products of the first ten years of the Pottery's life, even though it is obvious from the text of this chapter that great quantities of ware had been produced with considerable commercial success. The royal order gives a positive and specific date for the production of certain classes of goods which can thereby be identified. Nevertheless, it is still true that compared with the two great potteries mentioned above, Spode and Wedgwood, there is very little documentary history on Davenport, either concerning the history, or even more so of the wares. Unlike these two firms, there are no factory pattern or shape books and none of the precious historical documents in the form of account books, order books and other business papers which are so abundant at, for example, their contemporaries Minton. We have to rely very heavily on the personal papers of John Davenport to piece together the story of these years of outstanding success.

Shortly after the royal visit, a three-sided close of terraced cottages for the workpeople was built. These seem to have been attractive dwellings with small front gardens, and a central pediment dated 1807. The appropriate name of Prince's Square was given to the development, which alas no longer stands. The site the houses occupied is close to what is now Longport railway station.

Further expansion took place in 1809 when the large earthenware manufactory of Walter Daniel at Newport was acquired. Its location can be seen on the map shown as Plate 1. The factory was used for the production of earthenware, though it is not known if this means that all earthenware production was transferred to Newport and porcelain alone made at Longport. This seems unlikely, but there have been suggestions that this might account for the use of the place name Longport as a mark on some of the early porcelain wares. It has also been suggested that black basalt might not have been manufactured until such a time as it could be somewhat isolated from the production of finer wares. This could have been done in the post-1810 period at Newport. These are theories and we may never know the true answer. It is perhaps amusing to speculate on what would have been the reaction of John Davenport if he had learned that in the 1930s his Newport factory would be the home of Clarice Cliff's BIZARRE range. He would probably have approved – BIZARRE was a very profitable product! And some of his own wares of the early nineteenth century were highly colourful.

The word 'acquired' was used above as the precise status of Davenport in the Newport factory at this date is obscure. A Sun Fire Insurance policy of 22 December 1809 discovered by Harold Blakey and published by him in the *Journal of the Northern Ceramic Society* 3 (1978–9) begins as follows:

838698
Walter Daniel Senr. of Hassell Hall in the Co. of Chester Gent. Walter Daniel Junr. and John Davenport of Newport in the parish of Burslem & Co. of Stafford, China, Glass and Earthenware manufacturers. On a house and offices adjoining at Newport aforesaid not exceeding £625. Statuary work therein not exceeding £25. Barn stable and chaise house adjoining not exceeding £100. The above are in the tenure of the said John Davenport. The following in the tenure of John Davenport & Co. Viz. South range of potworks, warehouses near not exceeding £400 . . .

The policy then goes on to detail the East, West and North ranges with a total value of '£2250 being insured on the within mentioned property in like manner in the Royal Exchange Assurance offices is hereby allowed and agreed to.'

Two points arise from this policy. It has been suggested that Daniel and Davenport were partners in this Newport factory. There is no evidence other than this policy to associate them in any way, so that a formal partnership seems very unlikely – if it existed it never reached the pages of the *London Gazette*. What seems more likely is that the Daniels retained ownership of the factory at the date the policy was taken out, but that Davenport & Co (more correctly John & James Davenport) were the tenants – as indeed is indicated clearly – and the sole users of the premises. So far we have not been able to trace the precise date when Davenport actually purchased the factory, but they certainly were the owners when they sold it in the 1850s (see p. 61).

The second point concerns 'a house and offices adjoining'. This is surely Newport House, as marked on the map; in due course this was to become the residence of Henry Davenport, but it is very likely that John Davenport himself lived there before he purchased Westwood in 1813.

Mr Blakey also discovered the insurance policy taken out on the Stoke-on-Trent potworks occupied by John Harrison. The total insured in the name of John Davenport (significantly) of Newport in the Co. of Stafford Gent. was £400. The policy No. 835987 was taken out on 6 November 1809.

A second policy taken out on 22 December 1809 by John Davenport 'of Newport in the parish of Burslem and County of Stafford, china, glass and earthenware manufacturer' is also recorded in full by Mr Blakey. It is worth reprinting in part for it relates to 'his buildings consisting of potworks, Glass work Steam Engine house and ware houses situated at Longport in the parish of Burslem aforesaid in tenure of himself and partners excepting the mill and building marked D on a plan lodged in the Royal Exchange office and also excepting hovels, ovens, slip kilns or slip houses in the works aforesaid but including a new range of buildings Nos 100 & 105 not described on the said plan. Not exceeding £5900.' Then follows a lengthy list of buildings included in the schedule which ends with 'Household goods wearing apparel, printed books and plate in his now dwelling house and offices adjoining at Newport aforesaid, not exceeding £400 . . .' This would seem to confirm John Davenport's residence at this date at Newport House, a point strengthened by an earlier reference to a 'house and offices adjoining the said works [i.e. Longport] late [inserted in pencil] in the tenure of Jas. Davenport private not exceeding £600'. It would seem that the potter's house with the kiln apparently in the back garden (Plate 3) had been forsaken by both John and James Davenport. The latter is known to have been in Liverpool for a period and was resident in London for some years before his death in 1822 (see p. 23). The total value of the insurance as specified on the Longport properties was £9550.

On the same day (22 December 1809) 'the stock and utensils in all or any of their workshops and warehouses at Longport aforesaid' were insured for £4000. To which had been pencilled over £8000 and the additional note 'No stock or utensils in the hovels ovens sliphouses and slip kilns in the above mentioned works included in this insurance.' Once more we have tangible evidence of the scale and extent of the manufacturing activities of Davenport at this period.

Thus ended a decade of almost unbroken success. The premises he insured in the last days of 1809 were far more extensive and valuable than they had been in 1800 – never mind in 1794 – and at the age of 45 John Davenport must have felt that he had succeeded in many of his ambitions. His Private Ledger shows that 'Sundry Christmas boxes' cost him £5 12s 0d whilst on 11 February he settled his account for 'Geese 24s 9d'. Christmas that year must have been convivial as his wine account notes that in 1809 he had made 60 bottles of elder wine, and there are records of payments for beer, port and madeira. He can readily be forgiven for toasting the success of his enterprise in the previous decade.

2 The Davenport Family

It would seem most appropriate at this juncture to say something of the Davenport family. As was stated earlier John Davenport had married in 1795 shortly after he left Liverpool and established himself as a manufacturer at Longport. His wife Diana was thirty-one at the time of their marriage, John thirty. We have no direct evidence as to the happiness or otherwise of their union. And perhaps it is none of our business! However, together they produced five children who were to play their parts in the future both of the family and the factory.

It is appropriate to step aside from the direct history of the factory having reached the year 1810, for in little more than a year after that period of high success Diana Davenport died. I have no references to this event in any of John's letters except that in the letter to his grandchildren quoted on p. 50. There are however some jottings in the Private Ledger which record sums of money paid to her. On 9 December 1807 for example 'Mrs D.' received £22, the purpose is not stated, and in 1809 several sums are recorded for amounts which vary up to £50. There is little else of a personal nature, and as far as we are aware no portrait of Diana Davenport exists. It is entirely negative evidence, but nevertheless true, that John Davenport never married again and died a widower some thirty-seven years after the death of his wife.

The eldest child of John and Diana Davenport was Elizabeth. Born in 1795 she married Sir John Bent of Liverpool, whose name occurs from time to time in the Foxley papers but who had no direct involvement with the Pottery. Sir John Bent died in 1857 and Elizabeth in her eightieth year in 1875.

The second child was the eldest son John. He was born in 1799 and as far as can be established he was never active in the management of the Pottery. He was educated at Worcester College, Oxford and was called to the Bar in 1828. He was married the following year to Charlotte the daughter of George Coltman of Hagnaby Priory in Lincolnshire. After the death of his father in 1848 he went to live at his father's country house Westwood near Leek, but left there in 1855 when he purchased the Foxley estate in Herefordshire. There are important papers relating to this purchase and the estate in general in both the Herefordshire and the Staffordshire County Record offices. It is worth noting that the Foxley estate had at one time been owned by Uvedale Price whose writings on the 'Picturesque' had been so influential in the late eighteenth and early nineteenth centuries. The Foxley estate still contains some of the trees planted with such care for their picturesque effect by Price.

John Davenport II had six children. The eldest, John Coltman Davenport, died in 1858 and thus the estate passed to his younger brother the second son George Horatio Davenport MA on the death of John II in 1862.

This branch of the family, though largely unconnected with the Pottery (the Revd G. H. Davenport was concerned in its final years, see p. 65) is of particular importance because of the continuity it provides. The Foxley estate remained with them, and though Foxley House was demolished in 1948 (an illustration of the house appears as the Frontispiece of the *Hereford Journal* of 1902), the estate still comprises some 4,000 acres and provides together with the factory site our closest link with the founder. It was Major John L. Davenport who deposited the most valuable Foxley Papers in the Hereford County Record Office, without which our knowledge would be very much poorer. Upon his death in 1962 the estate passed to his son Major David J. C. Davenport, who takes a lively interest in the potting activities of his forebears and in their history and that of his estate. It was personally a great pleasure to visit him and see the fine portrait of John Davenport which provides the admirably appropriate Frontispiece to this book, and also to see a similar portrait of John II. He looks an altogether less severe man than his father! It is pleasant to record that although the potting activities of the family ceased entirely over a century ago, the land that they acquired from making the pots which we admire is still in the possession of a descendant of the factory's founder. As is indicated in the Acknowledgements we are very grateful to David Davenport for his enthusiastic interest and for making the Foxley papers so readily available to us. Historical researchers are not always made so welcome!

John Davenport II's other four children were Harry Tichborne Davenport, who became MP for North Staffordshire and died in 1880, and three daughters, Mary Ward, Diana Eliza, and Charlotte Lucy: these are the three grand-daughters of John Davenport to whom he addresses the delightful letter quoted on p. 50. Amongst the Foxley papers was one of those items which always intrigues researchers, but are totally irrelevant to their main area of study. In this case it is a diary written by John Davenport II in 1855 when he visited his son John Coltman who was serving in the Crimea with the British army. Temptation was resisted and the reading of this was reserved for a future occasion!

John Davenport's second son was Henry Davenport. Born in 1800, he worked in the business all his adult life. The Foxley papers contain quite a few letters addressed to Henry from his father, and though some are in the usual cantankerous vein, Henry does seem to have earned the grudging respect of his father. We know nothing of his early life and schooling, the first specific reference to him being in a letter dated 7 July 1817, at which date his father clearly regards him as part of the firm. He writes:

Dear Henry

I have sent instructions to James Sherwin to proceed immediately to St. Petersburg, and if you desire to go with him lose no time in getting down to Hambro'...

You have expressed a wish once to accompany some officer to this same place – is my reason for making you this offer – Mr Sherwin you will find with Jos'h Davenport at Grosse Strasse No 59 in Hamburg – the route you take I leave to your Judgment ...

The implication of this letter concerning Davenport's overseas trade will be commented upon later. There is no confirmatory evidence as to whether Henry actually made what in those days must have been a somewhat arduous journey.

It was to Henry Davenport that Henry Pontigny turned when his acrimonious quarrel with John Davenport was at its height, as is indicated in the letters quoted on p. 34. As the latter became more absorbed in the management of his estates from the mid 1820s and with politics and the election of 1832 it was Henry Davenport who took over the day-to-day management of the Longport factory. Indeed, at some time after 1830 the formal title of the firm was changed to Henry & William Davenport & Co. In 1834 it was in Henry and William's name that the Top Bridge pottery of Robert Williamson & Co. was purchased, but he was not to enjoy the ownership of his new factory for long. On 13 November 1835 he 'met with his death by a fall from his horse'. His addiction to hunting – he was Master of Foxhounds at Baddeley Edge – had proved fatal.

Henry Davenport never married and seems to have been a likeable character. He lacked the harshness of his father. His life had been easier having been born into considerable affluence, and though his father chided him frequently for laziness and lack of attention to business detail, the remarkable scenes recorded by the *Staffordshire Advertiser* at his funeral bear testimony to the respect and possibly affection in which he was held by the people of his native area. This account written on 21 November is worth quoting in full:

FUNERAL OF THE LATE HENRY DAVENPORT ESQ.

It was our painful duty last week to record the sudden and accidental death of Henry Davenport Esq. of Longport. The remains of this gentleman were deposited in a newly made vault, in St Paul's Church Yard, on Thursday morning last. This was a day such as

has seldom or never been witnessed by the oldest inhabitants of the Potteries, and such as will not be soon forgotten by either young or old. The expression of public feeling in Burslem, Tunstall, Longport and Cobridge, certainly surpassed anything of the kind we ever witnessed on any similar occasion. The manufactories were closed. The shops, too, we believe, without a single exception, were either wholly or partially closed; and every house we noticed had the window blinds drawn down – the customary expression of mourning. From eleven to twelve o'clock the inhabitants of the town and adjacent places were seen in all directions moving towards the burial ground, until not less than ten thousand persons were collected in the church, the churchyard, and the roads leading from Mr D's house to the church – even the tower of the church was filled with spectators – looking down upon the mournful procession as it passed. Shortly after twelve o'clock the workmen of Messrs Davenport came in a body respectably dressed, and formed themselves in a line on each side of the way leading to the church, that the procession might pass without obstruction. The procession was by express wish of the family small and select, consisting, principally, of the personal friends of the deceased, and the intimate relations of the family. Among the family carriages we observed that of Thos. Kinnersley Esq., E. Wood Esq., H. H. Williamson Esq., J. Wood, Esq. &c. &c. The clerks and other principal servants of Messrs. Davenport closed the procession. The Rev. J. Cooper read the burial service in the church, and the Rev. J. Noble at the grave. The workmen, arm in arm, formed a circle round the vault, and as the remains of him to whom they were accustomed to look up with respect as their employer, were deposited in its dark and solitary chambers, the tear fell from many an eye, and the deep drawn sigh of sympathy and of sorrow heaved many a breast. Such scenes are monitory and we trust will not have been witnessed in vain. His remains were deposited in the right hand niche of the lowest range in the vault. The niche was afterwards closed with a stone flag, on which was a brass-plate, with this simple inscription –
HENRY DAVENPORT, ESQ.
Died Nov. 13 1835
Aged 36.

A remarkably evocative piece of journalism.

The date of birth of John and Diana's fourth child, their second daughter, Mary, is not recorded, and nothing is known of her except that she married Josiah Gaunt of Leek who was a manufacturer of silk. Mary appears to have died in 1831.

The fifth child and youngest son was William, born in 1805. The Foxley papers contain many letters either to William from his father John, or about him. In these latter his father constantly complains of William's lack of diligence. For example in 1831 he writes from London, 'What am I to do with Will. He is of no use to me here – at least but little – He has had new clothes – the lad is very attentive and obliging . . .' (Foxley 57). 'The lad' in question was twenty-six years old at the time. Later that year John Davenport's tone is even less pleasant. He writes, 'I think you noticed to Master William what I said about his first and last letter since he left London, and you may add to it that I shall care as little about him as he cares about me. . . .' (Foxley 64). As will appear in the later narrative of the development of the factory William does not emerge as a very sympathetic character. His father may have been an extremely difficult man for whom to work, but there are human aspects to his character which, however curmudgeonly he appears at times, ultimately redeem him as a person. One never feels that William Davenport had these redeeming features in his personality.

On 11 July 1832 William married Marianne the daughter of John Wood of Brownhills. Their union – as the Victorians would have expressed it – was fruitfully blessed with issue. They had nine children. Of these only Henry the eldest son played any significant part in the management of the Pottery. He was to inherit the Works in 1869 on the death of his father, and as will be made plain in the narrative of that period he seemed singularly ill-suited to the responsibilities of running a business. Thus, whereas during his father's lifetime the prosperity of the concern continued, when Henry took over a decline set in, which may well not have been of his making, but which his abilities and temperament made him quite incapable of controlling and reversing. He was unmarried and when one reads in the *Wood Correspondence* of the parlous state to which the Pottery had been reduced and the ineffectiveness of 'Mr Henry's' response one cannot help feeling pity for a man who clearly would have much preferred the quiet life of a country squire or parson to the hurly-burly of the competitive market place. He seems a kindly and sympathetic character, quite out of his depth.

William Davenport's other children were all girls; Mary, who in 1863 married Edward the eldest son of Sir E. Manningham Buller of Dilhorn Hall; Emily Anne, who married her cousin Reginald Newcombe Wood in 1871; Constance Clementina, who married Charles Rivers Bulkeley of Clewer Lodge in 1875; Agnes, who in 1876 married Hugh Ker Colville of Armfield, Sterling; Alice Jessica, who also married a Manningham Buller, this time Frederick Charles Lt.-Col. in the Coldstream Guards in 1881. The three remaining daughters, Diana Elizabeth, Sarah Ellen, and Marianne Henrietta all remained unmarried. They lived together at Camp Hill and as the document quoted on p. 65 shows they were involved with their brother Henry in the rescue attempts of the 1880s. There is also a record that true to the fashion of the period for 'china painting', the ladies at Maer were adept at painting horses' heads upon china plates.

William Davenport had succeeded his elder brother Henry as Master of the Baddeley Edge Hunt, and in the 1840s revived the North Staffs. Hunt of which he was to be Master of Foxhounds for twenty-seven seasons. His residence was the now-demolished Longport Hall (Plate 8). In 1843 he bought from the Wedgwoods the Maer estate where he was to live until his death in 1869. Ten years earlier he had succeeded his other brother John as High Sheriff of Staffordshire, when John moved to Foxley. Although he did from time to time attend to factory business in his own way (see p. 54), William Davenport was a typical country gentleman. His only real interest in the Pottery was in the income he could draw from it. He totally lacked his father's dedication to the actual business. In this fashion, so familiar in the history of English manufacturers of the late Industrial Revolution, he was preparing the way, albeit unwittingly, for the death of the enterprise which his father had desperately struggled to establish and make prosper. William Davenport's death at Maer Hall is reported in the *Staffordshire Advertiser* for 12 June 1869.

8

Other members of the Davenport family also took part in the business. The most important of these, James Davenport, has already been noted (p. 14). He was John Davenport's partner from 1797 when he was only twenty-one, until his death at the comparatively early age of forty-six on 6 July 1822 at his home in Salisbury Square, London. In the early days of their association, James, who also, of course, was not a practical potter but a merchant, lived at Longport and would almost certainly have attended the factory daily. He appears also to have been a fairly frequent visitor to Liverpool and it was from there that he reported to John Davenport in the earliest dated of the family letters in the Foxley papers. On 13 November 1812, he writes, 'As to the General business here, the En'ware department is done as well as it can be by Fynney, the Glass business appears to have suffered . . .' (Foxley, 1: other parts of this letter are quoted on p. 286).

By the time of this visit to Liverpool it is likely that James Davenport was permanently settled in London. The *Staffordshire Advertiser* for 30 May 1812 announced a forthcoming sale in Longport on 25 June of the furniture and effects of James Davenport consequent upon his taking residence in London. The house he occupied was in Salisbury Square and remained his residence until his death. John Davenport on his own not infrequent visits to London seems to have stayed with James in Salisbury Square whenever he visited the capital. Thus the role of James in the business seems to have been akin to that of a modern marketing manager keeping his eye on the London showroom. In 1818 new London premises were acquired at 82 Fleet Street (Plate 9), an address previously occupied first by John Turner, and then by the well-known china merchants James Mist and Abbott & Mist whose names appear on some Davenport porcelains (see p. 216). In 1818 the showroom was leased by Abbott to J. & J. Davenport for ten years. It was still being leased to Davenports in the 1860s. (Further details are given in Bevis Hillier's book, *The Turners of Lane End*, 1965, p. 66). We may never be able to assess accurately the part played by James Davenport in the early success of Messrs Davenport, but it could well have been considerable. After all John Davenport could not be everywhere at once and he seems to have placed little faith in many of those who worked for him. There are documents in the Foxley papers (S 45) relating to James Davenport in the period 1816–26 including matters relating to the settlement of his estate. These have not been examined in detail, but a document records that 'by the late

8. Longport Hall, the residence of William Davenport. From a print dated 1843. (Lockett Collection)

9. The Davenport London showrooms at 82, Fleet Street. From a drawing by James Findlay, c.1845.

23 · The Family and Factory

Co-Partnership Concern, for James Davenport's share due to him £39,727 14s 6d. 10 April 1824.' Signed by J'n Davenport Exor., and the residual legatees Joseph, James (jun.), John (jun.), and Uriah. James Davenport died a wealthy man.

With the death of James Davenport other younger members of the family became more prominent. It is not necessary to trace all these in detail, but one young man, James Davenport Junior, nephew of the James Davenport written of above, seems to have something of the enterprising Davenport spirit about him. In 1820 he wrote, presumably to John Davenport, from Liverpool on 21 January as follows:

Sir,

I received your letter and feel very sensibly the justice of your remarks on the subject of my conduct while at Longport, which I must acknowledge was such as to cause your just reprehension, tho' at same time I cannot omit to state that, a conduct so highly improper on my part and so seemingly persisted in did not arise from any bad motives or from any inattention to the welfare of the concerns, had less austerity and censure been used to me in the early part of my career a great part of it might have been avoided, the fear which I was continually in prevented me from doing my duty as I ought to have done. I regret much that such has been the case as such as opportunity can never occur to me again of establishing myself to such advantage – I hope, however, by my future conduct to regain your lost opinion. I must appeal to Mr Fynney to appreciate the value of my services here who I am confident cannot say my exertions are withheld or given in that unpleasant way which you think they are, as Steel is left here I shall now have my hands full although we are not doing much at present, I came here in April and have had the sum of £20 to this period. I shall be well satisfied with whatever terms you think proper to fix either with Mr F. or myself.

I take the liberty also to name to you my Brother Uriah who has been here 5 years and is 19 years of age and as Mr Fynney is unwilling to part with him to Hambro' or to my Uncle [in London], *if you thought proper to put him on a small salary for a term of years it would be an encouragement to him. I have no doubt he will husband it well.*

I am Sir,
Your Mo' Hble' Sev't
Jas. Davenport Jun.

This masterly letter has a most modern ring to it; fear, austerity and censure drove the poor lad to excess. It was all John Davenport's fault really!

James Junior's artful letter must have made the peace with John Davenport, and perhaps the latter's rebuke had the desired effect, for the next letter in the records which has survived from James (3 September 1823) is a model of commercial acumen and businesslike efficiency. After details of collecting monies owed to them James writes 'I have to return to you my thanks for your advice as to my projected establishment at Brussels . . . I am yet of the opinion that Brussels would be preferable to Rotterdam, you might do the Wholesale Trade from thence (or rather from Antwerp) where goods might be kept at a very trifling expense . . .' (Foxley, 17). The upshot of this correspondence was that James Junior did establish some form of agency in Brussels, but it is not known for how long this lasted. When next we hear of James sometime after 1825, he is working at the Hamburg establishment together with the brother he recommended from Liverpool in 1829, that is Uriah, and another brother Joseph.

Further details of the important Hamburg showrooms are given on pp. 35–6. Quite how long James and his brothers remained in Hamburg is open to question. There were certainly further upsets with James as late as 1831 (see p. 36). But as is indicated in the section on the Hamburg warehouse James replaced Joseph as the person in charge there sometime in 1832. In a private communication to me some years ago Mr Merrick V. F. Bousfield of Formby reported his research into the Liverpool Census returns for 1841 in which there is a James Davenport listed as a China Merchant (in the age range 45–9) living at 3 Great Mersey Street, Kirkdale, Liverpool (then a very wealthy area).

The house is in the name of Uriah Davenport (45–9): also listed are Uriah's wife Elizabeth (30–4) and their six children aged from three to eleven, together with three female servants. Uriah's occupation is given as Iron Founder and in the 1841 Trade Directory he is described as 'of Davenport, Grindrod & Patrick, Naylor Street and Coburg Dock.' By 1845 the Davenport name had disappeared from the firm's title, and we know of no later references to this branch of the Davenport family.

One of Uriah's daughters was Mr Bousfield's great-grandmother. It does seem highly likely that these were the two Davenport brothers who had worked together both in Liverpool and at Hamburg and had now returned to Liverpool, where the Davenport showrooms and warehouse were an important and integral part of their business.

This lengthy résumé of the various family members who were directly or indirectly connected with the pottery in its ninety-year history is far from complete. But the ramifications were widespread and over the years we have received many letters such as that quoted above from people descended, sometimes quite remotely, from one or other branch of the Davenport family. Like all families they seek to find out more about their ancestors and one can only recommend those who are seriously interested to pursue their research in the archives at the County Record Offices in Hereford and Stafford, and in other sources quoted in the bibliography. It is only possible in a publication such as this book to reprint and describe a very small fraction of the material which is available on the lives and commerical activities of the Davenports.

3 Politics and Country Life

In the year that his wife Diana died, 1811, there occurs the first documentary evidence of John Davenport's involvement in what might loosely be called political activity. The Government led by Spencer Perceval – who incidentally has the unique distinction of being the only British Prime Minister to have been assassinated – was rumoured to be about to impose a tax upon earthenware and porcelain. The Staffordshire potters were greatly alarmed. A document was prepared, 'OBSERVATIONS on the Proposed TAX on PORCELAIN and EARTHENWARE particularly as Relative to THE STAFFORDSHIRE POTTERIES.' It reads in part:

In consequence of the great alarm that has been excited, by the rumour of an intended Tax on porcelain and earthen ware, Mr SPODE and Mr CALDWELL, have been delegated to attend in London, on behalf of the Staffordshire Potteries; and who, without taking upon themselves to pronounce, on the general inexpediency or impolicy of subjecting to direct taxation the Manufactures, and more especially such, as are in a peculiar degree, the produce of mere labour or of art, respectfully beg leave to submit the few following Observations, on the important subject immediately under consideration.'

There then follow 18 paragraphs of argument to justify the statement that 'the manufacture of earthen ware may, from its nature, be justly deemed deserving of particular protection and encouragement, inasmuch, as it is an absolute conversion of raw materials, the produce of this Island, and of little or no value themselves . . . into an article, constituting a considerable and valuable branch of national commerce.' Success depends upon cheapness, a tax would harm this, it would be difficult to collect, it would damage the export trade particularly that to America; when fully working there are 110 manufactories in Staffordshire employing 10,000 to 15,000 persons; there are the buildings, all the ancillary trades dependent upon the industry, including the coastal shipping trade. The plea – worthy of any modern vested interest lobby – ends with the statement that though 'the manufactures of porcelain and earthen ware . . . are still only, in a comparatively infant state . . . there is good ground to hope, that if duly fostered and protected, and left to take their course, they will eventually be found to rival, if not to excel, the best productions of other countries; and to maintain their station in the market, should the manufactures of the Continent be re-established.' (Wedgwood papers 29/20989–21026).

On the day that this was published, 8 May 1811, John Davenport replied to a letter from Josiah Wedgwood II who enclosed a letter from Mr Caldwell and enquired if it would not be advisable for the Committee to meet at the Roebuck on Wednesday.

Longport 8 May 1811
Sir

With three exceptions only the whole country is opposed to the Tax . . .

In the statement I noticed it to be said that the manufactory of E'Ware &c was still in its Infancy, I could not agree with this part of it – my opinion is that it is on the decline without an Export trade and every other encouragement which can be afforded, there is no country but what is able to produce within itself a good substitute for the commoner articles, and for the fine we are yet much behind our Neighbours the French in elegance and taste and the Chinese in price and value.

But I am wandering and ought perhaps only to have thanked you for your kind attention.

I am very respectfully
Dr Sir your Mo Hbl Sev't Jn Davenport   (Wedgwood papers 29/20843)

This civil tone in the correspondence did not last for long. Davenport became involved in selling horses, harness and carriage to Wedgwood and the haggling over the price was fierce and not very polite. 'Your horses are too high priced', writes Wedgwood. '. . . they are remarkably healthy and free from vice or blemish of any kind, well broke in and very good tempered', retorts Davenport. The price they eventually agreed was disappointing to Davenport – 'your offer is very much below the value' – and the subsequent letters between the two on the tax problem seems to reflect the acrimony of the equine transaction.

On 14 June Davenport accused Wedgwood of bad faith in proceeding with a meeting in his absence and passing resolutions of which he disapproved:

. . . it would be uncandid if I did not say in reply that . . . I am not at all satisfied with the proceedings which have been taken . . . I shall have no objection to state privately & publicly what have been my views and my feelings on the occasion.

The recriminations rumbled on (fuller details are recorded in *Transactions of the English Ceramic Circle* 12 Pt 2, 1985) and Josiah Wedgwood emerged with some dignity from the altercation, ending a letter of 3 July with the words, 'I am sure there could have been no intentional failure in respect towards you.'

The final act of this little drama shows John Davenport in one of his more petulant moods. Towards the end of a long letter written on 15 July to Wedgwood he declares:

A few days ago a Man called upon me with two papers one he said was a subscription for a plate, the other for the expenses on the Tax business, the latter I would have paid him could he have informed me what I had to pay, the former I mean to reserve for a more important occasion when the services rendered will be less equivocal, and when a greater display of successful Talent may call forth my gratitude, that period may not be far distant . . .
(Wedgwood papers 31/23255)

A very full account of the tax affair by Rodney Hampson is contained in the *Newsletter of the Northern Ceramic Society* 54, June 1984, which reveals that John Davenport did pay his share of the expenses (£3) but did not make any contribution to the subscription for the presentation of Silver Plate to Spode and Caldwell. Davenport also seems to have inferred that some of the potters were in favour of the proposed taxes and Thomas Minton was forced to deny publicly in the *Staffordshire Advertiser* of 1st June that he had been 'the inventor and promotor of the intended duty upon porcelain and earthenware.' John Davenport can never be accused of courting easy popularity with his contemporaries! The proposed taxes on porcelain and earthenware, and one on coal, were never introduced but the incident does highlight the truculence of John Davenport on occasions (though could this have been a difficult time for him with his wife either ill or having recently died?). It also emphasizes the difficulties experienced by potters in exporting wares during the Napoleonic Wars. The Government may not have needed to raise the proposed taxes in the Budget of 1811, but the following year resources must have been at an even greater stretch with the War of 1812 against the Americans. This war was regarded with considerable apprehension by exporters who feared the loss of one of their best markets. Davenport seems to have made the best of a bad job by producing wares for the American market decorated with portraits of their heroes who had fought valiantly in the struggle against the British (see pp. 160–2).

The year 1812, however, marked another significant milestone in the life of John Davenport. On 2 July a contract of purchase was drawn up whereby John Davenport 'of Longport, Staffs. potter and glassmaker' agreed that a sum of '£775 and £44,725 to be paid' for 'The manor of Westwood with appurtenances' and Westwood and Wallbridge. At the age of 47 and for a very considerable sum of money he had become a country gentleman with an important estate. There has been some confusion about the date of the purchase and the price paid. Sleigh records that it was purchased on 19–20 March 1813 of the Hon. William Booth-Grey of Duffryn for £15,500 and this date and amount were repeated in my 1972 Davenport book and elsewhere. The Foxley papers (D 399, S 19) give the figures indicated above which obviously include the entire estate. Sleigh's figure may relate simply to Westwood House and his date to that of completion. Plans of the estate are also to be found in the Foxley papers at Hereford. The house was to be John Davenport's main home for the rest of his life (Plate 10) and the purchase and occupation to signify a very real change in his status from 'potter and glassmaker' who lived hard by his works in the industrial environment from which his wealth derived, to wealthy landowner and country gentleman who also owned a manufactory. That he was not always sure that the move had been a wise one from the business point of view was cogently expressed by him many years later in a letter to his son Henry who had tried to persuade him to return to London. On 26 January 1831, he writes:

As to my residence at Westwood I know that you would not recommend it only that you conceive it would result to my advantage – but I see no advantage myself – either in comfort or saving – and it would have been well for us all if I had never seen it – You see what the introduction of Game Cocks &c has done for us – which we should never have seen but at Westwood and you know what our trade has suffered by the attraction it afforded to affairs of Sports rather than business. I am speaking of myself & others but the observation could be applied to you . . . (Foxley 62)

However, in the early days at Westwood his attention to the details of business, especially to the marketing and selling of his goods, was undiminished. We are fortunate to have a record of one of Davenport's most important employees at this period. John Haslem in his book *The Old Derby China Factory* (1876) writes of James Thomason who for thirty years was cashier and commercial manager at the Derby factory. Before going to Derby in 1815, he had been a traveller for Davenport since 1809. He clearly was a remarkable man, and provides another example of John Davenport buying the best expertise he could, as was the case with Lakin and Grafton. The importance of Thomason's contribution in the period 1809–15 is difficult to measure but it must have been very considerable. This was a period when exporting was almost impossible and only the vigorous pursuit of orders in the home market could have assured the firm of continuing success. It is always easier to work in the home market in times of difficulties: debts are easier to chase up, and delivery times are a fraction of those for an export order. Personal attention to the customer is more easily managed also. In every respect Thomason seems to have been an excellent servant of both the Davenport and

10. Westwood Hall *c.*1865, from a drawing by Mrs Trafford of Swythamley (reproduced in John Sleigh's *Leek*).

Derby concerns. Haslem's description of his travels for Davenport are worth quoting in full, they relate to a Yorkshire journey made by horse and gig:

He started on what was called his Yorkshire journey on the 18th of March, 1813, and returned on the 24th of May, a period of sixty-eight days, during which he visited seventy-five towns, called on one hundred and twenty-three customers, slept at sixty-one different inns, travelled nine hundred and fifty-seven miles, and took orders to the amount of £1,521. 11s. 3½d., his expenses on the road being £57. 12s. 8½d. Among the towns he visited on this occasion were Lichfield, Burton, Derby, Ashbourne, Bakewell, Matlock, Alfreton, Mansfield, Chesterfield, Sheffield, Wakefield, Huddersfield, Halifax, Bradford, Leeds, York, Pontefract, Doncaster, Gainsborough, Hull, Lincoln, Boston, Spalding, Lynn, Norwich, Yarmouth, Lowestoft, Ipswich, Colchester, Bury St. Edmunds, Newmarket, Cambridge, Peterborough, Stamford, Newark, Nottingham, Loughborough, Leicester, Market Harborough, Northampton, Daventry, Coventry, Birmingham and Uttoxeter. Several similar journeys were performed by him yearly and he generally did business to a larger amount than on this occasion. Thus on the Yorkshire journey in 1811, his orders reached a total of £2,839. 18s. 8d. and in 1812, £1,954. 4s. 6d.

John Davenport must have found a man as diligent and trustworthy as Thomason hard to replace, for no matter how efficient and innovatory the manufactory was, unless the wares were sold in the quantities he was able to achieve, the business would soon founder.

That Davenport himself as a former merchant was acutely aware of the importance of marketing and selling is manifest time and again in the surviving evidence. He was also considerably upset by anything that resembled the breaking of agreements on prices and any resort to unfair competition. Thus on 9 May 1814 he wrote to Josiah Wedgwood II at Etruria as follows:

The list of prices which have been printed, published and distributed, contrary to the express conditions of agreement at the Meeting are now in the hands of the dealers and merchants and not having it impressed upon them that this list contain'd the lowest class of prices much inconvenience has arisen from an understanding that they are the regular prices of the Trade in general without regard to the quality of the article.

It is also a known fact that these prices are not even now adopted by some Houses in the Trade, for instance Mr Spodes, who with few alterations continues to sell Blue Printed Table ware at the old prices. We feel therefore that we must be exonerated from our pledge of abiding by the prices agreed upon at the Meetings, of which we think it proper to give you notice in order that you may take such steps in the business as you consider necessary.

> We are
> Sir Yr Hb, s'vt
> Jn & Jas. Davenport.   (Wedgwood papers 29/20863)

Davenport's threat of unilateral action in retaliation for Spode's alleged breach of the price fixing agreement brought a swift response from Wedgwood. He replied from Etruria the following day:

I have called upon Mr Spode today with Mr Rogers, Mr Ward & Mr Stevenson & he acquainted us that immediately on finding his mistake, he corrected his prices to the List and has taken no orders since at the old prices. He will send his price list tomorrow to Mr Rogers that any gentleman may satisfy himself as to his present prices.

A second letter now affected by damp and with an illegible date reiterates much of the above and states that he, Josiah Wedgwood, 'begs to inform you that Mr Spode has corrected his price' and adds that 'if your resolution [not to adhere to the list] was principally founded on Mr Spode's not adhering to the list, I hope you may see reason to change it.'

John Davenport was clearly pleased by the speedy response to the pressure put upon Spode and his own reply of 11 May is for him positively fulsome:

Sir, We are much obliged to you for the trouble you have taken to set us right as respects Mr Spode's prices, and for the promptness with which you undertook it – The writer is sorry he was out of the way yesterday or he would most willingly have accompanied you to Mr Spode . . . [he then continues in an expansive and very informative mood] *. . . with respect to Cr. Col.* [cream coloured or creamware] *we were not very anxious, it is a staple and will find its value, but with regard to Blue Printed Table ware we conceive the case very different for if Mr Spode's large stock of that article gets all at once into the Home Market which it would naturally do at reduced prices, the future supply would be wanted chiefly for his patterns, which, of course, other manufacturers must adopt at the great expense of new plates* [for printing] *– or must look out for new Markets and new connections – We have begun to feel this inconvenience in the loss of our principal customer in that line – we hope this will satisfy you that we shall not readily and without just cause do anything to lower the prices of Earthenware.* (Wedgwood papers 29/20865)

Clearly Davenport regards Spode as the market leader in blue printed wares at this period, a judgement which would not occasion much dissent from modern collectors. It is also evident that the leading manufacturers realized the dangers of cut-throat competition and acted speedily to redress any possible imbalance in the market. Perhaps subconsciously they were acting upon the commercial wisdom expounded by Josiah Wedgwood when he wrote in 1771 'low prices must beget a low quality in the manufacture, which will beget contempt, which will beget neglect, & disuse, and there is an end to the trade.'

With the end of the long wars in 1815 the prospects opened up of renewed export markets and, as we shall see later, Davenport was in the forefront of Staffordshire potters in this aspect of business, but first the coming of peace had to be celebrated in the appropriate manner. We are told by Ward that the former Major Davenport headed a procession together with his Manager James Mawdsley, they both wore glass hats specially made for the occasion and carried Davenport glass walking-sticks. The procession walked from Longport to Burslem and was accompanied by 'a band of music which was connected with the works.'

The man so proudly leading his workers in the victory march was now a fifty-year-old widower with five children, the owner of two potteries and a glass works, a large country estate and a considerable fortune. Twenty years of endeavour had achieved all this, but his ambition still burned brightly and the next twenty years, a period of peace not war, were to be crowned with even further successes.

4 Warehouses, Agencies, and Exports

The ending of the war presented John Davenport with renewed opportunities and challenges. It is important to realize, as was emphasized earlier, that Davenport was first and foremost a merchant, and it is instructive to look at the warehouses and agencies he established through which his foreign trade was conducted.

The original base for all his activities was Liverpool. It was here he started his association with Thomas Wolfe, and here that his own first independent 'Staffordshire Warehouse' was established in 1790 (see p. 10). The researches of Mr Patrick Latham in the local Liverpool records reveal a long connection between the port and various members of one or other branches of the Davenport family. For example in 1766 a Richard Davenport had a mug warehouse on the South Side of the Old Dock (he is later recorded as a cheese and corn merchant); a Christopher Davenport of Dale Street is listed as merchant in 1769; a William as a wine merchant also of 1769. Significantly, although John Davenport's first address in 1790 is given as 46 Hurst Street, by 1796 this was changed to 51 Old Dock, exactly the same location as Richard Davenport occupied in 1766. John Davenport remained in various addresses on the Old Dock, Canning Place (45, 46, 47, and 50 as well as 51 are recorded, which are surely all in the same block of buildings) for the whole of his lifetime. The firm was to retain the Liverpool showroom and warehouse, which was generally referred to as Canning Place, virtually until the final closure of the Pottery in 1887. Plate 11 depicts the building as it appeared in 1829. Meanwhile in the 1805 Gore's *Directory* the 'Staffordshire Warehouse' is listed for the first time as being in the occupation of John and James Davenport.

Research undertaken by Ronald Brown in the City of Liverpool archives has produced further evidence of Davenport's activities in Liverpool and we are grateful to him for permission to publish some of this information for the first time here. The ledgers of Liverpool Select Committee Finance (352/MIN/Fin 1, p. 308) for 3 July 1809 record 'that the following leases be approved and recommended sold. John Davenport, House East side of Park Lane.' This 'house' appears to have been used as a warehouse though it could also have contained living accommodation and been used as such by John and James when they visited Liverpool. It was probably from this house that James wrote the letter quoted on pp. 23 and 286, and James Junior the apologetic letter of 21 January 1820 quoted on p. 24. The partnership used the Liverpool warehouses not only as crucial components in their overseas trade, but also as a regional base, and the records show

11. 'A View of Buildings between Frederick Street and Park Lane' c.1829. The Warehouse and Showrooms in Liverpool at the 'Corner of Old Dock Quay', usually referred to as Canning Place. (Courtesy Ronald B. Brown and Liverpool Public Libraries)

that the City purchased considerable quantities of pottery, porcelain and especially glass from the Davenports. Thus on 28 January 1814 the Treasurer is authorized to discharge the account of J & J Davenport 'for Earthenware and Glass £30. 17s. 4d.' and on 9 November 1822 'J & J Davenports for china jugs etc £37. 10s. 6d.' The glass sales are much more important and are dealt with in the chapter on glass (pp. 281–92).

It would appear from the somewhat fragmentary surviving evidence that the Davenports were not entirely suited with the management of the Liverpool business and the premises. The presence of James Junior and Uriah Davenport there in 1820 and the relatively small volume of business recorded has already been noted on p. 24. Subsequently on 28 May 1822 Henry Davenport wrote to his father about the business there:

Dear Father,

. . . Fynney [Mountford Fynney, later the Liverpool partner] *. . . left early next morning for L'pool, thus putting an end to my journey thither. I will have him up again before long for I cannot fix any prices there, I shall not have any support. I think an Agency will do as well in L'pool as a Co-partnership; it would not answer with evryone* [sic] *but I am sure he will act in every respect as if the concern was his own . . .'* (Foxley, 13)

It seems likely that Henry's advice was acted upon and for the time being Fynney acted as their agent until the reorganization of 1825. Henry wrote from Liverpool on 21 August 1823 enclosing a statement of account of sales and further reported:

To put in full lease the Corner Warehouse late Mr Wolfe, the Corporation ask four hundred and sixty pounds fourteen shillings, and one shilling per yard pr Annum ground rent to the front, & confine you sixty feet in heighth [sic] *of Building. As regards the Capital necessary for this Concern Fynney thinks that from thirty to forty thousand pounds will be quite ample, exclusive of Buildings and fittings up . . . Mr Fynney thinks that in rebuilding all the Show Rooms might be on one floor, that is the Glass, China & E'ware in one large room the whole size of the Buildings or with slight partitions as you may think proper. He says that the Park Lane Warehouse would not be wanted and that it might be let for about 70 or 100 pr annum or possibly a little more . . . I have had some conversation with John and Uriah & they say they shall leave it entirely to you to arrange matters as you think proper, the only alteration they seem to wish is in their lodging . . .*

I am dear father
Y'r dutiful Son,
H'y Davenport (Foxley, 16)

It would seem likely that some form of lease was taken on Wolfe's former warehouse which almost certainly adjoined part of Davenport's own property, the joint warehouse thus being the one depicted in the 1829 engraving (Plate 11). To further complicate matters the Corporation records contain notes of further leases, and though it is not always possible to pinpoint these precisely on a map (names and numbers changed somewhat alarmingly at this period), it is worth noting these leases to give an indication of the extent and importance of the Liverpool rooms. By the time this next set of leases were negotiated John Davenport was in partnership in Liverpool with the ever-reliable Mountford Fynney: the document dated 14 April 1825 quoted on p. 42 gives the relevant details.

From the Minute Books quoted above Mr Brown has extracted the following:
29 February 1828 [p. 251]. *Mr John Davenport re leases.*
John Davenport of a warehouse at the corner of Old Dock Quay and Park Lane and a house on the West side of Frederick Street.
16 May 1834 [p. 496]. *Mr Davenport having submitted the proposed elevation of his intended buildings on the South side of Canning Place resolved.*
1 August 1834 [p. 250]. *A letter from John Davenport Esq're having been read requesting*

that at considerable expense in ornamenting the front of his premises on the South side of Canning Place, the Corporation would be pleased to renew the leases of the two premises without fine.

22 August 1834. A letter from John Davenport Esq. on the subject of the lease of the premises on the South side of Canning Place stating the inconvenience which will occur to him by giving up the right of Warehouse doors, in the freehold works, and proposing to sell his reversionary interest to the corporation and to take the whole of the premises under one lease.

29 August 1834 [p. 546]. The Surveyor reported that the estimated value of the reversionary lease to John Davenport would be £252; the Corporation to give a lease of 75 years for the same and the adjoining property.

The Surveyor's suggestion was agreed to on 26 September 1834.

The inference of this documentary material was that it was not until 1834 that Davenport negotiated a full seventy-five-year lease on their major Liverpool warehouse after what appears to have been a major rebuilding, possibly that first indicated in the correspondence of Henry Davenport in 1832 quoted above. At all events Canning Place was to remain as the firm's Liverpool base until the collapse in the 1880s. It was to play a major role in the further development of their transatlantic trade in the future.

As noted earlier the factory manufactured many items in earthenware, china and glass specifically for the City of Liverpool. One such 'magnificent dinner service for state occasions' was noted by the *Pottery Gazette* for 1 March 1893 in a retrospective article on Davenport. Examples of this service apparently still survive in Liverpool and three punch bowls from the service are illustrated in *The Connoissseur* for June 1910, p. 88. It would seem to be the same service noted in the *Liverpool Post and Mercury* for 21 April 1931. Under a somewhat misleading sub-heading of 'Liverpool china as gift to New York,' we read 'to mayor Walker of New York, the Lord Mayor will hand some beautiful examples of Davenport china as a gift to the City of New York from the city of Liverpool. This china which is a hundred years old but in perfect condition, consists of a pair of three-tier cake stands, each on a broad base bearing the city coat of arms, and the whole delicately decorated with floral designs in which the Rose of Lancashire figures. The colours which are still very definite and appear to have lost little of their original freshness, include soft browns, blues, pink and white on a background of cream. The cake stands are to be enclosed in a glass-fronted case which will bear an inscription on a gold plate.' A fitting present of Davenport wares from the city in which they had transacted so much business to a city to which they had exported so much ware.

If we turn now to the London showroom, it will be recalled that the first notice of such a place occurs in Wedgwood correspondence of 1807 (see p. 16). Again the move from the Shakespeare Gallery to 82 Fleet Street in 1818 has been noted earlier. The management of the London rooms was to cause endless trouble to John Davenport and the Foxley papers contain many letters the principal burden of which is the difficulties being encountered in London. As almost always with Davenport, personality clashes seem to have been at the root of the trouble. In 1820 Henry Pontigny started work at the London office. At this date the management would have still been in the safe hands of the trustworthy James Davenport who was permanently residing in Salisbury Square. Upon his sudden death in 1822 the management at Fleet Street seems to have become the responsibility of Pontigny. A year later Pontigny's son Victor joined the firm. There is no indication in the Foxley papers of anything untoward at this stage. Indeed, rather to the contrary, for when the major reorganization took place in 1825 Henry Pontigny became John Davenport's partner on London.

The story of the deteriorating relationship is fully revealed in the Foxley papers and it was recounted at length in my 1972 Davenport book. Thus it would seem a work of supererogation to repeat these admittedly fascinating letters. The matter can be simply summarized. Pontigny was an exuberant character, beginning a letter of 26 Oct.

1825 to Henry Davenport thus: 'Old Spode is melted. He has published a New List, which I shall get as soon as I can. We must filigree him again to punish him for plaguing us so much . . .' His weaknesses which so infuriated John Davenport are partly revealed later in the same letter when he asks, 'I wish you would let me into the secret of the difference of value between the same articles in Ironstone & China . . .' (Foxley, 38). A really competent salesman would not have needed to ask after at least six years in the job!

On 12 April 1826 Pontigny wrote a long and bitter letter to Henry complaining of his father's 'Malignity' and that 'he has insulted, vilified me openly, his turning me out of the House, has been common talk of all the neighbourhood' (Foxley, 43). Some of his complaints do seem to have an element of justice as when he argues that 'it is ridiculous to say that we must sell for what we can get. We must have a price arranged for the times and carry on trade with some system . . .' It would seem that John Davenport, freed from the day-to-day supervision of the Longport factories, spent more time than ever in London at this period, and with his well-known proclivity for being unable to trust subordinates or to delegate with an easy mind, he made life very difficult for those supposedly in charge. It is a phenomenon not unknown in modern business and political circles. However, this kind of acrimony was injurious to the business and the following year after further recriminations a Memorandum of Agreement between Henry Davenport and Henry Pontigny was signed on 19 June by which Davenport purchased all Pontigy's interests in the concern for £8,500. The dissolution of partnership appeared in the *London Gazette* the following day. This was not the end of the end of the matter. Pontigny seemingly had not been paid by John Davenport as late as 31 May 1828 when he wrote despairingly to Henry (for the full text see *Davenport Pottery & Porcelain*, p. 15).

The troubles with the London warehouse were not yet over. On 7 January John Davenport was enquiring of Henry: 'But as to London I must ask you what is to be done with the management of this concern? I cannot undertake it and as to Victor Pontigny he is, if possible, more trifling and addling than even was his father – he does really nothing, yet is always busy . . .' (Foxley, 59). Less than a year earlier on 22 April 1830 John had written to his son William 'Henry & I both think that now our China is so fine we ought to have some sort of standing in the West End, some one to show it and sell it, if not a concern wholly of our own.' (Foxley, 76). Nothing seems to have come of this suggestion.

John Davenport maintained his vendetta against Victor Pontigny. Writing to his son Henry on 26 January 1831 he ends a long letter with a marvellously damning phrase: 'The trade here [London] I think may be mended, but not without a better direction – Victor like his father, will never get a shilling in the mug trade' (Foxley, 62). He returns to the attack on 21 March 1831: 'he continues as shuffling and trifling as ever' (Foxley, 18). He even suggested that they might as well give up the London concern altogether. Victor Pontigny hung on and further insults flowed his way on 21 September: 'he is the completest trifler in existence', and the following day 'he will never astonish anyone in the Mug Trade, whatever he may do in the Orchestra or quizzing room' (Foxley, 64).

The survival of Victor Pontigny is surely an indication that Henry Davenport was unwilling to be bullied by his father, but there clearly was something amiss about the London concern for there to have been so much acrimony over the years. We have only one indication of the level of business going through London at this period. In 1835 Victor Pontigny, clearly stung by fresh allegations from John Davenport that he 'never gets a shilling for this concern' forwarded a balance sheet of exports for the half year ending 30 June 1835:

Export to Spain	856. 15. 8.
to Italy	310. 13. 10.
	1,166. 19. 6.
to Sundries	1,191. 11. 2.
	£2,358. 11. 2.

London profit & above Port Invoices – say 15 pc (full) £353.15.0. which is £707.10.0. profit p. annum. (Foxley, 74)

There are no further references to the London warehouse in the period up to the death of John Davenport so we must assume that after the death of Henry Davenport in 1835, the preoccupation of John with his career as an MP and his subsequent retirement to Westwood, the new management of William Davenport & Co. was satisfied with London's contribution, or simply they did not care as much as John Davenport had done.

Liverpool and London were the two main showrooms in England. Overseas trade was conducted normally through agencies, but in a number of instances the Davenports managed premises of their own. The main establishment was in Hamburg.

The first documentary reference noted to a Hamburg depot is contained in the letter dated 7 July 1817 giving Henry Davenport instructions about a journey to St Petersburg (quoted earlier on p. 20). It is unlikely that a Continental warehouse would have been established much earlier because of the disruption occasioned by the Napoleonic Wars. Additional weight is given to this belief by one of several documents discovered by Ronald Brown in the Staffordshire County Record Office (D. 3272/1/4/29–30). This is a co-partnership agreement between 'Joseph Davenport of the City of Hamburgh, Dealer in China, Glass and Earthenware,' and both John and James Davenport of Longport, Manufacturers of the stated items. The Agreement was for ten years whereby Joseph was to live on the premises providing the cost was not more than £200, and to continue to do this whilst he was unmarried. Accounts to be rendered on 25 December each year. Five per cent was to be paid on all monies invested. This agreement was dated 14 December 1818.

A further agreement (D. 3272/1/4/29–30) of exactly two years later (but not signed by James) gave Joseph Davenport half the profits, John and James the other half. Following the death of James fresh dispositions were made in 1826 and on 18 November articles were agreed between Joseph Davenport of Hamburg and Henry and William Davenport. The business was to be known as Joseph Davenport & Co., and to continue in Hamburg and also at Lübeck (which appears to have commenced sometime in 1826). This was a seven-year agreement and a special clause provided that John Davenport's interests in the business was to terminate on 1 January 1827. Joseph Davenport was to receive 3,000 Hamburg Marks for his exclusive use and as compensation for treating the customers of the said Concern. An interest of five per cent was to be paid on all monies invested (D. 3272/1/4/1/31). This evidence clearly points to Joseph Davenport being the senior partner in Hamburg at this date (not James junior, as stated in my 1972 Davenport book) though as indicated earlier, at some time in this period both James Davenport junior and Uriah were working in Hamburg with their brother, and James did take control in 1832.

That Hamburg was an important element in the whole Davenport enterprises is clearly evident from all the relevant documents. Like London and Liverpool, it must be stressed that the Hamburg outlet did not only sell Davenport wares. They certainly marketed these as one of their primary functions, but both glass and ceramics of other manufacturers were traded and the scale of the merchanting side of the various Davenport subsidiaries is an aspect which could well provide further interesting research. They were running a quite complex integrated business combining the manufacture, export, and selling both wholesale and retail of ceramics and glass through a considerable number of outlets in this country and abroad.

Hamburg was a key component in the selling chain. In 1828 Henry Pontigny informed Henry Davenport 'You will hear with surprise that your father with Mrs. D. & William are fairly on their way to Hambro' in the steamer William Jolliffe.' Knowing John Davenport this would not be purely a family reunion!

But as with many Davenport matters things did not proceed entirely smoothly.

In 1831 James Davenport junior, who had a decade earlier caused difficulties at Longport, was apparently back in Liverpool and causing further trouble. On 3 October John Davenport wrote to Henry:

'In a conversation with James D- last I was vexed to observe a most deadly and rancorous feeling towards Fynney . . . and I think it right to advise you of it – He complained of Fynney's personal conduct towards him & others in L'pool . . . the sore is probably Fynney having been admitted into the concern instead of himself – He vilified McClean the protege of Fynney as a great rascal & drunken so that he was often turned out of the straw by Fynney himself . . . I fear he is very narrow in his feelings and disposition, a very different man to his Brother Joseph – and more like to his little brother Uriah – I scarcely know what you will do with him. But sift him and analyse him thoroughly before you trust him far – Joe is worth a thousand of him in every way – He will be more open with you than me . . .'

Whatever John's misgivings in October 1831, by 14 July the following year the situation had changed. A letter of that date to Henry enquires:
What is become of Joe & what should be done with him? Our affairs as you say are all abroad – our energies however should rise with our difficulties – This used to be the case with me and now I dont fear half as much a voyage to Hamburg as a Canvass in the Potteries – will you write to James D. – or shall I proposing to him to take the Hamburg concern, and then try to bargain with Joe for his interest – it should be more fitting for Will to take up some part of our disjointed affairs than to think of Marrying at present – if the Hamburg house fails us we shall be deeply injured – for Fynneys bad debts & the bad debts here [London], *profits are quite out of the question . . .*

A vintage John Davenport letter, which earlier had stated:
we are all alarm here, 14 decided cases of Cholera in Town . . . Things here will be in a bad state, all trade paralyzed – I really believe we arrived at a most important crisis & that we shall have convulsions in every part of the Empire. In Ireland a rebellion is almost certain. Foreign powers will interdict all commerce with our Shores now they are infected, and what that may lead to, God knows – would it not be wise to hoard a few Guineas . . . (Foxley, 68)

Just a week later on 22 July 1832 he wrote again to Henry, an indication of the urgency with which he viewed the Hamburg concern, but this time without the alarmist hyperbole:
James has arrived & we have consulted on the best manner of affecting that which is so desirable & so essential to us all. As it appears by a letter from Uriah that Joseph has left the House, & is now with him in [perfect quietness?] *I trust that you will have no difficulty in arranging with him as proposed . . .* (Foxley, 70)

Then follows three sides of detailed legal and financial transactions which will be involved in transferring the Hamburg business into the hands of James from those of Joseph who apparently has given up the job, possibly through illness. As noted earlier both James and Uriah were back in Liverpool for the 1841 Census return. It is not known who had charge of Hamburg at this date.

There is one set of interesting figures contained in the letter. The Johannes Strasse is given a net cash value of £3,560, and the net income from the premises is recorded as £311 per annum.

There are a number of other references to the Hamburg concern in various parts of the Foxley papers, but a sufficient indication has been given of its importance and of the manner in which the family, whatever may have been its failings, were extensively used as working members of the business. As is noted later (p. 63) the Hamburg connection lasted until very late in the factory's life; that at Lübeck apparently outlived it.

Reference has already been made to the visit to St Petersburg in 1817 (Foxley, 35). What was achieved here is not recorded. Nor do the Foxley papers contain any reference to 'the finest series of services of earthenware, china and glass ever turned out in the Potteries . . . that made for the Emperor of Russia – every piece was ensuite, and bore the Imperial arms' (*Pottery Gazette*, 1 March, 1893). Is the 1852 earthenware plate shown in Plate 128 a survivor of that service? But this is to jump ahead to a later period. In the time of John Davenport there is more documentary evidence such as the long letter of 6 July 1822 (Foxley, 14) from Samuel Hopkins who had been acting for four years as Davenport's agent in Messina, but who now wishes to return to England. James Davenport junior, as we have seen (p. 24) established himself in Brussels for a period around 1823. In 1828 (Foxley, 51) John Davenport wrote to Henry 'to pay more attention to the Rio orders to have them done in the very best manner that we may establish a regular trade, even a monopoly of the trade to that place – It is far preferable to any round Cape Horn or to Mexico.' Spain and Italy (Foxley, 74) have also regular documented trade and it would seem likely that either through London or more directly through one of the Continental agencies the various Davenport partnerships traded with most countries in Europe, and as we know, at a later date with India too.

If London, Hamburg and Lübeck were the focal points of Davenport trade to the Continent and even further afield to the East, Liverpool held the key to the transatlantic trade. The first reference to Davenport wares in the United States has kindly been reported by Nancy Dickenson in connection with her research on the papers of Ferguson & Day, merchants of New York. It clearly indicates some of the hazards of exporting wares such considerable distances with the transport available at the time. It is also a salutary reminder of the problems of securing a just settlement of monies due when the lines of communication are so extended. The reference comes in a letter to Ferguson & Day written on 20 February 1807 from George Gilchrest, a merchant and exporter of Liverpool, who complains that he is having difficulty with extracting payment from Ebetts & Gale who had a china store at '71 Pearl' in New York City. The letter reads (in part):

I doubt not you have used every exertion to terminate this business as favourably as possible, but the abatement made by Ebetts & Gale is a very serious one indeed & from the enclosed letter I received from Messrs. J. & J. Davenport on the subject, a house of first respectability here, whom I purchased them from, you will perceive they will allow nothing whatever for breakage. Now it is customary to have claims of this kind made upon them, as the ware was of the best quality, regularly packed, & shipped in good order – I have also had the opinion of several other dealers . . . but find I can claim nothing for breakage & as they observe it is inevitable in a voyage to America . . . you will therefore perceive that I shall lose the abatement of upwards £80 Stg. instead of a profit unless you are enabled to recover something from Ebetts & Gale – and beg you will endeavour to do so, it is nothing but just to expect an allowance from them – If any of the Crates were of bad quality, samples of the crazed ware should have been sent. The observation you made in a former letter that they perhaps were b'ot at auction. I made every enquiry respecting but found all the Crates per Ontario were landed & reshipped pr same vessel to New York . . .

It is not known if Mr Gilchrest was recompensed by Ebetts & Gale who had originally complained of both damaged and inferior ware. Exporting was not, as one might say, all plain sailing.

The next reference to the American trade is an advertisement (reported by Rodney Hampson) in the *Staffordshire Gazette* for 10 May 1814 requiring a packer and an 'outdoor clerk' in the earthenware store 'in British America'. From what has just been noted we could infer that these posts were probably in Ontario or possibly Montreal. It could easily have been through this route that the Davenport wares printed with the portraits of the heroes of the War of 1812 (see Plates 133–4) were distributed to the United States. At this date, and indeed for another decade of more, there is no indication that Davenport had a regular agency in the USA, but all the archaeological evidence is that Davenport wares were being imported for some time before any formal agency was established.

This supposition is supported by other evidence. Elizabeth Collard in her fine book *Nineteenth Century Pottery & Porcelain in Canada* notes an auctioneer's advertisement in the *Novascotian* for 6 December 1827, offering for sale amongst the household furniture 'a dinner set, DAVENPORT WARE, 247 pieces'. As Mrs Collard comments, 'Davenport became a household word' throughout North America. By 1828 John Davenport seems to have been actively exploring the possibility of a more permanent presence in America. On 26 January he wrote to his son Henry:

Fynney must look for some one to go to the US: – he can spare Everard for a twelve month – and our surplus stock would sell at Auction there better than in London . . . [he adds with another swipe at his old adversary] also as to Pontigny going to Spain – I don't think it would do much good for us . . . (Foxley, 53).

Three years later on 21 January 1831 John Davenport is still concerned about the American market. Writing to Henry, he notes:
What we have first to ascertain is the actual value of a piece of our Wares in the United States for unless a profit can be made we should not attempt to take up that trade – But I must remark that the quickness of returns compared with those from S America & the E Indies would make less capital necessary . . . (Foxley, 61)

John Davenport returned to the theme a few weeks later in a more general sense in a letter of 21 March to his younger son William:
Making goods, as I observed some time ago to your Brother, is but a small part of the duty of a master, perhaps the least, for the gains there come by small matters, while the property, by sales and consignments, is put at risque in heavy sums, and requires the exercise of a sound judgment & clear understanding with the parties, who are intrusted with it – Besides when you are carrying on with a party, of whose responsibilities you have doubts – the results are always like this – the dealers order goods, which you delay, or do not send at all, because the remittances from your agent are not duly transmitted to you, & so you lose the trade . . . a foreign trade can never be conducted with success unless the most minute and continual attention is paid to what is going on in the Sales, & in the collection of the monies at the periods when they become due. (Foxley, 81)

This realistically hard-headed attitude had probably been the reason why John Davenport had never formally taken premises in the United States, despite the obvious attractions compared with the South American trade and that to the East Indies. It may have been his influence that persuaded Henry & William Davenport to establish a formal agency agreement, which seems to have been entered upon by them in the early 1830s. The agents were to be the New Orleans firm best known as Henderson & Gaines. This connection is fully authenticated by a special mark which appears on wares handled by the American firm (Plate 12). However, recent research in the United States has indicated that pieces have been found in collections or excavated which bear the mark of two previous partnerships, Hill & Henderson who traded in the period 1822–34 and Henderson, Walton & Co. in 1834–6. It was only in 1836 that the partnership of Henderson & Gaines was established and this continued until 1866. The pieces date-stamped 1836 tie up nicely with this long-lived partnership, but the new evidence found by Art Black and Cynthia Brandimarte, published in *Research Notes* by the Texas Parks and Wildlife Dept (Nov. 1987) and reported by George Miller would indicate that his son had acted upon John's suggestions in 1831 and established the New Orleans connection at some time after 1831 and before 1834. This was to last at the maximum until 1867, though Black and Brandimarte report the latest datable excavated piece as being from 1853, though as this was a design registration mark, the actual vessel could have been made later. They speculate that the arrangement may have been terminated by the Civil War. One further point is worth noting from this most informative paper on the various Henderson partnerships. The authors record: 'In addition to the name and address variation noted above, the printed mark also occurs in a variety of colors. These marks occur on vessels with printed designs (transferware). Known transfer designs which occur with these importer marks include CHINESE PASTIMES, RUINS and the SCOTTS ILLUSTRATIONS series, all known Davenport designs.'

As a postscript to the above, George Miller also reported a research paper published in January 1988 by Leslie C. Stewart-Abernathy subtitled 'Perspectives on the Antebellum Ceramics Trade from a Merchant Family's Trash in Washington, Arkansas.' Amongst the material excavated from the trash of the Blocks of Washington Arkansas, a prominent family of merchants from the 1820s to the 1860s, was Davenport pottery with the marks of both Henderson, Walton & Co. and Henderson & Gaines and date marks from the 1830s into the 1850s. The paper also reports 'archaeological finds of Henderson-related importer's marks are known from Arkansas, Louisiana, Missouri, Oklahoma and as far west as California.' It would appear that Davenport chose wisely in using Henderson & Gaines as their agents in New Orleans. Perhaps it hardly need be added that examples with these marks are very rare in Britain and the authors cannot recall having seen pieces of either 'Ruins' or 'Chinese Pastimes' with the additional New Orleans importer's mark. It is very gratifying that our knowledge of Davenport's activities can be further increased by both documentary and archaeological work in the United States.

There is certainly a paucity of information on trade on this side of the Atlantic and systematic research of the kind reported above and that done by Mrs Collard in Canada would be most valuable in throwing light on Davenport's trade with North America. Mrs Collard was able to glean many references from such papers as the *Montreal Gazette*, which on 14 June 1851 reported a sale 'alongside the brig BRITONS PRIDE of 50 crates of assorted earthenware from the well-known house of William Davenport & Co. of Liverpool'. Later in the same year the *City of Manchester* put in at Montreal and a sale was held of 64 crates and H'hds assorted earthenware also from Davenport (Collard, *op. cit.*, pp. 243–4). These excerpts and those which follow relate to a period after the time of John Davenport, but it was felt sensible to draw together all the available evidence relating to trade with North America in one place. There is so little evidence from the later period in the British archives we have consulted that to separate the material artificially did not seem advisable.

Finally in this survey of American trade it should be noted that at some date as yet unknown the Davenports opened a New York showroom. It would seem certain that the date of this could be established from documentary research in the United States, but so far as we know this has not been done. There are no references in the Foxley documents that we have seen. The first mention is in the Wood Papers relating to the 1880s, but obviously the New York showroom had been established before this.

Two final transatlantic snippets. In 1975 a correspondent reported to me a plate in his possession of pattern 2226, royal blue, gold and white with the impressed DAVENPORT mark of the 1870+ period. Additionally, it was marked with a printed red mark: GILMAN COLLAMORE & Co. UNION SQUARE, NEW YORK. Again this would seem to be the mark of a retailer or agent that Davenport used on a sufficient scale to make the engraving of a special mark worth while. An 'Oriental' shaped octagonal jug of the very popular pattern 6060 of *c.*1880 in the Jennifer Moody collection also has this mark, which is placed in a broken circular band around a very elaborate anchor surmounted by a crown (Plates 13A, B).

As has been indicated there is plenty of scope, especially it would seem in both documentary and archaeological material, in the United States for further research on

12. Mark of the New Orleans importers, Henderson & Gaines, *c.*1836.

Davenport's trade with North America; the agencies and showrooms established there, the sales and other commerical outlets, and the type of ware exported and the clients who purchased them. It would be gratifying if this brief section were to act as a stimulus to a researcher with access to the material on the American side to give us at some future date a much fuller picture of this fascinating aspect of the factory's work. It would be a suitable challenge for some member of the Keele University International Summer School to undertake!

13A. Porcelain jug decorated with the popular pattern No. 6060, in the style of Crown Derby, c.1875–85. (Jennifer Moody Collection)

13B. Mark of Gilman Collamore & Co., Union Square, New York, on the jug above. (Jennifer Moody Collection)

5 John Davenport – The Later Years

The consecutive narrative was temporarily abandoned at around 1815. In the discussion of the family and of the trading practices of the firm we have covered much of the ground in the years that followed. However, certain items do call for further comment. Moreover the period from 1815 until *c.*1835, when to a very large extent John Davenport had ceased to have much day-to-day contact with the factory, are years of the highest achievement in his career. The exports markets were open to him, the reputation of the firm was high, his bone china was now of an excellent stable body and his family were coming to an age when they could be of service to the concern.

Commissions for services for important occasions continued to be received. Indeed one very intriguing reference appears in *The Connoisseur*, November 1909 as follows:

UNIQUE DINNER SERVICE made for perhaps the greatest banquet of all time (DAVENPORT CHINA), given to Russian Czar, Prussian King, Bourbon Louis XVIII and Prince Regent, June, 1814, at the Guildhall. Guaranteed. Specimens and price, for lot, or pieces, Connoisseur office or A. Ring Esq., Pandora Lodge, Seaview, I.W. Would accept £80 for the lot.

Even allowing for advertising hyperbole, this is an attractive prospect, and the price would not deter a modern collector! Alas, we have been unable either to trace this service or any further references. However the service made for George IV on his accession is better known and was described in the *Pottery Gazette*, 1 March 1893:

On the accession of the Prince to the throne, His Majesty entrusted to Mr Davenport the manufacture of the china services to be used at his coronation banquet. Both as regards richness and the quality of the workmanship, the effect was superb, to the gratification of both the manufacturer and his employees. The King caused it to be made known to Mr Davenport that he was highly pleased with the satisfactory manner in which his commands had been carried out, the artistic taste being most commendable. This was the first occasion that the royal crown was used in the stamping of Davenport china.

A few examples of this service still survive at Windsor Castle and a tureen from the Lockett collection was illustrated in *Staffordshire Porcelain*, Pl. 226. The service has a simple blue border, the Royal Arms, and the tureen finial is in the form of a crown.

Just before the accession of George IV the radical agitation which had been increasing steadily since the end of the Wars reached a new pitch with the so-called Peterloo Massacre in Manchester on Sunday 16 August 1819. Eleven people were killed and over 400 injured when the yeomanry charged the crowd of some 60,000 who had come to hear 'Orator' Henry Hunt. John Davenport writing on 19 August comments on the incident:

This chastisement of the demagogues at Manchester although severe will I trust prove wholesome. How monstrous it is that the poor people who want more work and better wages should be told and persuaded that a Parliamentary reform will procure it to them – At Coventry they have been more consistent, the remedy there has at least been more applicable to the disease. My opinion is that the masters have not (particularly in the North) done for their labourers what they might & ought to have done. (Foxley, 25)

Interesting sentiments from a man who was later to become a Tory MP.

Somewhat amusingly there is also a letter in the Foxley papers (No. 7, 16 May 1820) written by a Thomas Bamford to John Davenport with some interesting reflections on Radicalism as manifest in the factory of Josiah Wedgwood. He writes:

I visited Mr Wedgwood at Etruria last Saturday, it is needless to say I was 'Most graciously rec'd' – But very much disgusted by the chalk writing in every part of the premises – such as Mr Wilmot Brown for ever &c &c – why not have wrote Equality for ever – levelling for ever – No Governors to watch for our good – no Masters to render to the honest labourer his hire – and thereby feed *him with wholesome* food *– and furnish comfortable* clothing *– no Wives to thwart our designs and interrupt our* Jovial Glass *– no Children to* trouble us *with their manifold* wants *and* complaints *– 'Hunt for ever' – who had the courage and humanity to* turn *Wife and Children out of* doors *– and take an* harlot *and has the* goodness *and* honesty *to give us the necessary information respecting the above named* tyrants *and Oppressors –* . . .

A delightful piece of invective which no doubt would have amused Davenport especially as it would reflect somewhat badly on his fellow potter Josiah Wedgwood. One cannot imagine John Davenport tolerating Radical slogans chalked on the walls of the Longport Works!

    As was pointed out previously, from as early as 1817 Henry Davenport began to play an increasing part in the affairs of the concern. In the 1822 letter quoted on p. 32 (Foxley, 13), Henry includes a typical remark: 'You may be on the lookout for a bookkeeper, the animal we have here will have notice to leave in a few days, you would not bear him a week, he is a double Marmot, he sleeps both winter and summer.' The Davenport correspondence is never boring.

    In a more serious vein, the death of James Davenport in 1822 and the entry into the firm of Henry and Victor Pontigny together with the growing importance of Fynney's work at Liverpool led eventually to a complete reorganization of the structure of the business. This was formally recorded in a circular letter to clients:

Longport Pottery and Glass Works
Staffordshire. 14th April 1825

Sir,

    I beg to inform you that from the time of the decease of my late Copartner Mr James Davenport, I have taken into Copartnership my son Henry Davenport, who has for some time the Direction of the Manufactories in Staffordshire, Mr Mountford Fynney, who for many years has managed our Concerns at Liverpool, and Mr Henry Pontigny with whom I have long been connected in London.

    From the 1st May next, the Business will be conducted under the following Firms.
At Longport . . . John Davenport, Son & Co.
At Liverpool . . . Davenports, Fynney & Co.
In London . . . Davenports, Pontigny & Co.
    I am very respectfully,
    Sir,
    Your obliged humble Serv't
    J'n Davenport.   (Foxley, 29)

    Pontigny's share in the concern was an eighth. Thomas Kinnersley held a quarter share. These arrangements were not to last for long. By the end of the year Kinnersley was in severe financial difficulties and John Davenport was able to offer security for him which enabled the Bank of England to lend Kinnersley £80,000. But early in 1828 Kinnersley was finally bought out of the business for some £17,000, thus severing the link which had lasted since Davenport entered the Kinnersley bank nearly fifty years earlier. The Pontigny partnership did not last long either, the dissolution of that partnership being reported in the *London Gazette* on 20 June 1827 (p. 2650). The cost of this was some £8,500 which John Davenport bitterly resented paying. Further details and quotations from letters concerning these partnerships are given in *Davenport Pottery &*

Porcelain. Similarly a number of personal letters to Henry and William from their father dealing both with family matters and the conduct of the business at this period were also quoted, and to make room for new material have not been repeated here.

The year 1830 was an especially important one in the history of the factory. For with the death of George IV, the new reign brought renewed Royal patronage. William IV, who it will be recalled had visited the factory in 1806, was pleased to order from Davenports a dessert service which was used at his Coronation banquet. All the correspondence relating to this service has already been published in my previous book, pp. 78–84, but it is worth quoting again part of a letter sent by John Davenport to his son William on 20 November 1830:

Dear Will,

The King has requested to have the Group completed with a red, & white rose, shamrock, thistle, & leek, – tied with a Union Riband – I am getting a drawing made here to save time. I regret my instructions were so badly attended to, for these people don't like trouble – I learn that four or five services are now ordered – we shall I fear be the last to complete his Orders . . . We shall have trouble with this thing – I believe however that our specimen stands first – Flight & Barr are doing theirs in a blue ground . . .

I am your affect' father
Jn Davenport (Foxley, 79)

There were other problems before the service was completed which John Davenport did not hesitate to point out in detail: 'the Bouquet is not in the Centre of the plate and the painting which appears over-fired . . . the Stems are poor and thin the White Rose not well managed . . . ' (Foxley, 58)

John Davenport need not have feared. There were only two rival services, that produced by Flight Barr & Barr, details of which and illustrations thereof may be found in Henry Sandon's *Flight & Barr Worcester Porcelain 1783–1840* (1978), and that produced by the Rockingham factory, so severely delayed in the manufacture that it was only delivered to William IV just over a month before he died in June 1837. Full details of this service are in Alwyn and Angela Cox, *Rockingham Pottery and Porcelain 1745–1842* (1983). Davenport clearly was not the last to complete the order. Unfortunately, there appears to be no record of the cost of this service.

There is no doubt that it was very well received. The Duke of Wellington on a visit to Trentham Hall in September 1830 was reported in the *Staffordshire Advertiser* (25 September) to have visited Spode and Wedgwood and 'the extensive china and glass manufactures of Messrs Davenport at Longport . . . What appeared to excite great admiration were some very splendid and highly finished specimens of services ordered by His Majesty which in style and execution were allowed to excel anything which has been seen in this country.' It would seem that the Duke had a preview of the designs which were to be submitted for Royal approval a couple of months later. On 24 September 1831, the *Staffordshire Advertiser* carried a lengthy description of the service, and noted that a Royal patent had been issued appointing Davenports 'Porcelain Manufacturers to Their Majesties'. This proud title was incorporated in the firm's marks on porcelain wares until the end of William's reign (see mark P 8 on p. 209).

Plate 14 illustrates one of the low comports from the Royal service, showing very clearly the bouquet in the centre with the floral emblems of the countries of Great Britain. The other shapes are all illustrated in *Transactions of the English Ceramic Circle* 9 Pt 1 (1973). In 1855 there were 187 pieces still at Buckingham Palace though some were reported damaged and cracked. At some later date, further damaged pieces were withdrawn from the Royal Inventory and examples have been offered for sale both at the beginning of this century and more recently in the 1970s. Thus the determined collector has a chance of acquiring a piece of this finely decorated Royal service. Although some damaged pieces have been removed and disposed of over the years, the remainder of the

14

service is still kept on display at Buckingham Palace and despite some rather alarming stress cracks which have appeared over the years the service is still a splendid sight, which we had the privilege of seeing set out on the Library shelves in the room adjoining the Household Breakfast Room, where with only occasional temporary removal for decorating, it has been displayed and admired by many visitors to Buckingham Palace for well over fifty years.

The autumn of 1831 must have been a particularly gratifying period of his life for John Davenport. He had successfully completed yet another commission from a member of the Royal family, and on this occasion for the reigning sovereign who had appointed him a Royal Manufacturer. Shortly before receiving this honour his fellow potters had paid him a deserved tribute. On 16 July 1831 the *Staffordshire Advertiser* published a letter which was addressed to John Davenport and signed by many of his fellow potters. It urged him to stand for election to Parliament, together with Josiah Wedgwood, when the Reform Act was completed and the area was entitled to elect two members of Parliament. His acceptance of the nomination and the support of his fellow manufacturers is also noted in the paper.

Polling in the election took place on 11–12 December 1832. The candidates were Davenport and Wedgwood for the Tory cause, the Radical George Miles Mason and Richard Edensor Heathcote. A full account of the whole election is given by Reginald G. Haggar in *The Masons of Lane Delph*. As with most events associated with John Davenport it was not without acrimony. In his election address (a copy of which is preserved at the City Museum, Stoke-on-Trent) he rebuts the 'malignant aspersions' of his opponents who apparently had accused him of bigotry in politics and religion and as being opposed to the 'Education of the People'. On the hustings when Davenport spoke 'missiles were profusely thrown . . . inflicting some severe contusions on several gentlemen.' The windows of his committee rooms and those of some of his supporters' houses were smashed. Mason accused him of bribing the voters as did John Henry Clive in a 155-verse mock-Bible poem on the election. It seems that the spirit of Eatanswill was very much alive at this first Parliamentary election in Stoke. In the event he and Wedgwood were elected fairly comfortably. He entered Parliament, 'the highest honour attainable to an English commoner' as he expressed it, at the age of sixty-seven. He retained his seat in the election of 6 January 1835. When a further election was necessitated by the death of William IV in 1837 he was (according to Ward) 'reluctant to be put again in nomination, on account of his age and infirmities, but was prevailed upon to comply with the wishes of his friends, to nominate and re-elect him without any personal trouble or expense.' There were again apparently disgraceful scenes, but Davenport was duly elected along with his fellow potter William Taylor Copeland. He could hardly have

14. Porcelain comport from the dessert service made for William IV. The comport rests on four gilt lion's paw feet. Dimensions: 13½ × 9¼ × 4½in. (ht), 1830. (By Gracious permission of Her Majesty the Queen)

44 · The Family and Factory

been a very active member in this Parliament for all commentators seem to agree that he retired and settled in Westwood in 1838. Certainly he did not contest the 1841 election. This political aspect of Davenport's career has been researched by Gilly Thornhills, and the University of Keele Library holds an unpublished dissertation 'John Davenport the Politician' (1984).

John Davenport's entry into politics occurred at a time when the Longport factories were already under the title of Henry and William Davenport & Co. but John remained the owner and though he spent most of his time in London, the Foxley papers still contain many letters from John Davenport to both of his sons on pottery and family financial matters. It would seem that he could not let loose the reins, or more likely could not forbear to offer gratuitous and possibly totally unwanted advice to them both. Some of these letters have already been noted, quotations from others appeared in my 1972 book or 1973 E.C.C. article and a few extra items will be recorded later in this chapter. Taken together they do however give the lie to the oft-repeated statement that John Davenport retired from active concern with the Pottery in 1830. It was a least five years if not more before that came to pass.

It is only an assumption that he ceased active participation in Pottery affairs $c.1835$ or later. The assumption is based upon the lack of letters after that date in the Foxley papers. It could however, be argued that the death of Henry Davenport in 1835 was the turning point. He and his father had always enjoyed a better relationship than that which existed between William and his father. With Henry dead, William took full control at Longport and the firm was titled William Davenport & Co. Moreover John was now seventy and an MP and he may well have either despaired of influencing William or been told to mind his own business. There is of course another explanation, and that is that John Davenport continued his frequent epistolary advice, but the letters were not preserved at this date by William, as many clearly were by Henry, and thus they have not found their way into the archive. Thus a lack of evidence could easily lead us to false assumptions about the relationships within the Davenport family in the period following Henry's death. For whatever reason the 'Pottery letters' file in the Foxley papers ends with letters written to Henry in 1835, and we thus have to look elsewhere for information.

Fortunately there are many other documents in the general Foxley papers at Hereford. And it is from one of these that we learn of the purchase of the Williamson factory in 1834/5 sometime before the death of Henry. As the use of these buildings chiefly concerns William Davenport the purchase will be studied in the next chapter.

When John Davenport finally retired to Westwood $c.1838$ he was seventy-three years of age. He was still active in his mind, and indeed very active in business and property matters, and he kept his accounts as strictly as ever. He may well have played little part in the activities of the Pottery and the glass house, but he still continued to draw very considerable sums from the concerns, as a statement he drew up in 1845 signifies. From an undated and unaddressed memorandum we read (in part):

Account of my co-partnership Assets:-

Jun 30 1838–Dec 1845.   *I have drawn out of the concern say about £90,000*
Since June 1838 to Dec. 1845   *I have invested the above and other Monies in:*

  Land: Abbey Birchall
  House, Gardens   *£45,000*

  Canal and
  Railway shares   *£71,000*
  Railway bonds

Total invested on private a/c £116,000
This includes your T & M [Trent & Mersey] *& 40 of your G.J.* [Grand Junction] *Canal shares.*

1838 June 30th By balance   £178,428-2-7d.
1846 Buildings to be valued say   £ 25,000-0-0d.
Share of profits say 8 years   £ 60,000-0-0d.

                                                     £263,428-2-7d.
                          Less   £ 90,000-0-0d.

                  In the concern   £173,428-2-7d.

*This W.D. seeming objects to, though he has never spoken quite out – I shall not give it up – but without taking stock we cant take it will not be more, but may be less.
[In pencil is added underneath:]   *116,000* [total investments]
                                              173,428 [his share in concern]
                                              289,428

This last total is in effect his assets and income over the eight-year period of his 'retirement'.

    These are astronomical sums in modern money. He had invested something like £10 million in the eight years, and whilst taking no active part in the concern (as far as we know) had received something approaching half a million a year from it.

    In the same year (24 March 1845) he had made a will. In this he left sums of money to his daughter Elizabeth Bent, and his 'faithful servant' Margaret Martin and 'all the residue of my personal estate and effects . . . to my said son John absolutely . . . And I give devise and appoint unto my said son John his heirs and assigns all my real estate whatsoever . . .' John was also appointed Executor. This was manifestly unfair to William, but as the statement of accounts quoted above indicates, he and William were still apparently at odds. He must have had second thoughts for he altered the will without the witnesses being aware that he had done so. A codicil of 18 March 1848 signed in a somewhat shaky hand was very important for it made what in all justice can only be regarded as sensible provision for William. To him he bequeathed:

. . . *all those my Earthenware Manufactory, Glass Works, Dwellings houses and other erections, Land and premises with appurtenances situate at Longport . . . in the occupation of William Davenport & Co. . . . and also a piece of land lying opposite the said Glass Works called Williamson's Brickbank . . . and also the Freehold land, Crate shops, Saggar Houses, Messuages, Dwelling Houses or Tenements hereditaments and appurtenances known by the name of Middleport and extending from the Trent and Mersey Canal to the lane leading to Newport House . . . and also that slip of land near thereto and adjoining the said Canal with the Flint Ark and other buildings standing thereon . . . And being all the real property I am possessed of in the parish of Burslem aforesaid except my Newport House, Works and land purchased by me from Walter Daniel and a piece of land thereto and adjoining to the lane leading to Newport House aforesaid purchased by me from Hugh Henshall Williamson and others – To such person and persons for such estates and in such manner as my son William Davenport shall by any deed or writing not Testamentary appoint and in default of appointment to him and his assigns for his life . . .*

    John Davenport had not long to live after signing this codicil to his will. He died on 12 December 1848 at the age of 83. He was buried in the graveyard of Leek Parish Church where in April 1841 he is recorded (Foxley, S 19) to have purchased all the lands etc., tithes and pews, the property of George Yeldman Wilkinson for the sum of £31,250. The church (Plate 15) has a simply inscribed tablet to him by the west door. In the graveyard to the south-east of the church may be found the headstone illustrated in Plate 16 which under the name of his father Jonathan and his mother Hannah bears the words:

their son JOHN DAVENPORT
of Westwood
was buried in the vault
December 18th 1848,
aged 83 years.

15. The Parish Church, Leek. (Author's photograph, 1987).
16. The tombstone of John Davenport in Leek Parish Churchyard. (Author's photograph, 1977)

His obituary in the *Staffordshire Advertiser* (16 December 1848) records:

He entered the Potteries an almost friendless youth; but he had resolute determination and persevering industry on his side and he lived to attain the summit of

47 · The Family and Factory

commercial eminence and fortune . . . Much of the fortune thus honourably acquired has been employed in the purchase of properties capable of improvement, and his favourite estate of Westwood is an instance of the judicious application of capital to agriculture. Thriving plantations and fruitful fields cover hundreds of acres, which not many years ago were comparatively sterile . . .

Of himself he had spoken in 1834:
I am not loth to acknowledge that I began in the world with as few prospects as any of my contemporaries . . . in that line of business in which, by the blessing of God, I have been eminently successful . . . by patient and persevering industry and probity . . .

Our judgement today?

We are more fortunately placed to make a judgement upon him as a man, a potter and as a business man, than we are of almost any of his contemporaries. We have the abundant evidence of his own pen in personal letters and accounts, in addition to the pots which his factories produced. Few other potters have left so much personal material other than the Wedgwood family, and research into the Davenport archive is always more rewarding than the somewhat dreary trudge through the statistics of sales and the bare, dry bones of partnership agreements between men who seem totally anonymous. More than any other potter I have ever studied John Davenport is 'real'. In this way a collection of his pots has a life and meaning of a special character. We can still visit the canal-side factory site; go to Westwood, now a private girls' school; make a pilgrimage to Leek and see his memorial and grave, and read his most personal thoughts written to those closest to him. In this way the people behind the pots we admire in our cabinets take on as much significance as the pieces themselves. Though I suspect that John Davenport himself would regard this attitude as wholly and inappropriately sentimental!

In assessing his importance as a potter, we have to remember that as far as we know he had no experience as an actual practitioner. He was not a potter. Yet time and again in the correspondence we see his unfailing eye for what makes a good pot - which means an aesthetically attractive one, as well as one that will sell well. Two outstanding examples of this are to be found in letters written to Henry his son in 1834 when he was in his seventieth year, but with critical faculties as sharp as ever.

This order is for Amsterdam – I had much talk with the man [Oppenheim] *who says if encouraged he can do much business . . . The plate Blue & gold with Landscape is very Good – the Landscape might have been lighter and not so yellow or Autumn as he called it – I think the sky too formal* [rounded] *– the top of the tree to be the highest – It is very beautifully painted altogether – the distance is nicely managed – the foreground capital – it is the stiff appearance of the sky by one or two touches which should have been left out – I state this because he said that the landscapes were much liked, and that in that and figure painting we were much behind the French – our flowers, insects, and gilding he thought superior – Try and get into a light yet good and finished style in Landscape, the High finishing being confined – Give your Painter a Lecture at length on this subject – if we can beat the French out of Holland and Belgium we shall find a good Market – the Saucer is not good, the Gilding* [a small drawing at this point] *bad here, what I call under Glaze – the Buildings in the Landscape some of them are very stiff – and for such small things too much work in them.* (Foxley, 71, 7 June 1834)

Comment is superfluous on such a masterly discussion of a pot and its sales potential. Similarly, in a letter of 19 July 1834 (Foxley, 38) John Davenport exhibits a precise and detailed knowledge of pottery techniques, but shrewdly allied to marketing opportunities for the wares. Again he is writing to his son Henry: 'I have been here all day engaged with our Travellers, on the subject of prices & patterns – that is new patterns of Blue Table Ware in which we are behind Mintons and Ridgways – What is wanting is the exercise of more Judgement in the selection of Patterns . . .' (The remainder of this letter is printed in full on pp. 134–5).

When one reads such a detailed analysis of a piece of blue printed ware it seems very clear that whatever may have been John Davenport's defects, a lack of knowledge of what made a desirable and saleable pot was not one of them. As a potter he knew his trade.

Which inevitably brings us to his abilities as a businessman. Enough indications have already been given as evidence of his immense success in this direction. He knew the essential principles of a regular disciplined work force; of subordinates who were both loyal and capable; of a product range that was neither too daring nor too dull to sell effectively. He was an excellent accountant and trained others to be perpetually vigilant in curbing expenditure and collecting monies due. Occasionally, his enthusiasm for thrift becomes laughable and he almost appears to be overplaying his own prudence. Thus on 7 January 1828 he is concerned about the volume of paper used at Longport and admonishes Henry 'wastepaper in the House at Longport . . . amounts to *a very serious sum.*' And quite hilariously he had addressed Henry on 27 December 1825 (Foxley, S 45).
Dear Henry

Franklin says, 'If you would know the value of money, try to borrow some' – for the first time in my life, I have tried to borrow and have been refused, ergo, I now know the value of money better than I did before and have come to the determination to economize in every department . . .

Two or three weeks ago I thought I wanted a new hat and a new coat & I have now discovered that I can do very well without them – & on everything I look round and exclaim as did the old Grecian 'what a great many things there are in the world of which I have no need.'

. . . Take care of your money when you have it . . . what you do lay out lay it out well, don't part with a shilling when sixpence will serve the turn. I have actually changed all my penny pieces into half pence for the beggars and [heater?] *men.*

Tell Mary what Franklin says further, 'a fat kitchen makes a lean wife'. Let her look close to the dripping pan – & see that there is a good lock on the ale barrel – let her pay her butchers bill on the instant & get the odd quarters in weight taken off and the odd [pence?] *abated – let her count her eggs 13 to the dozen & buy her butter 20 ozs to the pound.*

I fancy I have too much Health for I do almost without sleep – I don't know how it is for a week back I have not averaged above three hours a night . . .

I suppose we have to accept this as a serious letter and not an exercise in self-mockery!

It was Davenport's ability to seize an opportunity, to be ever alert to make a sale, or to buy a potentially profitable investment which were his chief business assets. Thus as early as 10 May 1830 he wrote a most perceptive note to William (Foxley, 70):
. . . the Wharf will not readily let I fear – These Railways alarm everyone who has to do with Wharfs & Canals & Warehouses – for if goods can go as cheap to London & etc at the rate of 15 Miles an Hour, as they do now by Water Conveyance, much warehouse room will not be wanting.

I am desirous to sell the Grand Junction shares . . .

The Manchester to Liverpool Railways opened in 1830. It was not long before John Davenport had 'Railway shares and Railway Bonds' in his investment portfolio, to add to his already very considerable self-made fortune.

As a politician he made no mark. His Membership of the House seems to have been more honorary than distinguished. He made but one speech.

Finally, as a person, one cannot but agree with Reginald Haggar's epithet when he called Davenport 'an old curmudgeon'. He was a hard, gritty capitalist, who had made his mark, indeed a very considerable fortune, by his own efforts. He had none of the advantages of birth which he gave to his own children. We may be amused by his apparent meanness, and yet some of his contemporaries viewed him slightly differently. Simeon Shaw spoke of him as 'one of the most enterprizing and successful Manufacturers. Of his worth as a private person, the numerous instances of his benevolence are the best testimonials.' Miller described him as 'a man made for the circumstances and times in which he lived, and he was a man who made circumstances bend to his progress in life.' He may not have radiated a warmth of character which his son Henry did, but he most surely commanded respect.

The evidence upon which we base our judgements is always partial and thus two recently discovered items in the Foxley Papers put the somewhat humourless-looking man who stares firmly ahead from the portrait which is our Frontispiece into a much more attractive light. The first is his Commonplace Book dated 1817 (S 47). On the cover it says it is 'equally adapted to the Man of Letters and the Man of Observation; the Traveller and the Student, and forming an useful and agreeable Companion on the Road; and in the Closet.' In it John Davenport has written, usually in longhand, but sometimes in either code or a type of shorthand, quotations which have caught his eye in his reading. They come from Byron, Wordsworth, Coleridge, Reynolds, Rousseau and many others. They are in English, French and Latin and cover topics such as Abstraction, Attention, Commerce, Conduct, Government, Game Laws, Inventions, Portugal, Poor Laws, Poets, Sermons, Taxation, Taste and Volcanoes, just to take a random dip through the text. The entries reveal a man of surprising breadth of view and education considering he left school at the age of six (or so it is said). A man of some refinement, both of taste and feeling. He may have been rough, tough and abrasive, but he read the classics of both ancient and modern literature, bought books and pictures. In his travelling, and in his spare time, he clearly cultivated the finer areas of life.

Finally let John Davenport reveal another facet of his character in this letter written to his granddaughters in 1845 (Foxley, S 45).

My Dear Mimmie
My Dear Dear Di &
My Dear Dear Dear Lucy

I can't afford three letters & this must serve to tell you how glad I was to hear of your late arrival home. I have to tell Mimmie that you leaving me has made me feel very lonesome & dull notwithstanding her saying that [?] as I was accustomed to being too much alone. She hoped I should not feel the want of them.

As for Di Di I have to say that as this is the reason for hiring our servants I must give her notice that she is too big and too fat for a Tiger & she may take the place of Cook as she proposed, but she must set about taking lessons from Nip Robson in the Cuisiniere Royal. If Nip R. has not a copy I can send her one.

Now as to the little girl Lucy I offer to her the place of Tiger. She is better fitted for it than Di in size as well as figure and constitution – if she accepts my offer she may ask Mamma to order the witch tailor to make her a proper suit, blue jacket & red trousers I believe was fixed upon, but let there be plenty of sailor buttons & gold lace all over it – & not to forget her Hussar cap and feather so that we may cut a dash in the park & now I have no more to say at present – only that I will be a good master & am now My Dear Girls your Affec Grpa

Jn Davenport
Westwood 8 Dec
My wedding day
50 years ago.

6 William Davenport & Co., 1835–69

The death of Henry Davenport seems to have been a turning point in the history of the firm. The Company now fell into the hands of William Davenport and was to remain with him for the next thirty-four years. His relationship with his father appears at the best to have been an ambivalent one, but lack of specific documentary evidence makes it unwise to speculate further about their relationship in the remaining thirteen years of John's life.

Shortly before William took sole control a very important acquisition was made which added considerably to the holdings of the Davenports and to the firm then titled Henry & William Davenport. This was the adjacent pottery of Hugh Henshall Williamson. There are a considerable number of quite complex documents in the Foxley papers relating to this transaction which throw an interesting light on the history of this site of which more remains to be seen today than of the Longport Works. It is that area on the Hargreaves map immediately to the north of the bend in the canal above the word Longport (Plate 1) which is clearly visible on Plate 21. Plate 17 shows another part of the rear of the existing buildings from the canal. The factory site is now owned and worked by Price's teapots. A view of another range of buildings including the last surviving bottle oven on the site appears as Plate 18. This is really an historic site whose origins can be traced back in the documents just as far as the Longport works.

The first reference in the abstract of title (Foxley, S 42) records that in 1774 the 'Old or Upper Potworks', belonged to one Luke Bennett. It is referred to as 'All that piece of land or Ground commonly called Cross Croft containing by mensuration 2 acres 1 rod 7 perch or thereabouts, more or less, situate at Longbridge, in the parish of Wolstanton [in the margin is entered, 'This was a mistake it is in the parish of Burslem and the place is called Longport and never was (we believe) called Longbridge'] aforementioned then or late in the holding or occupation of Thos. Lockett his assigns or undertenants. . . .' This old or upper potworks had obviously been built before 1774. It was sold for £137 12s 6d at that date to Hugh Henshall, then of Turnhurst in the parish of Wolstanton. Mr Henshall afterwards sold part 'of the said piece of land to the Company proprietors of the Navigation from the Trent to Mersey for the purposes of their canal &c. . . . on other part of the said land Mr Henshall erected an extensive set of potworks with a Dw. house adjoining and subsequently erected another dwelling house licensed as an Inn called the Pack Horse and the remainder was occupied as Wharfs on the Banks of the Trent & Mersey Canal . . .' Once more we can visit the precise spot and see the

17. Part of the Top Bridge Works as seen from the canal (now Price's Teapots). (Author's photograph, 1987)

18. Part of the Top Bridge Works and surviving bottle oven. A typical canal-side view of the back of an old-established Pottery. (Author's photograph, 1987)

51 · The Family and Factory

'Dw[elling] house adjoining', now the Duke of Bridgewater Inn (Plate 19) and Longport Wharf on the banks of the canal (Plate 20).

Hugh Henshall made his will on 4 August 1810 and 'Gave and devised unto his nephew the said Hugh Henshall Williamson all the potworks called the Old or Upper Potworks with the Wharfs in occupation of Henshall & Williamson.' From 1827 onwards these were worked by Robert Williamson, but it was Hugh Henshall Williamson who initialled the Articles of Agreement drawn up on 10 December 1834, by which Henry Davenport 'doth hereby agree to purchase at or for the price of Two Thousand Pounds all those potworks, erections and buildings, heretofore erected and built . . . and together forming one set of potworks lately in the holding of Robert Williamson & Co. and now of Henry & William Davenport & Co.' Payment was to be made on 1 May 1835. It would seem from this document that the Davenports were already in occupation by December 1834, but I have found no other documentary confirmation of this. It is also not known whether Henry purchased the property out of his own pocket, or together with William, or if they were in any way financed by John Davenport. Henry did not live long to enjoy the fruits of the expanded business which passed to his partner and brother William. This Works became known as the Top Bridge Works. As will be noted again later, the Pottery was finally sold to Mr T. Hughes in 1881 for completion in March 1882 for the sum of £3,100. The Duke of Bridgewater Inn was sold earlier in 1876 for £1975.

Whilst considering the acquisition of additional factory space, we can also note that the next factory along the canal, the Bottom Bridge Works belonging to Edward Bourne, was bought in the early 1849s by William Davenport & Co. Plate 21 shows the

19. The Duke of Bridgewater Inn, the 'Fine Dwelling House' originally erected by Hugh Henshall sometime after 1774. (Author's photograph, 1987)

20. Longport Wharf, built by Hugh Williamson on the banks of the Trent & Mersey canal. (Author's photograph, 1987)

21. The remains of the Bottom Bridge Works, on the right across the canal from the remaining bottle oven at Price's factory. (Author's photograph, 1987).

only surviving remnants of this factory, on the right hand side of the picture across the canal from the Williamson Works and the bottle oven. This too was eventually sold off in the decline of the 1870s. It was purchased in 1876 by Edward Clarke for £7,500.

In 1836 after the purchase of Williamson's factory, William Davenport & Co were the largest enterprise in Staffordshire with some 30 ovens: Copeland & Garrett had 25 and Wedgwood only 15 (Rodney Hampson, 'Ovens Galore', *Northern Ceramic Society Newsletter* 34, June 1979). That Davenports enjoyed great prosperity and prestige was never more amply demonstrated than shortly after the accession of Queen Victoria in the following year.

Alas, we have not found any personal correspondence in the Foxley papers which can add to the description in the *Staffordshire Advertiser* of 11 November 1837 of the banquet given by the City of London in the Guildhall for the young Queen. This was a most sumptuous and remarkable occasion which the paper describes in full detail. Fascinating though the description is of the dinner with the '220 tureens of turtle, the fifty boiled turkeys and oysters . . . the 140 jellies . . . the sixty baskets of mince pies and the 30 baskets of brandy cherries' not to mention the musical arrangements with Mr Jepp playing the Serpent and Mr Handley the 'Cornet-a-Piston', it is the crockery which matters!

After a full description of the gold and silver plate used at the banquet, the report continues:

The China and cut glass were provided by Messrs Davenport, of Fleet Street, and it is but justice to that establishment to state, that although the order was not given till the 13th ult. owing to their incredible exertions it was completed on Monday last, and forwarded to town from their factory in Staffordshire.

The dessert plates for the Royal table, are of white china, with vine border in gold, and a wreath of oak leaves and acorns in raised matt gold, around the rim. A medallion at the top contains the Crown, and another at the bottom the City Arms emblazoned in their proper colours. In the centre are the letters V.R. in a handsome cypher, surrounded by an enamelled wreath of flowers of the most brilliant tints and exquisite workmanship. There are twenty four of these plates, which we understand are valued at ten guineas each, and they certainly form a hitherto unrivalled specimen of the perfection to which the manufacture had attained in this country.

Colour Plate II shows an example of this service, apparently from the description given, one of the 24 made for the Royal table. Clearly there would be no time to devise new shapes and this very characteristic moulding is one of the stock shapes for this period. The plate illustrated is in the Los Angeles County Museum and it is marked with the 'Royal', 'Manufacturers to their Majesties' mark (P 8). With William IV dead, this would be one of the last occasions upon which they could legitimately use this mark of Royal approbation.

The glass provided by Davenport is noted in Part Four, but it was not merely 24 ten-guinea plates which the factory provided so quickly. The report continues:

For the entertainment generally there were furnished by Messrs Davenport [then follows a description of the glass, as given on p. 287. The report continues]. *The china was a pure white ground to correspond with that provided for Her Majesty's table, the patterns being extremely chaste and void of all ornament, with the exception of a vine border in raised gold surrounding the rims, handles, &c.*

There were '500 large plates, 750 soup ditto, 1,500 pie ditto, 1,200 dishes (various sizes), 100 soup tureens, 200 sauce ditto, 50 dessert centre baskets, 200 compotiers, 500 ditto plates, 750 ice ditto &c.'

An impressive quantity of ware supplied by Davenport, as was the glass order. One can hardly imagine John Davenport not being in the thick of this activity. He was still an MP and not yet 'retired to Westwood'. But there is no evidence of his involvement in the surviving documents and no mention in the above report about his having been present at the Banquet at which the wares of his concern were used. Thus in the absence of any evidence to the contrary, one must record this as the first undoubted triumph for William Davenport & Co. Collectors might well look out for examples of this chaste china, with the raised gold vine border.

The absence of family records make it difficult to continue with any kind of consecutive narrative for almost the entire period of William Davenport & Co. In my 1972 book considerable use was made of quotations from that remarkable book *When I Was a Child* written under the pseudonym of 'An Old Potter' by the Revd Charles Shaw. His book was published in 1903, but described incidents of his childhood in the 1840s. The savage conditions he wrote about may well have been a description of one or other of the Davenport factories. The reader is referred to Shaw's work which was reprinted in 1969, but he does present us with what appears to be an authentic description of William Davenport and details a specific incident at the Davenport factory which are worth retelling here.

He writes of 'a later employer' (presumably William Davenport) who:
very occasionally came through the shop with a tall silk hat on, a swallow-tailed coat and shining boots. His habit was never to stop a moment, but to look up and forward, over the heads of the workpeople, with his hands under his coat tails, which tails were incessantly tossed, looking as if he had come on parade to show the awful or sublime contrast between his special humanity and that of the drudging humanity around him. . . . This swallow-tailed coat 'master' . . . some years before was a warehouseman. (Shaw, p. 75)

It is true that William Davenport had served as a warehouseman in London, Liverpool and at Longport. Charles Shaw however, leaves no doubt that he is describing William in a second excerpt. He writes:
My maternal grandfather [James Mawdsley, Davenport's manager, c.1815] *was honoured by his employer, while my father was ruined by the same employer's son. This was done with such calculated deliberation and with such force of animus that, as I shall show, it gave me residence in Chell, where I began to have experience of the new Poor Law. . . . My father, as I have stated, was a 'painter and gilder'. He worked at Davenport's. A new manager there introduced new methods of conducting business. For one thing he introduced female labour in a department which had hitherto belonged almost exclusively to the men. This new competition was resisted, partly as an innovation and partly because of the serious reduction in wages it involved.*

The men resented and resisted the change. They struck work with the winter before them, and with no organisation on which to depend for assistance. They had no resources whatsoever . . .

I suppose my father must have been a sort of ringleader in this strike, for many years after, I saw a letter from his brother-in-law, who was one of the managers of the works, to say that, if he did not give up the strike, Mr. D. had told him he would ruin him, and force him and his family into the workhouse. This bitter prophecy became bitterly true. Such intimidation in those days could easily be carried out by employers . . . It appears that my father would not be 'intimidated', nor would he desist in his efforts to maintain the strike. So we were indeed driven into the workhouse. I have sometimes wondered whether a direct Nemesis was sent to balance this sorry, reckless piece of vengeance. It would be easy to unfold a harrowing tale of what followed this man's wild revenge in his family history. . . . the year that man drove my father to the workhouse, I have since learned, he bought an estate for about £200,000. Yet trade was so bad he had to reduce the wages of his painters and gilders [the estate would be the Maer estate bought from Wedgwoods in 1843, though probably not for this price] *. . . I will not say how Nemesis has worked since, but that estate belongs to no descendant of his today* [the Maer estate was sold at auction in 1886].

Making due allowance for the lapse in time and the accumulated bitterness this is still a powerful indictment of William Davenport and his attitude to his workpeople. On the other hand their action in striking without any organized support and at the onset of winter was hardly sensible. This was the period of considerable unrest in the Potteries. Factory conditions left much to be desired and the periodic demands by the Chartists and others for further Parliamentary reform produced recurrent unrest. This took the form of meetings and petitions, but the movement for factory reform was often difficult to disentangle from that for improved Parliamentary representation and thus trade union activists often tried to use discontent with wages and working conditions to further political causes which were relatively remote from the immediate problems of earning sufficient to feed and clothe a potter's family. There were specific attempts being made to reform some of the worst abuses in the factories. One of the most widely supported was the agitation to regulate more closely the working hours,the age of working and the conditions of child workers. Charles Shaw, who was a Methodist Minister when he wrote his book, presents the view of a young and clearly bitterly exploited young worker. There is another perspective, that offered by the official reports presented to Parliament.

In the Parliamentary Papers 1843, Vol. XIII, entitled *Children's Employment, Royal Commission, Second Report, Trades and Manufactures* is printed the 'Report by Samuel Scrivens, Esq. on the Employment of Children and Young Persons in the District of the STAFFORDSHIRE POTTERIES; and on the actual State, Condition, and Treatment of such Children and Young Persons.'

As the material relating to Davenport has never before been published in ceramic reference books the evidence of the four children examined and that of the works superintendent is given in full.

Messrs. Wm. DAVENPORT AND CO., Longport.
No. 257. John Demcile, *aged 13:-*

I run moulds for Hamel Tilstone; have done so seven years, always in Mr. Davenport's factory. I go to Sunday-school top of the hill; never went to day-school above twice or three times. I cannot read or write, they teach me in the spelling-book at Sunday-school. I do not know how long I have been there, 'tis ever since it was opened [two years]. *My father has been dead eight years; he was a kilnman in regular work. Mother did nothing; I've got five brothers and sisters; one works in packing house, another works at Mayor's* [Mayer's] *as painter, another is at Venables as squeezer, the other stops at home; she goes to school at Dale Hall. I remember what I did before I came to work, and when father was alive – nothing; sometimes run about the streets at play. I come to work at six, and according how I get up. I go home according what I may have to do, sometimes six or seven, and at nine when I'm very much wanted. Hamel is very good to me, he never 'laid' on me. I get my breakfast at home; have coffee or tea and bread and butter, and treacle, just as it happens. I go home to dinner, and get tatees and bacon, not often beef; I am allowed an hour and a half at dinner. I only take half an hour, because I'm wanted back to Hamel to finish my work. I am paid by the week 3. 3d. If I work till nine at night I get just the same. Hamel is paid by the quantity he makes.*

No. 258. Thos. Massey, *aged 13:-*

I work in the warehouse; have been employed about six years. I can read; I can write a little. I go to church school to learn on Tuesday nights; I went to day-school about six months before I came here, I go to Sunday-school now. I come at half-past six in the morning, to get the fires in, fetch coals up, and then begin to work in the sorting-room. I go home at six o'clock; I work now and then 'till nine at night. I get play days at Easter and Whitsun, and Christmas, and at wakes and races. I would rather work 15 hours than 12, because I am paid for it half a day extra. I carry home my wages to my mother; she does not allow me any thing out. Father is a turner; he is not at work now; he did work with Mr Davenport, at Bottom Bank, master turned him away through his drinking; he loves drink too well. I have got six brothers and sisters, one paints, another runs moulds, another works at a farm house; all of us live at home except the last. I get 3s. 6d. a week, the others bring home 9s. 6d., which together makes 13s. The family lives upon what we bring home. Mother is a very good and careful mother; she is asthmatical and cannot go out of doors; she used to tread lathe.

No. 259. Alfred Downs, *aged 12:-*

I run moulds for John Dysche; have worked altogether about a year. I can read and write a little. Went to day-school at Newcastle National; go to Sunday school now at Longport. I come at six o'clock in the morning, and go home at six; I stop now and then till nine. I get 3s. 3d. a week; I get no more if I stop till nine. John Dysche pays me for the week if he does not work, it is his own fault, he stays away sometimes to play, and goes to a burying. He is very good to me; he gives me a 1d. every week. Father is a squeezer, and works in this Bank. I've got seven brothers and sisters; one works in biscuit oven, another is a painter, another runs moulds, the other three stops at home; mother looks after them. I have plenty to eat and drink, and more clothes than what I have on.

No. 260. Margaret Clewes, *aged 13:-*

I am paper cutter for Elijah Webster; come at six and half-past, and go home at six, seven, eight and nine. I get 3s. 6d. a week, and if I work overtime 3d. at the end of the week. When I come in the morning I wash dishes, get the fire in, and slack, and bring the water in pots and jugs, for washing dishes after breakfast or dinner. . . . Master will not allow us to carry the water for the large tubs, men do that . . . There are three presses a-gate [in action] *in our room, but four altogether; the printer is just dead, and his press is not employed. The man I work with behaves very well to me; some of the others curse and swear sometimes, and called the girls bad names; Elijah Webster is a good man he never swears. The women behave well to me; I'm certain they do not use bad words, or encourage it in the men. I stay in the work-room to breakfast; I get the half hour allowed me; I also get my dinner here in the work-room and take 20 minutes to it, and then begin to work again; I never play in the room in my dinner hour. I never do any needle-work; I can sew and hem; I do sometimes my pinbefore* [pinafore] *and bottoms of my frocks. Mother mends my stockings, but I mark them. My father is my step-father; he beats marl for grandfather, who is a saggar-maker. There are six children with me, two brothers turn jiggers the other three stops at home with mother. I am very tired when I get home if I work till nine o'clock. I would rather work up to nine o'clock, because the 3d a week finds me in clothes; I give it to mother, who puts more to it for this purpose. If I was to stop work at six o'clock I should go to school and learn to read; I am sure I should, if mother would let me. I'm poorly off for clothes, that is the reason I do not go to chapel sometimes. I get bread and butter and tea for breakfast, tatees and bacon for dinner, sometimes beef.*

No. 261. Moses Lees, *aged 50:-*

I have been the superintendent of Mr. Davenport's works about 11 years; I make up the wage-book of the people, and pay their wages in the shape of bills, called wage-bills, that is, with the names of 10, 15, or 20 persons, with their respective amounts carried out, which they get changed where they can; some go to the ale-house for it, where they are expected by the landlord to expend a certain quota in consideration of the favour. Boys and girls are included in these wage bills, but whether they drink I do not know. I think it is a bad practice, but if we were to pay in change many of them would still go to [the] *public house. We pay them in the shape I have stated because it is more convenient, for such is the difficulty of obtaining silver and copper for the number of people we have to pay, that before we got it we should be obliged to pay a great per centage. We have five distinct premises engaged in the manufacture of china, earthenware, and glass, and have, at a rough guess, from 1200 to 1400 hands, many of them children; we have but few very young, and these are the jiggers, paper cutters, and mould runners; master, I think, has an objection to take them too early. My opinion of the competency of children so engaged (educational) is that they may be improved if the parents paid more attention to them. Generally speaking they are ignorant, though I do not think we have much to complain of here; of the four who have been examined, two out of the four can read. Our machinery is well fenced off, and no children have business upon those premises, or are allowed to go near it. We are well supplied with drains, which empty themselves into the canal at the back of the works. Our privies for the people are private, and separated for the sexes by a wall, the doors being opposed to each other. On no consideration do they interfere with each other; if they did I have no doubt that the parties would be discharged. We have a number of apprentices that are bound by stamped* indenture; *I believe we are in this particular an exception to the general rule, as other manufactures bind their children by* paper *only; but I cannot speak with any certainty.*

Moses Lees.

Rooms lofty, spacious, well ventilated, healthy and clean.

To modern ears some of those statements sound horrific. Two of the four children interviewed had begun work when they were but seven years old. They rarely seemed to get their full lunch hour. It was quite frequent to work from six in the morning to nine at night, a fifteen-hour day winter and summer alike, and in some cases no overtime pay was given. The wages even of the children were not paid to them in cash, they had to go to the public house to cash their wage bills. It all seems to confirm what Charles Shaw had said. And yet by the standards of some other factories in the Potteries this was a good report. But to read these stories of the grinding hard work endured by children so young for what was really a pittance, puts into perspective the success story of John Davenport and his family. It adds another dimension to our appreciation and understanding of the pots we so much admire in our own cabinets.

Labour relations at the factory continued to be a source of concern, and it is interesting to observe the fluctuations in attitudes over the years. It is perhaps unfair to William Davenport to lay blame for bad working conditions and poor management entirely at his door. Increasingly after the purchase of Maer he seems to have lived the life of a country gentleman. The factory was left in the hands of managers or what Shaw called 'Bailees'. William had succeeded his brother Henry as Master of Foxhounds at Baddeley Edge, he revived the North Staffs Hunt and he was a local notable. He laid the foundation stone for the new Burslem Town Hall in 1854 and gave money for a new organ to be installed therein in 1864. As Shaw has indicated, William spent but little time at the factory, he was remote from his workpeople and their concerns. Thus there is no mention of his presence in November 1847 when the workers at the factory met to celebrate Mr William Meigh having worked for Messrs Davenport for fifty years (*Staffordshire Advertiser*, 27 November, 1847).

In 1850 the factory was brought to a standstill by a strike. The *Advertiser* reported on 17 August that a demand for higher prices by 50 of the hollow ware pressers at Davenport's factories at Longport and Newport had led to the works being closed for a fortnight. As a result some 1,500 were now out of work as Davenport had closed all their four factories (technically this would be termed a 'lock-out'), and were now seeking other pressers to take the place of those on strike so that the works could be opened up again. Over a month later the same paper reported on 28 September that the strike had ended and that there had been a general return to work a couple of days earlier. 19 men had lost their jobs and their places had been offered to others to start at Martinmas. The report concludes that the six-week strike caused 'considerable annoyance to a large concern conducted for so many years in a liberal spirit.' This latter observation is an interesting independent judgement. It seems to be borne out by a letter which appeared in the *Advertiser* on 22 March the following year 1851. It was from the Flat Presser's at W'm Davenport's New Bridge Bank to the editor of the *Potter's Press* contradicting an article of his of 15 March. In this the editor had stated that at Davenports the men are galled into almost an open turnout because of the delay in paying wages on the 'Good from Oven' system. The pressers assert that no delay occurs and there is no disposition to turn out [go on strike]. Quite who prompted the writing of this letter we may never know, but clearly the unrest of the previous year had not entirely subsided and there must have been rumours in the district of dissatisfaction. The system of payment 'Good from Oven' was a particularly vicious one which worked entirely to the advantage of the employer. The workmen were not paid for any articles they had fashioned however perfect they were when they left their hands, if they did not come out 'Good from Oven', where errors by a drunken fireman, or the vagaries of the wind direction could cause a firing to be unsuccessful. Davenports were not unusual in operating 'Good from Oven', and payment by bills exchangeable in public houses as described by Mr Lees to the Inspector Samuel Scrivens in 1843, but both practices were open to serious abuse and were highly disadvantageous to the workers. Astonishingly, 'Good from Oven' was not finally abolished until 1964. (Fuller details of these practices and the labour disputes of the time may be found in the books by Burchill and Ross, Dr John Thomas, W. H. Warburton, and Harold Owen listed in the Bibliography.)

By the time the last letter quoted above had been written the country was agog with expectation about the Great Exhibition due to be opened by Queen Victoria on 1 May 1851. It has always been something of a mystery as to why Davenports did not exhibit at the huge show in Hyde Park. Rodney Hampson has carried out detailed research on this matter, but though he has unearthed several very interesting items from the local newspapers, no firm evidence is forthcoming to explain Davenport's absence from amongst the exhibitors. To summarize Mr Hampson's research, it would appear that William Davenport together with William Copeland, Herbert Minton, John Ridgway and others was appointed a member of an early local committee the formation of which was reported in the *Staffordshire Advertiser* on 17 November 1849. He was not however present on this occasion. On 5 February following (1850) six 'Commissioners' including William Davenport were selected to represent the Potteries in London. In May of that year manufacturers were invited to state what they would exhibit and what space they would require, and town meetings were held in Hanley, Burslem and in June in Stoke and at none of these meetings was Davenport either present or mentioned. Clearly at some time between the end of 1849 and May 1850 Davenport had decided he did not want to exhibit. Were the labour troubles at the factory which culminated in the Strike in August 1850 the inhibiting factor? Possibly, but it seems more likely that Davenport conceived that the expense and effort of mounting an exhibition, especially when his products could certainly not match the grand, spectacular and showy nature of those of Minton and Copeland would not bring him an adequate reward. At this period the factory eschewed the adventurous and innovative approach of Minton under Arnoux. They made no parian, as far as we can tell, and no majolica or other historicist wares which Minton and Copeland amongst others had embarked upon. Davenport's porcelain wares were of a high standard but they were serviceable, rather than spectacular exhibition pieces. The earthenware, much of it made for export, was well below the standard of many Staffordshire contemporaries. It was good serviceable crockery for use in all climes and conditions. It was not what one would term 'Exhibition standard'. If this is how William Davenport and his manager's felt then perhaps it is the explanation for their absence. They were doing very nicely thank you, without the fancy frills and expense of exhibiting their wares in a Crystal Palace. It is worth noting in passing that Davenport wares may have found their way into the Great Exhibition on the stands of the china and glass retailers and wholesalers, but we have no evidence of that.

Davenport did not ignore the Exhibition. On 28 June some 160 of Davenport's workmen together with their friends took a special train to London to view the Exhibition. The *Staffordshire Advertiser* reported that Mr Davenport paid for their lodging, breakfast, supper and 'an ample allowance of stout' for the whole week which they stayed. Mr Davenport's large warehouse in City Basin was arranged into dormitories and fitted up with bedsteads. Omnibuses took the workers to the Exhibition each day. On their return they presented to William Davenport a silver cigar case and a wine flask (appropriate gifts for his tastes?) which were inscribed, 'Presented to William Davenport by his workmen as a mark of their respect and to testify their appreciation of his kindness in enabling them to view the Great Exhibition of 1851.' The *Advertiser* reported that the men had formed a fund of £600 for the visit – what I suppose we should now call a 'kitty'. With this and free stout for a week from William Davenport it must have been quite a party! The Davenport workers were incidentally the 'first body of men from the Potteries' to go to London. After the visit of Wedgwood, workers there presented their employers with gold pencil cases, and Robert Neason, the organizer of Minton's visit, received a handsome writing desk. I expect William Davenport was quite suited by his cigar case and wine flask.

The celebrations were not quite complete. In November a banquet was held at the Longport Works when 250 workmen with their wives, etc. dined to commemorate the trip to the Great Exhibition. The Chairman of this gathering was J. Wedgwood Esq., and also present were Mr W. Davenport and family, John Davenport [jun.] and family, Sir John Bent Esq. and Lady Bent [Elizabeth Davenport], Mr Wood and family, etc. Testimonials were presented to Mr Shirley (the manager at Longport) and Mr Allen the manager of the London House. A porcelain wassail cup suitably inscribed was also presented to each of them. About 150 wives and daughters were admitted (according to the *Advertiser's* report of 15 November), and dancing continued until 2 a.m.

Reading the report of the visit and the celebrations thereafter cannot but leave the impression that although the everyday lot of the ordinary worker was far from acceptable by modern standards, the situation at Davenports at this difficult time was not unmitigatedly harsh and repressive. A really brutal employer would not have paid for 160 of his workers to spend a week in London, especially when the factory was not even an exhibitor.

It is quite likely that the guiding spirit behind both the visit to London and indeed of the organization of the factory itself at this time was the Manager Joseph Shirley, to whom the workers had made the presentation noted above. We have very little evidence of him, but my fellow author drew my attention to two items which seemed to indicate his importance in the firm, and to support the earlier contention that William Davenport left the Works very much in the charge of his managers. The first item is in the *Londoniad*, that curious poem by Lidstone published in 1866. The entry on Davenport starts by giving the firm's addresses in Longport, London, Liverpool, Hamburg and Lübeck (221, Schüsselbuden) and continues:.

Thro' Arts Ceramic shall th' Muse enchant with song, Port
And Ocean in all climes for the giant firm of Longport . . .

The poetry is too excruciating to quote in full, but continues to rhapsodize on Davenport's overseas trade:

'*And, too, all Society's less'ning grades they supply*
With Goods to suit in ev'ry market under the sky.
Arms, Crests for Families, Companies, Nations we trace . . .
Ancient Ware resuscitated, who introduced the new,
And the doubtful renovated? O, Davenports, 'twas you . . .
It was my dream of Hope at roseate eve and early,
To have upon my unique list th' eminent Squire S-----y.

As Geoffrey Godden commented, no mention is made here of William Davenport, only of 'Squire S[hirle]y'.

The second item is an obituary notice for Joseph Shirley. This is alas, undated and the source not given. However, thanks to the prompt efficiency of Rodney Hampson and the University of Keele Library, it can be recorded that Joseph Shirley died on 8 March 1876. The notice, parts of which are printed below, and which probably comes from the *Staffordshire Sentinel* (it is not from the *Advertiser* whose short notice appeared in the issue 11 March 1876) is incorrect in several particulars. For example, Shirley was baptized at Hanley on 25 August 1813, the son of Jesse and Jane Shirley and thus is unlikely to have been born in 1812. Being born in 1813, he was obviously older than 30 when 'old Mr John Davenport' died in 1848. Despite these factual inaccuracies the general tenor of the piece is clearly indicative of the high regard in which Joseph Shirley was held, and of his important role in running the business.

DEATH OF MR. SHIRLEY

It is with deep regret we have this week to record the death of Mr Joseph Shirley, late of Port Hill, near Burslem' [in the *Staffordshire Advertiser* he is interestingly stated to have been 'of Longport House', the house hard by the factory, once the residence of John Davenport himself] *manager at the pottery works of Messrs. W. Davenport & Co. The deceased gentleman, who had resided in the district all his life, was born in Hanley, in the year 1812. . . . His father, who was clerk at the Old Church, was an earthenware manufacturer at Hanley. When quite a boy, the deceased Mr Shirley was placed in the office of the Messrs. Davenports, in the time of old Mr John Davenport. As an errand boy the honesty and perseverance of Mr Shirley was fully appreciated by his employers, and he was at the age of 21 appointed cashier. At 26 years of age he was made manager of the works, and a few years after the death of Mr Davenport he was chosen as general manager of all the branch houses of the firm, so that before he was thirty years old he had the entire charge of one of the largest houses of business in the kingdom. He was apparently in his usual health on Saturday morning last when he paid the employees their wages. He was however taken ill in the afternoon. . . . His death has cast quite a gloom over the neighbourhood. As a business man his straightforward and sound business-like habits won the confidence of all with whom he was brought into contact, particularly with his employers, and as a gentleman was highly esteemed and respected by the workmen under his control, as well as by a large circle of family and outside friends, in fact generally by the inhabitants of Burslem and the immediate locality* [then follow further details of his work for church, the Conservative Association, etc.]. *His remains will be interred in the family vault in St. Paul's churchyard today. . . . the coffin, which is a very handsome one, has been made by one of Messrs. Davenport's joiners, and the coffin plate engraved in a very elegant manner.*

It is clear from the foregoing that Joseph Shirley had played a major part in the guidance of the firm for many years. It is also worth remarking that he not only served John Davenport for many years but would have seemed to have been given the general managership sometime after William Davenport had assumed control. He, of course, outlived William, and must have seen the problems which he bequeathed to his unfortunate son Henry grow ever more pressing. When Joseph Shirley died in 1876, he was 63 years old and had been 'Mr Henry's' manager for the past seven. A worrying responsibility for a man of his age.

After his death, the post of General Manager seems to have passed either at once or shortly afterwards to another Shirley, his son John who was born 16 March 1846, the second child of Joseph and Lydia Shirley. And so the dynasties continued, the Shirleys father and son managed the factory, the Davenports father and son owned it. In past accounts of the history of the concern, insufficient credit has been given to the Shirleys for their part in the successes of the Davenport factory. But by the same token, must they not also share some of the responsibility for both the decline in technical and product innovation, and to some extent for the financial turmoil which dogged the enterprise in its last twenty-five years or more? These are difficult and debatable matters and a true assessment is perhaps not possible, and may well be unfair, when fully documented evidence such as the Accounts of the firm are not available for study.

In the years since my 1972 book was published diligent researchers such as Rodney Hampson, Ronald Brown and Diana Darlington have closed some of the gaps in our knowledge of the history of the factory. But there is still one period for which there is almost no documentary information. That is the lengthy stretch from the 1851 Exhibition to the death of William Davenport in 1869. Even the ever helpful pages of the *Staffordshire Advertiser* have little more than isolated snippets. It is possible that lurking somewhere in the Wedgwood papers there are references similar to those in the 1810–20 period. Sharon Gater, Research Assistant at the Wedgwood Museum, Barlaston has kindly sent me copies of a correspondence from one of Wedgwood's foreign agents A. J. Hoffstaedt from the later 1840s in which references are made to Davenport's wares and the kind of inter-potter trading which was shown to be common between Davenport and Wedgwood in the 1810–20 period which was noted in the *Transactions of the English Ceramic Circle* for 1985. There may be more but they do not provide a rounded picture. So far the Foxley papers have yielded nothing significant on the factory. What we appear to be lacking are the private papers of William Davenport, though there are some title deeds and papers relating to marriage settlements in the Stafford County Record Office. There is no documentation comparable to that on John Davenport in the Foxley papers and Henry Davenport in the 1870–88 period in the Wood papers. Without such material we are reduced to speculation.

It would seem in order to suggest that the firm prospered in the first twenty years of so of William's management. But the sparse surviving evidence is that thereafter things did not run entirely smoothly. For example on 9 July 1856 the *Staffordshire Advertiser* carried the announcement: 'To be sold. Noble pile. First class warehouses and house in Canning Place opposite the Customs House and near the Docks, now and for a long time occupied by William Davenport & Co. China, Earthenware & Glass warehouses and showrooms, who will show the premises – fixtures and fittings. To be sold. Apply Ward, Son & Collier Sons, Newcastle, Staffs.' Presumably nothing came of this for the Liverpool showroom at Canning Place features considerably in the 1880s correspondence. Nevertheless, it must surely be a sign of difficult times for the management to even contemplate giving up Liverpool which had been so important to their trade for so long.

The following year the Newport factory was advertised for sale in the *Advertiser* (10 January): 'To be let Newport House late in the occupancy of Joseph Alcock . . . and the Earthenware Manufactory on the Trent & Mersey canal near Newport, now occupied by William Davenport & Co.' Immediate possession of both house and Works was offered. Prospective purchases were to contact Joseph Shirley at Longport, or Ward & Sons the solicitors. This sale almost certainly did go ahead. William had not lived at Newport House for some time, he had obviously rented it to Joseph Alcock. Now it and the factory were disposed of. After years of expansion, the slow and painful process of contraction had begun. William Davenport did not live to see the worst days of decline, but when he died at Maer in 1869, a respected figure throughout Staffordshire, he must have had more than an inkling that the business empire founded by his father would be fortunate to survive his son. William Davenport has left us none of the personal memorabilia which so entertains and enlightens us in the life of his father. He seems to have been a somewhat wayward youth, perhaps a rebel against his father's over-strict control. He also lacked the guidance of a mother, for Diana Davenport died when he was only six. But even making such allowances, the evidence, and it is admittedly very incomplete, points to a rather self-centred man who lacked his father's vision, drive and enterprise, who was content to reap the rewards of the work of others. He had inherited a go-ahead thriving firm, frequently patronized by royalty. His legacy was a factory which had been left behind technically, and in the provision of new and exciting shapes, forms and decoration. There were no further royal commissions after 1837: those went to Mintons and others. Under William Davenport the firm gradually stagnated, prosperous it may have been for long periods, but William had no commitment to innovation or to exerting that drive for sales which so characterized his father. It is a familiar story expressed succinctly in Lancashire as 'clogs to clogs in three generations'. The delights of country living, and the style of a country gentleman took its toll. The foundations were thoroughly undermined when William Davenport, whose death is reported in the *Staffordshire Advertiser* of 12 June 1869, left the concern to his son Henry.

7 Henry Davenport and Davenports Ltd, 1869–87

As we approach the final years in the life of the Pottery we are again fortunate in having a good range of contemporary documentary material at our disposal. The most important source is the voluminous correspondence known as the Wood Papers. These are letters addressed to Edmund T. Wedgwood Wood, the brother of Mrs William Davenport, from the Newcastle solicitor S. Herbert Cooper. Wood also retained a number of letters and other documents relevant to the history of the manufactory. The letters cover the last ten years of the factory, 1877–87, but also contain much material relating to the more general business affairs of the family. They are full of fascinating insights into the Victorian world of business, but many are irrelevant to our main theme.

The story that can be related from this correspondence was told at some length in my 1972 book and the reader is referred to that for the full account, as it seems unnecessary to repeat all the intricate details of the efforts which were made in that decade to salvage the concern. For the sake of completeness, however, it is worth outlining the main events.

There is almost no evidence of any kind to indicate precisely what happened to the factory in the first few years after the death of William Davenport in 1869. His only son assumed control – if that is not too strong a word to describe his almost total lack of interest – and production and the selling of goods continued through the usual markets of Liverpool, London, Hamburg, Lübeck and New York. Judging by the wares themselves, the factory had settled for second best, there was no venturing into the production of such fashionable items as pâte-sur-pâte. Just mass production of routine wares, though the porcelain services maintained a good standard of finish and decoration.

William Davenport's major legacy to his son and the remainder of his children seems to have been debt and mortgaged property. The mortgage debt in 1869 was given in a document of 1878 as £45,620. In the intervening years property had been sold, most notably the Lower Bridge Works for £7,500, the Duke of Bridgewater Inn (£1,975), the Greyhound Inn (£1,100), and other property had brought in some £42,767 11s 7d, but payments out by the Trustees of William's will to his married daughters of their inheritance still left a mortgage debt known as the 'Longport' mortgage of £29,691 1s 5d. A valuation of the property made on 6 December (printed in full in *Davenport Pottery & Porcelain*) shows that the total value of stock at Liverpool, London and Longport was valued at £50,000 or thereabouts. Clearly there was no need for them to manufacture another pot for some considerable time!

At this point a prospective purchaser came forward, David Chadwick MP, and detailed negotiations with him dragged on into 1880 before being finally abandoned (again full details are in my earlier book). Some remedial action was taken. In March 1879 the London showroom at 82 Fleet Street was given up and the stock of china, earthenware and glass was disposed of at a sale at Phillips (*Pottery Gazette and Glass Trade Review*, 18 March 1879). It would appear from later documents that a London establishment, probably on a smaller scale, was maintained at 32 Ely Place. In the summer of 1879 Longport Hall was sold at auction to a Mr Hook for £4,650. Longport House which was also on offer remained unsold and the solicitor Cooper expressed his regret and the annoyance of the Bank that Mr Henry's overdraft was still so great. The position was not eased when Mr Hook's cheque paid as a deposit on Longport Hall was dishonoured.

Henry Davenport seems to have moved through this very serious financial crisis with an unruffled air of serenity. Cooper writing to E. T. W. Wood reports telling Henry 'I cannot exaggerate the critical nature of your position, altho' I fear you will not believe me, & I am satisfied that nothing but the most prompt and businesslike action on your part can arrest a Catastrophy.' The catastrophy of which he writes is succinctly summarized later in the same letter (Wood papers, 3 January 1880):

Mr Henry will find himself ruined. The Bank is most pressing and hostile in its tone . . . I cannot but feel that one single writ, issued by any one & for even a comparatively small amount, might involve a petition in Bankruptcy.

Mr Henry does not appear to appreciate his position; strongly as I have spoken & written to him on the subject, & now I feel that two courses only are open to me – one is to carry out, under your advice, the sale that has been agreed to & the other is to ask Mr Henry to seek professional advise elsewhere.

The negotiations to sell the business to Chadwick dragged on and eventually foundered. Throughout the correspondence at this period there is a tone of almost sheer desperation as Cooper and Wood strive to save something from the wreckage both for Henry Davenport and for the factory and the workers who are dependent upon it for a living. On 29 April 1880 Cooper notes 'I wrote you hurriedly yesterday to relieve your anxiety as to the wages for Saturday next.' The sale of Maer is proposed, the abandoning of Liverpool, but no decisive action seemed to be possible whilst Henry Davenport vacillated, and until honestly audited accounts were presented to the prospective purchaser.

The attitude of Henry Davenport is admirably summarized in a letter from E. T. W. Wood to David Chadwick dated 28 May 1880:

I think you know the circumstances under which Mr Henry Davenport is parting with the business. His father who realised a large fortune by it never intended him to continue in it – he was not brought up to it – he neither understands or cares for it, and in my judgement he will do well to dispose of it even at the very low figure mentioned in the prospectus, for he has no children, and no near relative able to take the concern off his hands.

The negotiation with Chadwick failed largely as a result of a properly conducted audit which revealed that figures presented to him were inaccurate: 'a loss of £8,553 was concealed.' Thus in the summer of 1880 there was a strong possibility that the Bank would act 'to pay the Ladies off [that is the four unmarried daughters of William Davenport their long-delayed inheritance], and having thus taken everthing into their own hands, to break Mr Henry up and know the worst of their position.'

In the event Mr Henry was not 'broken up.' In September he sold his 'reversionary share in the residual personal estate of the late Mr John Wood now represented by the sum of £66,591 4s 10d Consols to Mr Mountford Wood.' On 3 January 1881 Cooper was able to announce the sale of the Top Bridge Pottery 'to Mr T. Hughes for £3,100, the purchase to be completed on 25 March next.' The purchase price was to be paid directly to 'the Ladies'. (All the daughters of William Davenport had been left £5,374 5s 8d each. The married daughters had received their share, but the four unmarried 'Ladies' had not.)

The slimming down of the business progressed apace. In a five-day sale from 24–8 January 1881 inclusive 'The First Portion of the very valuable Stock of China, cut glass services and Beautiful Ornaments, by order of Messrs William Davenport & Co. which will be sold by auction, at Eleven o'Clock each day, on the Premises, Canning Place, Liverpool' was advertised. The catalogue of this sale has survived, but somewhat disappointingly it is not possible to separate the Davenport products from those of other manufacturers in the 1200 lots which were offered for sale. This is a pity for the lots are reasonably fully described, but no pattern numbers are given, and the only clues as to origin are notes such as 'Pair of French china candelabra' or 'Jasper ware flower stand' (no marked Davenport jasper is known, so one assumes this is by another maker).

Clearly Henry Davenport was bestirring himself and he earned this tribute from Mr Cooper on 17 May 1881. 'I cannot say too strongly how satisfied I have felt at the care and consideration Mr Henry has shown since July last, and at the loyal manner in which he has adhered to the task he then set himself . . .' With remarkable expedition considering his past hesitancies and uncertainties a new plan was evolved and on 9 August 1881 a new company, Davenports Limited, was formed. The company had a capital of £40,000 and the Memorandum of Association was signed by Diana Elizabeth Davenport, Sarah E. Davenport and Marianne H. Davenport all spinsters of Camp Hill ('The Ladies' of the earlier letters), and by Harry T. Davenport, MP of Hem Heath, Trentham, Staffs, Revd R. Mountford Wood, Albury Rectory, Tring, George W. Wood, Major Warley, Brentwood, Essex, and Revd George H. Davenport, Foxley, Hereford.

The Company was to have five Directors, E. T. W. Wood, H. T. Davenport, MP, Maj. G. W. Wood, Alfred Henry Dashwood 'formerly of Stamford Hall now of Longport, Gentleman' and one other to be nominated by the other four.

The Company was to act as both Manufacturer and Dealer in a long list of ceramic wares and was to acquire Henry Davenport's Longport factories as the manufacturing base. The new Company had contracted virtually to John Davenport's early site of Unicorn Bank and the Glass Works.

The *Pottery Gazette* of 1 October 1881 carried the following announcements:
LONGPORT, STAFFORDSHIRE, September 23, 1881.
Dear Sir,

I beg to inform you that I have converted my business at Longport, London and Liverpool into a Company, the capital of which has been subscribed by members of my own family with one or two friends, and that the same will from this date be caried on under the style or title of 'DAVENPORTS LIMITED.' All debts due to or from the late firm will be received and paid by the Company.

Thanking you for your support in the past and trusting that the Company will receive an extended share in your orders,

I am,
Yours respectfully,
HENRY DAVENPORT
Trading as Wm. DAVENPORT & Co.

The second letter also from Longport on the same date reads:
Dear Sir,

In succeeding to the old-established business so successfully carried on by Messrs. Wm. Davenport & Co., we desire to assure you that it is our intention to maintain in every way the high reputation of the late firm of excellence of Manufacture and Elegance of Design, while by the constant introduction of New Shapes, Styles, and patterns we hope to secure an extended measure of your support, which it will be our endeavour always to deserve and retain.

Yours respectfully,
DAVENPORTS LIMITED.
JOHN SHIRLEY, General Manager.

These two letters appeared beneath a decorative advertisement reproduced here as Plate 22.

There is a good deal of documentary material relating to the formation of the Company in the Wood papers including valuations and the like. Ronald Brown drew my attention to other material relating to the 1881 sale and formation of the Company in certain papers of the Newcastle Solicitors Rigby, Rowley & Cooper deposited in the Stafford County Record Office. It will be recalled that it was S. Herbert Cooper who acted for Henry Davenport throughout the business. These papers, which all bear the reference number D3272/1/4 and then a further individual number, include mortgage documents of the period 1869–85; papers relating directly to the sale of the works in 1881; the title deeds of various estates; and several marriage settlements, as well as quite a substantial volume of other papers on various aspects of the Davenport family. For our purpose the most interesting is contained in the papers relating to the 1881 sale. Here may be found a large-scale plan of the Longport site in 1881 and an accompanying schedule of fixtures (D 3272/1/4/1/27). In total no fewer than 140 separate 'shops' or 'Chambers' are itemized. It would be tedious to detail them all. They follow the normal types of rooms found on a large potbank, ranging from the five printing shops, through the Blue warehouse to the Porous warehouse, the Foot Bath Makers place, the Mould Chamber in Lustre Shop, the Old Iron Place, the Strip House (both Common and China), the Topping Shop which was next to the Womens Painting Shop and so to the Hot House and via the Blacksmiths Shop to the Lodge and the Office and Waiting Room. A similar document (D3272/1/4/1/22) gives the schedule for the Glass Works at the same date.

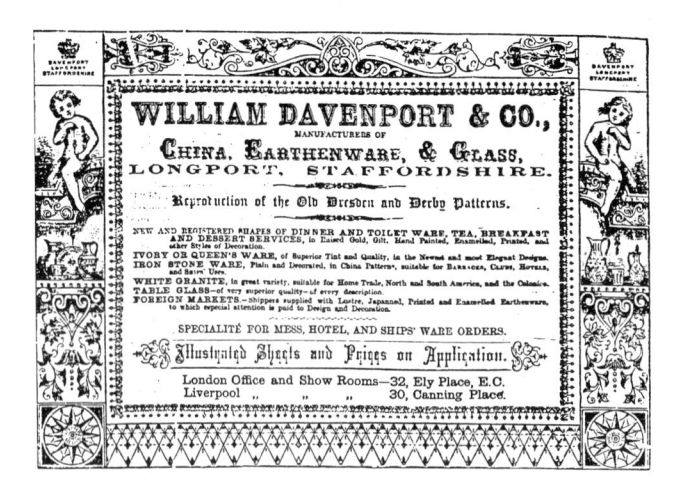

Could the new management succeed with a slimmer organization and without the burden of debt? The answer seems to be yes – and no. In the short run the annual balance sheets show a profit in 1882 of £4,649 18s 4d. The following year there was working profit of only £1,742 with a loss of £541 reported on the New York agency. Stocks however, were significantly higher and there was an ominous note about 'the late depression of trade.' By the following year the accounts showed a total loss of £6,338 2s 2d. There were losses on consignments to New York and Permanbuco, stocks were even higher and the value of goods manufactured was, naturally, considerably lower.

Henry Davenport too was still deeply in debt and the Wood papers continue to reveal his desperate financial plight (further financial details of these last years are in the 1972 book).

In 1885 the balance sheet reported 'the great depression in the Potting Trade has continued throughout the past year.' There were heavy losses at Longport and New York, and only the smallest of profits in Liverpool. The end was in sight. The Directors and the Solicitors were now seeking for a suitable time to sell. They were clutching at straws. Cooper reporting to Wood on 3 October 1885 writes:

A return of trade in the District might enable the Directors to dispose of the business as a going concern, which certainly could not be done now. It was thought that Spring is the time to sell [the cry of the property vendor throughout the ages!] ... *and in any case the Works should be carried on till then, and that this might at all events be done without a loss.'*

So potting continued but strictly on the understanding that this was only a temporary measure until a more opportune time came to dispose of the Works as a going concern.

The difficulties at the factory were in no way secret and the local papers have frequent references to the state of affairs. In 1886 it was resolved to dispose of the Maer estate, of which a rough valuation of 15 July reads:

22. Advertisement for William Davenport & Co., *Pottery Gazette*, 1 October 1881.

'Timber £15,000, Fixtures including organ £11,000, 1st Sept. 3,042 acres. House £30,000, Woodland £310 per acre.' The sale of Maer was in many ways symbolic. Bought from the Wedgwoods when their fortunes were at a low ebb in 1843, it was now the Davenport family and factory which were in a parlous state, whilst the Wedgwoods were enjoying something of a renaissance.

Work continued at the factory throughout 1886, but the end could not long be delayed. The hoped for revival of trade was a chimera. The end came, not in a neat and tidy fashion, but apparently as the result of a petition by Mintons in the Chancery Division on 19 February to wind up Davenports Limited, reported in the *Pottery Gazette*, March 1887. The same issue carried a preliminary advertisement announcing that the Longport business and the Ely Place showrooms in London were to be auctioned sometime in April as a going concern. According to the same source a Receiver was appointed, and in March 1887 all manufacturing ceased. The *Gazette* further reported in May that no bids had been received at the auction. In July the Receiver offered 4s in the £ to those with claims upon the Company.

These last few months could well form the subject of a quite separate study in business history as a once famous firm struggled to survive and then to arrange the disposal of the remaining assets to the best advantage. We have not seen any detailed documentation such as the letters of Cooper from this period, though there must have been plenty, which may well have survived and now await the attentions of a business or economic historian. It would be a most fascinating project. There was of course another dimension in that were the works to close permanently, there would be serious repercussions for the livelihoods of hundreds of workpeople in the Longport district. This aspect does appear from time to time in the consideration of those involved in the negotiations. After the failure to attract a bid at the auction, the Directors through Cooper advertised that the firm would be sold by private treaty as a going concern ('china, earthenware and glass manufactory') and invited offers (*Staffordshire Advertiser*, 30 April 1887).

None apparently was forthcoming, and the Pottery presumably lay idle through the summer months. Both the *Pottery Gazette* and the *Advertiser* reported in July that the Receiver and Manager invited offers for engravings and blocks etc. And the same papers noted in September that efforts were being made to float the works as a Co-operative Society. This proposal seems to have been abandoned fairly quickly because of a lack of funds. There seemed to be no other option, the concern would have to be 'broken up' and sold piecemeal.

In the *Staffordshire Advertiser* of 24 September there appeared the first of a series of weekly advertisments for the sale of the factory. On 29 October 21 lots in all, including the whole works, were offered for sale as the *Advertiser* described the proceedings:

On Wednesday afternoon Mr Samuel Edwards offered for sale by auction at the Town Hall, Burslem, the Longport Glass and China Works formerly owned by Davenports, together with two family residences and a number of building lots. There was a good attendance but the vendors were again disappointed in effecting a sale of the property, the maufacturing and other principal lots not attracting a single bid. The only lot sold was No. 14, a piece of building land 509 square yards on a site on the main Longport to Burslem Road.

The 'family residences' were (Lot 4) a house opposite Trubshaw Cross in the tenancy of A. H. Dashwood (one of the Directors), Lot 5, Longport House, in the occupation of W. W. Dobson. Neither, of course, was sold on this occasion, but appear to have been disposed of privately subsequent to the sale.

The failure to sell the factory and the glass works must have been a severe blow. There could now be little hope of disposing of them as going concerns. That this was evident to the Receiver is confirmed by a series of advertisements announcing the forthcoming sale of almost the entire contents of the factory and glass house, all the machinery, materials, fixtures and fittings. The Glass Works contents were the first to be sold on Monday and Tuesday, 28 and 29 November 'And Following Day if necessary' (see p. 291 for details). The sale was to be conducted by a different auctioneer, Mr H. Steele. His three adverts in the *Staffordshire Advertiser* are worth publishing in some detail, though a substantial excerpt from the first advert has been included in the section on 'Miscellaneous and Later Earthenwares' where it is more appropriate:

DAVENPORTS (LIMITED) CHINA and EARTHENWARE MANUFACTORY, LONGPORT, BURSLEM. Highly important and Unreserved SALE of valuable COPPERPLATE ENGRAVINGS, BLOCKS, CASES, and WORKING MOULDS, PRINTERS' PRESSES, FIRE ENGINE, CANAL BOATS &c.

Mr H. STEELE has received instructions to SELL by AUCTION, on the Premises on Monday, Tuesday and Wednesday, December 12, 13, and 14, 1887, and Following Days.-

The whole of the very choice and valuable Stock of COPPER PLATES, MATERIALS, UTENSILS, BLOCKS, CASES, and WORKING MOULDS, BOARDS, FIRE ENGINE, CANAL BOATS &c. comprising the blocks, cases and working moulds of some of the finest and best shapes and most saleable patterns in the home and foreign markets [see p. 194 for full details of these].

. . . The MATERIALS consist of Oxide of Zinc, Glaze, Colours, Muriatic Acid, Nitric Acid, valuable sponges &c.

The UTENSILS comprise 18 Printers' Presses, Dipping and Glaze Tubs, Gilders', Turners' and Throwers' Wheels, Whirlers, Jiggers, 1,500 Boards, Saggar Shords, about 6,000 Biscuit and Glost saggars, Steps, Stools, and a large quantity of Sundries appertaining to a large and well-appointed Manufactory.

Catalogues are now ready, price 3d each (to admit two persons), and can be obtained at the Manufactory; or at the Offices of the AUCTIONEER.

The Manufactory is situated within five minutes' walk of Longport Station, on the North Staffordshire Railway.

On view Wednesday and Thursday, December 7 and 8, from Ten to Four.

Sale Each Day at One o'clock prompt.

The AUCTIONEER solicits a punctual attendance, as the days are short and the Lots numerous. The Copper-Plates will be divided between the three days, and will be offered punctually at Two o'clock. The Shapes will be sold on Thursday, the 15th.

Auctioneer's Offices, Queen's Chambers, Burslem. (Staffordshire Advertiser, 26 November 1887, p. 8)

The second and third notices appeared in the *Advertiser* on 17 December. As some of wording is repetitious, they will not be reproduced in full.

CONTINUATION of SALE. – In Liquidation – DAVENPORTS LIMITED, CHINA and EARTHENWARE MANUFACTORY, LONGPORT, BURSLEM.

Mr HENRY STEELE will SELL by AUCTION, on the Premises, on Monday, Wednesday, Thursday and Friday, December 19, 21, 22, 23, 1887 the whole of the Unsold MATERIALS, BOARDS, CLAY, GLAZES, COLOURS, FIRE ENGINE, WEIGHING MACHINERY, CANAL BOATS &c. as follows.-

The list of materials and utensils hardly differs from that printed above, and probably represents lots not reached at the earlier sale.

The third notice perhaps more than the other two brings home how total was the collapse of the Concern. The buildings were being stripped not merely of useful potters' items such as saggars and sponges, or valuable cooper plates and moulds, but gutted of all machinery as the sale notice makes clear:

In Liquidation. – DAVENPORTS LIMITED, LONGPORT, BURSLEM. – To

MANUFACTURERS, FLINT-GRINDERS, USERS of STEAM POWER, &c – Important SALE of Capital STEAM ENGINES, BOILERS, STEAM PIPES, POTTERS' CLAY PRESSES, FLINT-PANS, COLOUR-PANS, JOLLIES, JIGGERS, SLIP-HOUSE PUMPS, BLUNGERS, PUG MILLS, STEAM PIPES, &c.

Mr H. STEELE has received instructions to SELL by AUCTION, on the Premises, on Tuesday December 20, 1887, the whole of the valuable POTTERS' MACHINERY, including.-

Engines, Boilers, Pug Mills, Slip-House Pumps, Blungers, &c. excellent Beam Engine, 20in. cylinder, and steam piping to ditto; large Beam Engine, 2ft. 6in cylinder, 6ft stroke with governors, &c, as fixed [and so the list continues through '820 yards of 1½in. steam piping' to '3 Batting Machines, 11 Printers' Stoves, 2,100 ft. Steam Piping at Saggar House, &c.]

Sale at One o'clock. Auctioneer's Office, Queen's Chambers, Burslem.

Thus totally ignominiously, by the order of the Receiver, was dispersed the very heart of the factory established nearly a century earlier by John Davenport. The very words 'In Liquidation' would have filled him with humiliation – and anger.

The rest of the story can be briefly told. Hardly had the sale been completed than former competitors were advertising their acquisitions. Thus on 2 January 1888 E. Swann of the Globe Pottery, Tunstall in the *Pottery Gazette* stated, 'Special attention is called to my purchase of DAVENPORT'S Patterns, as per list, any of which can be supplied on their 'BAMBOO' shape.' The patterns were: ITALIA, MIKADO, HARROW, HERON, FERN, FOLIATE, MYRTLE, NORTON and JAPANESE HAWTHORN (see p. 194). Wengers were swift to follow, the supplement of the same publication reported on 1 February that 'Mr A. Wenger, Helvetia Works, Hanley, had purchased a large number of the copper plates.' In February Wengers advertised 55 of the former Davenport patterns which he was willing 'to sell, hire and to match the colours and supply the shapes used with the following patterns (the list of patterns was printed in full in *Davenport Pottery & Porcelain*, p. 70). In the *Gazette* of April Mr Charles Ford of Cannon Street, Hanley, announced that he now owned all Davenports badges and crests coppers. Perhaps of more significance was an announcement in the same issue that 'the whole of the Works have been purchased by Thomas Hughes of the Top Bridge Pottery, Longport . . . he has advertised the Glass Works to let.' Presumably this was a sale by private treaty, which following the big auction sales would have enabled Hughes to purchase the stripped manufactory for a fraction of the asking price as a going concern. No documents have been noted giving these details, but they surely exist in one or other of the three main collections of papers.

In the *Pottery Gazette* of 1 October 1888, John Hughes of Cobridge called attention to his purchase of 'the whole of the valuable pattern books belonging to the late firm of Davenports Ltd.' Present-day ceramic historians and collectors would dearly love to know what became of these 'valuable pattern books.' They may still exist tucked away in some forgotten corner of an attic or lumber room, somewhere in Staffordshire. Their rediscovery might well throw important light on some of the many unsolved problems concerning the early Davenport wares. One lives in hope!

The same journal reported a month later that 'Mr Thomas Hughes has moved to the very extensive factory, lately occupied by Davenports Ltd.' It was to remain in the firm's possession until 1957 when it was taken over by Arthur Wood & Sons. As we have seen (p. 13), they demolished much of the main part of the factory, but have retained some of the earlier buildings. Visiting the site, which as was remarked earlier seems to add another dimension to our studies and our collecting, one can still find down by the canal bank shards and wasters discarded over a hundred years ago. Plates 23 and 24 illustrate some of these forlorn but fascinating fragments of better days. They were gathered by some of the American members of the 1987 Keele University International

23

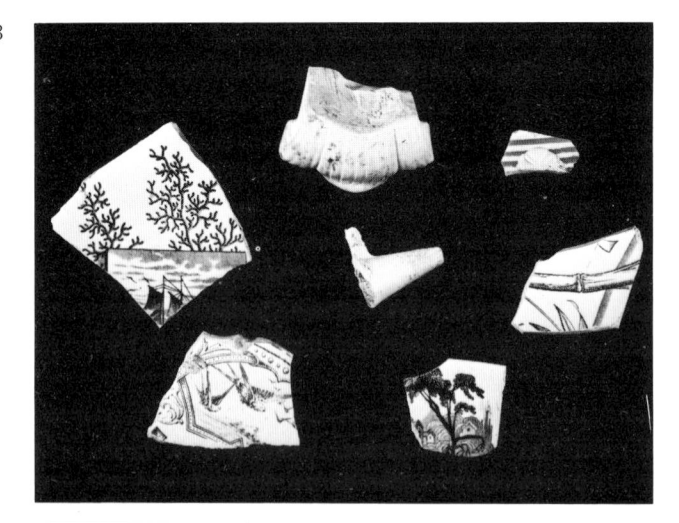

24

Ceramic Summer School and kindly donated for the purpose of illustration in this book. The Summer School on 'John Davenport and his Contemporaries' was timed to celebrate the centenary of the closure of the factory. We hope we paid fitting tribute on that occasion. In 1994 the City Museum at Stoke-on-Trent will mount an Exhibition to celebrate the bicentenary of the founding of the firm. Perhaps by then the site will have been excavated and the pattern books found.

Even if this is not the case, the researches of so many collectors and scholars has prevented the fate which the *Pottery Gazette* of 2 January 1888 seemed to fear:
To all interested in the noble craft of the potter, it is lamentable when such historic and valuable plant, engravings and designs as those of Messrs. Davenport's are scattered, and that a name, honoured by our forefathers, and familiar in all parts of the world as a household word, is all that is left as our heritage of the great firm of the past.'

A century later far more than the name lives on. That assuredly does, but so too does the work of the artists and craftsmen, men, women, young boys and girls, in the treasured examples of their skill which adorn the cabinets of hundreds of collectors who are proud possessors of cherished items of Davenport 'China, Earthenware and Glass.'

23. Selection of shards found on the factory site, August 1987.

24. Selection of shards, some with marks, found on the factory site, August 1987.

Part Two :
Earthenwares and Stonewares

8 The Earthenware and Stoneware Marks

The factory was not entirely consistent in its marking of wares. In the early years a reasonable proportion of wares remained unmarked. The problems associated with this fact are discussed in the individual sections on the wares. Of general concern is the question as to when the word Davenport was first used on earthenware and stoneware pieces. Traditionally, it has been argued, by myself and others, that this name mark was used from the early days, that is before 1800. However, some recent discussions have centred upon the use of the word Longport on early bone chinas, and not the family name. Some collectors believe that the name Davenport was not used until after the Royal order of 1806. Geoffrey Godden reviews the evidence for and against this view in the section on porcelain marks.

With the earthenware and stonewares, a similiar thesis would imply that no wares were produced bearing the family name before 1806. Thus the only Davenport items which can be associated with the period 1794–1806 are either unmarked or carry only the impressed anchor, mark E 1. Personally, I cannot accept this line of reasoning as applied to the early creamwares and, say, the cane wares. To me they have every appearance in terms of shape and decoration as having been made sometime in these first twelve years. This said, there are problems, and quite serious ones about using the impressed marks E 2 and E 5, for dating the wares. They seem to have been used on wares over a much longer period than I suggested in *Davenport Pottery & Porcelain*, and there is very considerable overlap in their use. Items in the same service have been noted carrying both marks, as well as others with combinations of E 1 and E 2 and E 5.

Despite these reservations on marking and the difficulties of attempting to use the different marks to try to date pieces accurately, which really is fraught with snags, the marking at the factory does not pose too many problems after 1820 at the latest. By this time most items seem to have been marked, and clearly so, with the family name. The marks reproduced below are not by any means a complete list. They constitute those most used, with just a few of the interesting variants which are indicative of many similar examples, especially those associated with printed and pattern names.

E 1. Impressed. The anchor alone is normally regarded as the earliest of the marks used c.1794–1820 at least. Some items with this mark appear to carry decoration of a much later date. It is important to note that the impressed mark has to be made in the clay state, before firing. It could well be some considerable time before such pots were taken from the biscuit warehouse and decorated. This could account for some of the discrepancies.
This mark has been found on some items in a service, other pieces of which were marked with E 2 and E 5, which could indicate some components of services manufactured at different dates, but assembled and decorated later.
In the past few years a number of pieces, mainly wares with a coloured stoneware body or of terra-cotta, have been noted with a very tiny impressed anchor. Most of these pieces are from the 1820–30 period and do not appear to fit into any known category of Davenport manufacture. Caution is required, not all 'anchor alone' marked pieces are of Davenport origin.

E 2. Impressed. This mark impressed in lower case letters is normally taken to be an early mark. However, a date span of c.1798 to at least 1820 seems to be the minimum in which to place wares so marked.
As indicated above. Wares so marked, but carrying decoration which would appear to be

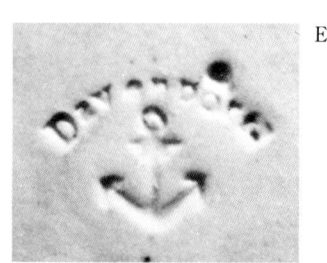

72 · Earthenwares and Stonewares

much later are encountered (see Plate 164 for a puzzling example). On the whole, this mark does seem to appear on wares which one would date earlier than those on which E 5 is found. But there is considerable overlap, as the splendid basalt teawares indicate (Plates 60–4).

E 3. Impressed. This mark is impressed in lower case letters in a quite distinct curve. It would seem to date from the period *c*.1800–20 but is rare.
To date this mark has only been noted on blue transfer printed wares.

E 4. Impressed. Again in lower case letters, but in a straight line. Some variants have been noted with large and long marks of almost two inches being recorded. Again *c*.1800–20.
This like E 3 is a rare mark, and it too has only been noted on printed wares.

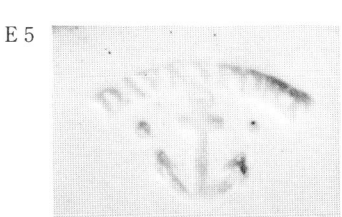

E 5. Impressed. A similar mark to E 2 but in upper case letters.
We cannot recall having seen wares so marked which one would readily date to before *c*.1815. The use of this mark especially on stonewares seems to have continued until at least 1860 and possibly beyond.

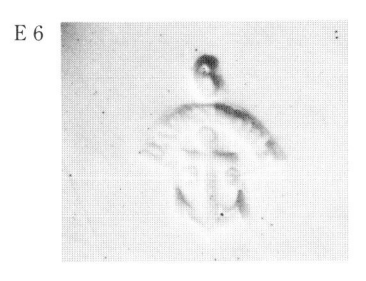

E 6. Impressed. Similar to E 5 but with numbers either side of the anchor which denote the last two digits of the year of manufacture, in this instance 1836.
This system seems to have started *c*.1830 and continued to *c*.1860, when other forms of dating appear as on E 15 and E 16. Curiously, there appear to be far more pieces dated in even years than odd. Thus 1836 is a very common date, so too is 1844, but 1839 is very unusual. There seems to be no satisfactory explanation for this, but a number of correspondents have commented upon it. The numeral which normally appears above this mark could be either the potter's personal tally mark, or possibly the month of manufacture.

E 7. Printed. The very rare printed mark of the partnership of Henry and William Davenport *c*.1832–5. By this date the use of pattern names on the back stamp was coming into practice at Davenports. This would seem to be a relatively early example of its use.

E 8. Printed. This is a typical pattern mark of the William Davenport & Co. period, which basically was continued throughout the factory's life. Similar marks, with different pattern names, can thus date from *c*.1835–81. After this date up to 1887 the words Davenports Ltd may be found on newly engraved patterns. Older patterns would still bear the earlier mark, as these were engraved on the copper plate.
It is not always easy to date such marks as they occur over such a long time span, and other features such as shape, type of pattern and general finish have to be assessed before a tentative date can be assigned.

E 8A. Many pieces do not carry any pattern name. They simply bear the word DAVENPORT printed in capital letters, in the manner shown in E 8. These marks are usually printed in the dominant colour of the print on the piece, blue, black, green, etc. and again appear to date from *c*.1835–87.

E 9. Printed. An uncommon mark found mainly on blue printed wares. Probably confined to the period *c*.1810–35.

E 10. Printed (the impressed mark is also visible). This splendidly bold mark is featured on the Christ Church Preston plate of 1852 with 'Wreath' border (see Plate 166).

Earthenwares and Stonewares

This pattern was one of those singled out for mention in the 1887 advertisement for the liquidation sale of copper plates (see p. 194). The mark is, of course, unique to this pattern, and is representative of literally hundreds of such pattern name marks.

E 11. Printed. The most commonly found stone china mark, and probably the earliest. Usually printed in blue, but has been recorded in red. First used *c*.1815, and still found on wares made in the 1870s.

E 12. Printed. Less common than E 11, but still a frequently found mark.
Again this mark was probably used almost from the first production of stone china, *c*.1815 or a little earlier. It too is found on wares of a quite late date, nearly always in blue.

E 13. Printed. This is a somewhat rare stone china mark. It is printed in puce and is usually found on good quality dinner wares of the 1820–40 period, but not exclusively so.

E 14. Printed. An elaborate printed mark. Very rare. Noted in connection with stone china pattern 51 as illustrated in Plate 99, and with one or two other highly decorated tablewares.
The very few examples noted seem to fall into the period 1820–35.

E 15. Impressed. Another quite rare mark found on stone china of the period *c*.1855–80. Too few examples have been noted to be positive that this mark was not used before the mid 1850s. The year numbers are impressed as part of the mark.

E 16. Impressed. A quite common mark of the late period.
Note the change of name to OPAQUE CHINA and the fact that the year numbers appear above the anchor, though not always very legibly. The earliest date is *c*.1850 and dates into the 1880s are recorded.

E 17. Printed. Another variant with the name given as STONE WARE, and the pattern name BLOSSOM. The accompanying wares appear in Plate 169.
The impressed year number on these pieces is not readable, but the general appearance would suggest *c*.1850 or possibly a little earlier.

It should be noted again here that some high quality, usually ornamental, stone china pieces, have been recorded as carrying the printed china mark P 5 (the brown strap mark). Theories abound as to why this should be, but no idea capable of positive proof has yet been advanced. It should be stressed that the marks illustrated here are *not* reproduced to scale.

The seventeen marks recorded above are by no means the entire repertoire of the factory's marks. There will be, as previously stated, literally hundreds of individual

74 · Earthenwares and Stonewares

pattern name variations from the 1830s onward, such as E 7, E 8 and E 10. Some are shown in Geoffrey Godden's *Encyclopaedia of British Pottery and Porcelain Marks*, Nos. 1185–7. Other variants including an example of a Davenports Ltd mark are shown on the shards illustrated here on Plate 24, and on the example E 18 below. Doubtless collectors will know of others, and will hasten to inform us of them.

We conclude this survey with an interesting mark **E 18** which has the impressed mark W. Davenport & Co. Longport. 3:81 (for March 1881), and also a printed mark for the new company, Davenports Ltd. Longport, associated with the pattern MERSEY. This is in effect a double marking, the piece presumably made under the old company and then decorated and marked again by the new when they took over the stock and blanks.

Not all wares which carry the Davenport name were made at Longport between 1794 and 1887. Certain very unusual items stand alone such as the fine jug in the British Museum which bears the inscription, THIS IS THE FIRST ARTICLE MANUFACTURED BY CHARLES DAVENPORT. NOVEM'r 16th 1798 (see *Northern Ceramic Society Newsletter* 62 (June 1986) and 64 (December 1986) for details). As was noted earlier those companies which bought up Davenport copper plates continued to use them for many years, and thus wares made well after 1887 bear such names as HOBSON'S DAVENPORT, and similar names as indicated on p. 69. The name has also been used in this century. In the 1950s pieces were issued with the mark Davenport's Fine Bone China, England, and A. Wood & Sons have more recently quite literally traded upon their location by using the name Davenport Pottery Co. Ltd. There have been other potters or pottery dealers apart from Charles Davenport in 1798 who quite legitimately used their own name of Davenport on the wares they made or sold. There have also been other potters who, again perfectly legitimately, used an anchor as part of their own mark. Incidentally, it has never been entirely satisfactorily explained why John Davenport first used an anchor, unless it was to mark his close connection with Liverpool and the sea across which he hoped to export vast quantities of his goods.

Thus the presence of an anchor or the name Davenport does not always betoken a piece made at the factory which is the subject of this book. *Caveat emptor!*

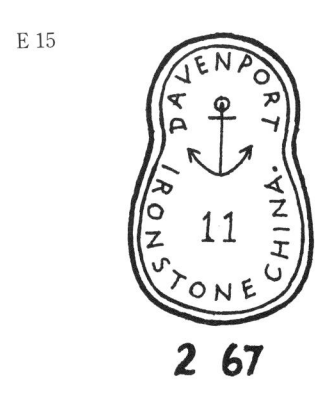

9 Creamware and Pearlware

When John Davenport took over the Longport Unicorn Bank factory in 1794, he did so at a time of great expansion within the Staffordshire pottery industry. The foundations built by Josiah Wedgwood in the period 1760–90 were secure and there were vast opportunities for enterprising manufacturers in the 1790s. For Josiah Wedgwood and the firm he created, the truly great days were past. Josiah himself died in 1795 and the leadership of the industry passed to a new generation amongst whom were the familiar names of Josiah Spode, Thomas Minton and, as events were to prove, John Davenport himself. For all these potters the staple of their prosperity in trade was the production of large quantities of saleable earthenwares. At this date this meant creamware, pearlware and underglaze blue printed ware, which of course was done on a basic pearlware body.

We do not know if John Davenport began to manufacture from the very first when he took over the pottery, but it is likely that he would proceed cautiously at first. He was after all an experienced trader and would have many wholesale and retail outlets already well-known to him, and his knowledge of the best-selling lines would enable him to gear production to these areas. These are inferences about Davenport's likely attitudes, but they seem to be borne out by an examination of what he did actually produce. In this section we shall deal with creamware and pearlware, made during approximately the first thirty years of the factory's life, that is up to the early 1820s. The blue printed wares will be left to a later section.

By 1794 creamware was well past its heyday. It will be recalled that Josiah Wedgwood had complained to his partner Thomas Bentley as early as 6 August 1779 that Lady Dartmouth and her friends 'were tired of creamcolor,' adding in tones of sheer exasperation, 'and so they would of Angels if they were shown for sale in every chandler's shop through the town.' Wedgwood's answer to this was to develop a ware which he christened 'pearl white.' This as the name implies was a ware whose appearance was white and not cream-coloured. It is worth noting that recent research by George Miller and others (summarized in the Northern Ceramic Society exhibition catalogue *Creamware & Pearlware*) would seem to prove that other Staffordshire potters had, prior to Wedgwood, developed a ware of which the glaze had been made a bluey-white by the addition of cobalt. Jugs bearing dates of 1775 and 1777 are recorded and the trade Directories of the time refer to manufacturers of 'China Glaze' ware which seems to have been the accepted trade name for what Wedgwood 'developed' in 1779. However, it is the term he used, pearlware, which has passed into accepted usage. 'China glaze,' which so accurately expressed the ambition of the potters to emulate the superficial appearance of porcelain, has been forgotten.

What is important for the study of Davenport's wares is to realize that creamware of the kind we associate with Leeds, Wedgwood, and others – the lovely teapots, the massive centrepieces, and the delicate pierced plates, comports and baskets – were yesterday's wares. Lovers of creamware may regret this, but it is a fact. Davenport's creamwares have interesting characteristics of their own, but they cannot be compared, like for like, with their earlier counterparts. What should also be realized, is that, as far as we can tell, Davenport was on the scene too late to make any of the 'traditional' early pearlwares. By this we mean those wares which have a very blue glaze and which conventionally are decorated with underglaze blue painted designs of the *Chinese House* pattern with its endless variations on the basic picture of tree-fence-house-fence-tree. These and the Chinese ladies with parasols do not appear to have been part of the Davenport repertoire. The pearlwares with which this chapter is concerned are wares in which the body has been made of somewhat whiter firing clays than were used for the conventional creamwares, but which above all have a glaze which where it gathers in slight pools can clearly be seen to have a blue cast, rather than the creamy-yellowy tone of the glaze on the creamwares. It should be stressed however, that even by 1794, let alone ten years later, the dividing line between what was creamware and what one should more accurately call pearlware is extremely hard to define. Visual examination is the only method of assessment and the glaze on many pieces is almost colourless. Perhaps it does not matter all that much. There doesn't appear to have been any settled factory policy as to which wares were finished in a creamware glaze and which with a pearl, though it would seem that where one has a complete or partial service for comparison, the two types of glaze were not mixed in the same service. The difference is readily discernible if you 'mix' pieces in this way. One cannot be dogmatic about the matter, but it does seem that more of the factory output was finished in the pearlware glaze than in the cream. This is something which has only been remarked upon in the last few years and certainly the distinction was not made in the relevant section of my 1972 book on Davenport. Thus, while every effort will be made in this section to distinguish between the cream and pearl finishes, where examples are not now available for examination, being in private collections or taken from old catalogues, it is more than likely that pieces will have been described as creamware, which now I think would be more accurately termed pearlware.

As a last word of introduction it should be noted that as time passes, and certainly by 1810, Wedgwood and other potters developed a 'whiteware.' Whilst some of these white wares, including Wedgwood's often have a bluey glaze, many have a really white body over which there is a clear glaze. There is good evidence that Davenport followed this fashion and a significant output from the factory was by the 1820s in whiteware rather than either cream or pearlware. It is for this reason that this chapter will concentrate upon those wares which appear to date from the period before the mid 1820s. The later examples of creamware, pearlware and whiteware appear in chapter 16.

As stated earlier very few 'traditional' types of creamware can be attributed to Davenport. Plate 25 however shows a plate decorated with underglaze blue flower paintings in the fashion of the 1780s. The piece has a faintly discernible impressed lower case mark and so far nothing similar has been noted. It is just possible that this was a replacement done by the factory to match an earlier service made by another pottery.

25. Lobed creamware plate painted underglaze in deep blue. Diameter: 9½in. Mark E 2 (faintly impressed). (Lockett Collection)

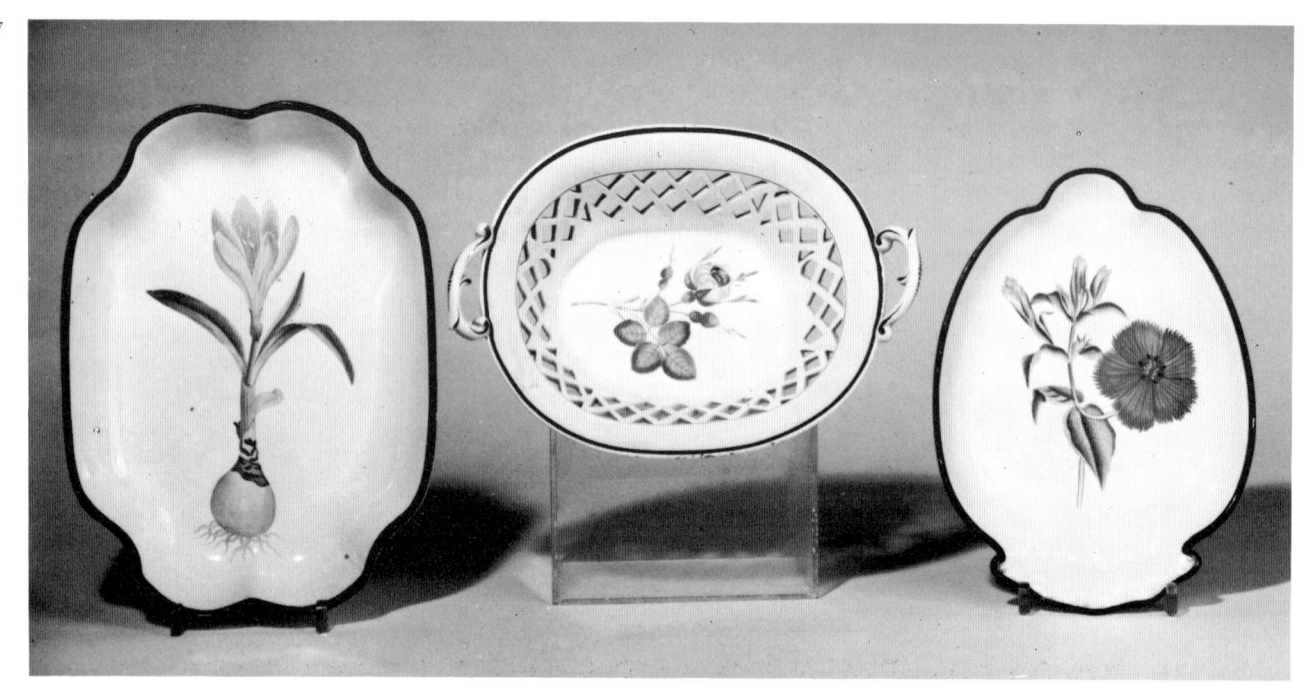

Another interesting, and apparently early piece, is that shown in Plate 26. Otherwise plain, the rim is most attractively moulded with animals. These two are unusual items and don't conform to any generally accepted pattern. What is really quite remarkable is how limited is the range of wares produced in creamware and how few variations there are in the shapes within this range. This limited range fits in with our understanding of the commercial attitude of John Davenport. He was extremely cautious with his money and it would appear that once he had settled upon a serviceable and standard set of shapes – and this is especially true of the dessert wares – he was not anxious to incur the expense of additional moulds and the like just to be able to offer a variety of shapes and sizes to his customers. Variety was achieved by decoration. There is a wide range – almost bewilderingly so – of decorative treatment, but on basic shapes which hardly change over the years, and indeed which are used not only for the cream and pearl wares but upon other earthenwares such as the chalcedony, and even find their way into the early porcelain production.

The basic shapes are all shown in the illustrations. A dessert service at this period would consist of a specified number of plates, of low comports or dishes usually in square, oval, heart-shaped and rectangular form (Plate 27). In what appear to be the earliest services, these are of simple regular shape (see Plate 237). On the slightly more

26. Close-up of the border of a very rare creamware plate, moulded with animals in cartouches (sheep, pig, greyhound, cow, horse and dog), otherwise undecorated. Diameter 9½in. Mark E 2. (Iwass Collection)

27. A group of finely-decorated pearlware dessert wares. Marked with both E 2 and E 5 (on different pieces). (Courtesy Christies's)

28.

29.

28. Creamware dessert tureen and stand with an unusual finial form. Pattern 125. Ht 6½in. Length 7¼in. Mark E 4. (Diana Darlington Collection)

29. Pearlware dessert tureen painted with KING-BIRD-OF-PARADISE (lid) and THE EAGLE OF MONTEVIDEO (body). Ht 7in. Unmarked. The reverse side of Colour Plate IV. (Hacking Collection)

common and later version, the basic shapes are modified by moulding which forms embryonic handles (Plate 27). In addition there would be a raised or footed comport (Plates 48 and 238) and cream and sugar tureens with their accompanying ladles, that for sugar being pierced. Finally there would be fruit baskets, not as so frequently described chestnut baskets, again with their accompanying stands. The early Davenport examples of baskets and stands in both cream and pearlware are usually pierced as can be seen in the illustrations. The handles vary a little. The standard forms are either twisted rope or a very simplified form of rustic handle with spurs on both the inner and outer edges. Very occasionally the tureens and the side dishes or comports are pierced also (see Plate 57). The tureen finial too is standard in shape (Colour Plate III), though an interesting variant can be seen in Plate 28. Ice pails or ice cream containers might also have formed part of such a service, but I know of no examples in either of the early simple shapes. Other pieces are occasionally encountered. The very fine circular tureen, decorated with enamelled birds (Colour Plate IV and Plate 29) would at first glance seem to be the centre piece of a supper set, but as it was found in conjunction with two dessert comports (Plate 48) it can be regarded as an addition to the normal range of dessert wares, as can the very rare ring-handled tureen (Plate 30). These relatively simple shapes and forms, based loosely on contemporary silver examples, were made in both cream and pearlware,

79 · Earthenwares and Stonewares

30.

31.

32.

30. Unusually shaped pearlware tureen painted with 'Thrush' (cover) and 'Redstart' (body), and a plate decorated with NUMIDIAN-CRANE-OR-DANCING-BIRD. Mark E 2. (Courtesy Christie's)

31. Leaf-moulded pearlware dessert tureen enamelled in bright colours. Ht 6¼in. Length 7¼in. Mark E 2. (Diana Darlington Collection)

32. Pearlware leaf-moulded plate decorated in bright natural colours. Diameter 8¼in. Mark E 2. (Alan Cleaver Collection)

Earthenwares and Stonewares

33.

and seem to have persisted for at least twenty years if not longer. As was stated earlier their apparent variety is achieved by the various forms of decorative finish.

At some date possibly after 1810 new dessert ware forms were introduced. These were very flamboyant, and hardly accord with the element of the neo-classical restraint that remains in the so-called Regency period. The wares in question are elaborately moulded in leaf form, and stylistically seem to hark back to the Rococo period, or even to look forward to its re-emergence, the Revived Rococo of the 1830s. So although there is no positive documentary factory evidence that the leaf-moulded wares are from the period c.1810–25, their decoration, marking and the comparison with contemporary wares seem to indicate this date span.

Whenever they were made these pieces are certainly stunning. The tureen and stand in Plate 31 is marvellously coloured and that in Colour Plate V with the bunch of grapes finial is quite breathtaking – if not entirely to the taste of those who like their pots to be characterized by 'elegant simplicity'. A whole service with plates in coloured leaf form, and both high and low comports of moulded leaf form, painted in what could be called bold – some might say brash or bizarre – colours was sold some years ago in London and is now believed to be in America. Incidentally, plates from this type of service can be either moulded overall (Plates 32–3) or have only the rim in overlapping leaf form (Plate 34). The ice pail (Colour Plate VI) gives a good indication of the remarkable richness of this particular dessert form.

Turning to other wares made in cream or pearlware, we find far fewer examples. Teawares were probably made, and a number of teapots are known, such as that in Plate 35 which is of the standard form for the period c.1800–15 and the so-far unique early pearlware example in Plate 36, but cups and saucers have not yet been recognized, though they are known in chalcedony, cane ware and porcelain from the same period, and thus one would imagine would be produced in cream and pearlware. The route to recognition and attribution of such pieces must lie through a comparison with the shapes occurring in the materials already mentioned, as it is unlikely that marked teacups and saucers will be found from this early date.

33. Large pearlware dessert dish moulded in leaf form and brightly coloured. 12×10in. Mark E 2. (Godden of Worthing Ltd)

81 · Earthenwares and Stonewares

34. Pearlware dessert plate moulded with overlapping leaves on the rim. Painted in monochrome with a picturesque ruin. Diameter 8¾in. Mark E 2 with 'Donevan' (sic) in red script. Presumably this indicates an item ordered by the Dublin retailer James Donovan. (Lockett Collection)

35. Pearlware teapot of old oval shape, printed overglaze with a floral pattern and additional enamelling. Ht 5in. Overall length 9¼in. Mark E 2. (Lockett Collection)

Dinner wares too are known. A full service with a painted border in the Wedgwood style was reported from a sale room some years ago. The sauce boat and attached stand in Plate 37 is an example of the kind of dinner ware produced. But it has to be said that such wares are rare. The Iwass collection contains a pearlware tureen with just a blue feather edge decoration, but one looks in vain for the great creamware tureens that typify Wedgwood's dinner services, although isolated plates may be noted from time to time.

In nearly every other type of ware made by Davenport jugs are prominent, but not in cream and pearlware. The one, two and three pint jugs so familiar in white stoneware do not appear in either cream or pearlware. It may be that Davenport satisfied demand with the stone china, chalcedony, porcelain, and white stoneware items, but it is strange that not until much later do we find earthenware examples, which after all were produced in vast quantities by other manufacturers.

On the other hand, with typical Davenport idiosyncracy they produced quite large numbers of bulb pots in cream and pearl ware. These follow the usual D-shaped form, though with some variation both in size and proportion of straight back to curved front. The chief element of variety however, is provided by the handles and lids. The three basic handle forms, the attached ring, the dolphin mask and the rustic or crabstock are all depicted in the illustrations (Plates 38–41). The tops, where they have survived, are generally of flat form with holes into which the bulbs would be placed: the more elaborate variant with the moulded sockets for the bulbs and the curious kind of handle for lifting the top can be seen on the three splendidly decorated pieces from the Darlington collection shown in Plate 41.

Other forms are rare. The quintal flower horn (Plate 42) is the only known example in pearlware (a pair of lustre examples was sold at the Dorchester Fair some years ago). A pearlware Portland vase decorated with Chinese figures has also been reported, and most unusual of all are the objects described in the *Connoisseur*, June 1963, 'an extremely rare set of four pottery quail boxes and covers *c.*1820, contained in a circular nest, each bird is beautifully modelled with feathers in relief, and coloured yellow

36. Pearlware teapot of unusual form. Decorated with pattern 245. Ht 4¼in. Overall length 9½in. Mark E 2. (Diana Darlington Collection)

37. Creamware sauce boat and attached stand. Pattern 442. Length 8in. Mark E 5 (Lockett Collection)

83 · Earthenwares and Stonewares

38

39
40

41

beak and feet, brown feathers flecked with yellow and grey underbody. The nest has a centre of soft pink and a raised border of grasses in shades of green and brown. The bird boxes are 3 inches high and the nest, which is impressed marked 'Davenport' with an anchor is 10¼ inches in diameter.' Surprisingly this is not a unique item and the example

84 · Earthenwares and Stonewares

42

43

38. Two pearlware bulb pots, both decorated with brightly coloured enamel border patterns, unnumbered. Note the slight differences in the basic shape. Both have attached ring handles. Ht (L) 4¼in. (R) 4⅜in. Marks both E 2. (Lockett Collection)

39. Pearlware bulb pot decorated with an enamelled anthemion motif in brown and red. Attached ring handles. Note the somewhat thinner and taller form than those in Plate 38. Ht 5⅜in. Mark E 2. (Diana Darlington Collection)

40. Creamware bulb pot with finely enamelled monochrome picturesque landscapes. 'Bronzed' dolphin handles. Ht 4¾in. Mark E 2. (Lockett Collection)

41. A garniture of three pearlware bulb pots and covers, attractively painted with polychrome picturesque landscape. Bronzed rustic, or crabstock, handles. Hts L and R 6¼in., centre 7in. (Diana Darlington Collection: photo courtesy Sotheby's Sussex)

42. Pearlware quintal flower horn with 'peasant enamel' painting on the body. The terminals in Pratt-type underglaze colours. Ht 8⅝in. Mark E 5. (Diana Darlington Collection)

43. A remarkable pearlware quail's egg cup suite, with 10 cups and covers in a circular dish. Fully coloured. Mark E 2. (Courtesy Royal Pavilion Art Gallery & Museum, Brighton)

illustrated in Plate 43 comes from the Willett collection in Brighton.

It was indicated earlier in this section that though there was only a limited range of shapes produced in the dessert ware range the variety of decoration more than made up for this. Several types of decoration seem to have been favoured by the factory. The conventional border patterns familiar from the wares of Wedgwood and other potters feature on many items of Davenport cream and pearlware. There seem to have been special patterns reserved for these wares ranging from 1 to that on the creamware sauce boat and stand which at 442 is the highest so far recorded. Good examples of the type of pattern are shown on the three pattern plates illustrated in Plates 44-6.

Other attractive forms of decoration are depicted in the illustrations, and it is worth drawing attention to some of these. Colour Plate II is decorated with extremely well-painted leaves in autumnal colours. This type of decoration has been found on several different dessert services, and not all done by the same hand. So it would seem that this decoration, which incidentally has never been noted in connection with a pattern number, was a speciality at the factory and at least two if not more painters or

85 · Earthenwares and Stonewares

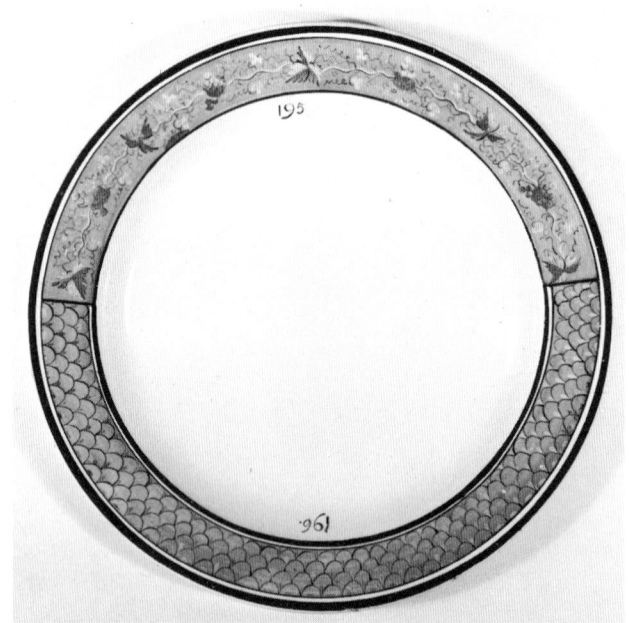

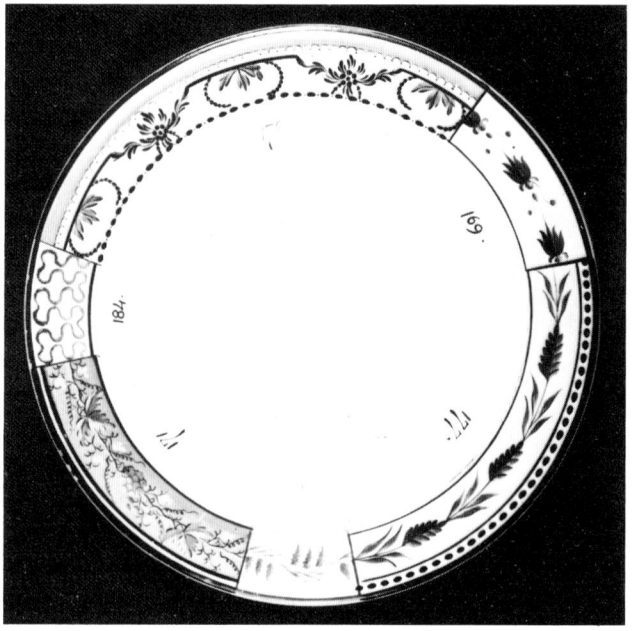

paintresses were able to work in this fashion. The dessert plate in Colour Plate VII is rather different in that it has a blue printed osier or basket weave pattern as a background to a very remarkable and colourful leaf decoration. The shape of the plate and the lack of a foot-rim indicate a fairly early date for this piece c.1810–20.

Most factories at this period used Curtis's *Botanical Magazine* and other such books of botanical prints as sources for decoration on ceramics. Davenport followed this trend. There is indeed quite a range of treatment in floral decoration with many examples known of specimen flowers on all types of body from porcelain to chalcedony. On creamware and pearlware, as one would expect, a number of different 'styles' have been noted. The word styles is used deliberately as in a matter of straightforward copying from a published (and probably coloured) print the idea that one can recognize the hand of an individual artist is not a belief to which I personally subscribe. The whole manner of factory organization in the large potbanks of the early nineteenth century was inimical to the 'great artist' approach. The painters and paintresses did not sign their work at

44. Creamware pattern plate showing specimen border patterns in the range 59–67. Mark E 2. (The late Stanley W. Fisher)

45. Creamware pattern plate showing patterns 195 and 196. Diameter 10in. Mark E 2. (The late Rupert Gentle)

46. Creamware pattern plate showing border patterns in the range 169–84. Mark E 2. (The late Stanley W. Fisher)

86 · Earthenwares and Stonewares

47.

47. Pearlware dessert baskets and stands. Finely painted with coloured central cartouches of country scenes. Note the characteristic three small monochrome flower groups on the border. Unmarked service. It has been carefully examined and is unmistakably Davenport. (Courtesy Edward C. Monsson, Los Angeles)

Davenport at this time, nor indeed at most of the factories, and unlike the Derby factory where signed sketches and pattern books exist which assign specific patterns so numbered to specific painters, no documents of any kind are available to help us to discriminate between the work of the artists at Davenport. There have been several attempts to identify individual 'hands,' but they have not met with much success. It is, of course, perfectly natural to want to assign a particularly fine decoration to a named artist. It is a matter of scholarship and connoisseurship to so do, it is also commercially very helpful. Above all one would like to pay tribute to the skill and artistry of those involved in the decoration of the work we so much admire. Alas, in the present state of our knowledge of Davenport this is just not possible.

Two examples may suffice. The decoration on the part dessert service in the Monsson collection (Plate 47) is truly fine. It has been suggested that it is the work of Daniel Lucas Senior who is recorded by Haslem as having worked at the factory, 'in early life . . . at glass and china painting.' Given that the pots seem to date from the period c.1805–15 and that Lucas was born in 1787, it is possible that he was the artist responsible. But a comparison with paintings attributed to him later (1820–40) when he was working at Derby does not really take us any further. They do not seem to me to be by the same hand. Indeed, it would be surprising if an artist was painting in the same fashion over a period of thirty years or more. Be that as it may, given our present very limited knowledge all that can be said is that we do not know the artist responsible for these delightful landscapes. A second example concerns paintings of flowers and birds. Several, such as that in Plates 48–50, have the name of the bird or flower neatly painted in capital letters on the back of the piece. The curiosity is that on some of the very finest examples each word in the title is linked to the next by a hyphen thus: 'EAST INDIAN-BLACK-CAPPED-LORY.' Not unnaturally the work of this man or woman has become known as that of the 'hyphen painter'. But no name can be given to him or her.

The wares just discussed in the Monsson collection do focus attention on another aspect of Davenport decoration in this period. Together with a few of their equally high-quality contemporaries, Davenport landscape decoration of this period reflects the then fashionable 'picturesque' painting which had such fine exponents, especially in water-colours, as Francis Towne, Gainsborough, Constable, Crome, Turner and a host of other well-known names. This addiction to picturesque scenes was amply catered for, not merely by the paintings produced by the artists named, but also through the medium of the published print. The scenery of the Lake District, Derbyshire, Wales, and to a lesser extent Scotland, had replaced the Italian vistas favoured by those who had experienced the Grand Tour in the eighteenth century. The poems of Wordsworth and his contemporaries also helped to create an intellectual backcloth which further enhanced the demand for the Romantic and the Picturesque (which, of course, are not by any

48. Pearlware footed dessert comport decorated with a painting of the EAS'T INDIAN-BLACK CAPPED-LORY by 'the hyphen painter'. The title on the fore edge of the dish relates to a second bird not visible in the photograph. Length 11in. Ht 4½in. Mark E 2. (Hacking Collection)

49. Close-up of the title of the bird in Plate 48. (Hacking Collection)

50. An interesting dessert tureen decorated in colours by 'the hyphen painter' with a NARROW-LEAVED-NARCISSUS (base) and SQUILL-BELL-FLOWERED (lid). Though this piece is unmarked, the combination of the handle and finial forms, the overall shape, the three small monochrome flowers on the stand rim, and the hyphenated title, make this undoubtedly Davenport. Ht 6½in. (Hacking Collection)

88 · Earthenwares and Stonewares

means the same thing). For the potter however, the books of prints of *Views in Cumberland and Westmoreland* etc. were ideal material from which to copy scenes to paint on pots. The Davenport artists were no exception. Unlike the flower and bird painting, these early views were apparently not named, but there is little doubt that they were taken directly from published prints. There is also little doubt, as can be seen in the illustrations to this chapter and to those on porcelain, that the factory had several very accomplished artists on its staff. A close examination of the monochrome painting on several bulb pots, plates and other items which superficially would seem to come from the same hand indicate quite different technical approaches to the task, and thus it would appear that several artists were capable of achieving the high standard that is evident on the wares. It should be added that the Picturesque style was much more free in approach and finish than the rather laboured, meticulous and topographically accurate style adopted by the artists at Rockingham and Derby at a somewhat later date. The painting on these early Davenport wares of all classes is very much in the fashion and manner of contemporary water-colourists, and as such is one of the most attractive and lively styles to be found on English wares of the early nineteenth century (Plate 51).

I have commented earlier on the sad fact that we are unable to pay our respects to the artists simply because we do not know their names. In just one case this is not so. Marked Davenport wares are recorded with the signature of the painter William Absolon of Yarmouth (Plate 52). Absolon was not a factory artist. He bought Davenport wares 'in the white' and decorated them, and those of other suppliers, at his home in Yarmouth. The Davenport wares we have examined are all named flower studies and all painted in what John Howell describes as 'a blackish sepia and washed in a pale lustrous green'. Further examples and a discussion of his work may be found in Mr Howell's article in *Transactions of the English Ceramic Circle* 10 Pt 5 (1980) and 12 Pt 2 (1985).

The range of decoration at Davenport on their creamware and pearlware is quite considerable; floral and geometric border patterns, birds, flower and landscape studies constitute the chief elements, with the unusual coloured leaves, and some interesting examples of a combination of blue printed and brightly painted decoration. Further examples of this type are given in the chapter on blue printed wares. As was indicated earlier, there is much more variety in the decoration than there is in the shapes of the wares. Nevertheless, the quality of both the potting and the decoration is almost always very high. In the wares of his period, one gets the distinct impression of good

51. Creamware plate decorated in monochrome with the typically free approach of the water-colour 'Picturesque' artist. This is a much 'sketchier' approach than that, say, on the bulb pot Plate 40. Diameter 7¾in. Mark E 2. (Lockett Collection).

management, of quality control, and an eye not merely for what will sell, but for what will serve to enhance the reputation of the manufactory. These feelings are certainly not always present when one examines some of the later wares.

Finally, in this section, we must make a note of the marks found and their significance. It is certainly not clear cut as to which marks were used at which time. I have always assumed, and still do so, that the earliest mark used on any of the earthenwares was the anchor alone, impressed (E 1). Unless the factory marked none of its early wares, then it is reasonable to assume that wares carrying this mark may be dated to *c*.1795 onwards. At some point, as yet unclear, the impressed mark 'Davenport' (lower case) over an anchor was introduced (E 2). The introduction of this mark did not apparently end the use of the anchor alone, for services are known with both marks on different pieces. It has been argued that the lower case mark bearing the family name was not introduced until *after* the Royal visit of 1806. This might apply to the porcelain wares as my fellow author argues in chapter 17, but personally I find it very difficult to substantiate that every piece of Davenport creamware and pearlware marked with the family name must date from after 1806. The corollary of this is that all the wares made in the factory between 1794 and 1806 are either unmarked or marked with the anchor alone impressed. My own belief is quite firmly that at some date, possibly as early as 1800, the family name mark was being used on creamware and pearlware (and also on the stoneware bodies) and that the anchor alone continued to be used contemporaneously for some time, the length of which is as yet undetermined. The fact of the matter is that we shall never know for certain unless factory records are discovered which give us a clear indication, or dated wares are discovered found in conjunction with the mark we have just discussed.

The use of the family name mark in upper case letters (E 5) again presents problems, which we touch on in chapter 11. It would appear – and we can say no more – that the upper case mark was introduced somewhat later than the lower, but that for quite some time the two were being used contemporaneously. To clarify matters a little,

52. Creamware dessert dish painted in sepia with a flower spray named on the reverse 'Arbae a Fratex'. Length 8in. Mark E 2 and 'Absolon Yarm'th' painted. (Courtesy Victoria & Albert Museum)

90 · Earthenwares and Stonewares

I know of no wares with the upper case letters which one would confidently date as pre-1806, whereas there are many wares which seem to date from the 1820s which may be marked in either the lower or the upper case manner. As with some of the other controversies and difficult points, perhaps in the end it does not really matter. What happened in the dingy workshops of the factory on a brutal winter's afternoon, will never be known to us. Nor can we expect early nineteenth-century manufacturers struggling with the problems of securing payment for goods sent to St Petersburg or New York to be precise in the marking of wares. They would not confiscate all the lower case stamps on 1 January 1810 say, and forbid their further use on pain of dismissal! Potbanks were human workplaces and all kinds of strange and unscientific practices went on. When one reads of the terrible living and working conditions of the time, not to mention the vagaries of the kiln, it is a miracle that so much ware of beauty was produced. We should be thankful that so much of the fine creamware and pearlware made at Longport has survived to this day. Our cabinets give testimony to the skill and craftsmanship of the Davenport potters and artists, even if the dates and labels we attach to the pieces are based more on reasoned deduction than historically demonstrable certainty.

10 Coloured-body Earthenwares

One of the most distinctive classes of early Davenport earthenwares is that which can be called coloured-body ware. It is perhaps as well to state at the outset that there are several shades of colour involved, ranging from an orange body to a quite light stone colour. The best known are certainly the orange body pieces. Recent research by Diana Darlington in the Royal Archives has produced the 1807 orders which have been quoted elsewhere in this book. Amongst the wares sold to the Prince Regent following his visit in 1806 are:

> *2 Pot Pourres Calcedony Painted in Flowers*   £5   10   0
> *3 Jarrs Large & less ditto ditto*   4   4   0
> *1 ditto Calcedony Painted Flowers & Black ground*   1   10   0
> *1 Ditto ditto Painted Flowers & Etch'd Lustre*
>   *Fruit, ground colord, & wash'd with yellow green &c*   2   2   0

Additionally, there is an entry for:

> *2 Portland Vauses, Etch'd Figures*   4   4   0

Although there has been some debate on the interpretation of the word 'calcedony', there seems little doubt that what is referred to is the orange coloured body with which we are familiar, principally in Davenport teawares. This seems to be confirmed by a contemporary reference in the Notebook of Thomas Brameld housed in the Victoria & Albert Museum where we read:

> *Bodies used By T.B. May 1808*
> *Chalcedony or Orange*
> *32 White Slip*
> *8 Flint*
> *20 Red or Yellow slip*

It is clear from this that John Davenport was not alone in producing chalcedony or orange body ware at this period, though as far as I am aware no marked example of

53. Portland vase in the chalcedony body decorated with a picturesque country scene. Ht 7⅛in. Mark E 2. (Iwass Collection)

54. Part of a tea service in the chalcedony body: the inside of most of the vessels is covered with a creamware slip. All decorated with monochrome landscapes (see text). Teapot, overall length 11⅜in., ht 4¾in. Coffee can, ht 2½in. Cup, ht 2⅜in. Saucer, diameter 5¼in. Sugar box, ht 4½in., length 6½in. Cream jug, ht 3½in., length 6in Salt, ht 3½in. Slop bowl, diameter 5½in. Mark E 2 on teapot; stand; cream jug and sugar box only. (City of Liverpool Museum)

Brameld's chalcedony has been recorded. It is also worth noting that during this precise period Thomas Lakin was in a position of responsibility at the Davenport Works. Subsequently, c.1810, he left to establish his own business, and one of the products for which he was best known was a light orange coloured body ware. With his knowledge of the chemistry of potting, it is reasonable to assume that Lakin had a strong influence on the type of ware produced by Davenport especially in the coloured-body range. It may be of interest to note that in the posthumously published *Valuable Receipts of the Late Mr Thomas Lakin* (Leeds, 1824) the following is found: 'Process 13. To make a Calcedony Body. Take 32 Parts of Yellow Clay, 10 Parts of Cornish Clay, 4 Parts of Flint. . . . Process 42. To make a Calcedony Glaze, take 65 Parts of Litharge, 40 Parts of Cornish Stone, 20 Parts of Flint, 6 Parts of Frit. – Process 32.' There is an added note: 'The three coloured glazes as above, require using about the same consistency as the cream colour glaze, and will stand the highest temperature of heat in a common glazing oven.'

Returning to the Royal order we can note that a marked chalcedony vase (Jarr) of the Chinese shape depicted in Plate 92 of *Davenport Pottery & Porcelain* exists in a Canadian collection. This is decorated with picturesque scenes rather than flowers, but these are set against a black ground as described above. The Royal order does not specify the body in which the Portland 'Vauses' were to be made, but we can illustrate in Plate 53 a fine, and so far unique, example in chalcedony from the Iwass collection. The combination of chalcedony and lustre has not been noted.

Vases and other ornamental items, including quite elaborate bulb pots (though not of typical Davenport form) have been recorded in the orange body. The great majority have been unmarked and though I think one can confidently expect to discover new ornamental forms in this body, it must be stressed that not all chalcedony wares emanated from Davenport, though it is reasonable to think of the factory as a first possible attribution.

The most usual items found in chalcedony are teawares. The service illustrated in Plate 54 is housed in the Liverpool Museum and comprises four saucers, seven cups, four cans, and the other major items as illustrated. The decoration is also typical being in monochrome sepia and consisting entirely of simple landscape designs. At one stage I felt that these were just imaginary, made-up scenes, but the more one studies the books of engravings from this 'picturesque' period the more one realizes that even the simplest scene was not beneath the attention of the artist. Thus what looks to us like a totally anonymous country scene, can appear, for example, in a set of Ackerman prints as 'Nr. Twickenham' or whatever. It seems more than likely that these quite arresting and charming miniature landscapes were directly copied (usually unnamed) from books of prints which were so fashionable at the time. It is worth noting that in the Liverpool service only the major pieces carry the factory mark. None of the cups, saucers or cans is marked. This would seem a deliberate factory policy, but it does make identification of surviving pieces of this type dependent upon a knowledge of shape, and to a lesser extent, of decorative treatment.

Teawares certainly form the bulk of surviving specimens, with teapots in several collections having decoration of the landscapes, as illustrated; of a simple Greek key border pattern; of Egyptian motifs; and of variations of anthemion-type leaf decoration, as on the Stoke-on-Trent City Museum example illustrated in *Davenport Pottery & Porcelain*, Plate 21. Curiously enough this type of decoration has not yet been noted on other items of teaware.

A reasonable number of dessert wares has also been noted in the full orange chalcedony colour range. There are several plates in the Liverpool Museum collection, all decorated with monochrome landscapes including a replacement piece with the year code marks for 1856. The Lockett collection contains three rarities, a dish (low comport) of standard earthenware shape, and a plate, both of which have a landscape decoration painted in browns, green and yellow rather than in the usual monochrome. There is also a plate, from the Hartley Asquith collection, which is somewhat bizarrely printed in a deep orange with the well-known Bisham Abbey pattern (see Plate 110).

Other not uncommon wares made in the standard darker chalcedony are jugs of the type illustrated in Colour Plate VIII. These splendid pieces with the gold Greek key pattern and the picturesque landscapes may well have been part of an even larger set. But even three are sufficient to arouse the admiration, and probably the envy, of those who find this particular type of ware especially attractive.

Turning to the lighter body colour, almost a stone colour, we find very few teawares, indeed one can only recall a teapot in the Darlington collection (Plate 55), decorated with a Greek key pattern and interestingly marked with the impressed word WARRANTED which has also been noted on Davenport caneware teapots of the same period (*c*.1810) (Plate 67). Several dessert wares are known including a basket and stand painted with named flowers (illustrated in *Transactions of the English Ceramic Circle* 12 Pt 2, 1985) and several plates ensuite. There is also the very unusual service of which we illustrate two pieces (Plates 56–7). This service of which a raised comport, plates, dishes and most attractive cream and sugar tureens and ladles survive, has a most unusual decoration of a dotted leaf design which however pleasing to look at, must have been extremely boring to paint. Other dessert services are known with pierced plates and a simple border design. The tureen in Plate 57 gives a good idea of the delicacy of this particular form. Even without the cover it is a handsome piece. This stone or light buff-

55. Light chalcedony or stone coloured body teapot decorated with a bold Greek key design in black enamel. Overall length 10½in., ht 4½in. Mark E 1 and WARRANTED (impressed). (Diana Darlington Collection)

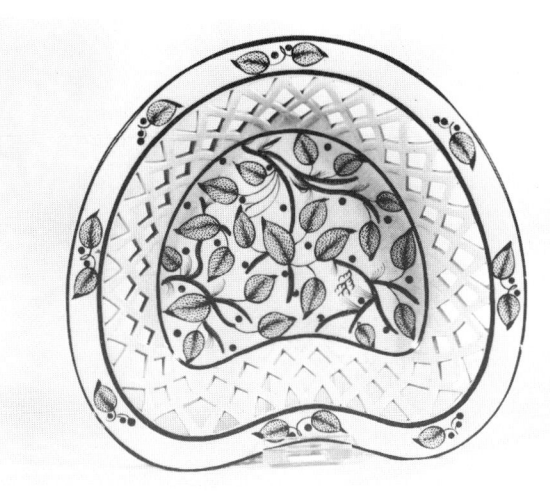

coloured body is again not unique to Davenport, and perhaps is not quite so characteristic as the darker chalcedony body.

We end this section with a note of a number of special items. In the Lockett collection is a jug in the chalcedony body bearing a print of Nelson signed 'T. Baddeley, Hanley.' Other similar items are also recorded. This piece is illustrated and discussed elsewhere (*Northern Ceramic Society Newsletter* 47 and *Transactions of the English Ceramic Circle* cited above). The piece is not marked, and the handle form is not precisely consistent with that of other Davenport pieces. On balance I would now describe this as possibly Davenport rather than 'probably'.

There is no doubt about the authenticity of the second item. At a recent National Exhibition Centre Fair in Birmingham there appeared a quite magnificent marked part dessert service in the chalcedony body decorated in monochrome red with marvellously painted and named birds. No one who saw the pieces could have failed to be impressed, they truly merited the old Pre-Raphaelite term of approbation, they really were 'stunning,' but so alas was the price! However, it was a privilege to see such splendid works and be reminded again that though the Davenport Pottery was by and large a very 'commercial' factory, they were also capable of a quality of work – in this case in a most unusual medium – which was equal to, indeed probably could not be matched by, any of their contemporaries, even by such giants of the trade as Spode, Wedgwood, and Minton.

The coloured-body wares were probably in production for a period of ten to fifteen years. It would be surprising if many could be dated to much before 1800, and, as they were the kind of ware much subject to changes in fashion, it is unlikely that any were being made as late as 1820. As we have indicated marking was somewhat irregular. Major pieces bear marks frequently, the lesser components of tea services and some of the plates in dessert services are found unmarked. Both the anchor alone impressed and the anchor with Davenport in lower case letters are known (E 1 and E 2). I know of no chalcedony pieces with the upper case name mark.

As stated earlier, I feel sure that there are many unmarked examples, some probably of decorative form, in this body as yet unrecognized. Certainly, if we go by the Royal order, we should expect to find vases with floral paintings additionally decorated with lustre or with a black background. The surprise would be if nothing new was found in the next few years rather than the contrary (see Colour Plate IX).

Finally, we illustrate two such unmarked pieces which are of considerable interest. The teapot in Plate 58, though of a shape which has not hitherto been recorded, has a typical Davenport spout, the acorn finial is known on marked wares, the strainer is also of a known form, and the decoration is totally in accord with that on marked pieces such as the Liverpool tea wares (Plate 54). There can be little doubt that this unmarked piece was made at Longport.

56. Pierced dessert service dish in a rich stone colour body, painted in monochrome black with a dotted leaf design. Ht 7¼in., width 8¼in. Mark E 1. (Lockett Collection)

57. Pierced dessert basket and stand (cover missing) in a rich stone colour body, decorated with a simple painted border pattern in puce enamel. Stand, 6½in×5in. Tureen, length 8in., ht 4½in. Mark both E 2. Plate (as dish in Plate 56) Diameter 8¼in. (Lockett Collection)

95 · Earthenwares and Stonewares

The unmarked jug in Plate 59 would appear from its shape, especially that of the handle which, alas, is not visible in this picture, also to be Davenport. The Christie's catalogue credited the decoration to Absolon of Yarmouth whose work was mentioned earlier (p. 89). The painting, however, is not really reminiscent of his work, and it is just possible that the piece was actually decorated in Lowestoft by Robert Allen who established a decorating shop there on the closure of the porcelain factory *c*.1800. (Details of his work can be found in the specialist books on Lowestoft by Geoffrey Godden, and on the Norwich Castle collection by Sheena Smith). It is unlikely that this is Davenport 'in-house' decoration, and there is ample evidence that the factory did sell wares to be decorated elsewhere. Again one would expect more of these to be positively recognized in the future.

58. Globular teapot in the chalcedony body, decorated with monochrome black picturesque landscapes, with additional gilding, Ht 5½in. Overall length 9in. Unmarked (see text) but with pattern number 60 in red script. The same pattern and number are found on a chalcedony sucrier in the Lockett Collection. (Diana Darlington Collection)

59. Jug in the chalcedony body decorated with a black monochrome scene of two boys fishing and inscribed A TRIFLE FROM LOWESTOFT. Unmarked (see text). (Courtesy Christie's)

11 Black Basalt

The term 'Black Basalte' first appears in the Ornamental Pattern Book of Josiah Wedgwood dated 1773. Like many other ceramic bodies, Wedgwood had refined an existing material and produced and marketed a ware of outstanding quality. Egyptian black was the name commonly used in the trade for the high-fired stoneware. Wedgwood was to write of his improved version, 'the Black is sterling and will last for ever,' a prophecy which so far has proved remarkably accurate.

It is not possible to say when John Davenport began to produce basalt. Extant examples are very rare and one would hesitate to date any of them much before 1805 on stylistic grounds, or much later than 1830. At the time of writing only a few more than a dozen positive and marked examples are known to the authors. Despite the publicity given to the wares by the Northern Ceramic Society's Stoneware Exhibition in 1982 and the Keele University Ceramic Summer School of 1987, little further information or previously unknown specimens were forthcoming subsequently. Thus the corpus of known wares is restricted to the following pieces which will be described in detail in order to facilitate recognition of unmarked examples.

The known marked pieces are: an engine-turned milk jug in the Stoke-on-Trent Museum (*Davenport Pottery & Porcelain,* Plate 16); the teapot (Plate 60); a similar but much larger version in a private collection; a sucrier in the Gunson Collection again with the same six sprigs as the preceding items but with a rouletted pattern on the upper rim and a fluted and crimped collar (*Transactions of the English Ceramic Circle* 12 Pt 2, 1985, Plate 94b); an *unmarked* sucrier with the identical six sprigs to those on the previous three pieces but of straight-sided 'old' oval form, set on an engine-turned base

60. Black basalt teapot with sprigged classical motifs and a widow finial. Ht 4½in. Mark E 5. (Lockett Collection)

61. Black basalt sucrier with fluted or crimped rim, widow finial and engine-turned decoration. Unmarked, but matching a larger piece in the late Nancy Gunson Collection (see text). (Alan Cleaver Collection)

62. Black basalt teapot with sprig motif of Mercury and Pan, within a sprigged frame of rose, thistle and shamrock. Ht 7in. Unmarked. (Hacking Collection)

with a top rim of rouletted diamond lattice shapes. On the evidence of the sprigs one should be able to class this as Davenport, but the shape is unknown, and the owner now confesses to 'doubts'! A marked waste bowl in the Darlington Collection again has the same six sprigs and a rouletted and crimped rim; whilst a similarly sprigged bowl, but without the crimped rim, is illustrated in Geoffrey Godden's *British Pottery: An Illustrated Guide*, p. 218. There is a teapot, sugar box, and cream jug ensuite decorated principally with engine-turned and rouletted decoration, but with the widow finial, fluted and crimped collar, and square handles, in a private collection; and a similar globular

63. Black basalt covered milk or hot water jug, sprigged with a scene of Vulcan, grape and vine leaves and rose, thistle and shamrock motifs. Ht 5¾in. Mark E 2. (Hacking Collection)

64. Black basalt covered sucrier, sprigged with a cherub (note the curious bowler hat he wears on the back of his head!), and other sprigs as in Plate 62. The attached ring handles are almost vestigial. Ht 6in. Unmarked. (Hacking Collection)

sucrier in the Iwass Collection. Two teapots were reported by Mrs Egerton Brown (*Transactions of the English Ceramic Circle* 5 Pt 5, 1964, Plate 263a), the piece illustrated is of a low drum shape with vertical engine-turned fluting and a simple button-like finial. There is the remarkable set from the Hacking Collection (Plates 62–4) recently discovered in Portugal. As can be seen this has a totally different figure 7 handle form, with sprigging of leaves on the lid, shoulder, and base as well as other features noted in the captions. Had not one of the pieces been marked, a Davenport attribution would have been most unlikely. Finally, at the time of writing, two basalt pieces were noted in the Zeitlin collection in Philadelphia, a sucrier and a milk jug, both of known shape and decoration.

These few examples demonstrate a wide range of treatment and shape, with two quite distinct types of sprigging and a number of variants on both the shape and form of engine-turned decoration. It seems likely that one can deduce from this admittedly small range that teawares were the only items made by Davenport in basalt. Moreover, it

99 · Earthenwares and Stonewares

is reasonable to suggest that much of the output was unmarked, as seems to have been the case with Spode, Minton, and a number of other prominent factories. Why this should be is not easy to explain, but the evidence of the range of shapes and decorative treatment would lead one to expect more examples to be forthcoming. Blocks and moulds were not produced for 'one-offs' in a material such as basalt.

The marks help us very little. All the pieces except the Hacking service have upper case impressed marks (E 5) which we tend to regard as a later mark than the lower case. The Hacking service, which on shape and style one might place later than some of the other pieces listed, has just one piece with the mark Davenport in lower case letters over an anchor impressed (E 2). Perhaps this is further support for the growing belief among collectors that whilst lower case marks generally appear on the earlier pieces there is a considerable overlap, and upper and lower case marks are used contemporaneously. In any event marked Davenport basalt remains a very rare commodity – even in Portugal! We would welcome news of other items.

12 Caneware and Terra-cotta

Caneware is a dry-bodied stoneware of a buff to tan colour which was being developed by Josiah Wedgwood during the 1770s. It seems likely that it was not perfected until certain technical difficulties were overcome by Wedgwood in the mid 1780s. It made its first appearance in the 1787 edition of the Wedgwood catalogue where it is advertised as 'BAMBOO or cane-coloured bisque porcelain.' The Turners of Lane End were other early producers of the ware, according to Simeon Shaw. (Fuller details of the development of caneware are given in the Northern Ceramic Society catalogue *Stonewares and Stone Chinas*, 1982.)

Once more the lack of any specific documentary evidence means that it is not possible to be precise as to when John Davenport first began to produce the ware. If we accept the evidence of Jewitt and Ward that the first products that Davenport manufactured were blue printed and cream/pearlwares, then diversification into other areas would follow as and when commerical success warranted it. On this basis, and that of both style and marks, it seems reasonable to suggest that caneware was introduced in the late 1790s. But one must emphasize – rather maddeningly – that there is no documentary evidence to support this assumption.

It should also be pointed out at this stage that the term caneware has been used somewhat loosely in the past to cover both the high-fired unglazed stoneware and the low-fired porous terra-cotta used for wine coolers (the section in *Davenport Pottery & Porcelain* needs emendment in this respect). In this section the two will be separately treated. Firstly, the true high-fired stoneware.

Caneware

The range of wares is quite considerable and new forms and decorative treatments are coming to light quite frequently. But this does not mean that caneware is not rare, simply that the range was quite extensive. We now know of no fewer than four teapot shapes.

65. Caneware teapot of low oval shape. Overall length 9in. Ht 3¾in. Mark E 2 and WARRANTED (impressed). (Lockett Collection)

101 · Earthenwares and Stonewares

66

67

All four are basically of the low oval shape, though with considerable variation in the form of handles, terminals and decorative treatment. Plate 65 shows a recently discovered example, the features of which are closely akin to those of the orange-bodied ware (Plate 54) and the early porcelain shape. The somewhat rounder shape of two examples decorated entirely with engine turning and – in one case – the addition of blue outlines, seems to indicate a slightly earlier date (Plate 66). The fourth shape is quite extraordinary consisting as it does of moulded leaves outlined in brown. This example has the additional interest of the impressed mark 'WARRANTED' on the base (Plate 67). The Lockett collection contains the sugar box to match the teapot (Plate 68) but to date no cups, cans, or saucers have been discovered to match this moulding. Indeed, the accompanying teawares for all these shapes are far from common. Simple Bute-shaped cups and saucers occur, some totally unglazed, others with glaze in the interior of the cup and saucer and blue line decoration. Coffee cans are also known (Plate 68) some

66. Left: Caneware honey pot and attached stand, brown enamel lines. Ht 5¼in. Mark E 2. Right: Caneware teapot (spout restored), blue enamel lines. Ht 4¼in., length 8½in. Mark E 2. (Both Lockett Collection: photo courtesy City Museum, Stoke-on-Trent)

67. Caneware teapot elaborately moulded with leaves lined with brown enamel. Note the remarkable handle. Spout slightly damaged. Length 9½in. Mark E 2 and WARRANTED (impressed). (B. M. & A. C. Walters Collection).

102 · Earthenwares and Stonewares

undecorated, but at least two examples have engine-turned decoration at the foot and enamel painted initials on the body of the piece (Plate 70). A can in the Agius collection has a simple but attractive floral border pattern on the upper rim. To accompany these tea wares small side plates are recorded, one bearing the impressed name of the Dublin china dealer DONOVAN. A most attractive and rarer piece is the custard cup (Plate 70), a beautifully potted specimen. A double-handled example is also known. The teaware range is completed by at least two cream jugs, one of which is of straight-sided 'old' oval shape which could indicate that a teapot of this form was manufactured. The second piece, also engine-turned, matches the low oval teapots.

To complement the teaware range large jugs occur decorated with a band of harebells and foliage on the upper rim, blue enamel lines and engine turning (*Davenport Pottery & Porcelain*, Plate 17). Honey pots in at least three sizes were made (Plate 66) and the remarkable eggcup stand (Plate 71) would be an asset to any breakfast table, and could easily have been accompanied by a covered marmalade or jam pot and attached stand, with blue line decoration and engine turning, which was displayed at the Blackburn Museum Exhibition in 1978. It is perhaps worth remembering that a very wide range of table items was made in caneware and the very fine display of Wedgwood canewares at Woburn Abbey reminds us of other items which we could expect to have been manufactured by Davenport in similar shapes and for similar purposes.

68. Caneware sucrier moulded with leaves outlined in brown enamel. Ht 4½in., length 7½in. (Lockett Collection)

69. Bute-shaped caneware. Unglazed saucer, diameter 5⅜in. unmarked; Cup, ht 2⅜in., unmarked; Plate, diameter 6in., mark E 2; Coffee can, ht 2½in. This group was purchased en suite with other similar sets in which only the plates were marked. (Lockett Collection)

103 · Earthenwares and Stonewares

70

71

There is certainly evidence that Davenport produced dessert wares in caneware. A pierced basket of the standard creamware shape was reported some time ago and both the accompanying stand and plates are in private collections. Nor must we forget the so-called 'pastry' wares. These items of which the small pierced piece in Plate 72 is a splendid example – similar round ones are also recorded – were glazed inside but unglazed on the exterior. There is ample historical evidence that these were being considered even before the severe grain shortages of the Napoleonic Wars made them both fashionable and functional. In 1786 Richard Lovell Edgeworth wrote to Josiah

104 · Earthenwares and Stonewares

72

73

70. Left: Caneware coffee can. Ht 2½in., unmarked. Centre: Caneware coffee can with blue enamel lines and initial E and engine-turned decoration. Ht 2¾in., mark E 2. Right: Caneware custard cup. Ht 2½in., mark E 2. (Lockett Collection)

71. Caneware eggcup stand outlined in brown enamel. Ht 6⅜in. Length 8⅞in. Mark E 2. (Diana Darlington Collection)

72. Small, oval caneware pie dish with pierced lid. 5×3¾in. Mark E 2. (Lockett Collection, from the L. A. Compton Collection)

73. Caneware bulb pot with slight smear glaze and brown enamel decoration, attached ring handles. Ht 4⅞in. Mark E 2. (Diana Darlington Collection)

Wedgwood, 'I think oval baking dishes for meat pies in the shape of raised paste pies . . . made of cane coloured ware, not glazed, but nearly as possible the colour of baked paste, would be saleable articles. If any should be made, be so good as to send me half a dozen. They should have covers.' This suggestion does not seem to have been acted upon immediately, but by 1795 such 'pastry wares' do begin to appear in Wedgwood invoices. As has been indicated Davenport pieces are known in several sizes in both the round and the oval forms. The moulds must have remained serviceable for many years as the large fully glazed example in *Davenport Pottery & Porcelain*, Plate 56 is date-marked for July 1864, long after the other pieces illustrated here were made. The fashion for canewares seems to have lasted little longer than the French Wars and one would hesitate to date any of the Davenport items discussed above to later than 1820.

    Finally in the stoneware range of cane-coloured wares we must mention the handled basket in the Liverpool Museum which has a wash of green enamel on the outside, in addition to engine turning (*Davenport Pottery & Porcelain*, Plate 14) and the inevitable bulb pots. That illustrated in Plate 73 has a slight smear glaze as well as the flecks of enamel decoration. A smaller example in the Lockett collection is fully glazed within and without, on top of an engine-turned design. There can be no doubt that the Davenport factory made a feature of bulb pots as they appear in almost every material which the factory produced. The last items to record are so far unique, the candlesticks illustrated in Plate 74. As they are very simple in construction and decoration, it must be assumed that quite a considerable number were originally manufactured.

    No attempt had been made in this section to separate out those wares which

105 · Earthenwares and Stonewares

74

have some glazing to the interior from those which are totally dry-body. The only exception is the last-mentioned bulb pot. Glaze on the inside of a vessel was a common-sense precaution, though strictly speaking a high-fired stoneware body should be impervious to liquid without further protection. There is however, a class of wares which are coloured-bodied and are fully glazed, but of which some pieces are of a stone or cane colour. These pieces do not appear to be of the stoneware body and thus have been treated separately in the section on coloured-bodied wares.

Terra-cotta

This word has been used to indicate the cane-coloured wares – often with a reddish tinge – which were low-fired and deliberately made to be porous. The principal item which Davenport made in this fashion was the wine cooler. William Evans in *Art and History of the Potting Business* (1846) writes of vessels 'used for coolers of water butter and wine. . . . These articles are baked in a very slow part of the oven; and after being immersed in water till saturated, on any substance being placed therein the cold caused by evaporation reduces the temperature of that substance to a soft palatable state.'

Several different forms of wine cooler are known to have been produced by Davenport, and once more these seem to date predominantly from the first thirty years of the factory's existence. The most sought after bear the likeness of Admiral Nelson on one side and a ship and battle trophies on the reverse. This model (Plates 75–6) has satyr mask handles. A similar handle form can be seen on the pair of coolers (Plate 77) on which the very clean and crisp moulding is of vine leaves and bunches of grapes. Another highly desirable design is that shown in the Liverpool Museum (Plate 78) where the painted decoration shows an interesting cultural conjunction with a Greek key design on the upper rim and Egyptian motifs on the body of the cooler. As can be seen these pieces have dolphin mask handles. They clearly owe their inspiration, if only at second hand, to Napoleon's Egyptian campaign of 1798–9, and the great interest which this aroused subsequently in the antiquities of Egypt. Variations have been noted in the painted symbols in the designs. The Royal order of December 1807 contained the following: '24 Egyptian porouse Wine Coolers, Emboss'd &c. 10/6 £12 : 12 : 0'.

The dolphin mask appears again on a pair of coolers in the Cleaver collection on which the only other decoration is in brown enamel outlines on the mask and brown lines at the upper and just above the lower rims. Similar dolphin masks appear on coolers with a sprigged decoration of the familiar 'Topers' scene (*Davenport Pottery & Porcelain*, Plate 12) and on a most unusual pair of coolers in the Miller collection. These are rather incongrously decorated with a transfer printed scene on the familiar 'Chinoiserie Ruins' pattern. Obviously this has been fired on the surface of the ware, but as there is no glaze

74. A pair of caneware candlesticks enriched with blue enamel, stained with use. Ht 6½in. Mark E 2. (Lockett Collection)

75. Terra-cotta wine cooler moulded in high relief with a portrait of Admiral Lord Nelson. The handles are Satyrs' heads. Ht 10in. Mark E 2, *c*.1800–10. (Courtesy City Museum, Stoke-on-Trent)

76. The reverse side of the Nelson wine cooler, moulded in high relief with naval trophies. Dimensions and mark as above. (Courtesy City Museum, Stoke-on-Trent).

75

76

on top of the fired print it appears as a rather faded black colour. Another variant in the Walters Collection has satyr head handles and the body entirely covered with fluted engine turning. It is likely that other forms will come to light, but as can be seen from the foregoing, all the pieces appear to have either satyr head or dolphin mask handles. All the pieces that have been examined have been marked with the lower case impressed mark (E 2). Curiously, the mark, for no apparent reason, appears twice on the transfer printed coolers. 'Topers' pieces are usually of smaller dimensions than the others.

77

78

77. A pair of terra-cotta wine coolers moulded with a grape and vine decoration, handles as Satyrs' heads. Ht 9½in. Mark E 2. (Lockett Collection)

78. Terra-cotta wine cooler decorated in brown enamel with a Greek key border and Egyptian symbols. Handles moulded as open-mouthed dolphins. Ht 9½in. Mark E 2. (Courtesy Liverpool Museum)

79. Terra-cotta butter cooler and stand, modelled with leaf forms, the handles as cows' heads. Diameter 7in. Mark E 5. (Hacking Collection)

108 · Earthenwares and Stonewares

79

Following William Evans's list, we have seen several butter coolers such as that illustrated in Plate 79 in a soft terra-cotta body with moulded decoration. Upper case marks have been noted on these pieces, as well as lower. It seems likely that other objects were made in this body: for example a globular flask, most curiously decorated with a matt white and blue enamel decoration (a later addition perhaps) was recorded. The piece had been bored through the base and wired for service as an electric light holder. In that condition not a particularly desirable object.

Although wine coolers are not particularly easy objects to display in a domestic private collection – they sit rather uneasily with delicate bone china teaware – nevertheless they are well worthy of the attention of collectors. Davenport seems to have been one of the largest producers of this type of vessel, if one judges by the surviving marked examples from contemporary factories such as Spode, Wedgwood, and Minton. The Davenport coolers certainly perform their allotted function admirably!

13 White Felspathic Stoneware

White stoneware jugs, sprigged with a hunting scene, must be amongst the most familiar items of Davenport to most collectors. The material, felspathic stoneware, seems to have been first developed by the Turners of Lane End. Their superb jugs sprigged with scenes such as the 'Archery Lesson,' the 'Cock Fight,' and 'Falstaff in a basket' are the direct precursors of the Davenport article.

Another strand of stoneware development led to the thinly potted and translucent wares which have been given the rather misleading generic title of Castleford wares. The title is misleading as it is unlikely that the Yorkshire firm were the foremost manufacturers of the ware. However, be that as it may, the production of teapots and other vessels of the Castleford type is not a development which Davenport seems to have undertaken. So far no wares of this kind can be attributed to the factory, although some pots with the typical blue lines of decoration also have characteristics in the form of sprigs and finials etc. which are similarly found on marked Davenport wares. This has resulted in the occasional very tentative attribution 'possibly Davenport.' However, at the time of writing, no positive conclusion can be drawn.

The known marked wares stick to a fairly easily recognizable pattern and these white stonewares were probably initially produced within the first few years of the factory's life. There is a Davenport trade catalogue in the Spode archives which indicates that the sprigged hunting jug was still being offered in the 1880s. If these wares were still being manufactured at that date it is a record of astonishing longevity, but perhaps not altogether surprising as the design is still current on biscuit tins etc. to this day. Purely on stylistic grounds one would have said that the majority of the stoneware jugs and mugs were made up to and possibly including the 1830s. It is certainly a surprise to find them still in the catalogue another half century later. Intriguingly, if 'hunting' jugs were being made as late as the 1880s, how were they marked? Most of the extant examples have the impressed lower case mark, only a few have the upper case. Does this signify that these impressed marks were in use much later than anyone had hitherto assumed? At this stage it is not possible to be positive, but there is no gainsaying that the jugs were on offer in the 1880s and unmarked and 'positive' Davenport jugs are not often encountered.

We have written elsewhere of the hard commercialism of the Davenport factory under John Davenport. The production of white stoneware seems to present a perfect example of this. As far as we are aware there were just three designs available to customers, the hunting scene featuring 'The Kill,' 'The Stag Hunt,' and 'The Topers.' That is a really economical way to run a factory! All three designs are illustrated in the accompanying plates. Furthermore, and again we are speaking only of known marked wares, there seem to be only four handle forms used: the 'traditional' Davenport (Plate 80), which took two forms, one with a straight thumb rest and the second with a slight 'flick' upwards in the rest (Plate 81); the 'Hunting Horn' (Plate 82); and the indented handle which stands away from the neck of the jug (Plate 84). Of these three handles, the hunting horn has only been found on wares decorated with the 'Stag Hunt' sprigs, whilst the indented handles seem exclusively associated with the 'Topers.' Another example of the rationalization or perhaps one should say simplification of production.

The wares decorated in this fashion cover a relatively limited range. There are jugs in very many sizes. They may have additional engine turning in a number of variations, and most are enriched with bands of blue or brown enamel usually at the neck. A few are further embellished with gilding, and both 'The Kill' and the 'Stag Hunt' are occasionally found in an enamelled version. It must be stressed that although the range of designs may have been limited, the quality of wares was every bit as high as that

80. Jug in white felspathic stoneware sprigged with 'The Kill'. Note the flat thumb rest on the handle and the small inner spur. This piece has been carefully coloured in enamels. The rest of the scene appears in Plate 83. Ht 4¾in. Mark E 2. (Courtesy David Golding)

81. Mug in white felspathic stoneware, finely sprigged with 'The Kill'. Compare the slight upward 'flick' on this handle with the preceding illustration. The rim is gilded and the whole piece is of the highest quality. Ht 5in. Mark E 2. (Diana Darlington Collection)

82. White felspathic stoneware mug with 'The Stag Hunt' sprigged onto a dark brown enamel ground. Note the extraordinary handle in the form of a hunting horn. (The remainder of the scene appears on a jug in Plate 9 of *Davenport Pottery & Porcelain*.) Ht 3⅜in. Mark E 2. (Diana Darlington Collection)

83. Left: Felspathic stoneware jug, with only a very slight lip, sprigged with the scene of 'The Kill', and with a silver-plated lid. The handle is an unusual variant with the thumb-rest pointing backwards, and with no inner spur. Ht 6¾in. Mark E 2. Right: Small mustard pot (lid missing) sprigged with a scene from 'The Kill'. Ht 3in. Mark E 2. Both have blue enamel at the neck. (Hacking Collection)

111 · Earthenwares and Stonewares

produced by their contemporaries. The sprigs are sharp and usually very clear-cut especially on the earlier pieces, and though the enamel may have flaked a little on some pieces, generally it has stood the usage of time remarkably well.

Mugs are also fairly numerous with all three scenes represented, though 'The Kill' is the most frequently encountered. Again these are in several sizes. One very unusual piece is that in Plate 82 which has the background in brown with the white sprigs of the 'Stag Hunt' scene clearly contrasted. So far this appears to be a unique example and the use of the hunting horn handle makes this item particularly fascinating.

There is at least one class of stonewares with a semi-matt brown ground and a variety of different sprigs. These wares are very well produced and though at one time they were confidently labelled Herculaneum, there is no real evidence to support this attribution. Some of the wares with these characteristics also have handles in the traditional Davenport shape, but no marked pieces are known, and that form of handle is a very simple and effective one to use so that it is not uncommon at the period. Thus it seems unlikely that the mystery class of white sprigged stoneware can be attributed to Davenport. It is also well known that many other factories used these specific sprigs, especially the 'Kill.' Only the most exacting scrutiny can enable one to recognize the distinctions between the various manufacturers' sprigs. It is really necessary to place the wares side by side to make the proper comparison, and even then the general shape and specific details such as the handle and characteristic details of the turning are more likely to give a correct attribution than reliance on any minute variations in the sprigged design. In the case of Davenport, the general shape of the objects and certain of the handle forms are a better aid to attribution on unmarked wares.

Generally speaking, marking is fairly consistent, and both upper and lower case impressed marks are found (E 2 and E 5). The impressed anchor alone (E 1) is also known on at least one definite Davenport jug. In the light of other evidence mentioned above, it would be unwise to use the impressed Davenport mark as a reliable guide to

84. Two white felspathic jugs sprigged with scenes of 'The Topers'. Both have brown enamel at the neck. Note specially the 'indented' handle form, encountered only on 'Topers' wares, and the quite sharply pointed lip. Hts 6½ and 5¼in. Marks both E 2. (Hacking Collection)

112 · Earthenwares and Stonewares

85. White felspathic stoneware circular flower or garden pot, sprigged with 'The Kill'. Blue enamel on the ring handles which stand just proud of the surface, also at the rim and base. Ht 5in. Mark E 2. (Iwass Collection)

dating a piece of felspathic stoneware. The material was also used for making mustard pots (Plate 83), and the larger covered jugs with metal mounts and lids, but no spouts, also illustrated. These probably did service as storage jars. Three rather rare forms should also be mentioned. Firstly garden pots such as that illustrated in Plate 85 were made. There is also a large jardinière sprigged with the 'Topers' scene in the Miller collection. And it would certainly not surprise me to learn that a D-shaped bulb pot had been found in felspathic stoneware. The only other recorded shape in the material is a mortar in the Lockett collection which is illustrated in the Northern Ceramic Society catalogue *Stoneware and Stone Chinas,* Plate 221.

Davenport stoneware then is not uncommon. It is very well potted and on the thinner pieces there is a good degree of translucency. It is, however, as far as we can ascertain, limited in the range of objects produced: to date no Castleford-type teapots and no Turner-type vases. But then it would make good commercial sense to limit the range to the sturdier items which would suffer less damage in the journey overseas which was the destiny of so many of the wares produced at Longport. If the customer wanted extra embellishment it was cheaper to gild the piece than go to the expense of producing new moulds to provide a wider range of sprigged designs.

However, having said this, there are other wares in the Davenport repertoire in porcelain and basalt of which the sprigged designs have not been encountered in felspathic stoneware. It would not be surprising if research such as that being carried on by Mr Jack Hacking and others did not result in the discovery of hitherto unrecognized stoneware pieces made by Davenport in this material, which was undoubtedly very popular and saleable in the first three decades of the nineteenth century.

Earthenwares and Stonewares

14   Stone China

It is now generally accepted that the origin of stone china lies in the patent taken out in 1800 by John and William Turner. The material they made, usually marked Turner's Patent, is a hard, compact, dense-bodied and usually opaque fabric, which bears a passable resemblance of the coarser forms of Chinese export porcelain. It was clearly intended that the patent body should secure the market heretofore served by imported Chinese wares.

The Turner brothers went bankrupt in 1806 and though Simeon Shaw writing in 1829 seems to indicate that Spode bought up the patent and began to manufacture the ware, Leonard Whiter, the distinguished historian of the Spode factory, argues that Spode did not introduce their stone china until 1813/14. Both Reginald Haggar, who first discussed the point, and Geoffrey Godden agree that sometime after 1806 and before 1813, Miles Mason and his sons were making a form of stone china. This was formalized in 1813 when shortly after the retirement of Miles Mason from active business, Charles James Mason took out the famous patent for Ironstone China. It need not concern us here that the patent specification was inaccurate and that the ware Mason did produce could not have been made from the ingredients specified. C. J. Mason was like that! It was probably not long after Mason and Spode began to produce the ware that Davenport entered the market. We have no specific documentary confirmation of this until 1818 when, as is clear from the letter quoted below, they had been making a rival to Mason's ironstone for some time. On 12 January 1818, Child & Co. china dealers of Edinburgh wrote to John Davenport. The letter is worth quoting in full for the insight it gives, not only Davenport's activities, but also into the methods of trading current at the period, especially those of C. J. Mason, whose habit of selling at auction greatly upset the established china wholesale and retailers.

At last the Masons have open'd out their Forty Hhds. *Stoneware and China here, and are selling by Auction, which circumstance of course for ever closes our Account with them. We fear it will, in some degree, injure our demand, but we must do the best we can, relying upon your support, for our mutual interest. We succeeded in competing for the Sale of two Dinner Services by the superior appearance of your No. 6. which we hope will not be allowed to fall off in whiteness, which is a great object.*

We are of opinion that it would be a politic measure to Change the name of it to 'Metallic Porcelain' as we must now Cry down the Ironstone, at least the patent *and it will warrant any one to do so as in fact it is now* bad earthenware.

Can you get us anything in ware for Masons to match up. To avoid suspicion they might be sent to Liverpool, for thence by sea to Glasgow and readdressed.

We fear it is Masons intention to have a permanent Connection here with an auctioneer. If so we must devise some plan for opposing them. Say what you think of changing the name of the Stone ware and inform us the price of Breakfast and Tea ware No. 6 and the Broseley Pattern.

We shall reply to your letter in a few posts. In the meantime,
We are
Dear Sirs,
Yours truly,
Child & Co.

On the cover of the letter is written 'Davenports Improved Ironstone' and 'Davenports Improved Metallic Porcelain.' Both have been crossed out. There are many points of interest in this fascinating letter which we will touch upon later in this section. In a more

86. Group of octagonal stone china jugs brightly decorated in underglaze and overglaze colours, snake or hydra-headed handles. These jugs are called 'Oriental' in an 1880s factory price list. Hts 4½, 7, 5½, 3½in. Marks E 11 in blue, *c.*1820–30. (Lockett Collection)

general sense it is worth noting that Davenport did not change the name of the product; it remained as stone china. It seems rather rich that Child & Co. complain so bitterly about Masons's activities, and then calmly asked Davenport to arrange to secure ware from Masons to be sent to them by a devious route. A salutary reminder that both potter and merchant were in business to make money, and yet another example of inter-potter trading at which John Davenport seemed so adept.

Turning now to the wares themselves, it seems likely that stone china was produced from *c.*1815. For how long is somewhat problematical. There are examples of wares with marks which contain the words 'stone china' or 'ironstone' which seem to date from the 1870s and beyond. Indeed the familiar hydra-headed octagonal jug (Plate 86), given the title 'Oriental' is still being offered in a catalogue which dates from the 1880s. On the other hand there is very little true stone china which one would care to date after the 1850s. Most of the stone china-type wares from the mid century onward bear the impressed mark E 16, which contains the words 'Opaque China' or some such variant. It must be remembered that the factory carried out a huge overseas trade and really durable wares of the 'Granite' type were essential to withstand the buffetings of journeys of many thousands of miles before they reached their customers. Thus we delude ourselves if we expect a factory of the size of the Davenport enterprise to produce only one type of body over a very long period of time. There is no such thing as a standard Davenport stone china body. In this respect the comments of Child & Co. quoted above are instructive. There are some Davenport stone china pieces in which the body is very fine and the surface finish very white indeed. These pieces could, at a glance, easily be taken for English porcelain. This whiteness is a quality which was being encouraged by Child. Conversely, there are very many pieces including large and important decorative items the basic body of which has a very blue/grey hue. These match the typical appearance of Turner's Patent and Masons Patent Ironstone China.

If we examine the wares with the conventional stone china marks (E 11–15) we find that the patterns are almost all of the Imari type. That is, they are based upon Japanese porcelain prototypes, with decoration normally comprising some form of conventionalized floral pattern. The typical examples illustrated show the familiar features of a strong, dark underglaze blue (termed an 'oven' blue in the Potteries)

115 · Earthenwares and Stonewares

87

88

supported overglaze with often quite bold – even brash – enamel colours in green, pink, orange, and red. Yellow is also occasionally used and many examples have gilding as an additional embellishment. Other patterns are found from time to time, such as the 'Broseley' mentioned in Child's letter, seen on a teapot in Plate 88.

It would appear that the factory used a separate pattern book for the stone china wares. The patterns (which do not match those of the normal creamware range) seem to start at pattern one and continue to pattern 145 or thereabouts. There are a number of examples recorded outside this range, but these are usually instances where Imari-type patterns from the bone china pattern book have been used on stone china. A commonly met example of this occurs with pattern 568 found equally on porcelain and stone china, but originally apparently entered in the bone china series. The soup plate in

87. Stone china plate decorated with a striking pattern (no. 35) in deep underglaze ('oven') blue and overglaze enamels and gilding, in a typical floral 'Imari-type' pattern. Diameter 9½in. Mark E 11. (Diana Darlington Collection)

88. Stone china teapot printed in blue with the 'Broseley' pattern (no. 142) with additional gilding. Note the curious flat-bottomed shape. Ht 4in. Length 9in. Mark E 11. (Lockett Collection)

116 · Earthenwares and Stonewares

89. Stone china soup plate decorated with the bone china pattern 568. Diameter 10½in. Mark E 16. (Lockett Collection)

90. Teapot, sucrier, and cream jug from a stone china tea service. Note the bone china shapes with the very idiosyncratic bifurcated handle. Decorated in bright colours and gilding with pattern 659. Teapot, overall length 10¾in. Sugar box, length 6in. Cream jug, ht 4in. Mark E 11. (Godden of Worthing Ltd)

Plate 89 is a stone china one with the pattern 568, and the teawares shown in Plate 90 are decorated with a somewhat similar pattern 659. This too is from the bone china range, and the shapes are better known in bone china (see Plate 201). The converse can also occur, and stone china patterns have been noted (No. 37 is a case in point) on porcelain of the period *c*.1820.

These patterns appear most frequently on dinner and dessert wares, though teawares are known, as is indicated again in the Child letter and is exemplified by the Broseley pattern teapot, and the wares of pattern 659 just noted above. Complete services were made in large quantities and Plate 91 shows part of a dessert service in the pattern No. 6 which Child & Co. were writing about. This popular pattern with birds and branches is well known in Mason's ware, but also is common on pieces from Hicks and

117 · Earthenwares and Stonewares

Meigh and several other potters. It can be seen to splendid advantage on the ice pail in Plate 92. Further examples from services are the shapes from a dinner service of pattern 135 on Plate 93, and another goodly range of shapes can be seen in Plate 94 of pattern 78. Collectors can therefore expect to find Davenport stone china in all the usual forms used at the table ranging from teapots, cups, saucers, plates, soup dishes to tureens, sauce boats, milk jugs, and a whole host of other utensils, with the octagonal jugs forming a large proportion of surviving hollow ware pieces. It would be tedious to attempt to describe the complete range of stone china service items.

There are, however, a number of real rarities which deserve individual discussion. The teapot illustrated in Plate 95 is most unusual bearing as it does Japanese figure subjects set against a matt brown ground. The dating of this piece is not easy. It bears the conventional stone china mark (E 11), but the subject is not one that is normally associated with English ceramics until the period of Japonism or Japonaiserie in the Aesthetic Movement of the 1870s. Identical decoration can be found on porcelain pot-pourris which one would again date to the 1870s. Very recently a stone china pot-pourri identical in decoration to the known porcelain version has come into the Hacking Collection. They are shown together in Colour Plate X. The porcelain piece carries an underglaze blue printed mark (P 5) common in the post-1845 period, but not before. It can clearly be seen that the printed and enamelled Japanese figures are the same. This would seem to indicate that the stone china mark of Miss Darlington's teapot remained in use for something like fifty years or more after its first introduction.

A further remarkable object from the Hacking collection is illustrated in Colour Plate XI. Several punch bowls have been recorded, one in the Ronald Brown collection with an Imari pattern (others similarly decorated have been noted over the years), and another decorated with printed and coloured figure subjects of Chinese children at play, that is, the pattern known as Chinese Pastime (see p. 137). However, the item illustrated is most unusual in that it is decorated with motifs painted in white slip, very much in the fashion of pâte-sur-pâte, or the imitations of Limoges enamels made by Mintons in the

91. Representative pieces from a stone china dessert service, decorated with pattern 6. Basket 10½in. long. Marks E 11 and E 12, c.1820. (Godden of Worthing Ltd)

92. Stone china ice pail and cover decorated with pattern 6, and with dolphin finial and handles. Ht 11¾in. Mark E 11, c.1820. (Courtesy Phillips)

93. Representative pieces from a stone china dinner service decorated in bright colours with an Imari pattern (135). Mark not noted, c.1820–30. (Courtesy Christie's)

94. Representative pieces from a typical Imari-style stone china service, pattern 78. Mark not noted. (Courtesy Sotheby's)

95. Stone china teapot with a brown ground decorated with printed and enamelled Japanese figures with additional gilding. Ht 5½in. Mark E 11. (Diana Darlington Collection)

118 · Earthenwares and Stonewares

Mintons in the late 1850s and early 1860s. A similar bowl, or possibly the same one was noted some years ago. It seems remarkable that so much time and ingenuity in decoration could have been expended on a vessel in stone china. It is perhaps an indication that we (surfeited with second-class ironstone plates) place a lesser value on the material than was the case a century and a half ago.

This contention is I think supported, not merely by recalling the vast range of decorative items made by C. J. Mason at his best, but also by considering some other Davenport stone china rarities. David Davenport has in his collection a vase of almost two feet in height, with cover, decorated with pattern 24 and finely finished with elaborate gilding on the handles, base, and finial (Plate 96). Potters did not waste gold on inferior materials. The Iwass collection also contains a fine large vase, with excellently executed

119 · Earthenwares and Stonewares

96

gilt patterns over a deep blue ground. The same collection also contains a most unusual pair of small spill vases, again with a deep blue ground and decoration in gilt. A curiosity of these pieces is that they are marked with the brown 'strap' mark (P 5) which is usually associated with porcelain of the 1820–40 period. There is no doubt however, that these fine spill vases are stone china.

In the section on underglaze blue printed wares we illustrate a wash bowl printed with a View of the South Bank (Plate 144). This view also occurs uniquely in our experience on a stone china plate in the Iwass collection marked in the normal way with the circular stone china mark (E 13). Another unusual item is an octagonal large tea or small waste bowl in the Cleaver collection, and Plate 97 shows decoration of the most refined kind with beautifully delicate gilding, fit for porcelain, executed on the stone china body.

These then are some of the rarities which appear in Davenport stone china, but as has been stressed earlier the bulk of production would be the serviceable tea and dinner ware. One such rather naively decorated cup and saucer carries the highest pattern number we have recorded from the stone china series, 145, and bears the interesting dealer's mark 'Sandbach & Co. King St. Manchester' (Plate 98).

We end this section with a reminder that occasionally one may come across plates, dishes, etc. which in addition to one of the normal set stone china patterns also bears an individual decoration. Such a piece is the plate (Plate 97) clearly part of a service made especially for the 49th Regiment. Similar regimental wares from other detachments are known, and in a Californian collection I was delighted to find a tureen, stand, and lid with a regular pattern but inscribed 'City of London Commercial Club.'

A number of additional patterns appear in *Davenport Pottery & Porcelain*, Plates 44–9 and are not repeated here. However, since that book was published a number of different stone china marks have been reported, some of them very rare, and these are given here in chapter 8.

96. Large stone china vase on a gilt-striped plinth, decorated with a typical Imari pattern (24). The handles are deep blue with a gilt scale pattern, the finial a recumbent lion. Ht 19½in. Mark E 11. (Courtesy Major Davenport)

97. Stone china plate beautifully decorated with a Chinoiserie scene (pattern 8) and delicate gilding. Diameter 8¾in. Mark E 11. (Godden of Worthing Ltd)

98. Stone china cup and saucer decorated with a colourful pattern of Oriental 'trophies'. Saucer diameter 5¾in. Mark E 11. Pattern 145 (the highest recorded in the normal stone china range). (B. M. & A. C. Walters Collection)

99. Soup plate decorated in Imari style (pattern 51) made for the 49th Regiment. Diameter 10¼in. Mark E 14 (very rare), c.1820–30. (Iwass Collection)

120 · Earthenwares and Stonewares

121 · Earthenwares and Stonewares

15   Transfer Printed Wares

A large proportion of the huge output of the Davenport factories during the approximate period 1795–1850 was made up of earthenwares, mainly but not exclusively of a useful nature, decorated by one of the transfer printing processes. At first such designs were printed on the once-fired (biscuit) body in cobalt blue, but by the 1820s other colours were being used for underglaze printed designs. These other, then novel, colours never succeeded in completely superseding the traditional underglaze blue printed wares, but Simeon Shaw noted in his *History of the Staffordshire Potteries* (1829) that:

Very recently several of the most eminent Manufacturers have introduced a method of ornamenting Table and Dessert Services . . . using red, brown and green colours, for beautiful designs of flowers and landscapes, on pottery greatly improved in quality and shapes formed with additional taste and elegance. This pottery has a rich and delicate appearance, and owing to the blue printing having become so common, the other is now obtaining a decided preference in most genteel circles.

Mr G. Bernard Hughes has written in his *English and Scottish Earthenwares 1660–1860* (Lutterworth Press, 1961) that these other colours were introduced in 1828 'when it was discovered that by mixing finely powdered yellow, green, red and black enamels with barbardos tar it was possible to transfer the designs in various shades of these colours without distortion or loss of brilliance.'

The basic printing process was by no means a simple operation. A team of skilled workpeople were employed and several factors play their part in producing a presentable finished printed pottery plate. Many people still decry printed wares, comparing a mass-produced earthenware example with a finely painted bone china specimen, but of course such comparison is meaningless, for the two articles were produced for quite different markets, the hand-painted bone china example being prohibitively expensive for the majority of the population.

Both crafts have their place in ceramic history and in the market's requirements. In basic terms a well-printed plate produced from a skilfully engraved and designed copper plate is much superior to a poorly painted specimen. There is no overriding advantage in hand-painting, only when the artist is a master craftsman. Such artists have always been scarce and demanded high wages – for a slow process. Few artists would be content to decorate a run of a hundred large dinner services with the same pattern, a task which may take months of labour.

The printing process obviously has its place and a very important one. It permitted long runs of plates and complete servies to be decorated with often tasteful and intricate patterns at a price that most of the buying public could afford. In particular such blue printed useful wares suited our large export market and many patterns were especially introduced for these important overseas requirements. One must always remember that Davenports' overseas trade was very considerable. It has been reported to us that in several early nineteenth-century American sites, the excavated fragments were mainly Davenport. Of the ordinary printed earthenwares probably more was shipped out of the British Isles than was sold in the home market.

It must not be thought that these staple blue printed earthenwares were produced without cost or trouble. This was far from the case, especially after *c.*1810 when the better class dinner services would have several related designs printed on the different articles. Even with the standard Chinese-styled landscape designs such as the basic Willow pattern, a set of twenty or more engraved copper plates would be needed, each engraved with a different size or shape. Obviously a copper plate for a circular

100. Dessert basket and stand, printed underglaze in blue with scenes from the Gothic Ruins series. Stand: 'Solitary Fisherman'. Dimensions: 10×7¾in. Mark E 2. Basket: (handles missing) 'Fisherman and Friend'. Dimensions: 10×7¾in. Mark E 2. (Lockett Collection)

dinner plate could not be used on an oval platter and each different size of platter, dish, or stand would need a separately engraved copper plate. None of these flat-ware copper plates could be used on a curved or shaped tureen body, where the contours had to be taken account of in engraving straight lines, towers, etc.

When it is remembered that a complete earthenware dinner service sold in the first quarter of the nineteenth century could quite easily run to well over a hundred pieces or in some cases to over two hundred, the complexity of the problem is underlined. We have for example an account for such a Davenport dinner service sold to Mr R. Beech in April 1812. This order for the underglaze blue standard series of designs called 'Gothic Ruins' (see Plate 100) comprised plates of three sizes; twenty-two oval meat platters or dishes in various sizes from about eight inches long to the very large examples of twenty inches or so; tureens, covers, and stands of two sizes, each with a ladle; four covered vegetable dishes; oval baking dishes of two sizes; a salad bowl; a 'Beef steak dish with water pan;' a cheese stand; a trifle dish; and two pierced drainers for the large meat platters. The 1812 buyer also ordered a matching dessert service which comprised a centrepiece or footed comport and stand; four fruit baskets and stands; eight shaped dishes (in two or three different shapes); and thirty-six dessert plates with a diameter of seven inches. In addition Mr Beech ordered a matching sandwich set. This last item would have comprised four curved segment dishes and covers encircling a central covered bowl. These sets were originally fitted inside a mahogany tray and are sometimes called supper or breakfast sets. They were very popular articles in the better class homes and they could be extremely complex. One such rather special and non-Davenport example is shown in Geoffrey Godden's *British Pottery. An Illustrated Guide*, Plate 308. Each different shape or size of object in all these services would need a separate engraved copper-plate.

Returning to Mr Beech's 1812 order, this then comprised over two hundred units of the blue-printed Gothic Ruins series of design. For this complete set of dinner and dessert ware he was charged £12 9s 5d. This sum is, of course, meaningless today unless we translate it into present day inflated currency or at least remember that a good average weekly wage at that period would have been about one pound. Part of his order has fortunately survived and is today housed in the Edward Dean Museum of Decorative Arts, Cherry Valley, California, USA. This service is made up of six different compositions in the popular Gothic Ruins series. It was not a single design service as for example a Willow pattern set would have been. At present eleven such related Gothic Ruin prints have been recorded (see A. W. Coysh and R. K. Henrywood, *The Dictionary of Blue and White Printed Pottery 1780–1880*, p. 137). This pattern was formerly known to collectors as the 'Fisherman series' but the 1812 account proves that the original factory title was 'Gothic Ruins' and, of course, ruins feature prominently in each print. Most of the pieces supplied in April 1812 bear the impressed upper and lower case Davenport over the anchor device, the standard mark of the period.

Other dinner services were of a lesser size. One supplied from the London showrooms at 82 Fleet Street in August 1827 by the London partnership of Davenports Pontigny & Co. comprised:

36 large Plates
12 Soup do.
12 Pie do.
1 Soup Tureen and stand
4 sauce do. do.
4 Covered Dishes
1 Salad Bowl
3 Pie Dishes
1 large Gravy Dish
11 flat dishes in sizes and
1 fish Drainer

This was described as '1 Dinner Set for 12' in 'Best Blue Printed . . . Pattern' and was invoiced at £5 15s 0d. The number of pieces, not including covers, was ninety-one, giving an average price of just over 1s 3d a piece, including large platters and the tureens. It is interesting to note that this service intended for twelve people comprised only twelve soup and pie plates but three times as many large plates. This was always the case, as there might well be more than one main course to be served. The seemingly large number of sauce tureens is also interesting and reflects culinary customs of the period.

When we consider the care and time needed to engrave a set of copper plates for a detailed and intricate dinner service pattern where perhaps ten or twelve entirely different views are needed, as in the 'Muleteer' design (see Plates 101 and 105) the cost would obviously be many times greater than it would have been for a simple and broadly-styled Willow pattern design.

101

124 · Earthenwares and Stonewares

Transfer Printing

Firstly, the master engraver or the factory owner would need to draw or paint all the designs, amending them to suit personal taste and the shape and size of the object that they were to adorn. In many but by no means all cases the basic pattern might be copied from a published source such as a book illustration or engraving but even then the design had to be adapted from a square or oblong format to one more suitable for round or shaped pottery objects.

Once the basic designs had been agreed, the laborious and time-consuming task of transferring such a drawing on to a copper plate could begin. Here one must remember that a washed-in foreground, for example, had to be rendered on the copper by closely packed dots or lines, for the colour could not be washed in by a brush but had to be held in such recessed dots or lines and so transferred to the ware. To engrave a set of copper plates for a reasonably intricate dinner service design might well take months rather than weeks and a team of engravers might be engaged on the task.

Large firms such as Davenports, Mintons, Ridgways, etc. no doubt had their own engraving workshop or departments which would be fully employed at all times, for the copper plates needed re-engraving or 'repairing' as they wore with use. The smaller firms relied on the services of specialist engravers to the trade, from whom they would purchase their sets of copper plates if and when they saw the need to introduce a new pattern. More often than not the smaller firms purchased copies of already proven saleable designs leaving the large firms to experiment with new styles.

This is not to say that the large firms always went their own way or were always innovators. This is far from the case. There was much to be said for issuing a market-proven popular pattern even when other manufacturers had been selling the pattern for years. You could for example sell further pieces to buyers who already owned some of that pattern and wished to enlarge their services or replace damaged pieces. Other sales might be made to persons wishing to have the same pattern on different objects or on new up-to-date fashionable shapes. The popular and usually quite early blue-printed pattern known as 'Chinoiserie Ruins' (Plate 102) was for example not only produced by Davenports but by Ridgways, Rogers, and Stevenson, to name only the manufacturers who sometimes marked their examples.

Once the sets of copper plates had been engraved or purchased, they had to be put to use, for themselves they are but useless slabs of copper. The successful charging and transferring of the engraved design onto the once-fired but unglazed blanks was a skilled task, taking time and trouble if the result was to be successful.

Many reference books will be found to give a résumé of the engraving and

101. Bordalou, transfer printed in blue with the 'Muleteer' pattern. Length 10¼in. Mark E 8A. (Courtesy The Wellcome Foundation)

102. An impressed marked 'Davenport' blue printed platter from a dinner service showing the popular pattern called 'Chinoiserie Ruins'. 20½×15¼in, c.1800. (Godden of Worthing Ltd)

transferring processes and these basic techniques should be understood by all those interested in collecting the finished article. A complete understanding of the difficulties and trouble involved will add materially to your appreciation of a good specimen and permit you to understand better the reason for the large number of unsatisfactory examples that are to be found.

Rather than paraphrase accounts that may not in themselves be trustworthy the authors here quote from contemporary accounts written by authorities who had practical experience of the pottery industry and of transfer printing under the glaze. Before quoting these it must be underlined that the process here explained relates to transferring under the glaze by the hot or press method. This is quite different from the various overglaze techniques including the bat-printing process and other cold processes. The reason why we call the underglaze method 'hot' will become apparent shortly. Our first contemporary account also mentions the bat-printing process. This is useful to show how totally different it was. However, Davenports carried out very little bat-printing, but see Plates 153 and 200 for its use on earthenware and porcelain.

Our first authoritative account is taken from Charles F. Binns's little book *The Story of the Potter* (George Newnes, 1898). In his chapter III the author, the son of R. W. Binns, founder of the Worcester Royal Porcelain Company, explained the process of transfer printing. He wrote, in part:

The process of transfer printing is extremely interesting on account of the many details to which careful attention has to be given. The copper plate, the paper, the press, the oil, the colour, and the ware must all be in proper condition if fine work is to be done, and it may not be out of place to give here some particulars of the work as now carried on.

Upon a pattern for printing being designed, the drawing is passed to the engraver, who prepares for it a suitable piece of copper. This copper is in the form of rolled plates about one-eighth of an inch in thickness. The preparation of the copper is important, for were the surface not uniformly hard it would wear unequally and speedily become useless. At one time the engraver had to trace every line of the designer's work, and transfer it laboriously to the copper, squaring and measuring if any alternative in size had to be made. It must be remembered that a drawing on paper is not usually prepared with sufficient accuracy to fit closely to every part of the pottery, but the work of the engraver is useless if not exact. To fit a plate is easy, but when such a piece as a milk-jug with undulating edge has to be printed, the matter is more complicated. The engraver lays morsels of wax all over the part to be printed, and then presses upon these a piece of tissue-paper. Carefully removing all wrinkles and making or cutting out all the gores, the paper is removed, and being laid out flat upon the copper-plate shows the required form. To this outline the design must be adjusted, and it is here that the difference between good and bad work is seen.

How often, in a cheap piece of printing, is the work evidently a make-shift! No special engraving has been made for the difficult pieces, but a straight length of print has been cut and bent out of all recognition in order to fit.

. . . The cutting of a copper for transfer printing is considerably deeper than for bookwork. The whole of the colour cannot be pressed out on the paper, and as a large body of colour is required for transferring, allowance has to be made in the depth of the engraving. And this is more the case for some colours than for others. A copper engraved for printing under the glaze must be a good deal deeper than one which is only used for enamel colours, because the stronger fire of the glaze kiln through which the first has to pass impoverishes the colours to a greater degree than does the other, so then an engraver always wants to know for what colour his copper plate is to be used before he can cut the pattern correctly.

Now to the printing room. In the centre of the room are the printers, each in a kind of cubicle. The man is not enclosed, however, except by his benches and stove and press. The press stands in front of him, and is like a large iron mangle. The rollers are iron, and so is the heavy plank which passes between them. By means of a long handle he works the upper roller round through half a circle, and this of necessity moves both the plank and the

103. An interesting 1860s photograph of a pottery print-shop showing the presses and young girl assistant. This is not directly related to the Davenport works. (Godden Reference Collection)

lower roller. At his left is the stove, reduced by engineering skill to a simple iron slab, hollow, through which waste steam passes, keeping it at an even temperature, just too hot to press the hand on. Beside the stove is a strong table, to which is affixed a sheet of copper upon which to clean his 'boss,' and upon the remaining side is a sloping desk for damping the paper.

This is how he sets to work. Taking the engraved copper plate, he places it upon the stove to get warm, and with his palette knife he takes a portion of the mixed colour and spreads it upon the copper. This colour has been mixed in a very stiff oil, so stiff that were it not for the heat of the stove it could not be worked at all. The object of this will be seen in the transferring. After carefully working the colour into all the details of the engraving, the printer scrapes the surplus away with a knife, and taking a pad or 'boss' covered with corduroy he wipes the surface of the plate perfectly clean. This boss he slaps now and then upon the sheet of copper which is fastened to his bench, and so keep it from becoming overcharged with colour. The plate, being duly filled and cleaned, is laid upon the plank of the press, and the printer, taking a sheet of fine tissue-paper, makes it thoroughly wet with a solution of soap and water and lays it down upon the copper. This requires great care, for the smallest crease in the paper would be detrimental. Now he lays a piece of printers' blanket on the paper-covered copper, and working the handle of the press, he passes the whole between the powerful rollers. Great pressure is thus exercised, and the saturated paper is forced into close contact with the colour in the engraving. The pressure removed, the copper plate is placed on the stove once more. As the copper grows warm the paper is carefully lifted by one corner, and as it peels off it carries with it an impression of the engraved pattern. So far the operation of printing, but now the transferrer must be brought into notice.

Seated down the side of the room at tables are a number of women and girls, two or three to each printer. The youngest of the party is called the 'cutter'; she fetches the print from the press, and with a large pair of scissors in her deft fingers she cuts away all superfluous paper, leaving the pattern on a long narrow strip. Meanwhile the senior woman, the transferrer, has coated the ware over with a fine varnish to ensure the adhesion of the print. Now she proceeds to lay the printed paper accurately in its place, adjusting it with a needle if necessary, and when all is in position the paper is pressed down with a piece of flannel. Stronger measures are, however, necessary to secure perfect contact, and with a tightly bound roll of cloth lubricated with soap one of the women rubs the whole print firmly and evenly. All being ready, the printed piece is immersed in a tub of water, when the paper floats away and the print is left upon the ware. Now the object of the stiff mixture of colour is seen. Were the colour soft enough to be used cold, it would not resist the action of the water; but, being heated, the cold surface of the pottery causes it to at once harden, and the water leaves it unharmed.

For both biscuit [underglaze] *and glost* [overglaze] *printing the process is the same, with but slight variation in the oil and varnish. Sometimes the ware is printed dry and a slight dusting of powdered colour is passed over the print, but these are minor deviations which do not affect the principles under which the work is carried out.*

A delicate use of this method of dusting was found in what has been termed 'bat printing.' This was carried on some years ago at Worcester, and received its name from the fact that a flexible 'bat' of glue was used instead of paper. The idea was that some engravings were so fine that no adequate effect could be got by printing in colour. The printer therefore took the oil alone, and filling the minute work with this, he used the ball of his thumb as a 'boss.' Cleaning the copper plate thus, he took the piece of elastic glue and squeezed it down upon the copper. No other force was needed, and of course no press could be used. The glue took up the oil from the engraving, and being then laid gently upon the china, the pattern in oil was transferred. This of course could hardly be seen, but some colour, generally black or purple, being reduced to a fine flour was softly dusted over the place with a piece of cotton wool. The oil attracted the powder, and the pattern stood revealed. It was then only necessary to fire the ware in the usual way to fix the print.

This 1898 description is reasonably straightforward and helpful. Many other descriptions, contemporary and modern, may be found in other books but few if any accounts go further and explain some of the practical difficulties which arise from printing under the glaze by the standard and accepted method.

One account does, however, explain some of these difficulties. This we feel is well worth quoting at some length so that present-day collectors will appreciate the complexities of the process. The following extracts appeared in Ernest Albert Sandeman's book *Notes on the Manufacture of Earthenware* (Crosby Lockwood & Son, 1901, reprinted 1917 and 1921). This is a manual of instruction and as such unknown to most collectors. Whilst some basic facts will repeat points made in Charles Binns's account, this practical manual does show that all was not straightforward. The engraving of the copper plate was but a start, they were the tools, now the workpeople had to transfer that design on to the ware. The extracts are from chapter XXIII.

The Printing Press consists of an iron framework which supports two hollow cylinders or rollers, between which is a planed iron bed or table on which the copper plate, engraved with the design to be printed, rests. The upper roller is furnished with screws on each side by which it can be adjusted and fixed at whatever distance may be desired from the lower one. It has a lever or handle attached to it which, being depressed, causes it to revolve, carrying the table with the copper plate on it between the two rollers. The upper roller is covered with thick flannel in either two or three layers. The flannel should be cut slightly shorter than the circumference of the cylinder, and the ends should be laced together with string, so that, as the flannel stretches, which it is sure to do, the string lacing can be tightened from time to time in order to keep the flannel tightly in position. It is as well to have two sets of flannels to each press, so that one set may be washed and dried while the other is in use, and with care they should last about twelve months.

Printing Stoves or Tables. The 'medium' or printer's oil that has to be mixed with colours to enable prints to be taken off has to be kept hot during the whole process, and for this purpose the old-fashioned system was to have flat stoves with an iron bat on the top, burning either coal or slack, to heat both the copper plates and the colours.

This method was unsatisfactory for several reasons. The heat was not equal, as sometimes the stove was allowed to get red-hot, burning the colour and damaging the coppers, and at other times, after fuel had been freshly put on, the heat was insufficient; these variations in heat were a cause of irregularity in the printing. There was also always a certain amount of dirt and smoke in the shop to which the carrying in of coal and the removal of ashes contributed.

The modern tables [this was written in or before 1901] *are heated by live steam under pressure, directly from the boilers passing through a coil or pipe cast in the iron slab which forms the table, and which, after being cast, is planed smooth. The steam, after passing through the table, is received by a steam trap, which by the action of a valve prevents any steam from wasting and only allows the condensed water to escape, one trap being sufficient for several tables. Each table is made sufficiently large to serve for two printers, and as each table is fitted with an independent tap, steam can be shut off when not required, and waste is avoided. The heat being easily regulated and always equal, there is no fear of burnt colour, and smoke and dirt in the shop are done away with.*

Copper Plates are in most general use for printing on earthenware, though of late years many manufacturers have employed plates made of zinc as a substitute. These are, of course, easier to engrave, as they are so much softer, but for this reason they wear out very soon, and the outlines are not so clean, nor are they suited to full patterns with much detail and shading. The copper plates are about an eighth of an inch thick, and vary in size according to the pattern, or according to the pieces which have to be printed from them. They are engraved with the aid of acids or electricity, or by hand with gravers, steel points, and punches. The latter is undoubtedly the more expensive method, but it is the more satisfactory, as not only must the design be delicately and finely cut, but it must be also deeply incised, or the plate will last a very short time, as the constant cleaning off of the colour from the plate with the steel knife wears it down. The colours being metallic oxides, however finely they may be ground, are always hard and slightly vitreous.

Engraving on copper is work which requires a considerable amount of technical training, but no amount of training will make a really satisfactory engraver unless he has artistic feeling for arrangement and design. Great attention should be paid in the first place to the production of good designs, and in the second to their proper reproduction in copper with varying light and shade.

Copper plates continually wear down with work, and to prevent this some manufacturers have the plates steeled and nickelled. No doubt this causes them to last rather longer, but when once damaged they require, as a rule, more repairing than ordinary copper. Plates, however, will always require repairing and recutting, if the printing is to be kept up at a high standard of excellence. Some printers are very careless, and cut and mark the coppers with their knives when removing the colour. These marks retain the colour, and when a print is taken off the plate they appear, and thus disfigure the design and give an unsightly and dirty appearance to the ware. Every copper should therefore be examined before it is handed to the printer, and after it is done with, or at every week-end, it should be again examined to see that it has received no unfair treatment, and if it shows signs of cutting and marks other than those that would be caused by fair wear and tear, he should be charged with the cost of repairing the damage.

If copper plates are not carefully looked after they will soon be spoilt and useless. It is surprising how soon copper plates diverge from the original design by constant repairing; so, whenever a new design is cut, the designer should always keep one of the first prints off it by him as a reference or guide for when the plate has to be repaired. These prints should all be pasted in a large book kept for the purpose, which will always serve as a reference. It is impossible to have clean and bright-looking printed ware unless the copper plates are kept in good condition, and nothing is more unsightly than coarse and dirty printed patterns.

The paper used for receiving the print from the copper plate is a sort of thin tissue paper. It must be strong, so that is does not break when sized or pulled off the copper plate. It must, when held up to the light, be quite free from holes, so that the design is solidly printed on it, and it should have a smooth surface without any hairs on it, so that when the print is transferred to the ware the paper does not absorb the colour, but freely leaves all the colour on the ware when it is washed off. It is important to have paper of the sizes required for the different pieces and patterns, so that the waste may be avoided, otherwise large paper may be cut up for printing small patterns, and the cost of printing will consequently be increased. The paper before being applied to the copper plates must be sized with a mixture of 1 lb. of soft soap and 2oz. of soda to a gallon of water.

   The colours are for the most part oxides of metals, and of late years great advances have been made in their manufacture; and there are many firms, both in England and on the Continent, who dedicate themselves solely to the manufacture of potters' colours for the use both under and over glaze. Formerly every potter manufactured his own colours, but now, owing to the improvements in their preparation, good colours can be obtained at moderate prices; and where ordinary colours only are required it is probably cheaper to buy, as colour-making takes up a considerable part of a manager's time, which often might be better expended in looking after the details of manufacture. Manufacturers who have colour pans will best employ them in grinding stain for the body and in the manufacture of the colours which they use in the largest quantities, as it will be found that it is not economical to make colours of which only a small quantity is required.

   . . . Cleanliness is most necessary in colour mills, and it is as well to grind up a few pitchers after a strong colour has been on a pan in order to thoroughly clean it before putting on another colour. Light colours should not be ground on a pan, from which a dark colour has been taken off, and it is best, when possible, to keep certain pans for certain colours. It is important that the colours should suit the glaze, and the manufacturer who makes his own colours has the advantage of knowing of what they are composed, and all metallic oxides that will easily dissolve and flow in the glaze must be avoided.

   It is not considered necessary to give recipes, as they exist by the thousand, and have been published again and again. They are usually of little value except to the expert, as the success of a colour generally depends more on its manipulation during manufacture than on anything else. . . . All colours, whether made on the premises or from whatever other source they may have come, should always be tested before they are put in general use.

   Printer's oil. For printing purposes all colours have to be mixed with what is called printer's oil, which is a thick, dark, treacly-looking substance, which causes the colour to adhere to the paper when laid on the copper plate and passed through the press. When the paper is pulled off the plate, the colour in the cavities of the copper sticks to the paper, thus forming the pattern. The paper is, in its turn, applied and rubbed on to the ware, which, being porous, absorbs the oil and colour. The paper is then washed off with water, but the oil prevents the removal of the colour from the ware. Almost every head printer has his own recipe for oil, by which he swears; one such recipe is annexed. . . .

> (1) 1 gallon linseed oil (boil and scum for about two hours).
>   30 oz. Stockholm tar.
>   1 oz. red lead.
>   1 oz. resin.

Add the above to the oil, and the whole to be boiled and scummed and burnt off three or four times. A large iron pot is best for this purpose, and a round wooden flat cover with a piece of flannel tacked on, with a long handle, will be required to put out the fire after the scum has been lighted in the pot. It is best to do all operations in connection with boiling oil in the open air, or in the centre of an empty oven, as the smell is rather overpowering.

   Printer's knives are used for applying and removing the colour from the copper plates. They are made of thin whippy steel, about 2½ to 3in. broad, and are ground quite sharp. They require skilful and careful usage, or the copper plates will be cut and destroyed by them. The copper plates should not always be held in the same position, but should be *turned round from corner to corner, as should the printer continually start cleaning off the colour with his knife from the same corner, he would wear away the part nearest the corner sooner than the rest of the plate, thus causing unequal impressions.*

Wooden rubbers are used for rubbing the colour over the copper plate to thoroughly fill the design.

A corduroy boss, or small cushion about 8 in. long and 3 in. wide, is employed to clean the plate after the bulk of the colour has been removed with the knife. The plate is thus left quite clean, the colour only remaining in the engraved part.

A long-haired brush is required to size the paper with.

The benches for printers to put their coppers, colours, &c., on should be arranged at a convenient distance from the steam tables and presses.

The transferers will require:-

A tub for every two presses, with a good supply of clean, cold water, the cooler the better, as the paper is washed off and the colour not softened as it would be were warm water employed.

Sponges, which need not be of very good quality, to wash off the paper, and a piece of pumice stone to rub off any spots of dirt or colour that may have soiled the ware.

Flannel rubbers, which are simply rolls of flannel of about twelve thicknesses tightly rolled up, about 13 in. long, and whipped about 10 in. up with thick packer's string, leaving at one end about 2½ in. of flannel, and at the other end about ½ in., hollowed out, in which the thumb can rest. A yard of flannel will make two rubbers, which should last about three months, as, when they wear down, the string can be gradually unwhipped. They require to be dipped in a little soft soap to make them slip smoothly over the paper, and not to ruck it up when rubbing it on the ware. A few small pieces of flannel are also useful for the same purpose.

A considerable amount of bench room is required, and on the bench opposite each transferer a leather pad should be nailed, on which she can rest the ware. . . .

The printer's team consists of a man who does the printing, and three women or girls: the transferer, who is the head woman, places the pattern in the proper position on the ware, and presses it slightly on; the apprentice, who rubs the paper firmly on to the ware; and the cutter, who receives the paper from the printer and cuts out the various pieces into the necessary shapes to fit the ware, and removes any superfluous paper.

Having mentioned the various appliances, we will proceed to describe the process.

The printer first takes his paper and cuts it to the necessary size for the pattern or plate he is using, and then with his brush sizes the paper over. He then places the copper plate on the steam stove, his colour having also been previously placed on the stove on an iron palette or 'Batstone.' The copper plate being sufficiently heated, he takes some colour on his knife and puts it on his copper plate and rubs it in with his wooden rubber.

The colour should be used of a stiff and not too liquid consistency; this makes the work harder, but it ensures good printing; if the colour is used thin the pattern is printed more in oil than in colour, and after firing it will have a faded, wishy-washy appearance. He then removes all the colour from the copper by scraping it with his knife, being careful that the edge of the knife does not catch in the engraving and cut and spoil the plate; after which any remaining colour is cleaned off with the corduroy boss, leaving the plate quite clean, though the pattern is filled with colour. He next places the copper plate on the iron table of the press, and as the plate is very hot, he has a small piece of leather with which he can lift it up comfortably, and he then deftly takes up a piece of the wet sized paper and lays it over the copper plate, care being taken that there are no wrinkles. The lever handle is depressed, the upper roller revolves, carrying the iron table and the copper with it between the rollers, and the paper is thus firmly pressed by the flannel covering on to the copper. The handle is then reversed, and the copper comes out of the press again with the table, the paper being now quite dry from the pressure of the flannel on the heated copper. The paper is lifted up carefully at one corner and pulled off the copper.

The printer has then to repeat the process. The paper is taken by the cutter, who cuts it into the shape required and hands it to the transferer; she applies it to the proper place on the ware, and slightly rubs it on with a bit of flannel, and then passes it on to the apprentice, who rubs the paper firmly on with the rubber dipped in a little soft soap. This requires very thoroughly doing, especially in the case of fluted or embossed work, so that the pattern is rubbed right into all the cavities. A stiff brush is often used under these circumstances instead of the rubber, with satisfactory results. It is best to leave the paper a little time on the ware before washing it off, and as a rule it is left till the evening, when all the women wash off the day's work together though it is better not to wash it off till the next day, as it thus gives the ware more time to absorb the colour, and this is especially necessary should the biscuit ware be rather hard fired.

Each printer should be furnished with a small copper plate with his number engraved twenty to thirty times or more on it, which he can print off every now and then, and every piece printed should bear the printer's number so that there is never a doubt as to who is responsible for the work. [Such printer's or team numbers seldom appear but some old examples of blue printing do bear various printer's tally-marks or symbols – a star or a small circle. Such marks were merely intended for internal quality control or the piece-rate payment. They are not necessarily unique to one manufacturer and do not therefore afford a reliable guide to identification.]

Cleanliness is most important in the printing shop, and the transferers should always keep their hands clean; nothing looks worse than ware with smudges of colour on the face or back of it, due to the transferer's fingers. Tubs, benches, and utensils should be cleaned every week, before being looked over, with sawdust and rectified spirits of tar. Patterns of which large quantities are required should be engraved on two or more plates, and the plates should never be allowed to 'get down,' but when partly worn should be repaired, so that the tone of printing may always be equal; otherwise, if a plate gets much worn and ware is printed from it, and then after the plate has been newly cut more ware is printed from the same order, the tone of colour will be quite different, and will not match. It is always best to use newly cut plates for the more delicate colours, such as matt blue, mauve, and pink, whenever possible, and afterwards, when slightly worn, for the stronger browns, blacks, and dark blue.

It has been seen that the printer can only take one impression off a copper plate at a time, and then has to go through the whole operation of filling it again with colour, &c., and for this reason it is necessary for economical working to arrange the patterns on the plates so that enough pattern will come off at each printing to decorate several pieces of ware.

Care must therefore be taken in deciding on new patterns that, besides being effective, they can be arranged in a suitable manner on the copper for working. Formerly, patterns were designed in such a way that it was necessary to have a copper plate for every individual piece, and thus to print a full dinner service twenty to thirty coppers were required; with proper arrangement four or five coppers should now be sufficient for doing the same work, as the patterns most in demand are sprig and flower patterns, which lend themselves readily to every class of piece, and thus one copper will suit several different purposes. If, in arranging a pattern, pieces of sprig, &c., have to be cut off, it is well to see if these bits cannot be applied to some other ware, such as bowls, basins, &c., which is of advantage both to the manufacturer, as he uses up prints which would otherwise be wasted, and to the printer, as he thus does more ware with the same amount of work. A well-engraved copper, with ordinary work and proper care, should last six months. . . .

Up to the present, most of the new methods proposed are for overglaze decoration, and this can never be so satisfactory or desirable for ordinary commercial purposes as underglaze. Underglaze decoration is practically indestructible, and though the colours are fewer in number than those that can be applied over glaze, their appearance is far superior. They have a deep rich colour, and one seems to be looking into them, more than at them, and they give much the same impression as when looking at a cut precious stone.

There is always a strong party agitating against the introduction of mechanical means on account of its tendency to kill individuality; and to a certain extent this is true; but on the other hand, as a printed pattern can be produced in an almost indefinite quantity, considerable time and money can be profitably expanded in producing a really good design, and surely a really good design executed in a satisfactory manner is better than a design executed by hand which probably has only the individuality of inferiority. The ordinary painted ware issuing from the English manufactory to-day is practically a reproduction of some pattern given as a sample to be copied, and the individuality usually consists in mistakes in copying it!

. . . Unfortunately, every man is not an artist, and who would prefer some 'pot-boiler's' crude, badly-executed daubs to a well-engraved proof copy of a really fine picture? This is perhaps carrying the matter too far, but at all events it shows that there is something to be said on both sides of the question, and that mechanical reproductions are not necessarily bad because they are mechanical.

Ernest Sandeman then gave in his following chapter a short account of the all important so-called 'hardening-on' process which had to be undertaken before the printed article could be glazed. He wrote:

It has been mentioned several times in the course of these notes that all ware which has been printed or painted with colours mixed with any greasy or oily medium has to be dried at a heat sufficient to evaporate these foreign substances from the pores of the ware, so that it has resumed its absorbent properties, and on being immersed in the glaze it will receive an equally even coating all over the piece. This is called 'hardening-on,' really a complete misnomer, as after the ware has been submitted to the heat, the oils used in applying the colours being driven off, leave the colour on the pieces in its original state of impalpable powder, which will come off if touched with the fingers ever so lightly, and care must be exercised in handling it before dipping to avoid smudging it. [This statement is not true of eighteenth-century Worcester or Caughley porcelain wasters of blue-printed articles, for when such fragments have been taken from the damp earth after lying there for well over a hundred years such 'hardened-on' cobalt will resist quite strenuous washing. It could be, however, that these and some other makers applied a very small amount of glaze to fix the colour before the main glazing was undertaken.] *To thoroughly dry out these oils it is necessary to raise the temperature of the ware to a red heat, and to obtain this object kilns are employed.*

Kilns, both for hardening on and for enamel or overglaze purposes, are built on much the same principles, the former, however, usually being considerably larger. A kiln is simply a fire-clay box into which pieces of ware may be introduced, and which can then be surrounded by fire and heated to the necessary degree without the pieces of ware coming directly in contact with the flame. The shape of a kiln may be compared to a railway tunnel, that is to say, it is formed by an arch supported on sides which are not quite perpendicular, but slope slightly inwards, so that the breadth at the bottom is slightly narrower than the breadth at the point from which the arch springs.

In building a kiln it is first necessary to secure a thoroughly firm foundation and then to decide on the size of the kiln to be built. This will depend on the quantity of ware that is to be fired at one firing, and must be governed by the rate of production of the printing and painting shops, and moderate sized kilns will usually be found the most useful. If very large kilns are used, it will often be found that there is not sufficient ware to fill them, and they either have to be fired partially full, which is waste of fuel, or they must wait over until the next day for more ware, which is loss of time. The number of the mouths will vary in accordance with the size of the kiln; formerly kilns were built with one mouth from the back to the front, the flues working through the top of the mouth arch, which was the system specially advocated in France, but now, by a different arrangement of the flues, the mouths are constructed at the side, by which means much greater regularity of heat in all parts of the kiln is obtained, and there is also less destruction to the brickwork and flues, and it is therefore more economical in repairs. . . .

Placing. The ware all being in the biscuit state can be piled up one piece upon the other, as long as the colour on one piece does not come in contact with another; dishes, plates &c., are kept apart by small biscuit supports called 'nibs,' the important point being to get as much ware as possible into the kiln. It should be piled up in such a way that it will not fall during the firing nor while it is being drawn. Some kilnmen use props and bats in a hardening-on kiln as they would in an enamel kiln, but there is really no necessity for this, unless the kiln is so exceptionally large that the weight of the ware would be likely to crush or crack the pieces at the bottom.

There is little art in firing hardening-on kilns, and almost any fuel will answer for the purpose, small coal and an admixture of slack being quite sufficiently good. There is no occasion for trials, the colour of the interior being quite sufficient guide, and when the heat has reached a dull red it is sufficient for the purpose, and the firing may be stopped. Care must be taken to leave plenty of vent for the exit of the vapour from the oils and for the steam from the water; the latter exists in considerable quantities, as in washing off the paper from the printed ware the pieces absorb a considerable amount of water, and should this steam be shut in, it is very likely to affect the colours, especially the more delicate ones, the glost fire to stand out in rough ridges as if insufficiently hardened on, or giving them a milky, washed out appearance, as if they had been carelessly printed. The clamins should therefore be left open for some time – in fact, the kilnman can always light his kiln before he has finished placing it – and by this means the ware is drying before the clamins are built up and considerable time is saved.

Drawing. Kilns may be cooled rapidly as soon as they are finished, though a certain amount of time must be allowed if there are many large pieces, such as dishes or basins in the front, to avoid dunting. The kilnman must be careful in handling the pieces, when taking them out of the kiln, not to rub the colour off them, not to smudge them by getting colour on his fingers. Nor should they be sent to the dipper when hot, as in this state the absorption would be greater, and they would receive a thicker coating of glaze than desirable.

Insufficiently hardened-on ware can generally be detected when drawing a kiln, as the colours after firing should have a dull matt appearance; if they look at all glossy the oil has not been properly driven out. After the glost fire it shows unmistakably, as the parts where any oil remains will not be glazed, will be blistered, or will be covered with small holes known as 'pinholes.'

After this 'hardening-on', the plate or other article may be glazed and fired yet again before it is ready to be sold. It is to be hoped that you will now have a greater respect for that blue (or other colour) printed plate and for the workpeople who created it. Lest the reader believes that the possible faults detailed in this old potters' manual be exaggerated, it is relevant to quote from a letter written by John Davenport on 19 July 1834, at a period when one would think that the Davenport firm had completely mastered all difficulties and was able to produce the basic type of blue-printed earthenware to rival those of any other manufacturer. But John wrote to Henry Davenport in the following manner:

I have been here all day engaged with our Travellers, on the subject of prices & patterns – that is new patterns of Blue Table Ware in which we are behind Mintons & Ridgways – What is wanting is the exercise of more Judgment in the selection of Patterns – we have been very successful in two lately viz the Rhenish Views, & the Leaf Border – and I am anxious to have something very good now fixed upon – It must be particularly studied in the Border in which much of the effect lays – White brought some Swiss Scenery which I send you, but it is too much like the last. On looking over much of the Ware, I must remark that a good deal of it is very roughly got up by the Workmen in the clay – badly printed with soft Oils, & badly laid on by the Transferrers – a good deal dirtied in the Glaze Tub in dipping – some much run together in the Blue, as I presume by being placed wet, or not properly dried before putting into the Hardening Kiln – the cockspur marks are very bad, & I think what you make now at Longport must be bung, as I believe Spodes & Mintons are. I have sent you down a China jar as the best way of explaining its defects – You will see how badly it is got up in the Clay from the Molds – no Sharpness – seams not rubbed down – no lining around the ornaments with a tool – the Handles hardly stuck on at all – and sent from Biscuit W'house without stopping the Spouts &c &c – the Blue badly laid on. But indeed ought such a piece to have been Ornamented in that expensive manner, if at all . . .

It should be noted that John Davenport was only referring to the blue printing and this was in July 1834, some six years after other underglaze colours had reputedly been introduced in the Staffordshire Potteries.

There were several variations on the basic blue printing process and these will be mentioned in the following pages, but first let us discuss or list some of the Davenport earthenwares which were decorated in the standard manner, by underglaze transfer printing in blue.

Underglaze Blue Printed Patterns

As has been indicated earlier, underglaze transfer printed wares were almost certainly amongst the earliest of the products from the Longport factory. It would seem likely that some of the earliest patterns were unmarked and consequently have remained unrecognized. Indeed Coysh and Henrywood in their *Dictionary* state, 'It is not clear when Davenport started producing blue printed wares, but known marked examples would appear to date from about 1810, although it is quite possible that unmarked pieces were made earlier.' Since that was written in 1982 most authorities would agree (including the *Dictionary's* authors) that a number of marked patterns have been discovered which one could date prior to 1810. Nevertheless, these are few and there are clearly further discoveries to be made about these early printed wares.

Most collectors are primarily interested in specific and identifiable patterns, and although it would be quite impossible to illustrate or even describe every single pattern and its known variants, we include here a quite lengthy list of patterns with details of where illustrations may be found and what variants to expect. For the purposes of this preliminary check list (we hope it will be added to over the years as fresh discoveries are made) the patterns described had all been introduced in the first fifty years of the factory's life, that is from 1794 to approximately the mid 1840s. It is not possible to be precise about this, but one can assert that during the 1840s printing colours other than blue became much more fashionable; that in the case of Davenport, the quality both of printing and the ware declined somewhat, and thus is of lesser interest to collectors, and significantly more patterns of this period carried a backstamp bearing the name of the pattern, thus making identification so much simpler. The later transfer patterns will be discussed in chapter 16 and a check list of pattern names is given there.

Notes on the Pattern List
1.   All the patterns in the list have been noted on known marked wares. It has not been thought necessary to give the mark in each case except where this helps to date the introduction of the pattern.
2.   In the earlier patterns, the same scene was used on wares of all descriptions, thus the 'Chinoiserie Ruins' pattern (Plates 113–14) many be found in the same form on plates, dishes, soups, even on a bulb pot. At a later date a limited number of engravings was used of different scenes which were placed on different items in the service. Thus the 'Gothic Ruins' service described in some detail earlier had only six different scenes

thereon, though it should be noted that additional scenes have been recorded on other items. As the Beech order was dated 1812 this gives an indicative date for the use of more than one scene on dinner and dessert services. At a somewhat later date, probably not much earlier than 1820, the factory began to use a multiplicity of scenes which varied with each item in a large service. The best example of this is the 'Rustic Scenes' series.

3.   As a consequence of the above the varied views in a given series can be identified as belonging to that series by the border pattern. It seems that though some views were very disparate in subject, items intended to be used together in a service would share a common border pattern. Thus where this is of especial significance we have directed particular attention to the border by which the series may be recognized.

4.   To eliminate tedious repetition, and because not every variant of a pattern is available to us, we have not attempted to describe every known variant within a long pattern series such as 'Mare and Foal'. A whole book could be devoted to that kind of activity and one hopes that one day it will be, by a devoted collector of Davenport blue printed ware. (It has been done for Spode by David Drakard and Paul Holdway, *Spode Printed Ware*, 1983.)

5.   The list contains a number of abbreviations where standard reference works are indicated. These follow the now accepted format of the Friends of Blue in their Club *Bulletin*:

Coysh 1 Pl. 34 = Plate 34 in A. W. Coysh, *Blue and White Transfer Ware 1780–1840* (1970)
Coysh 2 Pl. 23 = Plate 23 in A. W. Coysh, *Blue-Printed Earthenware 1800–1850* (1972)
Dict. p. 315 = A. W. Coysh and R. K. Henrywood, *The Dictionary of Blue and White Printed Pottery 1780–1880* (1982)
FOB = Friends of Blue *Bulletin* (followed by the issue number)
Godden Mark 1187 = G. A. Godden, *An Encyclopaedia of British Pottery and Porcelain Marks* (1964), mark number 1187
Godden BP = G. A. Godden, *British Pottery. An Illustrated Guide* (1974)
Godden I = G. A. Godden, *An Illustrated Encyclopaedia of British Pottery and Porcelain* (1966)
Little = W. L. Little, *Staffordshire Blue* (1969 & 1987)
Lockett = T. A. Lockett, *Davenport Pottery & Porcelain 1794–1887* (1972)
Williams = P. Williams, *Staffordshire Romantic Transfer Patterns* (USA, 1978)

6.   Pattern names often cause confusion. Again we have followed accepted FOB custom: that is, where the factory pattern name is known, often because it appears as part of the mark, this name is given unaccompanied; where there is no known factory name the title customarily used either by the FOB or in the *Dictionary* is indicated by (A), for attributed, after the name. In certain cases we have had to indicate a change in pattern name from an attributed one to the real factory title and this has always been made clear. The most obvious example of this is the pattern formerly known as the 'Fisherman' series which the document cited at length earlier reveals should be called 'Gothic Ruins,' which is how we have styled it. Unfortunately, the title 'Gothic Ruins' was used by Coysh (2 Pl. 22) for a scene which we now know comes from the 'Rustic Scenes' series. Discrepancies of this kind will be clearly indicated in the few cases when they occur.

7.   The patterns are listed in groups in alphabetical order. This should make it easier to identify a particular pattern. The groups are roughly chronological. Chinoiserie patterns are likely to have been amongst the earliest production and are listed first, then follow the English country scenes, foreign scenes, floral compositions, and a category for literary and commemorative items. All the patterns in these lists will have been produced before *c*.1845. The dates given indicate the probable date of introduction.

Chinoiseries

Amoy. Two Chinese ladies with a parasol. Noted in flown blue on a plate dated 1844 (Plate 145). Amoy was a Chinese port captured by the British in 1842.

Bamboo and Peony (A). Coysh 1 Pl. 29. A large platter is attributed by Coysh to *c.*1825–30. The pattern also occurs on stone china. The pattern had a long life, an example dated 7:78 (July 1878) being recorded. Clobbered or coloured-over examples are also found. Used on a variety of items.

Bridge and Temple (A). To the left an arched bridge, to the right a courtyard of a temple with small figure therein. Distant lakes and mountains. Recorded on a shaped dish with shell and gadroon motif. Marked with a scene of a Chinaman and palm trees with DAVENPORT printed in the centre (Godden Mark 1185). *c.*1835–45.

Chinese Banana Tree or **Chinese Beekeepers** (A). Miller and Berthoud, *An Anthology of British Teapots*, 1985, Pl. 717. A very large laburnum-type tree with pendant clumps of what look very like bananas to the left, beneath which two houses are seen. Two rather indistinct figures appear near a house on the right. This teapot is undoubtedly Davenport and has the interesting early feature where the lid finial is a ring handle in red. It is marked with the anchor alone, *c.*1800–10. The pattern has been noted on miniature wares.

Chinese Fishermen or **Fishing Family** (A). Dict. p. 114. This early pattern is illustrated as bearing the mark of the Irish retailer DONOVAN (impressed). It is also known with the word DAVENPORT impressed in very large letters (see mark E 4). The pagoda on the left has a large chimney-like structure, there are two anglers to the right seated, and standing in the foreground is a lady (?) angler with her rod on her shoulder. *c.*1795–1810.

Chinese Flag Bearers (A). G. B. Hughes, *English and Scottish Earthenware, 1660–1880*, 1961, Pl. 39. Two men are seen on a bridge in the foreground with fishing nets or flags over their shoulders. A boat is above the bridge and there are houses on an island beyond. To the right the pagoda has a large fenced courtyard or patio. Two figures are seen in a window. Hughes illustrates a typical Davenport basket stand, marked DAVENPORT impressed. Unmarked plates etc. have been noted. *c.*1800–10.

Chinese Garden Scene (A). Lockett, Pl. 30. Two Chinese figures appear in front of a single-story house. The border is floral. *c.*1825–30.

Chinese in Gazebo (A). FOB 19 p. 4. A pleasant pattern featuring a Chinese lady with a parasol. There is some indication that the pattern details change with the object. This pattern has not been seen by the authors.

Chinese Marine. A chinoiserie scene closely akin to that used by Mintons (see Dict. p. 82) has been reported on pieces in a marked service *c.*1835. The scene was named in an elaborate backstamp typical of the period. No further details are known and the pattern has not been seen by the authors.

Chinese Pastime. A number of patterns are known on wares with this title printed as a backstamp (Godden Mark 1186). Usually found in green, not blue, the scenes depict Chinamen playing dice, whipping tops, etc. About six variations have been reported. *c.*1840+. A stone china bowl has been noted with the print enriched with overglaze enamel colours.

Chinoiserie Bridgeless (A). Coysh 1 Pl. 27 and Lockett, *Transactions of the English Ceramic Circle* 9 Pt 1, 1973, Pl. 17c. A very common pattern with some variants. A man is seen in the doorway of a pagoda to the right. There is no willow tree, bridge, or birds. It has been found on dinner, dessert, and miniature wares. Early and quite long-lasting, introduced *c.*1795–1805. (See Plate 104.)

Chinoiserie High Bridge (A). Coysh 1 Pl. 30 and R. Copeland, *Blue and White Transfer Printed Pottery*, 1982, p. 16. Two pagodas are joined by a high bridge. There are three figures in the foreground. Widely used on items of dinner, dessert and supper ware. *c.*1810–15.

104

105
106

Chinoiserie Ruins (A). Coysh 1 Pl. 26, Little Pl. 22. This is a very well-known pattern with a somewhat weird church to the right beneath which are two figures, one seated and the other holding a parasol. The border is very similar to one used by David Dunderdale at the Castleford Pottery. Versions by both Rogers and Ridgway are illustrated in Dict. Pls 83–4. Stevenson is also recorded as having used the pattern. Davenport wares for dinner and dessert carry the pattern over a wide range of shapes, even a bulb pot is known (see Plate 105) and asparagus servers (Plate 106).

Dragons No. 2 (A). (See R. Copeland, *Spode's Willow Pattern and Other Designs after the Chinese*, 1980, p. 146, No. 31 for the Spode version.) This pattern is known on dessert and supper wares, both in plain blue and also with the hand-painted minute circles in red as illustrated (Plates 107–8). These thin dragons are very different from the Masons version (Coysh 1 Pl. 58), but very similar to the Spode, and almost indistinguishable from the Herculaneum (the Davenport and Herculaneum versions are shown together for comparison on p. 39 of *Herculaneum: The Last Liverpool Pottery*, the catalogue of an Exhibition held at Warrington Museum, 1983). The border is normally the Greek key. *c*.1815–20. Dict. p. 113 illustrates an example with DONOVAN enamelled in red on the base. This is almost certainly another of the many Davenport pieces made for the Dublin retailer.

View of the Imperial Park at Gehol (formerly called **Chinese River**

104. Oval, footed comport, printed in blue with the 'Chinoiserie Bridgeless' pattern. 10¾ × 7½in. Mark E 4. (Courtesy David Golding, Arundel)

105. Bulb pot, printed in blue with the 'Chinoiserie Ruins' pattern. Note the attached ring handles and the inner rim and the two 'rests' for the missing lid. To date no other factory is recorded as having produced blue printed bulb pots – and this is the only known Davenport example! Ht 5in. Mark E 2. (Lockett Collection)

106. A pair of asparagus servers printed in blue with the 'Chinoiserie Ruins' pattern. 3⅝ × 3⅝in. Mark E 2. (Diana Darlington Collection)

138 · Earthenwares and Stonewares

107. Tureen, plate and segmentally shaped dish from a supper service, printed in blue with the 'Dragons and Key' (or 'Dragons No. 2') pattern, with additional on-glaze enamelled small circles in red. Dish and lid, overall length 13in. Tureen and lid, ht 6½in. Plate, diameter 8in. Tureen unmarked; plate and dish E 2. (Lockett Collection)

108. Plate printed in blue with 'Dragons and Key' pattern (or 'Dragons No. 2') and red enamelled circles overglaze. (What a tedious task!) Diameter 8in. Mark E 2. (Lockett Collection)

Scene). Lockett, Pl. 22 and Coysh 1 Pl. 28. A Chinese junk sails on the river with buildings and figures on the far bank. The scene was taken from John Barrow's *Travels in China* published by Cadell & Davies in 1804. Widely used for items in services etc. *c.*1810–25 (Plate 109).

Willow. Lockett, Pl. 23. Over the years a number of variants were engraved and used but the basic design remains the same. In Dict. Pl. 343 an unusual example has the additional printed name SPANIARD INN on the rim. This may indicate it was made for the famous Spaniards Inn at Hampstead, a place which Coleridge, Byron, Shelley, Reynolds, and Dickens used in their respective eras. Alas only the latter could have used this particular piece as it is datemarked for 1856. The earliest marked pieces seem to be *c.*1805.

Other unmarked Chinoiserie patterns have been shown to us at Roadshows and seminars, but it has not been thought worthwhile to describe them as the attributions are

139 · Earthenwares and Stonewares

often tenuous. One item does warrant a special mention. In an article by Ivor Noel Hulme, 'Creamware to Pearlware: Williamsburg Perspective,' published in the Winterthur Conference report for 1972, both sides of a pearlware jug are illustrated. The pattern would appear to be 'Chinoiserie Bridgeless.' The handle shape also has familiar Davenport features being of the same form as that illustrated on the white stoneware jug in Plate 84. What makes the Hulme jug especially significant is that it is inscribed on the neck in overglaze black POCOCK AND ALLEN 1802. Mr Hulme made a tentative attribution to Swansea, but a Davenport one seems more likely. If this were to prove correct on inspection, then the combination of the handle shape, the date and the use of the print would be especially significant as no other Davenport pieces are known which can positively be dated this early. The lack of a mark would also be additional evidence that many of the earliest pieces were totally unmarked.

English Country Scenes

Bisham Abbey (A) (formerly titled **Tudor Mansion**). Lockett, 34 and Coysh 1 Pl. 31. Two men, one standing and one seated, occupy the foreground in front of a Tudor-type mansion which has a central tower to the rear. Most of the pattern is trees. The abbey is 7 miles east of Henley-on-Thames. It had a remarkably short life from establishment in 1537 to its dissolution in 1540, when it was granted to Sir Philip Hoby. The pattern is known in blue, in a pucey-pink, and rather startlingly in orange on a chalcedony body. It occurs on dinner and dessert wares. It was once thought that the building was Oxburgh Hall in Norfolk. *c*.1810–15. (Plate 110)

Cornucopia Flower Border (A). Dict. p. 94. This series is distinguished by the border which features pairs of cornucopia-like objects with stylized leaves and flowers. The central scene, of which several variants are recorded, all depict country scenes with buildings in the background and people to the fore. The version illustrated has a watermill with a man, a woman, and a child with a basket (Plate 111), another has a

109. A group of blue transfer printed plates. Top: 'The Villagers'. Diameter 9½in. Mark E 2. Bottom Left: 'Rustic Scenes'. Diameter 10in. Mark E 2. Centre: 'George III'. Diameter 8in. Mark E 2. Right: 'View of the Imperial Park at Gehol'. Diameter 10in. Mark E 2. (Courtesy Spencers of Retford)

ruined abbey somewhat similar to Tintern with a man on a donkey followed by a woman with a large hat wearing an apron. The printing is usually in a heavy darkish blue. *c*.1825–30.

Cows Crossing Stream (A). (See Dict. p. 96 for an unmarked version on a drainer attributed to the Cambrian pottery, Swansea, and FOB 61.) The same scene is recorded on a marked Davenport drainer and on a large dish 22 x 18 in. This has an elaborate floral border going into the central picture which depicts trees shading a wooden bridge on the left, with three cows standing in the stream centre. There is a man behind them on the bank at the side of the bridge and a prominent fence runs horizontally across the centre of the picture. There are buildings to the rear. A similar but not identical scene is illustrated in Godden BP Pl. 314. Clearly this scene was popular as it also appears in a Goodwins & Harris version marked 'View near Colnebrook' *c*.1825–30.

Fisherman Series see **Gothic Ruins**.

Fisherman and Ferns (A). This pattern was published on an unmarked jug in FOB 55, and in FOB 56 (Summer, 1987) on a marked twifler in the Iwass Collection. The fisherman is prominent in the right foreground, whilst a man and a woman chat by a fence on the left. A building with a round tower fills the background. A feature is the large spray of fern-like foliage, which Mrs Iwass likened to asparagus. This is the only scene recorded and it can be seen to good advantage on the somewhat battered teapot (Plate 112). As a general observation, though teapots are not uncommon at this period with the occasional sucrier, there is no record of tea bowls, cups, and saucers in these early patterns to accompany them. Surely they cannot all have been broken and thrown away? *c*.1810.

110. Large meat dish with blue printed pattern of 'Bisham Abbey'. 18½×13½in. Mark E 4. (Godden of Worthing Ltd)

111. Plate printed in blue with 'Cornucopia Flower Border'. Diameter 9½in. Mark E 5. (Private Collection)

Gazebo (A). A pattern has been recorded on a piece of marked stone china which is a close version to that illustrated in Coysh 2 Pl. 66, where it is shown as being from Pettys & Co. of Leeds. The Davenport version also has three cows in the foreground with a country house, a gazebo, and a church in the background. *c*.1825.

Gothic Ruins (formerly entitled **The Fisherman** series). This is the correct title as indicated by the Beech order noted earlier (p. 123). Unfortunately, the title 'Gothic Ruins' was used in the *Dictionary* for a piece by an anonymous maker, and in Coysh 2 Pl. 22 for one of the many variants of the Davenport 'Rustic Scenes' series. There should be little confusion as all the known correctly titled 'Gothic Ruins' also have fishing scenes incorporated in the design.

Seven scenes have been published. See Lockett, Pls 25–7 and Dict. Pl. 37. These have been given descriptive titles: **Fisherman's Tale** (Plate 113), **Fisherman and Fence, Solitary Fisherman** (Plate 100), **Fisherman and Friend** (Plate 100), **Fisherman's Advice, Fisherman with Boat,** and **By the River.** A number of additional scenes have been recorded:

Norman Tower (A). A small plate depicts a square church tower not in ruins, with a single figure fishing by the river in the foreground; the usual 'weeping' tree growing on the right and flowing over to the left.

Fishing Talk (A). A fisherman with a rod is talking to a woman, there is a basket of fish to their left, the water in front. A man behind them is reeling in a catch. There is a large ruin on a bank at the back with two figures nearby.

The Catch (A). On the lid of a water filter noted at the Britwell House sale. The ruin in the rear has what looks like a figure or statue in the pointed arch window to the right. In front is the usual lake or river scene with one fisherman reeling in and his companion on his knees apparently 'netting' the catch. Curiously the body of the filter which, of course, was large, was printed with parts of two separate prints; at the bottom was part of 'Fisherman's Advice,' the top of the picture was a completely unrecorded print of a very extensive and complicated ruin.

Peaceful Fisherman (A). On a small tureen in the Iwass collection. A tranquil scene by the river depicts a standing fisherman and this seated companion. On the opposite bank there is a cottage beside a church tower to which is attached a very short nave, beyond which is a building with a conical roof. Of particular interest on this piece are the handles which are painted all over in blue and moulded in what appears to be a likeness of Mr Punch.

These prints which obviously date to before 1812 (the date of the Beech invoice) are found not exclusive to one item in a service. Thus the Beech service, large though it is, contains only six different scenes. Scenes were interchangeable so that the same scene may be found on single or double handled dishes or on plates or parts of a

112. Teapot printed in blue with the 'Fisherman and Ferns' pattern. This is an early old oval shape, *c*.1805–15. Ht 5in. Length 9½in. Mark E 2. (Philip Miller Collection)

113. Part of a supper set printed in blue with the 'Fisherman's Tale' from the Gothic Ruins series. 10½ × 7¼in. Mark E 2. (Lockett Collection)

142 · Earthenwares and Stonewares

114

supper set. The border, where it occurs, remains constant. The scenes have so far not been matched up with any published illustrations, indeed the architecture is so wayward that one wonders if these are not purely imaginary inventions of an inspired engraver!

Mare and Foal (A). Coysh 1 Pl. 34, Dict. lists 4 variants on p. 237. The original pattern name was given because of the prominence in the design of a mare and foal on the edge of a river, a country house in the background (Plate 114). However, as further scenes have been noted, the common elements are the border pattern of flowers, in which a rose appears prominently, and the presence of a country house or cottage as a central feature. In addition to the four scenes listed in the *Dictionary* the following have been recorded:

A meat dish with a fisherman with rod in hand on an island, trees, and a country house in the background.

A plate with a traveller with a bundle of sticks accompanied by a dog approaches a cottage where two figures are standing, a large tree to the left.

A tureen stand with a large timber-framed house in the centre, cattle down to the river in the foreground, two figures seated fishing.

A large cottage orné is in the midground with a mounted rider talking to a standing figure, two cows in the foreground, a large tree to the left.

A tureen stand in the Lockett collection has two fisherman in the foreground, two large spreading trees to the right, and beyond the water a bridge with an ornamental wall either side and a modest country house beyond (Plate 115).

A pierced basket in the Cleaver Collection has the house in the background, two seated and two standing cows, and a seated man (Plate 116).

The series appears to date from *c*.1825 and wares date-marked 1848 have been noted. The border pattern is the key to the correct identification of this very attractive series.

Milkmaid (A). This design is very similar to Spode's familiar Milkmaid (see Drakard and Holdway, Pl. 702, p. 136). The Davenport version is illustrated in Godden BP, Pl. 318. The Iwass collection contains a fine small globular teapot also with this design, the chief features of which are the curious head-dress worn by the milkmaid as she milks the cow. There are sheep nearby. The border is floral with daisy-like flowers prominent.

Rural Scenery. This title is recorded in a cartouche as the backstamp

114. Plate printed in blue with the 'Mare and Foal' pattern. Note especially the border design. Diameter 9½in. Mark E 6 (for 1836). (Iwass Collecton)

143 · Earthenwares and Stonewares

together with the printed Davenport mark E 8A. It is on a plate with a raised border and scalloped edge, c.1835–40. A boy is seated with a collie-type dog in a rural setting with two cottages in the background, all surrounded by trees. Two different scenes are illustrated in the *Dictionary*: the jug on p. 315 has a very indeterminate scene featuring a humped-back bridge and Colour Plate XXIX there shows three youthful figures seated beside the water with cottages to the left and a seven-arched bridge and a sailboat to the right. The border is interesting, containing flowers and scrolls with cartouches of cottage scenes, and birds perching on the scrolls.

Clearly this is a multi-scene series with many more views to be recorded. Other makers used this title (see Dict. for details). To further complicate matters, FOB 60 shows a number of illustrations under the title 'Davenport Rural Scenes series.' This should have read 'Rustic Scenes' (q.v. below). We hope that the two series, which have quite different borders, will not cause confusion in the future.

115. Tureen stand printed in blue with a scene from the 'Mare and Foal' series. Diameter 7in. Mark E 5. (Lockett Collection)

116. Pierced dessert basket with interesting twig handles, printed in pink with a scene from the 'Mare and Foal' series. Overall length 11in. Mark E 5 (Alan Cleaver Collection)

144 · Earthenwares and Stonewares

II. Porcelain plate from the service prepared for the banquet in the Guildhall given for Queen Victoria in November 1837. Diameter 9⅜in. Mark P 8. (Courtesy Los Angeles County Museum of Art, donated by Alan Ross Smith)

III. Pearlware dessert tureen, attached stand and a ladle, finely painted with autumn leaves. Length 7¼in. Ht 6½in. Mark E 2. (Diana Darlington Collection)

IV. Pearlware dessert tureen painted with Green Winged Dove (lid) and The Poronopt'ere (body). Ht 7in. Unmarked. This is a known shape on marked wares. Of the three pieces found together, this tureen was unmarked, the comport (Plate 48) was impressed with E 2, and a third dish had E 1. (Hacking Collection)

V. Pearlware leaf-moulded tureen and stand. Ht 7in. Marks both E 2. (The Hacking Collection)

145 · Earthenwares and Stonewares

VI. Large pearlware ice pail with moulded and brightly coloured leaves. Ht 11¼in. Mark E 2 (Diana Darlington Collection)

VII. Pearlware dessert plate with blue printed osier pattern and brighly enamelled autumn leaf design. Diameter 7¾in. Mark E 2. (Lockett Collection)

VIII. Three jugs in the chalcedony body decorated with monochrome picturesque landscapes, gilt Greek key border and intertwining initials R. R. in gold script. Ht L to R: 5in., 7in. and 5½in. (Hacking Collection)

146 · Earthenwares and Stonewares

IX. A plant pot in the chalcedony body, finely decorated with monochrome flower paintings, and with bronzed dolphin handles. Ht 5¼in. Unmarked. (Godden of Worthing Ltd)

X. Two pot-pourri vases decorated with printed and enamelled Japanese figures and floral subjects. Left: Porcelain. Mark P 5 in blue underglaze. Right: Stone china. Ht 8½in. Unmarked. (Hacking Collection)

XI. Stone china bowl with blue ground decorated overglaze with Renaissance motifs in white slip in the manner of Limoges enamel. Diameter 8½in. Ht 4½in. Mark P 5 in brown: this 'porcelain' mark has been noted on quite a few highly decorative stone china pieces. (Hacking Collection)

147 · Earthenwares and Stonewares

XII. A Davenport earthenware multicolour printed plate from the coloured 'Muleteer' dinner service invoiced in January 1840, see Plate 139. Impressed Davenport and anchor mark with potting numerals for 1835. Diameter 7½in. *c.*1835–9. (Godden of Worthing Ltd)

XIII. An impressed-marked and printed earthenware platter from a large 'Romantic Castles' pattern dinner service, the central design printed in colours. Other pieces from this service are shown in Plates 140–2. 18½ × 14in. *c.*1835–40. (Godden of Worthing Ltd)

XIV. Two earthenware jugs, both with a nacreous lustre wash over parts of the pattern. Left: 'Nectarine' (pattern number 1411 A). Ht 8¼in. Printed cartouche pattern name. Right: Sea-green ground, exotic birds and lustre finish. Ht 8in. Mark E 6 (indistinct). Both *c.*1860. (B. M. & A. C. Walters Collection)

XV. Left: Plate decorated with 'peasant enamels'. Diameter 9in. Mark E 6 (for 1836). Right: Soup plate with printed and enamelled pattern 3029. Diameter 8¾in. Registered design mark and impressed date for July 1881. (Both B. M. & A. C. Walters Collection)

148 · Earthenwares and Stonewares

XVI. Oval Davenport bone china sugar box with characteristic handles and formal floral knob form (see detail). Length 8in. Retailer's painted mark 'J Mist N.82 Fleet Street' and pattern number 310, c.1810–12. (Geoffrey Godden, chinaman)

XVII. An attractive and superbly potted relief-moulded teapot. Ht 6¼in. Printed ribbon mark (P 5) and painted number 706, c.1820. (Geoffrey Godden, chinaman)

XVIII. An attractive Paris-styled marked Davenport trio. Far side view of handle, see Plate 215. Diameter of saucer 5½in. Ribbon mark P 5, c.1825–30. (Geoffrey Godden, chinaman)

149 · Earthenwares and Stonewares

XIX. An early Davenport bone china stand to a dessert service centrepiece showing the popular 'Table' pattern. 8¾×7in. Note late typical slight discoloration to the body. Painted 'Longport' mark, c.1805–10. (Geoffrey Godden, chinaman)

XX. The front and reverse of a pair of Davenport dessert dishes in the hybrid hard-paste body. Other pieces from this superbly painted set are shown in Plates 238–41. 8¾×6½in. Impressed 'Davenport' name-mark over an anchor, as shown, c.1807-12. (Godden of Worthing Ltd)

XXI. A marked Davenport ice pail (missing liner and cover), very well painted with flowers on each side and with wide gilt border. Ht 8in. Printed name and anchor mark (P 4), no pattern number, c.1810–15. (Godden of Worthing Ltd)

XXII. A large size Davenport bone china plate of superb quality, painted and gilt in a typical manner. Diameter 9¾in. Printed ribbon mark P 5 and pattern number 170 with painter's tally-mark of a small circle, c.1820–5. (Godden of Worthing Ltd)

150 · Earthenwares and Stonewares

XXIII

XXIV

XXIII. An ornate moulded-edged plate, well painted and with raised and tooled gilding. Diameter 9½in. Fruit named on reverse. Printed Royal mark P 8, c.1830–7. (Mrs Clarke)

XXIV. A colourful and superb quality Davenport porcelain dessert plate of typical moulded and pierced form. Diameter 9¼in. Pattern number 1062 with painter's tally mark. Printed ribbon mark in brown, c.1850–5. (Geoffrey Godden, chinaman)

XXV. A lobed-edged Davenport dessert plate from a magnificent service, painted with different flowers. Diameter 9½in. This moulded form was registered on 11 March 1856. Blue registration device with 'Davenport' below. Pattern number 1174, c.1856–9. (Graham & Oxley)

XXV

151 · Earthenwares and Stonewares

XXVI
XXVII

XXVIII

XXIX

XXVI. An early Davenport bone china open-topped vase, well painted with named birds 'Ortolan, de Cap de Bonne-Esperance' and 'Ortolan de la Louisiane'. Well-modelled branch handles finished perhaps with the mock bronze of the Royal order. Ht 6⅛in. c.1806–10. (Godden of Worthing Ltd)

XXVII. An attractive Davenport vase very much in the style of contemporary French porcelains, with biscuit porcelain handles contrasting with the glazed and gilt vase. Ht 9¼in. The flower painting perhaps by Gould or Steel. Printed ribbon mark P 5 and initial 'G', c.1820–5. See Plate 309 for reverse side. (Geoffrey Godden, chinaman)

XXVIII. One of a set of three bulb pots in the hybrid hard-paste porcelain. Ht 6in. A very characteristic Davenport shape, see also Plates 313–14. Impressed name and anchor device P 2, as Colour Plate XX, c.1807–12. (Christie's, now Lockett Collection)

XXIX. A magnificent display plate, the centre very well painted with a miniature portrait of Prince Adolphus Frederick, Duke of Cambridge. Diameter 10in. Printed scroll mark P 4, c.1825. (Private ownership)

152 · Earthenwares and Stonewares

117

118

Rustic Scenes (A). Dict. p. 317 (two examples), Little 23, Coysh 2 Pl. 22, other pieces are illustrated in FOB 12, 44, 48, 57, 60 (in which latter seven further scenes are shown). This is an important series, which can be identified readily by the border (Plate 117). This has a prominent flower with light leaves on the outside, a group of dotted stamens and then dark leaves on the inner rim. There is some ambiguity as to exactly how many variants are known, but it is certainly not far short of twenty. The scenes are all of a rural nature with two different watermill scenes, a number with cows and calves, sheep and, as illustrated in Plate 118 on a splendid supper set in a mahogany tray, a rather tired looking horse. Some scenes have fishermen, some 'Gothic' ruins (Plate 119) and other watermills, but the border is the linking theme and the rustic nature of the scenes. Introduced probably in the early 1820s the pattern had a long life and is known on dinner, dessert, and supper ware.

Tudor Mansion (A) see **Bisham Abbey**

The Villagers (A). Coysh 1 Pl. 33, Dict. p. 388. A group of three young people and a dog are on a grassy bank. One, a boy, is seated and apparently about to play the pipes (? or blow bubbles). c.1820. The pattern is known on dinnerware (Plate 120), on a jug, and on a fine footbath in the Diana Darlington collection.

Wild Rose (A). This is one of the most familiar of all blue printed patterns, named after the border. Dict. p. 400 records over twenty potters who used the pattern, but not Davenport. However, a marked Davenport piece is now known. The source print also illustrated in the *Dictionary* is of 'Nuneham Courtenay, Bridge and Cottage.' A curious feature is that the pottery print always features a man in the punt with his hat pulled down over his ears rather like a circus clown. This figure is not on the original.

117. Plate printed in blue with a view from the Rustic Scenes series. This is an interesting variant of the watermill illustrated in the *Dictionary*, p. 317. Note especially the border pattern for the series. Diameter 9¾in. Mark: the very rare E 3. (Iwass Collection).

118. A supper set in a mahogany tray printed in blue with views from the Rustic Scenes series. (Peers Collection)

153 · Earthenwares and Stonewares

Other views have been reported from time to time, as for example a fine coffee pot with a good print of two rather aristocratic children with a spaniel dog. And, as indicated, in certain series there will be many unrecorded patterns awaiting discovery. We end this section with two such scenes. The old oval sucrier (Plate 121) has ring handles and a charming rural scene with the two horses and the child apparently kneeling and collecting grass with which to feed them. In the absence of any border pattern it is not possible to assign this view to any of the known series. The teapot (Plate 122) has another delightful and unrecorded rural scene for which the title **The Seated Shepherds** (A) would seem appropriate. As far as I am aware this scene has not been linked with any other tewares.

Foreign Scenes

Classical Buildings and City (A). Little, Pl. 24. This scene of Venice or more probably Rome is said to have been designed by William Brookes of Port Vale, Wolstanton. It is rare.

Florentine Fountain. Coysh 2 Pl. 24. A large dish in light and dark blue tones. A crowned figure with a trident is prominent on the left of the picture, a rococo bridge and rather fanciful buildings to the right. Pattern named in cartouche backstamp. The border featuring butterflies has been noted with other scenes. Mid 1840s.

French Groups. A floral design with exotic birds similar to 'Asiatic Pheasants' (see Dict. p. 148, not illustrated).

Italian Verandah. The scene is named in the backstamp (Plate 123). Other examples are known printed in mauve on a plate year-marked 1836. The example

119. Plate printed in blue with a view from the Rustic Scenes series. Diameter 9¾in. Mark E 2 (Courtesy J. K. des Fontaines.)

120. Platter printed in blue with 'The Villagers'. Length 14½in. Marks E 6 and E 8A. (Courtesy Sotheby's)

121. Old oval shape sucrier (lid missing) printed in blue with a charming pattern of two horses and a kneeling figure. This is a hitherto unrecorded and unnamed pattern. Note the ring handles standing proud of the body, an early feature. Mark E 2. (Courtesy Alwyn and Angela Cox: now Iwass Collection)

122. Teapot printed in blue with 'The Seated Shepherds' (A), seemingly a hitherto unrecorded and unnamed pattern. Length 11in. Ht 6½in. Mark E 4. (Diana Darlington Collection)

154 · Earthenwares and Stonewares

illustrated is in the multicolour process, and a similarly colour-printed tureen in the Cleaver collection has several different views under the same general pattern heading. More research is needed on this range of patterns.

Mosque and Fisherman (A). Coysh 1 Pl. 32. This fine scene (Plate 124) is normally found with the somewhat incongruous border of roses over a lattice framework. The pattern has been noted on dessert and dinner wares on vessels of all kinds. *c*.1815–20.

Muleteer (See Plates 139 and 160). This very popular pattern has been illustrated many times on a variety of objects. It seems especially popular for toilet wares e.g. in Lockett Pl. 28 it is seen on a chamber pot, and in Coysh 2 Pl. 25 on a pap boat; there is a feeding cup in Dict. p. 135. Crellin, *Medical Ceramics* shows a bordalou (see also Plate 101) and mentions a commode in the Wellcome collection. The pattern is also recorded on dinner wares and mugs, cups, and other small items of tableware (see Colour Plate XII for its use in colour).

Persian Bird. Dict. p. 140, where a flown blue version is illustrated. The pattern is of two birds like herons, one in flight, the other amidst aquatic plants. *c*.1844.

Rhine or **Rhenish Views.** This would appear to be the factory name given to a series of views of which at least ten are known, some in pale blue, others in the multicolour version. The term 'Rhenish Views' is used in a letter by John Davenport (see

123. Dessert dish decorated with a multicoloured print in the 'Italian Verandah' pattern (so marked on backstamp cartouche). Stripes in blue enamel. 9¾×9½in. Mark E 6 (for 1836). (Lockett Collection)

124. Large dinner service dish printed in blue with the 'Mosque and Fisherman' pattern. Dimensions not recorded. Mark E 2. (Private Collection)

155 · Earthenwares and Stonewares

125

126

p. 134). Robert Copeland, *Blue and White Transfer Printed Pottery*, p. 22 notes that W. T. Copeland bought the copper plates for the Rhine pattern presumably in 1888 at the closing auction of the Davenport factory. He notes that there were different scenes for each object. It seems possible that these.are the same pattern. Though the scenes given the title 'Rhenish Views' are usually accompanied by a curious border of radiating lines bounded by a wavy edge, they have also been recorded with a rather undistinguished border which would appear to match the one illustrated by Mr Copeland.

We illustrate an example with the wavy-line border (Plate 125) which, to add to the confusion was illustrated in my original book under the title 'Swiss Fishing Scene.'

156 · Earthenwares and Stonewares

This latter title should now be abandoned. Examples with the wavy-line border are dated 1832 and 1836. A later version dated 1846 has the floral scroll border.

One final observation is that the multicolour versions of 'Rhenish Views' seem to have the wavy-line border but with the addition of small dark-coloured sprigs of flowers on the border, which also feature on some examples of the 'Italian Verandah' pattern. It is likely that the pattern remained in use for many years.

Romantic Castles (A). See Plates 140–2 and Colour Plate XIII. The pattern is known in both blue and white (possibly in other monochrome colours) and in the colour printed version. Once again the border is the distinguishing feature. It is a wide border of fir cone-like objects (some descriptions refer to them as strawberries) interspersed with florets on a lightly patterned coloured ground. As can be seen in the illustrations at least ten views occur on different items in the service. This is an interesting pattern on which very little research has been done. c.1836 onwards.

It is worth stressing that four patterns are relatively common in the multicolour version and they can easily be confused. They are 'Rhenish Views', 'Italian Verandah', 'Muleteer', and 'Romantic Castles'. The border designs are probably the best guide to attributing the correct series.

Snow Scenes (A). Plate 126. This teapot is printed with a scene which is also to be found on an unattributed egg hoop or ring shaped cup (Dict. p. 125). It is also referred to there on p. 340 under the title 'Snow Scenes,' and rather than cause confusion by adding further titles, we will use this one. As can be seen the central figure is wearing snow shoes and carries a staff. To his right is a gibbet-like erection and all the trees are covered in snow. This is an extremely rare piece, one other teapot is recorded, and a small plate. From research undertaken by Mrs Elizabeth Collard it would appear that the scene is adapted from 'the Ostiaks method of travelling in Winter' one of the illustrations in Thomas Bankes, *A Modern, Authentic and Complete Geography* (n.d.). The scene therefore is of Siberia, and not of the Arctic regions of Canada as collectors in that country had always hoped. The teapot shape, especially the handle, is noteworthy. c.1815.

Swiss Chalet (A). A small miniature round teapot with a crisp print of a Swiss chalet, to the right of which two small figures are silhouetted and with another chalet to the right and mountains in the distance, is recorded. The print does not seem, as yet, to fit any known series. In the *Dictionary* a Minton pattern is given this name, but it is quite different from the marked Davenport one just described.

Swiss Fishing Scene (a discontinued title) see **Rhine** or **Rhenish Views**.

Statuary. Plate 127. This jug is really very rare, bearing as it does the mark relating to the short-lived Henry and William Davenport partnership (E 7). The pattern too is not often seen.

Tempest. Plates 128–9. This rare item with the Russian armorial was published in my earlier book, but no other example has been reported to either of us or the FOB. It is just possible that this is an example from the service supposedly made for the Tsar of Russia (see p. 37).

Tyrol Hunters. Williams, p. 438. Two hunters hold guns, whilst a third is shooting. They wear Tyrolean attire with feathered hats in an Alpine setting. The border is floral. We have not seen this pattern, but it may not have been introduced until after the mid 1840s. A note of any pieces found on a dated body would be interesting.

View in Geneva. This pattern c.1840+ has been reported with the name in a backstamp cartouche. Groups of people and animals appear in front of stylized buildings, the nearest a temple or shrine. Three men and a child in one group, a man pulling a goat, two men and a dog, and a man on a horse. This pattern has not been seen by the author.

Floral Patterns

Hop. A pattern of hop vines noted on mugs and a coffee can. The mark is a

125. Plate printed in pale blue with the 'Rhine' or 'Rhenish Views' pattern. Diameter 10½in. Marks E 5 and E 8A. (Lockett Collection)

126. Teapot (cover missing) printed in blue with the 'Snow Scenes' pattern. The strainer on this piece is typical of many early Davenport teapots. It is raised from the body of the piece with holes around the edge of the raised rim as well as on the flat face of the strainer. Length 11¼in. Ht 6in. Mark E 2. (Lockett Collection)

cartouche formed from a single hop leaf with the pattern name. No date is recorded for this pattern which could well be after the mid 1840s. Not seen by the author.

Hydrographic. It is difficult to term this a floral pattern, but as there appears to be some kind of underwater floral symbolism in this design, it would seem an appropriate place to discuss it. The pattern is quite strange as can be seen from Plate 130. The wavy lines do give an impression of the ocean, but the other objects are not quite so directly aquatic. It is quite a rare pattern, only recently having been brought to the attention of printed ware collectors.

Orissa. Two vases feature in this pattern. One contains a large peony and other flowers issuing from the neck, and with Chinese figures painted upon it. The

158 · Earthenwares and Stonewares

127. Jug printed in blue with the 'Statuary' pattern. Ht 6in. Mark E 5 and the very rare printed mark of Henry & William Davenport E 7 (c.1832–5). (Lockett Collection)

128. Dinner plate with an armorial surmounted by a double-headed eagle. Diameter 9½in. Mark E 6 (for 1852) and the legend depicted in Plate 129. (Lockett Collection)

129. Close-up of the blue printed armorial on the Russian plate. The motto can be translated 'Glory to God and Life to Thee'. The single Russian word means 'Storm' or 'Tempest'. (Lockett Collection)

130. Tureen and lid printed in pale blue with the 'Hydrographic' pattern, and with additional gilding. 12×9in. Mark E 6 (for 1842). (B. M. & A. C. Walters Collection)

second contains a stick and a parasol. The border has three large sprays of flowers and three butterflies between them. Examples have been noted in a dark, flown blue with additional 'clobbering.' Godden Mark 1181a. c.1840+.

Vase of Flowers or **Flowers on a Table** (A). Both names have been used to describe a rather dramatic pattern featuring a large spray of flowers in a small vase on a table set in a small central cartouche. This is surrounded by three Renaissance urns, each containing three leaves. The urns separate three large floral rococo-scroll cartouches. The outer rim comprises a pattern of dots and circles with a looped lace-like motif at the rim. The pattern completely covers the surface of the plate. Variants of the vase and its contents are recorded. Examples date-marked for 1836 and 1844 have been noted.

Vase on a Wall (A). FOB 2. A large vase or urn with handles in the form of twisted snakes contains garden flowers with a tulip prominent to the right front. The vase is set on a portion of a brick wall. Tree tops are visible in the background. The border is of leafy scrolls suspended from rings which support clusters of apples and pears alternating with sprays and blossom. The border extends into the well of the plate. At least two examples with minor variations in the engraving are recorded. c.1835.

Literary and Commemorative

Unlike many factories which had an extensive overseas trade Davenports did not produce services decorated with views of North America in the manner say of Enoch Wood or Stevenson. A few items of specifically North America interest are recorded, and in this country these are extremely rare. At a somewhat later date commemorative pieces were made for Sunday Schools and the like and these will be noted in due course. The firm also made English topographical scenes, such as those of Great Yarmouth (see p. 179) and items in both porcelain and earthenware with views of English churches and other noted local scenes of interest. These too are later than the wares under discussion here.

Franklin's Experiments with Electricity. Illus. in *Transactions of the English Ceramic Circle* 12 Pt 2, 1985, and in D. and L. Arman, *Historical Staffordshire – An Illustrated Check-list*, Danville, Virginia, 1974, p. 210, No. 577 where a washbowl and

159 · Earthenwares and Stonewares

pitcher are shown under the title 'Franklin'. This pattern has a wide floral border and the central scene depicts Franklin flying a kite from which electrical sparks are issuing. There are buildings to the right and the name FRANKLIN is printed under his feet. The pattern dates from c.1830, and has been recorded in pink, purple, blue, and brown on pitchers, wash bowls, chamber pots, and other toilet items.

Franklin's Morals. Two examples are illustrated in A. W. Camehl, *The Blue China Book*, Dover reprint, 1971, p. 162 where they are listed as 'Maker unknown.' This is another rare series which is not often met with in Britain. The border which is common to this series is an ornate one of fruit, flowers, and leafy scrolls, but further identification is provided on the reverse of the pieces where the series name is printed together with the appropriate 'Moral.' The scenes are taken from *Poor Richard's Almanack*, a publication which ran for over twenty-five years. Camehl devotes a full chapter, pp. 158–71, to Franklin's Morals or Precepts or Maxims, and makers other than Davenport were responsible for the majority of unmarked pieces which are not uncommon. There are four Morals recorded on marked Davenport pieces:

The Eye of the Master Will Do More Work than Both His Hands;

Many a Little Makes a Mickle;

No Gains without Pains;

If you would Know the Value of Money Try to Borrow Some.

George III. Plate 109: a supper set dish is also illustrated in FOB 60. At the centre of the print is a likeness of George III crowned with laurels surrounded by a union wreath border of roses, thistles and shamrock set in a laurel border. Outside this is an array of farming implements. A dinner plate as well as the dessert plate pictured, and the supper set base has been recorded. The date is difficult to determine. The King died in 1820 and this could be to commemorate the end of his reign. It could just have appeared in 1810, the fiftieth anniversary of his accession.

Imperial Measure. *Northern Ceramic Society Newsletter* 62, June 1986. Though not exactly a commemorative, this rare design, which comprises the Royal Arms surrounded by a border of flowers and surmounted with the printed legend V. R. and IMPERIAL MEASURE, clearly has a significance beyond that of a mere blue printed pattern. Imperial measure superseded the old WINCHESTER WARRANTED by an Act passed in 1824. The mug in Plate 131 holds precisely two pints. The one pint version is also illustrated (Plate 132), and as can be see lacks the floral embellishment. I know of no other factory which produced blue printed Royal Arms mugs other than Davenport. These examples obviously date from after the accession of Queen Victoria in 1837, but probably not much after.

Captain Jones of the Macedonian. Full information is in E. B. Larsen, *American Historical Views on Staffordshire China*, 3rd edn, Dover reprint, 1975, Nos. 614, 758, and 759: the illustration of Jones is on a jug which is almost certainly not of Davenport manufacture. Two sizes of marked Davenport plates are recorded with prints in blue and black. The Smithsonian Institution in Washington has an example on a shell edge plate with the figure of Jones in the centre (Plate 133). Jones was the captain of the sloop *Wasp* which captured the British brig *Frolic* on 14 October 1812. However, both ships were later recaptured by the British and taken to Bermuda. At the end of the war, on his return to America Jones was regarded as a hero and given command of the recently taken British frigate *Macedonian*. The print is taken from *Analectic Magazine* II, July 1813, from a portrait by Rembrandt Peale engraved by D. Edwin.

Montreal. Lockett, Pl. 35: Elizabeth Collard, *The Potters' View of Canada*, 1983 pp. 28–32, cover colour ill. and Pls 15–16. This well-known print shows the steamship *British America* on the St Lawrence river with a view of Montreal in the background. The viewpoint is from St Helen's Island and appears to have been adapted from a series of views of the city by Robert A. Sproule published in 1830. The view occurs on plates, platters or meat dishes, bowls, the splendid basket and stand illustrated

131. A two-pint mug printed in blue with a floral border, the Royal Arms, and 'Imperial Measure'. Ht 5¾in. Mark E 8A. (Lockett Collection)

132. A one-pint mug printed in blue with the Royal Arms and 'Imperial Measure'. Ht 4¾in. Mark E 8A. (Godden of Worthing Ltd)

133. Plate printed with a portrait of 'Captain Jones of the Macedonian'. Diameter 9½in. Mark E 5. (Smithsonian Institution, Washington).

by Mrs Collard, and a number of other items. It is known in pale blue, pink, brown, grey, lavender, and black and also in a multicolour version. The border on the monochrome version is of flowers linked by scrolls below a narrow chain design with pendant dots. The full historical details of this splendid pattern are given by Elizabeth Collard. It is a rare and expensive pattern in Canada, and almost unknown in this country. Mid 1830s.

Commodore Perry and the Niagara. *Transactions of the English Ceramic Circle* 12 Pt 2, Pl. 97c. Full information is given in Larsen, *op. cit.*, Nos. 625 and 779: the illustrations of Perry on a jug is probably not of Davenport manufacture. Like Jones and Pike, Perry was a hero of the war in 1812. He captured the British fleet in the battle of Lake Erie in September 1813 even though his own ship was destroyed, by escaping to the *Niagara* and continuing the fight there. The print in black is known on a marked shell-edge plate, and it is from a portrait by Waldo, engraved by D. Edwin and published in the *Analectic Magazine* in December 1813. An example is in the Smithsonian Institution.

161 · Earthenwares and Stonewares

134

Pike, Zebulon Montgomery. Illustrated on a jug, not of Davenport manufacture, in Larsen, *op. cit.*, Nos. 629 and 782. This print is recorded on three different sizes of plate and in both black and blue prints on marked Davenport pieces. Examples are in the Smithsonian Institution, Washington (Plate 134). Pike was a general in the American army and an explorer and is said to have 'sighted' Pike's Peak, the famous mountain in Colorado, and to have explored as far as the Rio Grande. In the war of 1812 he was killed whilst leading the forces that captured York (Toronto) in Canada. His portrait is by Thomas Cimbrede, engraved by the artist and published in *Analectic Magazine* in 1814.

We can only speculate as to how the Davenport firm came to acquire and use the three portraits of the American heroes. What is perhaps even more surprising is that Britain's enemies should have been portrayed so heroically so soon after the end of hostilities – these pieces probably date from *c*.1815. It is well known that Wedgwood and many other potters of an earlier generation sympathized with the American revolutionaries, and doubtless such friendly feelings continued despite the 1812 dispute. And with John Davenport at the helm, so to speak, business was business. If the Americans wanted prints of their heroes, he would be happy to oblige – many of his contemporaries did likewise. It is however just possible that the Davenport plates were exported undecorated and printed in America.

Scotts Illustrations. This famous Davenport series has been much illustrated, most notably by Martin Pulver in *Antique Collecting*, March 1986. Mr Pulver illustrates the following scenes:

The Bride of Lammermoor 1. This is also illustrated in Dict. p. 55 and Williams 520.

The Bride of Lammermoor 2 (incorrectly titled on the back as Guy Mannering). Also illustrated in Dict. p. 325 where rightly the printed title is queried.

Guy Mannering. Also Dict. p. 166. A correct scene from the book.

Heart of Midlothian. Also Dict. p. 172.

Waverley. Also Dict. p. 395, where the illustration is of a plate with a printed Royal Arms mark with IRONSTONE below and the initial W and D on either side. The piece had the normal Davenport impressed mark and an indistinct date of 1860. The Royal Arms and IRONSTONE mark is rare, but a very similar version can be partly seen on the factory site shard in Plate 24. My 1972 book, Plate 36, showed a plate printed in two colours, the border green and the centre blue.

Legend of Montrose. See also Coysh 2 Pl. 23, Williams 519, and Plate 135.

134. Shell-edge plate printed with a portrait of 'General (Zebulon Montgomery) Pike'. Diameter 9½in. Mark E 5. (Smithsonian Institution, Washington)

Old Mortality. A rare print not previously published.

Rob Roy. See Also Dict. p. 304.

These wares have been found printed in various colours with date marks ranging from 1836 to at least 1860. They are also commonly found with the additional marks (see below) of the American importers Henderson & Gaines, 45, Canal Street, New Orleans; and also with the allied marks of Hill & Henderson and Henderson, Lawton & Co. (see pp. 38–9).

The derivation of the various scenes is given in the *Dictionary* and in Mr Pulver's article but basically they are taken from prints by Robert Cadell in the Magnum Opus edition of Scott's works published 1829–33. They must have been a very popular series, though their use, so far recorded, seems exclusively confined to dinner wares. Undoubtedly there are other scenes to be discovered. Illustrated here is the 'Legend of Montrose' scene which we principally show for the very characteristic and readily identifiable border pattern which is common to the whole series.

View on the Thames (A). *Transactions of the English Ceramic Circle* 12 Pt 2, 1985, Pl. 96c & d and FOB 54, pp. 6–7. This very fascinating view of the South Bank of the Thames is recorded on an earthenware wash bowl in the Lockett collection; a large octagonal stone china meat dish with well and tree moulding, and on a stone china plate in the Iwass collection. All the recorded prints are in blue. The wash bowl is date-marked for 1836.

FOB 54 records that the owner of the meat dish also possessed the source print which is titled 'View on the Thames' drawn by F. C. Turner, engraved by George Hunt and published 30 December 1836 (Davenport were quick off the mark!) by J. Moore of St Martin's Lane. The visible buildings are the now-demolished Shot Tower, Fowler's Iron Works, and the Old Red Lion Brewery, the flag on which reads GODINGS ALE BREWERY. Other buildings on both pots and print are named: J C STALL-SCHMIDT; MOORES MAHOGANY TIMBER MERCHANT; and PEACHE, but these and other details are not as clearly visible on the pots as they are in the original print on paper. This is a remarkable piece of historical evidence depicting the area now occupied by the Royal Festival Hall. The quality of the print on my bowl is very good and I feel confident that other items with this print will be discovered. I cannot imagine that it is a one-off service or for the Lion Brewery exclusively. The central scene only is shown in Plate 136.

We have noted several times that wares were printed *underglaze* in colours other than blue. However, it is worth noting also that some patterns appear to have been printed in

135. Plate printed in blue with 'The Legend of Montrose'. Diameter 9½in. Mark E 6 (for 1860?, rather indistinct) and the printed 'Scotts Illustrations' cartouche. (Lockett Collection)

163 · Earthenwares and Stonewares

colours other than blue with an overglaze print. This would seem to be an attempt to vary the finished appearance of wares at a date prior to that quoted earlier of c.1828 for the general introduction of underglaze printing in colours other than blue. The pattern Bisham Abbey is quite well known on wares printed in a pucey-pink and it is generally accepted that these pieces are pre-1828. Close examination of the wares is not conclusive, but it seems probable that the print was applied over the glaze. This is certainly the case with a very rare plate in the Lockett collection which is of the chalcedony body and which is printed over the glaze with an orange coloured transfer – a most unusual combination. A similar overglaze print can be seen on the teapot illustrated as Plate 150.

Another transfer printed item of great rarity is in the Cleaver collection. Mr Cleaver has a pair of tureens, for cream and sugar, complete with ladles, transfer printed underglaze in blue with a most unusual floral/geometric pattern and finished overglaze in pale peach, red, and black enamel (Plate 137). These are truly stunning items and it is really not possible to classify them under any of the headings we have adopted above. They make a suitably dramatic final illustration in this particular section.

We are conscious that in every category this list cannot be called definitive. New patterns are constantly being discovered, but we have tried to make it as comprehensive as possible within the limitations of present knowledge and the collections to which we have had access. The *Supplement* to the Coysh and Henrywood Dictionary is eagerly awaited (due 1989). It is possible that it will contain patterns not recorded here, particularly extensions of known series and new floral patterns. Let us hope that pattern

136. Close-up of the centre of a wash bowl printed in blue with 'View on the Thames'. (Lockett Collection)

137. Dessert service tureen, printed in blue and enamelled overglaze in a creamy peach, red and black. Ht 6½in. Mark E 2. (Alan Cleaver Collection)

names will be consistent between the two publications, otherwise confusion will be worse compounded!

Multicoloured Printed Wares and Flown Blue

While the vast majority of underglaze printed earthenware was in cobalt blue at the Davenport factories especially, several other colours were employed from time to time, chiefly after about 1835 as the manufacturers sought novelty. Such colours were transferred in the normal manner as has been previously described, the main difficulty being in the preparation of the colours and of the oil with which they were mixed. Such underglaze colours had to withstand and mature at a higher firing temperature than overglaze enamel colours.

The successful introduction of underglaze printing in colours other than blue was to lead to experiments to print in more than one colour; to endeavour to emulate a hand-painted pattern. For very many years various overglaze printed designs or outlines had been coloured in by hand but this was a time-consuming process and unless neatly carried out was largely unsatisfactory.

Several pottery firms in the mid 1830s or early 1840s were striving to print entirely multicolour designs. As a first step some firms including Davenports, W. Ridgway, and Enoch Wood & Sons used two different engraved copper plates. One would be charged with a given colour and applied to the centre of a plate or other article while the border design was transferred in, say, blue. The colours could be changed or reversed so that the central design was in blue and the border in perhaps green. The effect was novel and in most cases quite successful for the price required for such products. Davenports employed such two colour printed designs into at least the 1860s, sometimes using totally unrelated border and central prints!

In one such case the border design is printed in a pale green and the centre is printed in blue. The advantage of this simple trick was that existing copper plates could be used to introduce a novel variation. Little extra trouble or cost was involved as the border had always been applied separately: all that was needed now was that the two copper plates or parts thereof were charged with different colours. One example bears as part of the impressed name-mark the number 36 signifying that the plate was potted in 1836. This plate is, however, not necessarily the first one decorated in this style but the process was probably in use from the period 1835–8 onwards. Examples of this two-colour printing are surprisingly rare considering that it was used on large dinner sevices and probably also dessert services. The technique was applied mainly to earthenwares and much was exported (Lockett, 1972, Plate 36).

In connection with these two colour printed wares it has been suggested elsewhere that two separate firings would have been required, one for each colour. Our non-expert opinion is that this would not have been needed. It would have been the colour mixer's job to produce colours and oils that matured at much the same temperature, so saving one or more extra firings and the subsequent cost. The firing process was not only hazardous but was costly in time, labour, and coal. Josiah Wedgwood had in the previous century testified that it took ten tons of coal to fire one ton of earthenware!

It is certainly true that later in the nineteenth century the manufacturers were able to fire once the many underglaze printed colours then in use. Geoffrey Godden has, for example, an earthenware platter which has been used as a firing trial for twenty printed scraps all of different colours. These colours are named on the reverse Canton light blue, Claret, Brown, Chocolate, Plum, French Green, Grey, etc. we think all these colours were 'hardened on' in one fire and that they were subsequently fired once again after glazing in the 'glost kiln' - once not twenty times! The essays in the Pratt–Austin style of multicolour printing from 1851 onwards were also fired once.

This two-colour (border and central design) printing was soon superseded at the Davenport factories by a system relatively new to ceramics but not to printing in general. However, for a time probably both the old two-plate method and the new were in use at the same period. This is not to say that the use of two or more separate copper plates ceased at all factories, several continued to use this method up to quite recent times.

In the new colour printing process existing copper plates could still be used although some new ones were, no doubt, especially engraved for new multicolour printed patterns. This type of printing was practised at Davenport up to at least 1844 but had seemingly been practised elsewhere for a short period in about 1760.

In this novel technique a single engraved copper plate was charged with different colours, blue, two tones of green, and black according to the subject depicted in each area – blue for the sky, green for grass, etc. A plate for such a service is shown in Colour Plate XII. This bears a clear impressed Davenport name-mark, with the year number 35 for 1835 incorporated as part of a basic mark. Other parts of this dinner service are shown by Geoffrey Godden as Colour Plate V of his *Illustrated Encyclopaedia of British Pottery and Porcelain*. This service is important because the original account has been preserved (Plate 138), and from this we learn that the retail price for a 'Coloured Muleteer' dinner set for twelve persons was seven guineas, a price that included large soup tureens, smaller sauce tureens, covered vegetable dishes, large meat dishes and a range of at least thirty-six plates. The retail price of the large soup plates was 7d each, the smaller cheese plates were 5d. The factory price of these was probably little more than half these amounts. Here lies the secret of commercial success, a series of intricate colourful designs that could be mass-produced at low cost without the need to employ first-rate relatively well-paid porcelain painters decorating the less expensive earthenware tablewares. The basic Davenport 'Muleteer' pattern also occurs printed only in underglaze blue and such examples, no doubt, predate the 'Coloured Muleteer' version. The single colour blue version would also have been cheaper in price than the multicoloured services which are made up of two tones of green, blue, and the black outlines and dark shading.

We have just stated that this and other Davenport earthenwares were produced by charging a copper plate with different colours before the whole completely coloured design was transferred by paper on to the underglaze biscuit earthenware. It should be pointed out, however, that there are two schools of thought on the technique used. Some experienced and learned authorities are (or were) of the opinion that the method used was the little-known 'Pluck and Dust' technique.

In this case the copper plate would have been charged only with a slightly tinted thick oil. This would be transferred to the ware by paper in the normal way and the different parts of the design dusted over with powdered pigment to colour up the design. The basic system is much like Bat Printing except that paper is used instead of glue bats and the process is a hot one not cold printing. The 'Pluck and Dust' technique is well explained by David Drakard and Paul Holdway in *Spode Printed Ware* (1983), chapter 6.

We have examined the Godden examples closely, in particular the 'Coloured Muleteer' service with its many related designs, and I am firmly of the opinion that the service was produced from colour-charged copper plates not by the 'Pluck and Dust' process. The rather coarse engraved design is also what one would expect if this method of printing was employed. The engraving style is quite different to that which would have been used if oil was to be transferred - this permits a far finer engraving or etching of the copper plates. It should also be noted that in some cases including that of the 'Muleteer' the design is recorded printed in one colour (usually blue) only, and in this case the normal hot method would certainly have been employed. I believe the same copper plates were used for the new multicolour process, except that the plate was charged with more care and with three or four different colours.

The ceramic process which we have described is apparently well known in other non-ceramic printing circles. It is known by the French term *'à la poupée,'* which can be translated 'with the doll', the doll being the term used for the bundle of fabric used to charge the engraved copper plate, etc. with different colour inks. Mr Bamber Gascoigne in his excellent book *How to Identify Prints* (1986) states on his p. 26 that the technique was used for prints (stipple engraving, mezzotints, and aquatints) from the late eighteenth century onwards. He shows in colour (Plates 90–1 and in detail on his dust jacket) an *'à la poupée'* print of an elderly lady which was engraved in 1807.

It would, of course, have been comparatively easy to ink a copper plate etc. for transferring to paper, for the pigments do not need to be glazed and fired. This probably is the reason why the process was not adopted more generally to ceramics where thick oily pigments are required for underglaze printing. Still, the Davenport firm seems to have been reasonably successful, even if the technique was soon superseded or found to be too difficult and costly.

Returning again to ceramics, the 'Coloured Muleteer' design was really a series of related patterns: it is not a question of a single design but several going to make up the entire dinner service.

Apart from this dinner service design several others were treated in a similar way, ususally with attractive scenic designs such as Romantic Castles in the centre (Colour Plate XIII) printed in three or more colours, with an intricate underglaze blue border. These sets, or rather the remains of them that are now left to us, can be most attractive and they are very typical of their early Victorian period. Some of the scenic colour-printed dinner wares are shown in Plates 139–43 and Colour Plate XII. A single plate is in the Victoria & Albert Museum collection on display in the upstairs gallery (C415.1920) and another good example is on display at the Stoke-on-Trent City Museum. Other equally rare examples are floral in nature, such as the 'Indian Festoon' patterned plate show in Plate 144 which bears impressed year marks for 1836.

With these impressed year marks, it must always be borne in mind that these show only the year in which the blank plate was made. In this case it might have been potted on 1 January or on 31 December 1836, we have no way of telling. Also we cannot say if the plate was decorated within days, weeks, months, or even years of its manufacture. It should be understood that in the case of major firms they made large runs of plates, dishes, tureens, etc. and these remain in store rooms until orders were received for particular goods or patterns. Then the blanks were drawn from the store to be decorated. The potteries kept large undecorated stock but as little as possible of the costly finished ware. The impressed year marks then only show the earliest possible date that the piece could have been decorated and sold, not the latest. In most cases however, it is probable that the piece was completed in the same year, but there is no guarantee that this was the case.

It would appear that the Davenport firm produced a decorative range of these

138. Davenports & Co. printed bill head of 1840, with below the account for a colour printed dinner service with extra units. (Geoffrey Godden)

139

140

multicolour printed dinner wares, dessert services, and very rarely teawares in the mid or late 1830s and perhaps into the 1840s. The very rare teawares can be in a porcelain body rather than the usual earthenware. One such porcelain teapot has the unusual pattern mark 2/1001. Perhaps a special second series for this colour printing possibly started at 1000 or 1001. Our Longport firm was seemingly the only one to have used this method of charging a single copper plate to produce multicolour printed dinner and dessert services on a commecial scale, although other firms may have experimented with the process.

    It seems certain that the technique was time-consuming and therefore more expensive than simple one-colour printing. For in the normal way one thick colour is placed on the engraved copper plate and then forced into the identations with a special but large tool. With Davenport's system quite small areas had to be treated with different colours, a fiddly method at best. It has been suggest that the technique of charging the copper plate was much more complicated than that of simply rubbing in different colours.

168 · Earthenwares and Stonewares

141

142

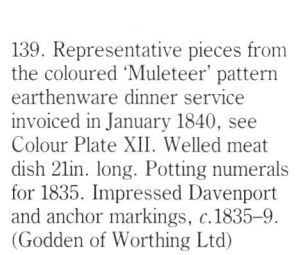

139. Representative pieces from the coloured 'Muleteer' pattern earthenware dinner service invoiced in January 1840, see Colour Plate XII. Welled meat dish 21in. long. Potting numerals for 1835. Impressed Davenport and anchor markings, c.1835–9. (Godden of Worthing Ltd)

140. Three multicolour printed plates from the large 'Romantic Castles' pattern service, see following Plates and Colour Plate XIII. Note the different designs on the various size plates. Diameter of soup plate (centre) 10½in. Impressed and printed Davenport marks, c.1835–40. (Godden of Worthing Ltd)

141. A vegetable dish and cover from the multicolour printed 'Romantic Castles' service shown in plates 140 and 142 and Colour Plate XIII. Dish 12¼in. long, c.1835–40. (Godden of Worthing Ltd)

142. A sauce-tureen with its stand and ladle all multicolour printed with typical Davenport 'Romantic Castles'. See also Plates 140–1 and Colour Plate XIII. Stand 9 × 7¼in., c.1835–40. (Godden of Worthing Ltd)

143. A marked Davenport dinner plate with multicolour printed centre but different border design to those previously illustrated. Diameter 10½in., c.1836. (Victoria & Albert Museum)

143

One authority has suggested that one colour was applied to the heated copper plate in the correct position, i.e. blue in the sky or water areas, and that this colour was then allowed to cool and coagulate before the surplus colour was cleaned from the surface of the copper. This was then reheated and another colour applied, and the whole process repeated for each colour.

This seems a very time-consuming process especially as the articles so

169 · Earthenwares and Stonewares

144

decorated were mainly dinner services with over a hundred articles in each. We cannot now say if this separate heating and cooling of the copper plate was necessary but we think not. The designs are in the main broadly engraved and the colours were applied to fairly large areas with seemingly little regard to keep the colour strictly within the correct area, and furthermore the colour applied to the pottery surface was that furthest in the recessed part of the engraving. This recessed pigment was well protected from any later movement of surplus pigment on the surface of the copper plate and we are of the opinion that the copper could well have been charged with the different colours in one operation, without the need to cool the copper plate after each colour was applied. We readily admit, however, that we have no first hand practical experience of the technique and no record seems to have survived to guide us.

Interesting as these Davenport essays in multicolour printing are, the system was soon superseded by an advanced technique which necessitated the engraving of a series of special copper plates, each one of which was to transfer a separate colour until the complete coloured picture had been built up on the unglazed object. By the time of the 1851 Exhibition this new technique had been mastered and wonderful examples were being displayed, mainly on the stand of Messrs F. & R. Pratt of Fenton. These Pratt exhibits were engraved by Jesse Austin, a designer and engraver who had been reputedly apprenticed to Davenports. Pratt & Co. and their main competitors Messrs T. J. & J. Mayer are mainly known for their decoration of meatpaste pot lids, but decorative desert services were also made. It would appear, however, that Pratt did not produce dinner services in this technique until a later period. It would seem that the cost of engraving the special sets of copper plates for such long services and the many designs and sizes of pattern required to complete such printed sets was prohibitive, bearing in mind the low cost of other earthenware services on the market. It will be remembered that Davenport used, initially at least, existing copper plates for their new style colour printed dinner services. The additional cost of the copper plates was therefore nil.

The late Cyril Williams-Wood, an authority on engraving and printing techniques, has written two articles which include mention of the Davenport multicolour printing process of charging a single copper plate with different pigments. These appeared in *Art & Antiques Magazine*, 22 November 1975, under the title 'Jessie Austin, Unsurpassed Master of the Transfer Print', and in *Collectors Guide*, July 1986, under the title 'Who Invented Polychrome Transfer Printing?' In the 1975 article he noted:

During the period 1835 to 1837 Davenports began to produce pieces decorated with prints in two colours, made from two separate copper plates, the impressions taken from

144. An impressed-marked Davenport dessert plate bearing a fine multicolour printed floral design, 'Indian Festoon'. Diameter 8½in. Impressed year numerals for 1836. (Godden of Worthing Ltd)

170 · Earthenwares and Stonewares

each being carefully registered on the ceramic article. This was a quite fundamental breakthrough in colour-printing of ceramics.

An early example dating from c.1835 is a pink and black dinner plate with a print in line and stipple. This was the work of Jesse Austin, and he first transferred by potters' tissue a print from the pink plate in the normal fashion, and when it had been dried he transferred on top a print in black from the master, or key plate. The result of this is that the buildings and flowers in the foreground have a pink tint, which the rest of the picture lacks. This proved to be not only a more versatile method than working from the single copper plate, but a very much quicker one.

In the City of Liverpool Museum is a Davenport plate with the pattern 'Geneva' printed in blue and black, with a green border on the condiments rim. This is back-dated 1836. [The Liverpool Museum authorities have been unable to trace this specimen up to the date of publication.]

It has not been uncommon in the early 19th century for two transfers in differing colours to be used on separate parts of one ceramic piece – such as a plate wth a black centre-picture and a blue or pink border on the condiments rim; but never before on a ceramic piece had one colour been superimposed on another as part of one picture. Whether this was the invention of Austin or of someone else in the Davenport factory is so far unknown. What is certain is that Austin developed the process and brought it to perfection – an achievement never equalled by anyone else.

We have been unable to trace any contemporary reference to the date (or year) of introduction of the so-called Pratt or Austin technique of multicolour printing by means of different copper plates, impressions from which were applied one on top of the other in perfect 'register.' The new manner of colour printing was certainly in use before 1847, the year often cited, as examples occur bearing the name-mark of Enoch Wood & Sons of Burslem, a firm which ceased trading in 1846. It can further be proved that the technique was being used before March 1845, for examples exist bearing the joint signatures of the Shelton (Hanley) engravers Alphonsus Toft and Jesse Austin. This partnership was dissolved on 25 February 1845, so such jointly signed copper plates must have been produced before this date. It is interesting to note that colour printed designs bearing the Toft–Austin joint signatures sometimes occur on pottery blanks seemingly potted in 1839, and the W. Smith & Co. impressed mark incorporates the year numeral 39. We cannot unfortunately be sure that the printed designs were added to the blanks in the year of their potting. Unfortunately, the overglaze marks added at the time of decoration do not bear a similar dating system. The impressed date marks were added especially to help control the chronological use of blanks in the store rooms.

The name of Jesse Austin is rightly and firmly linked with Pratt & Co. and with the story of pot-lids but it is relevant to give a very brief résumé of his career in this book. Jesse Austin was born at Longton in the Staffordshire Potteries on 5 February 1806, the youngest son of a family of twelve. He was apparently educated locally and was according to family tradition apprenticed to Davenports. If his apprenticeship was commenced at the age of fourteen and lasted for the normal term of seven years he would have been under training in the approximate period 1820–7, well before the multicolour printed designs we are discussing were introduced.

We are of the opinion that Jesse Austin probably remained with Davenports for many years after the apprenticeship was complete in or about 1827. At the end of his apprenticeship he would hardly have been fully trained and capable of setting up on his own account even if he was in a financial position to have done so. He most probably worked his way up the Davenport engraving department, being entrusted with more and more responsible tasks before he was able to design and complete his own printed subjects. His hand probably was at least partly responsible for the attractive Davenport printed designs of the late 1820s and early 1830s. He would not, however, have been by any means the sole engraver employed by this firm, as a quite large team must have been employed.

It is possible that Jesse Austin was responsible for the idea of charging the engraved copper plates with different colours to produce a multicoloured design. Certainly he would have seen the Davenport experiments in the technique and would have understood the difficulties and perhaps sought to introduce a more perfect method of production.

It should, however, be noted that as far as we know the Davenport firm did not proceed to use the new multi-copper plate technique. It is possible that this was introduced independently by Jesse Austin or by his early partner the little-known Alphonsus Toft, who may have also have been employed with Austin at the Davenport factory. On seeing the advantages of the new technique Austin (and Toft) perhaps decided to start their own engraving business and so, hopefully, make their fortunes.

We do not know when Jesse Austin left Davenports. He is listed as an 'artist and drawing master' at Hope Street, Shelton, in William White's Directory published in 1834. If this entry is taken to show that he was not then a mere factory-employed engraver, a quite tenable suggestion, it would mean that Austin was not in fact directly employed by Davenport at the time when their multicolour printed designs were being produced. He could, of course, have supplied the copper plates to the firm as an independent engraver. He was described as a 'Pottery Designer' in the 1841 census returns and was seemingly working under his own name in the summer of 1844 when he sent an example of his work, an earthenware plate bearing one of the 'Baronial Halls' series of prints, in this case Stow Hall, to the editor of the *Art-Union* magazine. Plates in this series sometimes bear the Design Registration device for the entry made on 15 August 1844, and some of the subjects bear Jesse Austin's signature, suggesting strongly that he was employed on his own account at this date. At about this period or soon afterwards Jesse Austin must have joined into partnership with Alphonsus Toft 'as engravers at Tinkersclough, Shelton Potteries.' Signed examples of true multicolour printing from two different copper plates bear the 'Toft & Austin' joint signature, but as previously stated the partnership was dissolved on 25 February 1845. Jesse Austin was later associated with F. & R. Pratt & Co. of Fenton.

We have in this chapter discussed the traditional printing methods and Davenport's designs and the rare multicoloured wares of the mid 1830s (which never fully superseded the traditional one-colour patterns) but we have still to discuss another puzzling technique. We here refer to the fuzzy or misty designs mainly of the 1840s which are known under the name 'Flown' or 'Flow' designs. They are puzzling on two accounts, when they were introduced and why they were (and are) so popular, especially in the important overseas markets.

As with the colour printing we have very little documentary evidence on the circumstances that led up to the introduction of the style. It may have been accidental, poorly fired 'seconds' or 'thirds' may originally have been shipped abroad at a low price and these caught the buyers' fancy on the account of their novelty and keen price! Soon the distinct misty printed designs were being especially ordered and made! This is merely a later theory but it is difficult to see what the wares were emulating or the reason for their mass production, if it were not to lower the basic price of the wares. It has been suggested elsewhere that these Flown or Flow-Blue designs were introduced to emulate the imported Chinese blue and white porcelains, but in our experience the blue Oriental examples are remarkable for the sharpness of the painting. The Chinese cobalt does not seem to run into the glaze, although on some nineteenth-century pieces the glaze is very thick and slightly bubbled giving a misty covering to the underglaze blue pattern.

Few British readers will know of these Flow-Blue wares for they are almost exclusively an export line. However, the technique and its merits or failure was discussed at some length in England at the period, an article in *Art-Union* magazine of June 1844 being the fourth part of a series of reviews on current ceramic productions. The editor made the following observations on this 'precious novelty'.

It would not be necessary to enter into any discussion of the merits of colour generally, had not our remarks in the former article on the present prevailing abomination, the 'floating blue,' or, as it is rather grandiloquently termed, the 'Kaolin fluescent wares,' induced the editor of the very able local paper published in the Potteries to enter on the defence of this precious novelty. Now, our first position is, that the effect is unnatural: no leaf, bird, beast, or flower is ever seen in such a light as to convey notion of its colour flowing away from it. The effect is very inaccurately described by the word 'floating,' which is sometimes given to the pattern instead of 'flowing,' a truly 'floating' pattern, such as is sometimes seen on Sèvres china, and particularly in one design, fresh in our memory, which represented water-plants in flower on the surface of a tranquil lake, may be exquisitely beautiful. But where are we to look for the archetype of a flowing pattern? The only place where we can find anything like it is in the wash-house, where the laundress squeezes the blue-bag over wet flannel, and amuses herself by giving a rude configuration to the discharged contents. The more perfect the flowing effect is produced the more preposterous is the ultimate result, because the more does it suggest the notion of the colour being in the course of being washed away.

This 'Kaolin fluescence,' like its kindred abomination in calico-printing, the immortal Diorama pattern, was discovered by accident, and being, a novelty, it took amazingly. Some patroness of fashion, indulging untrained caprice, declared that it was beautiful; and her opinion became as far removed beyond appeal as the laws of the Medes and the Persians. The manufacturers were forced into the adoption of the barbarism much against their will; for the colouring matter of the blue is costly, and the flow, being produced during the process of firing, is far from being certain in production. In fact, we have heard of instances in which manufacturers have lost from one-third to one-half of the contents of the oven from the failure of the flow. Consumers of course, must pay something additional for the lottery of chances in this costly ugliness; we wish it were possible to charge them an extra per centage for the indulgence of bad taste. The only thing that can be said in favour of this preposterous absurdity is, that it is difficult of production, and, as Doctor Johnson said in a similar case, it would be a blessing if it were so difficult as to be impossible.

Bad as is the style itself, the patterns originating from it are infinitely worse: all the absurdities of the Chinese, all the monsters of heraldry, all the incomprehensibilities of the Aztec paintings, are tame and sober in comparison with the brood of prodigies claiming the parentage of Kaolin fluescence.

Seemingly, however, the public in general appears to have liked these Flow-Blue printed earthenwares, for they form a quite large part of the Davenport output during the approximate period 1840–60. This mass production of Flow-Blue useful wares, usually dinner wares, is by no means limited to our factory: it was a standard production of most British potteries which catered for the export markets, and can rarely also be found on a china body. We have written Flow-Blue but the technique was by no means confined to underglaze blue printed designs. The treatment could be and was used, to a lesser degree, with most other underglaze colours.

The very description could also vary considerably, as could the recipes for the different preparation which included the flowing effect. 'Flow Powder', 'Flow', 'Flow Blue', 'Flown Blue', were all used and the official catalogue of the 1851 Exhibition used the description 'Flowered' seemingly for these wares – as 'Flowered Blue Chusan'. This could, however, have been a repeated error on the part of the compiler or by the typesetters who perhaps did not understand the term Flow-Blue. As already noted, the editor of the *Art-Union* used the term 'Kaolin fluescent ware'.

Various recipes for mixtures to induce the flowing of the blue into the glaze in a halo-like effect have been published. Flown Blue was mentioned as a 'recent introduction'

145

in connection with 'cheaper processes' in William Evans's *Art and History of the Potting Industry* (1846). His contemporary comments are of great interest:

I am fully aware, that the question with potting manufacturers, is not so much the advancement of the art, as the discovery of cheaper processes and cheaper materials, by which the present quality of manufacture can be wrought.

To this end the enquiry of nearly all practical potters is now directed. The flow, for blue, although of recent introduction, has undergone several changes. That, now in use by W. Ridgway, Esq., is considered to be the best. Instead of washing, or placing the flow in the saggars, it is introduced in the glaze; and a great saving of expense is thereby secured.

The flows have been sold, and resold at exorbitant prices, since first introduced in the potting manufacture. Those recipes were sold, on two succesive occasions, for £100 each time, and are now prized by the Messrs. Boyle, Dimmock and Meigh, as the best in use.

The technique was probably first produced several years before 1846, certainly it was being marketed in 1844. We have observed Davenport examples with year marks within the 1844–60 period.

An undated manuscript recipe book in the Godden Reference Library includes several mixtures. These were probably gathered from several different sources and it is assumed that the technique was widely understood, not a secret kept by one manufacturer only. Unfortunately we have no record of who introduced the flown blue method or at which factory it was first produced. Davenports was certainly a large manufacturer and several popular printed patterns are recorded as Davenport essays in this style. The Davenport basic underglazed printed designs include Amoy, Cornice, Cuba, Cyprus, Griffin, Ideal, Japan, Las Palmas Canaria, Montilla, Spanish Rose, Vine, and Watteau.

The recipes in the Godden book include:

Flow Powder for flowing blue.
10lbs Whiting
4lbs Red Lead
2lbs Salt.

Flow Powder for Blue.
10lbs Whiting
6lbs White Lead
2lbs Chloride of Lead.

145. Plate printed in flown blue with the 'Amoy' pattern. Diameter 10½in. Mark E 6 (for 1844) and pattern name cartouche. (Lockett Collection)

Flow for Mulberry.
2lbs Salt
1lb Nitre
1lb Red Lead.

    In using mix it with the saggar wash. The Wash is – 3 [parts?] Red Lead. 1 [part?] Stone.

Flow for Mulberry.
2½lbs Whiting
1lb Chloride Lead.

Most manufacturers probably had their own special recipes for the Flow Powder, to suit their own glazes or firing temperatures.

    The reader will find interesting information on the Flown technique and the patterns and their manufacturers in American reference books such as those written by Petra Williams. These specialist books include *Flow Blue China* I (1971), *Flow Blue China* II (1973) and *Flow Blue China and Mulberry Ware* (1975). These three titles were published by Fountain House East, PO Box 99298, Jeffersontown, Kentucky 40299, USA. We also recommend Mary Frank Gaston's book *The Collectors Encyclopaedia of Flow Blue China* (Collectors Books, Paducah, Kentucky, 1983). This American authority makes the interesting suggestion that the muzzy flown effect was first introduced in an effort to hide the joint marks in printed border designs.

    Davenport was certainly sending blue-printed Flown-type dinner services to India in the late 1840s, as evidence by the letter quoted on p. 188.

16 Miscellaneous and Later Earthenwares

The wares which will be discussed in this section are, in general, those which were produced after the retirement of John Davenport from active management c.1838. This is a purely arbitrary date and there is inevitably a great deal of overlap. Some pieces similar to those illustrated in this section were produced well before the mid 1830s, other wares which we have already noted in earlier sections, especially some of the printed patterns, continued to be manufactured almost to the end of the factory's life.

A case in point is of earthenwares decorated with lustre, which seems to have been used in one form or another for at least eighty years. The researches of Diana Darlington, using the 1807 Royal order as a starting point, seem to indicate that by that early date the use of lustre was well developed at Longport. In a lecture to the Northern Ceramic Society which will be published in Vol. 7 of the Society's *Journal* (December 1989) Miss Darlington drew attention to the various items in the Royal order which mentioned lustre, for example '2 Antique Jarrs Painted Lustre Landscapes', '1 Jarr Etch'd Lace borders in Lustre &c.', '2 Jugs & Covers Lustre Landscapes &c.' Using this documentary information, two teapots were illustrated, and though both were unmarked, they had a reasonable claim to be considered as Davenport. Confirmation of this was soon forthcoming as an earthenware cream jug decorated with a very attractive silver lustre pattern, in exactly the same form as the chalcedony one shown in Plate 54, appeared in a saleroom and subsequently at an antique Fair in London. So far no *marked* examples of early Davenport earthenware teawares decorated with silver lustre have been reported, but here clearly is a field for further research.

Other marked examples of silver lustre are rare. In my 1972 book, attention was drawn to the huge jug in the Liverpool Museum Collection. This massive piece, 25in. high and 65in. in circumference, was exhibited at the Blackburn Exhibition in 1978 where it drew much comment. It is inscribed 'Eyo Archibong Esquire'. The Museum card reads, 'Silver lustre jug, manufactured by Davenport for an African chief Eyo Archibong, Calibar. This is one of a dozen made to the order of the Chief to store rum.' It was presented to the Museum in 1912. Apart from the missing eleven jugs of Chief Archibong, there must be many similar, but unmarked Davenport silver lustre jugs, 'Jarrs', and probably teawares lurking unrecognized in private and public collections.

The wares just discussed above have all been items decorated with silver lustre (note that it would strictly be more correct to term this platinum lustre). Several other kinds of lustre ware, usually of a later date than those just mentioned are found more frequently. The most common is the use of pink lustre to provide colourful decoration: it occurs on both earthenware and porcelain, but we are only concerned with the former here.

It is not easy to date the introduction of this type of decoration, which was of course common in the industry well before the 1820s. (Details of the development of lustre may be found in Una des Fontaines, *Wedgwood Fairyland Lustre* (1975) and in W. D. John and Warren Baker, *Old English Lustre Pottery* (1951). The technicalities need not detain us here.) The best clue we have is the frequent use of pink lustre as part of the decoration of teawares carrying pattern number 701, the introduction of which one would date to c.1820. The three examples illustrated here are all later than this.

The earliest use of pink lustre we have recorded was reported by Diana Darlington at a major London Fair some years ago. On offer were two quintal flower horns with a very striking and accomplished all-over pink lustre resist floral pattern. They bore the lower case impressed mark E 2 and would seem to date from c.1810–20. But for the presence of the mark it is unlikely that anyone would have thought of attributing the

146. Representative items from a miniature earthenware tea service, decorated with enamel colours and pink lustre. Teapot ht 4in. Mark E 6 (for 1844 or 1848). (Geoffrey Godden, chinaman)

147. Earthenware plate decorated with a simple landscape in pink lustre. Diameter 10in. Mark E 6 (for 1844). (Lockett Collection)

148. Earthenware teapot decorated with lustre pattern 850. Ht 8¼in. Mark E 6 (indistinctly for 1847?). (Godden of Worthing Ltd)

176 · Earthenwares and Stonewares

146

147
148

pieces to Davenport. The wares are now apparently in an American collection. Doubtless other surprises await the observant.

Plate 146 shows examples from a small or miniature tea service decorated with pattern 701 in enamel colours and pink lustre. The piece is indistinctly date-marked for 1848 or 1844. The pink lustre was frequently used with small or miniature items. A more unusual form of decoration can be seen in Plate 147. This attractive if somewhat skimpy landscape is painted entirely in pink lustre. The piece is date-marked for 1844, somewhat later than one might have expected. The full size teapot on the other hand in Plate 148 is

177 · Earthenwares and Stonewares

also lustre decorated and has a pattern number of 850. The date mark though indistinct appears to be 1847. A further example may be quoted. In the Blackburn Exhibition a tea bowl and saucer with a very simple pink lustre design was decorated in pattern 896, but the body was impressed with a potting date of 1836. Perhaps all we can sensibly conclude from these apparently conflicting fragments of evidence is that the relatively few recorded pink lustre patterns on teaware remained popular for many years.

At least two further types of lustre decoration may be found on Davenport wares. Plate 149 is of a cup and saucer, cleanly printed in black with the 'Nightingale' pattern. The whole piece has then been washed over in a thin film of pink lustre, which one must admit is very effective, though this cannot be seen in a black and white photograph. The dating of this is problematical. The 'Etruscan' shaped cup is of the 1820s, the print in the style of the late 1830s and 40s. A second example of this technique of covering a print with a lustre wash can be seen on the attractive teapot in Plate 150. The charming print would seem to be in the same series as the 'Swiss Pastime' scene shown in Plate 177.

We know of no examples of marked Davenport with the popular copper lustre, which must have been used by scores of potteries for the innumerable jugs which used to decorate every mantelshelf. It would be surprising if Davenport were not in this market.

149. Small earthenware cup and saucer, 'Etruscan' shape, printed in black with the 'Nightingale' pattern (so marked in cartouche on reverse) and covered all over with a pink lustre. Diameter 4½in. Mark E 5 and pattern name, *c.*1830+. (Alan Cleaver Collection)

150. Earthenware teapot printed with a variant of the 'Swiss Pastime' pattern, washed over with a film of pale pink lustre. Ht 5½in. Mark E 8A. (Courtesy Mrs Gail Finney)

178 · Earthenwares and Stonewares

151. Group of chalk body wares decorated with an enamelled pattern of pink fronds and green trefoil leaves. Spill vase: Ht 4in. Mark E 5. Dish: 10×7¾in. Mark E 6 (for 1836). Jug: Ht 4½in. Mark E 5. (Lockett Collection)

However, marked copper lustre of any make is extremely rare and once more, it may well be that Davenport copper lustre could be revealed by a close examination of the shapes of unidentified wares.

The last type of lustre decoration to be discussed seems only to be found on relatively late wares. This is the nacreous or mother of pearl lustre. This may not be its correct name technically, but the effect of the lustre wash over the printed and/or enamelled pattern is to give a thin metallic sheen with very much the colour range of mother-of-pearl or even of petrol lying on water. The use of this film lustre was quite widespread on many Davenport patterns. It can be seen to good effect in Colour Plate XIV where both jugs have parts of the pattern finished in lustre. The patterns 'Ivy Wreaths', 'Ceres', 'Whampoa', 'Hop', 'Acanthus', and several others have been noted with this treatment, but one suspects that there are very many more.

If we turn from lustred wares, which cover almost the entire factory history, to some of the other finishes, we encounter a slightly shorter life span for most of them. In the letter quoted earlier on p. 34 (Foxley, 74: 13 August 1835) Victor Pontigny writing to Henry Davenport noted: 'I have been trying to persuade the folks at Genoa that we are now making CC [cream colour] quite equal to Wedgwood, & have obtained a trial – see order herewith – pray let it be very white and *light* & well made – with a little pains we shall get a footing in the market...'

The ware that Pontigny was describing hardly sounds like our idea of creamware, but it does closely resemble the body which the Bramelds of the Swinton Pottery called 'chalk body'. Plate 151 shows a group of objects made in the very white-bodied earthenware simply decorated with a shamrock-like pattern. This very white ware seems to have been used for a variety of objects and one commonly sees miniature tewares in this body (see *Davenport Pottery & Porcelain,* Plate 53 right, for an example). More ordinary tablewares are also known, such as the broth bowl and stand shown in Plate 152. The enamelled pattern on this bowl, 376, occurs on a miniature cup and saucer date-marked 1836. Somewhat rarer are items decorated as the spill vase in Plate 153 with on-glaze bat prints of scenes of Yarmouth. A coffee can similarly decorated with 'Yarmouth Bridge' is illustrated on the coloured Frontispiece of *Davenport Pottery & Porcelain.* Curiously, this is marked with the brown strap mark (P 8) normally associated with porcelain, yet another example to indicate that we should exercise great caution

179 · Earthenwares and Stonewares

when we try to use marks for dating, authentication, and attribution purposes. There is a considerable element of inconsistency and unreliability about Davenport marks. One would imagine that other resorts were featured in this way, but though such scenes are common on porcelain of the 1850s and 1860s, I can only recall having seen Yarmouth on earthenwares, and then, of course, of an earlier date. The collector will not easily mistake this white-bodied ware: it is both very clear white and very light in weight.

Moving from white to green glazed ware, one again finds Davenport following the renewed fashion for this finish which is evident in the 1820–60 period. Brameld, Ridgway, the Don Pottery, Wedgwood, and other firms made mainly dessert wares with moulded detail and a fresh, sparkling green glaze. For some reason collectors seem to shun these green monochrome pieces, preferring the multicoloured delights of majolica, a type of ware, incidentally, of which there is no record of Davenport having produced. Three examples of green glazed ware are illustrated in Plates 154–6. The plate and oval dish with twig handles and vine and grape moulding are probably from the same basic service design. The oval dish with overlapping leaves would be accompanied by plates of a similar design. These pieces are not uncommon, but no particular study seems to have

152. Broth bowl and stand in white (chalk body) earthenware decorated with pattern 376. Ht 5½in. Mark E 5, *c.*1830. (Courtesy City Museum & Art Gallery, Stoke-on-Trent)

153. Spill vase in chalk body ware. Bat-printed with a named scene of 'Pier and Roads Gt. Yarmouth'. Ht 3½in. Mark E 5. (Lockett Collection)

180 · Earthenwares and Stonewares

154. Moulded green glaze plate. Diameter 7¼in. Mark E 5. (Lockett Collection)

155. Green glazed dessert dish. 10×8½in. Mark E 5, c.1830–50. (A. E. S. Blyth Collection)

156. Green glazed dessert dish with moulded leaf design. 11×8¼in. Mark E 6 (for 1856). (B. M. & A. C. Walters Collection)

been made of them, and once more further research could well reveal an extended range of Davenport designs and shapes.

Moving to even darker wares, the semi-matt black, and painted earthenwares such as the three teapots illustrated in Plates 157–8, form a very interesting class. Most of the group seem to have been decorated with Japanese-style floral studies in bright enamel colours as on the teapots, but Chinese figure subjects and even dragons are also met with quite frequently. This is a type of pottery which people either truly detest – some find it funereal – or admire overmuch, often ignoring the obvious defects of rather crude enamelling which can spoil many examples. The range of items made in this finish is very large. Teawares preponderate, but as the collection in the Weston Park Museum, Sheffield reveals, coffee pots, plates, jugs, footed bowls, candlesticks, spill vases, and items from toilet sets were all part of the repertoire. A good collection of these wares was assembled by Cherry Gray for the Blackburn Exhibition in 1978, details of which can be found in the catalogue (item 122). The marks found are usually the single printed word DAVENPORT in blue or black (E 8A) with more rarely an impressed mark. Marks with readable dates are rare, though 1856 has been reported on several items.

157. Teapot with matt black ground and enamelled flower sprays. Ht 4in. Mark E 8A. (B. M. & A. C. Walters Collection)

158. Two drum-shaped, black ground and enamelled teapots. Left: Ht 1¾in. Unmarked. (Hacking Collection). Right: Ht 4½in. Mark E 8A (knob restored). (B. M. & A. C. Walters Collection)

Remaining with somewhat colourful wares, we turn to Colour Plate XV, where on the left can be seen a plate decorated in what is usually termed 'peasant enamels'. These are wares painted with a restricted palette in which most of the colours are underglaze (as in the so-called 'Pratt wares'), supported by some on-glaze colours, such as green where appropriate. The items so decorated are by no means sophisticated, but exhibit a pleasing naivety. Once again we have a type of ware which seems to have enjoyed a long life. The plate illustrated has a date mark for 1836. A pint mug with similar bold foliage and the words 'Success to Berbice' (a commercial venture in British Guiana we understand) would appear to date from the 1850s, and the saucer accompanying the miniature tea bowls in Plate 159 has the impressed date mark for 1867. These wares are not common, and always seem to be much later than one would imagine. It may well be that they were manufactured for an unsophisticated market: possibly most were exported, but they are rare, disarmingly attractive, and worth a place in any representative collection of Davenport.

In chapter 10 we wrote of the coloured-bodied wares produced in the 1800–25 period. The factory continued to make certain kinds of coloured-body wares for many years. Plate 160 shows a fine large jug of really rococo shape which is in a drabware body

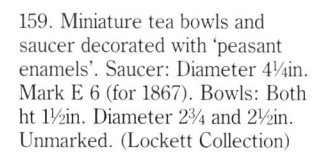

159. Miniature tea bowls and saucer decorated with 'peasant enamels'. Saucer: Diameter 4¼in. Mark E 6 (for 1867). Bowls: Both ht 1½in. Diameter 2¾ and 2½in. Unmarked. (Lockett Collection)

160. Large drabware jug with a lustre decoration and printed with the 'Muleteer' pattern. Extravagant rococo outlines. Mark E 5, c.1835–40. (Iwass Collection)

183 · Earthenwares and Stonewares

with additional lustre decoration. This is printed with the 'Muleteer' pattern. Other wares with a similarly stained body colour, especially blue, have been noted, mostly with additional decoration in the form of prints. These pieces are quite rare and date from the 1830s onwards.

Whilst still pursuing the theme of bright, bold, and colourful items the three Davenport Toby jugs shown in Plate 161 are worthy of attention. Such pieces are not uncommon, though there is considerable variation in the enamel colours applied to decorate the jugs. The coloured frontispiece of *Davenport Pottery & Porcelain* illustrates two such variants, and there is a good range of colour on the examples shown here. The model seems to be standard, what Toby jug buffs refer to as the 'Ordinary' Toby. Davenport Tobies do have one distinction, as almost uniquely amongst models of this period they carry the factory name. According to Vic Schuler in his book *British Toby Jugs* (1986) '95 per cent of all early Tobies do not have any marks on them.' Most jugs carry the mark E 5, but several dated examples are recorded. All seem to be from the 1830s with 1836 the most frequent date. It would be surprising if production began before 1830 and continued after 1848.

A much rarer Davenport model is that known as 'Drunken Sal'. Plate 162 shows a fine example of this figure which according to Mr Schuler is 'probably only made by Davenport'. He illustrates a differently decorated model on p. 90 of his book. When these pieces are marked they too carry date stamps indicating manufacture in the 1830s. This splendid large female Toby really is an unusual departure for Davenport, and the fact that it depicts a woman, that it is unusually large, and is marked, makes it a prime target for Toby jug collectors. It is rarely seen in collections of purely Davenport wares. An example sold at Sotheby's in November 1988 realised £1265, at least four times the price of a male Davenport Toby.

Even rarer still is a male Toby which depicts a red-faced toper with his mouth agape and large staring eyes, looking to his left and clutching in his raised hands a jug of foaming ale. The lip of the jug is level with his right cheek. He is wearing a very distinctive four-cornered hat, as opposed to the usual tricorn. This version is recorded by Mr Schuler as the 'Four Cornered Hat Toby' and is illustrated on p. 40 of his book. The only other example noted is somewhat differently decorated and was sold by Sotheby's Chester in 1980. Its present whereabouts is unknown. Fortunately the catalogue records the impressed date of 1840.

Mention has already been made of certain wares which, though from the shape

161. A group of three enamel-decorated Toby jugs. Ht 9½in. All marked E 5. (Spencers of Retford)

162. A 'Drunken Sal' Toby jug enamelled in colours. Ht 12in. Mark E 5. (Sotheby's)

184 · Earthenwares and Stonewares

163. Dessert dish with brown ground colour, sombrely but strikingly painted in brown, green, orange, yellow, black and white with a variety of leaves. 9¼ × 7½in. Mark E2. (Lockett Collection)

164. Pierced pearlware dessert basket, with printed and enamelled pattern, heavily gilded, bearing a label, 'Purchased at Lord Rosemead's sale Jan. 28/98', and in pencil '£25'. Overall length 10in. Mark E 2. (Hacking Collection)

and mark appear to date from an early period, carry decoration which on stylistic grounds it is difficult to associate with the period of potting. Two examples are illustrated. Plate 163 shows a dessert service dish of a standard form for the 1800–20 period. It bears an impressed lower case mark E 2. When first this was shown to various 'experts' it was pronounced Victorian and dates were mentioned in the 1870s. Other similar pieces have since come to light, including a pierced dessert stand in the Diana Darlington collection of the common form seen in Plate 47, and tureens in the familiar shape of Colour Plate III. Could these shapes have been in 'Biscuit Warehouse' for the best part of fifty years and then have been decorated? Personally, I think not. These leaf decorated pieces seem to have a natural affinity with other examples from the 1800–20 period which are illustrated in the creamware and pearlware section. Plate 164 shows an even more puzzling piece. Again the shape is the standard one for 1800–20. The glaze on this piece is somewhat crazed and looks oddly thick and very 'pearly'. It is the decoration however which is most mystifying. The central scroll is printed and enamelled over. The whole idea of such a scroll seems typical of the 1870s and the cult of Japan which was then fashionable. Personally, I cannot recall anything similar from the pre-1820 period. The rim decoration too is baffling. It is exceptionally well done in gilding. The shells too on the central painting are very well managed. How shall we date this piece? Shape and mark indicate very clearly a pre-1820 date, unless, perish the thought, mark E 2, the lower case mark, continued to be used throughout the factory's life! If we leave out this last suggestion then we have a pre-1820 shape with a decoration which the present writer feels is of a much later date. But is it feasible for the basket to have remained undamaged and undecorated for at least fifty years? There may be wares from other factories with a similar type of decoration which can very positively be dated to the pre-1820 period. That might settle the issue. Until then my own instincts favour a later rather than an earlier date for this piece. Is it perhaps an example of the use of an old mould and stamp long after they had passed from normal use? After all it is unlikely, to say the least, that on 1 January 1820 a manager would go round the factory and confiscate every lower case metal impress stamp! Sometimes we expect too much precision from the potters whose working conditions we have already examined. Would they be too bothered if the odd item was marked with an out-of-date stamp? They had problems of far greater immediacy than that. This is something of a hobby-horse of mine, but we do seem to expect the most minute scientific accuracy from often illiterate, half-starved, or sometimes two-thirds drunken workmen. They made their pots to satisfy their immediate bosses so that they would not be punished and could still draw their wages. They could never have envisaged the earnest discussions in which twentieth-century collectors and historians become involved over the minutiae of their daily toil. Perhaps we had better return to less complicated matters, two pots which carry a clear mark and date!

185 · Earthenwares and Stonewares

165

166

We have already discussed the 'Imperial Measure' mugs which feature the Royal Arms of Queen Victoria (see Plates 131–2). From the same period come Coronation commemoratives (Plate 165). The mug shown here has a portrait of the young Queen printed in blue, which can just been seen, and the words 'Queen Victoria. Crowned 28 June 1838'. What makes this piece especially interesting is that there is an additional inscription 'Success to the Town and Trade of Preston'. John May in his fascinating book *Victoria Remembered* (1983) states, 'this is perhaps, the rarest of all Victoria Coronation mugs.' Examples may be seen in the Harris Museum at Preston. A similar mug was brought for inspection at a recent BBC Antiques Roadshow. This too had the Royal portrait and inscription and the parallel expression of good wishes, 'Success to the Caledonian Free School, Liverpool'.

Returning to Preston, the plate in Plate 166 stands as representative of a goodly number of Davenport commemorative earthenwares, often of a relatively cheap quality, which must have been specially commissioned by churches and Sunday Schools. Unfortunately, no checklist of these has been kept, but examples relating to Tunstall in the Potteries, St George Street Chapel, Liverpool 1863, and to a chapel at Heaton Mersey in Stockport come to mind. This particular Preston example is of a good quality ware with a dated 'Opaque China' mark for 1849 which fits nicely with the 1852 commemorative date. The border pattern is 'Wreath' and the extraordinary anchor mark is shown on p. 74 (E 10).

Production for commissions of what we now term commemoratives must have

165. Blue printed mug, bearing a portrait of Queen Victoria and the words 'Queen Victoria Crowned 28 June 1838. Success to the Town and Trade of Preston'. Ht 3in. Mark E 8A. (David Golding Collection)

166. Plate printed with 'Wreath' border pattern and a picture of 'Christ Church, Preston Erected A.D. 1836 Enlarged A.D. 1852'. Diameter 10½in. Mark E 16 (for 1849) and E 10 (Wreath). (B. M. & A. C. Walters Collection)

186 · Earthenwares and Stonewares

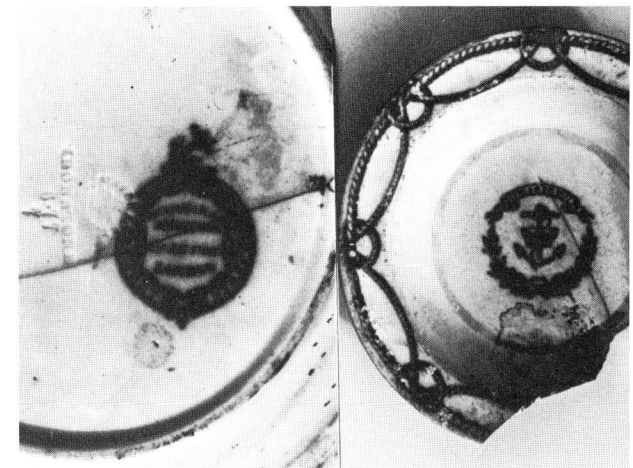

provided a reasonable amount of business for the firm. Just how lucrative such orders were is open to question. Each church, school, ship, regiment, or hotel would require at the minimum the engraving of a special copper plate for either a picture of the building or at the very least, as with the Victoria Coronation mug, a separately engraved inscription. Sometimes the order would appear to have been for a whole dinner service with the individual requirement of the customer very much to the fore. A fine example of this is the gravy boat in Plate 167. The border pattern is standard, but the central pattern with a view of the Hotel Royal, Aarhuus and the supporting emblems delightfully labelled 'Restauration' and 'Billard' as well as the owner's name and the location, would require an individual copper plate engraving. Once again we see Davenport catering very specifically for the export market.

Although there are a fair number of earthenware 'commemoratives' of this kind, there were probably more made in porcelain, and these decorated with on-glaze prints, usually of churches, often bear the name on the back of the china dealer in the town for which they were destined. This does not seem to have been the practice with the pottery items. A collection of speciality or commemorative wares would be a fascinating one for the collector to pursue. The truly dedicated enthusiast might have some difficulty in adding an example such as that shown in Plate 168 to the collection. These battered fragments were recovered from the bed of the sea where they had lain since the ship for which they were commissioned, the *Pomerania,* sank more than a century ago. A sub-aqua collection really would be unique!

As well as specifically individual wares such as those for churches, regiments, and families, the factory did seem to make a very conscious effort to provide appropriate wares for the various export markets it served. We have already noted the prints of the American heroes of the war of 1812 (p. 160) and the detailed instructions which John Davenport relayed about the requirements of the Amsterdam trade (p. 48). Another perspective on Davenport's foreign trade is provided by a letter written by a John Wardle to John Lockett the Longton potter. Wardle writing on 17 November 1846 from Liverpool is clearly passing on to Lockett the results of some industrial espionage upon which he and an accomplice have been engaged. He writes: 'I enclose you a list of prices copied by Davenport bookkeeper from the last assortment they sent out to Ceylon'. Some time later he is still engaged in his nefarious activities writing on 25 April 1848: 'The reason I have not answered your esteemed favor [*sic*] of 19 inst. sooner is I have been waiting opportunity to have access to Davenport's sales books and I now subjoin a copy of some adventures of theirs to the Markets of Bombay Calcutta and Madras. I find they are very similar aportments sent to each of those markets . . .'

He then details some of the wares with comments indicative of how Davenports approached the specific requirements of their overseas clients – a concern

167. Gravy boat with fixed stand printed in blue with 'Hotel Royal Ved F.R. Larsen Aarhuus'. The emblems inscribed 'Restauration' and 'Billard'. Length 8½in. Ht 6in. Mark E 8A and E 6 (indistinct, but could be 1836). (Lockett Collection)

168. Two views of a damaged plate salvaged from the S.S. *Pomerania* which sank off Folkstone in 1878. The marks on the left indicate a potting date of May 1877. The printed mark gives the London and Liverpool showroom addresses. On the right, the front of the plate with the wreath and anchor motif labelled 'Marine'. (Photos courtesy Peter G. Weatherly, Folkestone Branch of the British Sub-Aqua Club)

187 · Earthenwares and Stonewares

for the customer which probably paid handsomely: '1 Hhd of Earthenware all of Light blue pd Ware or 1 table service complete . . . Also Hhd of Dinner ware same quantity are sent of Flowing blue *NOT* landscape patt'ns, these are objected to . . . They never send either Chamber ware or Breakfast & Tea ware of the flowing blue . . .'

The conclusion of this letter is worth quoting in full as it indicates both Davenports trading methods with overseas clients and their care to study the market as regards patterns and types of ware.

I find they do not sent any Willow ware, Persian painted or Cream Color'd ware to any of those markets, or Tappies, but I think Tappies or Rice dishes light blue P'd would take there, I ascertained Davenport have not yet made any consignments to these markets but what they have sent has either been thro a Captain that could be depended upon and accustomed to those markets and they divide profits with Davenports, but the prices given with the discounts given is how they are invoiced to them, I understand as soon as the vessels arrives out, the goods are sent to the public sale rooms and if the assortments are made up suitable, there is generally good sales for them, I would especially point out to your notice that they do not like any patterns with human figures, animals or landscape patterns. Such patterns as plants, flowers, chintzs or anything of bold in stripes or plaids would find more ready sales. The last shipment but one Davenports made to Bombay they sent 2 Dinner sets quantity as given of E'ware best white glaze with 2 Gold lines, also 2 Dinner sets E'ware filled in, & 1 Hhd of Breakfast and Tea ware white and gold. I always noticed when I have been waiting on any Gent. from Bombay that has been making a selection of goods for his own use or for his private speculations they mostly prefer'd the plain white & gold ware, some plain blue Chintz Patt'ns saying that those patt'ns looked cool for a warm climate . . .

(Document in the City Museum Stoke-on-Trent: Mr Wardle's punctuation is non-existent and a little has been added to make the document readable)

One can readily imagine the Liverpool warehouse shipping orders to a great many countries, both East and West, from Bombay to Lima, New York to Sicily at this period. For each market there were special requirements and when we realize just how extensive were their overseas commitments, it is no surprise that the range of products was so great. Moreover, with what seems at this period to have been a very thriving and assured overseas trade, one can understand why the firm appears somewhat unadventurous compared say, with Mintons and Copelands who made great efforts at the international trade Exhibitions. Davenports had a world-wide market. It may have been the lower end of the market as far as quality goods were concerned, but it was a most lucrative one, and enabled them to have a wide product range without risking too much on speculative and innovative ventures. As a policy it was eminently successful at least until the 1860s. Thereafter, their lack of product innovation and the preoccupation with the middle to lower end of the market for their earthenware may well have been a major contributory factor to their eventual downfall.

Returning specifically to the wares, it must be obvious that it would be impossible to cover the entire range of the later wares, especially as there is so much overlap from the pre-1840 date. Typical of this is the case of stone china which we have already discussed in chapter 14. There is some evidence that stone china wares, particularly the very popular pattern 142 (see Plate 88) were being made certainly into the 1870s. A somewhat down-market version was also on offer called 'Opaque China', and as was seen on Plate 168 a further variant was termed 'Ironstone'. Geoffrey Godden also reports a mark comprising the Royal Arms and supporters, with the words 'Davenport Longport Staffordshire' arranged above each other in a double-lined box and then 'Real Ironstone China'. Plate 169 shows a basket and stand printed with the pattern 'Blossoms' and yet another version of the basic wording, this time 'Stone Ware'. How significant these different terms are it is hard to say, but both visually and with regard to the structure of the material the conventional 'Stone China' would appear to be the highest quality body, with 'Ironstone' probably the cheapest. Some very good pieces were made in the 'Opaque China' body, but also some very routine examples have been noted. Neither the 'Stone Ware' nor the 'Real Ironstone China' are found very frequently, but would appear to be of a sound quality. As the earlier stone chinas become progressively more difficult to find and expensive to purchase, these later variants could well offer another interesting field for collection and research.

Plate 170 shows a fine pair of jugs which carry one of the normal stone china marks, but decorated with pattern 141. From their shape one would imagine that they dated from the post-1840 period. They can stand as representative of many fine quality stone china wares which were made, as earlier indicated, well into the 1870s. It does however appear that the other variants were the more plentiful in the last twenty years of the factory's existence.

Certain other types of ware continued in production over very lengthy periods and one occasionally meets glazed caneware pie dishes of the kind illustrated in *Davenport Pottery & Porcelain*, Plate 56, which is date-marked for 1864. Similarly, good quality jelly moulds are known from a very wide date span. Examples with the lower case mark E 2 could well have been made before 1820. Other moulds, still very much creamware in the finish, have been recorded with dates as late as the 1870s. The piece illustrated in the 1972 book, Plate 53, is date-marked for 1864. The jelly moulds present an interesting variety, we have noted examples formed as sheaves of wheat, a peacock, several varieties of fruit, as well as a number of simple patterned pieces.

White stoneware continued to be manufactured apparently until the closure of the factory. Some years ago a white stoneware circular bread tray with simple relief moulding was noted, with a year mark of 188? (the last number was too indistinct to read). In the Lockett collection is a white stoneware mortar, with the lower-case impressed mark E 2, and it really is impossible to date the piece other than by accepting a pre-1820 date for this form of mark. From its appearance, it could have been made in any decade from 1800 to 1880 (illustrated in the Northern Ceramic Society catalogue *Stonewares and Stone Chinas*, 1982, Plate 221). As was stressed in the section on white stoneware, the dating of wares is very problematical. Plate 171 shows another page from the 1880s Davenport London price catalogue. Clearly visible, and thus offered for sale is a jug labelled 'Hunting'. Apart from the lack of a 'kick' or thumb-rest on the top of the handle this is the typical Davenport white stoneware jug which (marked with both lower and upper case marks E 2 and E 5) had been in production throughout the century. How can one discriminate between a jug manufactured in 1800 and one made in 1880? It has to be assumed that the upper case mark E 5 was used on any jug made as late as the 1880s

169. Dessert basket and stand, printed in green with the pattern 'Blossoms'. Stand, 10×8in. Mark E 17 (Stoneware) and E 5. (David Golding Collection)

170. Two stone china jugs, pattern 141. Hts 7¼ and 8¼in. Mark both E 12, *c.*1840–50. (B. M. & A. C. Walters Collection)

189 · Earthenwares and Stonewares

(no 'Hunting' jug has ever been reported marked in any other way than E 1, E 2, or E 5).

One's impression that the better the potting and finish of an item, the earlier it is in date, can only be taken as a very rough and ready guide. This is yet one more avenue which needs further exploration.

For many years the factory seems to have made something of a speciality of miniature and childrens' wares. These range from whole dinner services such as the blue printed one illustrated as Plate 54 in *Davenport Pottery & Porcelain*, to childrens' plates and mugs such as the plate printed with the name 'Edward', also illustrated in the 1972 book on Plate 53. Four illustrations of similar wares are included here.

Plate 172 shows three blue transfer printed pieces, the details of which are in the caption. The delightful small central mug is typical of several similar items with quite unusual prints. The Jewish Museum in Manchester has a marked mug which features a Jewish pedlar and the City Museum in Manchester another small mug with an all-round decorative print. The small mug in Plate 173 is printed in black with the 'Gleaner'. This would seem to be one of a series, for in the Roger and Janice Chambers collection a small octagonal plate with a 'daisy' border, a few flower heads of which are touched over with lustre, is printed with another charming scene of a young boy holding a rake in his right hand and a watering can in his left. This is titled 'The Youthful Gardener', and is marked indistinctly for a year in the 1840s. The 'daisies' are not continuous as in most wares of this type but scattered over the rim with space between each. Most are 6-leaved flower heads, but at each of the corners of the octagon the flower is 8-petalled, and these are the

171. A page from an 1880s Davenport London price list showing a range of toilet wares and jugs. (Courtesy Spode Museum Collection Trust)

172. Three miniature or childrens' pieces, all blue printed. Left: Plate printed with the 'Friburg' pattern. Diameter 4¼in. Mark E 6 (year date indistinct) and printed pattern name mark. Centre: Small mug printed with scenes of children taking food and feeding a goat. Ht 2½in. Mark E 8A. Right: Plate with a floral print. Diameter 3½in. Mark E 8A. (Lockett Collection)

173. Small mug printed in black with 'The Gleaner'. Ht 2½in. Mark E 8A. (Courtesy Mrs Una Charles)

ones which have lustre decoration. The plate measures 6in. diagonally corner to corner.

Closely allied to the above mug and octagonal plate are no fewer than four octagonal childrens' plates kindly reported by René Nicholls. These also had daisy moulded borders, picked out fairly indiscriminately with touches of pink lustre. Two were printed with birds, one boldly labelled 'Turkey', the other untitled. A third depicted two birds amongst plants and foliage and was entitled 'A Brother's Present'. The fourth was printed with an imposing building/cage before which a family group was standing, with the legend 'Zoological Gardens – Monkey House'. All these plates were marked with impressed and printed marks. The moulding on these is identical with the 6- and 8-petalled flower heads on the Chambers's plate. These are very rare examples, as none with precisely this moulding is illustrated by Maurice and Evelyn Milbourn, *Understanding Miniature British Pottery and Porcelain 1730–Present Day* (1983).

Very much more commonly found are miniature tea services of which we have already illustrated the examples in a lustre finish (Plate 146). The pieces featured in Plate 174 are printed in black with a sheet pattern in the form of a Maltese cross motif. Other patterns as well as the lustre finish have been recorded on these shapes which date from the early 1840s and were in use for at least fifteen years. It should also be recalled that Plate 158 shows a very small miniature teapot with the semi-matt black finish. A somewhat larger example is illustrated by the Milbourns' in colour on their Plate 5, p. 59.

Lastly in this section on miniature wares, pieces from a tea service printed with the 'Athens' pattern are featured in Plate 175. This is clearly date-marked 9.68, and though the wares may not have been decorated immediately, the pattern was still the second one listed by Wengers when they were advertising their acquisition of Davenport's patterns in 1888, giving it a life span of almost twenty years.

Before we finally turn to the later printed patterns in detail, an excerpt from an article in the *Pottery Gazette* for 1 September 1884 is worth quoting for the information it provides on the production at the factory in its last few years. In the section 'Buyers' Notes' we read:

On a recent visit to the show rooms of Messrs Davenport, Limited, Longport, we were shown a splendid collection of vases and violet pots, some having a gold ground, others a malachite green, while a third had a royal blue ground in various rich styles of ornamentation. The productions of this firm in the Crown Derby styles are so well-known that it will be sufficient to say that these formed a prominent feature of the goods displayed [most Crown Derby style wares were made in china, but some examples, including a splendid cabaret set have been noted in earthenware] . . . *A number of new dessert shapes were shown us, among the most striking being one named 'The Duchess' and another called*

174. Miniature teapot. Ht 4in. Cup and saucer and sucrier. Ht 3¾in. Printed in grey-green with a Maltese cross pattern. Mark E 8A and E 6 (year date indistinct) (Lockett Collection)

'The Imperial'. These are a kind of 'pierced' shapes, and are elaborately decorated [again probably predominantly porcelain wares]. A toilet set in china and gold, as used by Her Majesty, is worthy of note, while a déjeuner set in white china with solid gold handles looked exceedingly rich. A new toilet shape called 'Grecian', but the decoration of which is a passion flower is having a splendid run [see Plate 176 for the shape] and may be seen on view at the Health Exhibition. Another, styled 'The Antique', is also a shape that is selling well. Dinner services, whose number was verily legion, were shown to us, some special 'lines' for hotel and ships' use being among the number, while a neat set for the officers of the York and Lancaster Regiment in china and gold may be mentioned. The show of glass, too, which is here manufactured in all its forms is very extensive, and includes all the newest designs and colours. This firm have just opened a New York House at 45 Murray Street.

Though much of this report seems to refer to china products, the entry on the toilet wares is interesting. The range of earthenware toilet sets made in the 1870s and 1880s seems to have been very extensive. Examples of the shapes illustrated on Plates 171 and 176 are found quite frequently. The decoration is often flamboyantly bold. An example in the Bevis Walters collection is printed with the 'Acanthus' pattern and has the nacreous lustre finish described earlier in this section. There is a splendidly full set in a dark blue printed pattern at Whitwick Manor near Wolverhampton. Many items have become separated from the service to which they belonged and it is not uncommon to find Davenport chamber pots in collections of such articles – hanging from the rafters of a pub on one occasion – or like some of the large basins from toilet services, being used as rather grandiose bulb bowls. Soap dishes and toothbrush holders being more easily displayed find their way into the cabinets of collectors. Some years ago Mrs Jo Curtin reported a splendid water closet or lavatory pan, printed in blue with the 'Marine Chintz' pattern and carrying in addition the printed name 'J & R Milligan, 47 Cary St. London' and the printed factory name mark E 8A. More recently in the September 1988 issue (71) of the Northern Ceramic Society's *Newsletter* Dick Henrywood wrote of a similar portable water closet in stone china, printed with a geometric and floral trelliswork pattern, with the name inside the pan of 'Marriott Patentee, 26 Ludgate Hill and 89 Fleet St. London'. Dr Henrywood gives full details of Marriotts. He dates the piece which is illustrated to c.1826–42. Such objects intended for very practical purposes have rarely survived, but such is the present interest in these and similar toilet wares that they are unlikely to be thrown away on the scrap heap as part of the process of modernization, as once they so frequently were.

175. Group of miniature tewares, printed in blue with the 'Athens' pattern. Teapot, ht 5¼in. Mark E 6 (for September 1868). (B. M. & A. C. Walters Collection)

176. A page from an 1880s Davenport London price list, showing a range of toilet wares. Many of these match the names listed in the closing down sale of 1887. (Courtesy Spode Museum Collection Trust)

177. Small earthenware plate printed in black – slightly flown – with the 'Swiss Pastime' pattern (so named in cartouche on the back). Diameter 5¼in. Mark E 6 (for 1848). (Alan Cleaver Collection)

178. Large dish printed with the 'Floral' pattern in charcoal lilac. 20¾×16½in. Mark E 6 (for 1852).

The printed water closet pans brings us to the final group of wares to be discussed, the later printed patterns. In the earlier section on transfer printed wares, an attempt was made to record most of the known blue printed patterns. It was stated then, and can bear repetition, that once past the mid 1830s, the proliferation of patterns is so great that no serious attempt could be made to chronicle the complete range. Nor in some ways is it quite as necessary. Many of the later patterns, probably most of them, carry the pattern name as part of the back stamp mark, and several of these are illustrated in the mark section. Thus where more than one pattern is used in a service all the scenes bear the pattern name and consequently the problems of assigning scenes to a specific series is not fraught with the kind of difficulties we were wrestling with in earlier pages. However, it should be stressed that certainly by the 1860s the common practice was akin to that in the earliest days of the factory, that is, one basic pattern was applied to all items in every type of service. The expense of separately engraved scenes for each kind of item in a service was clearly uneconomic. For the purpose of this final summary of the later wares, a number of patterns have been chosen to illustrate the range, together with examples of the shapes which may be found to match the shape pages from the 1880s catalogue illustrated throughout the book in various places (see Plates 139–43 and Colour Plate XII for a number of printed patterns which appear to have enjoyed a lengthy life). Furthermore, by using the final sale notice of 1887 together with a similar list of

193 · Earthenwares and Stonewares

179. Earthenware plate printed with the 'Chinese Birds' pattern. Diameter 10¼in. Mark E 5 (c.1840–50). (Hacking Collection)

Wengers we can arrive at a list of patterns which is the nearest approximation we can make to those offered at the auction of 1887, when no less than eleven tons of copper plate engravings were sold which bore no fewer than 300 patterns.

The early part of the advertisement for the sale of 'the valuable COPPER-PLATE ENGRAVINGS, BLOCKS, CASES, WORKING MOULDS . . .' is quoted in full on p. 68. The rest of the notice is printed in full here here as it contains many shape names that can be matched to those illustrated from the shape book in the Spode Museum, together with many of the names of patterns, some of which are illustrated here, others of which may be in the collections of readers.

. . . the blocks, cases and working moulds of some of the finest and best shapes and most saleable patterns in the home and foreign markets, including, Chelsea, Oval, Bamboo, Victoria, Alexandria, Talbot, Brighton, Prussian, Embossed Grape, Devon, Peel, Clifton, Eldon, Empress, Albert, Stanley, Canova, Limoges, Sèvres, Embossed Maezina, and other choice DINNER WARE SHAPES.

THE TOILET SHAPES comprise Antique, Westminster, Dolphin, Grecian, Empress, Stafford, Peel, Paris, Cypress, Lily, Cactus, Berlin, Regent, York, Devon, Argyle, Tamworth, Sutherland, Atlantic, Niagara, Derby, Trent, &c.

THE TEA WARE consists of St. Denis, Canning, Devon, Bute, Embossed Fern and Lily, Tulip, Plain and Embossed Niagara, Devonia, Calais &c.

The JUGS and VASES comprise some of the most recent designs of the best modellers of the day.

The CHINA PATTERNS comprise Chelsea Oval, Victoria, Albert, Empress, Regina, Imperial, Canton, Paris, Wicker, Octagon, Dolphin &c. in DINNER and DESSERT WARE.

The DÉJEUNER SETS consist of Victoria, Round, Sutherland, Mayer, and other patterns.

Over 11 Tons of valuable COPPER-PLATE ENGRAVINGS, comprising about 300 of the most saleable patterns now in the market, including, Florentine, Osborne, Mikado, Eton, Burmese, Athens, Versailles, Bamboo, Ornate, Windsor, Spanish Rose, Moresque, Convolvulus, Cornucopia, Seaweed, Gothic, Syria, Sunflower, French Groups, Alpine Amusements, Lily, Clematis, Corea, Italian, Rhine Views, Mersey, Orient, Java, Paris, Wreath, Muleteer, Agriculture, Hop, Stork, Watteau, Florentine, Ostrich, Chinese Bird, Madras, Persian Ornament, Iolanthe, Delaware, Arabesque, Chantilly, British Scenery, Alhambra, Ceres, Pekin, Chinese Pastimes, Pagoda, Chinese Scenery, Floresque, Sheet Patterns, Conchology, Cyprus, Marine Views &c.

194 · Earthenwares and Stonewares

180. Cheese dish and stand, printed in blue with the 'Genoa' pattern. Overall length 7¼in. Mark E 8A and pattern name in cartouche, c.1860–70. (B. M. & A. C. Walters Collection)

181. Oval dish printed with the 'Eastern Birds' pattern. 10×8½in. Mark E 6 (for 1852). (B. M. & A. C. Walters Collection)

182. Soup plate printed and enamelled with the 'Java' pattern. Diameter 10¼in. Marks: pattern name and no. 3144, indistinct year mark for 1878. (B. M. & A. C. Walters Collection)

183. Sponge bowl or soap dish and cover from a toilet set painted with pattern 2905. Diameter 8in. Mark E 6 (for September 1878). (Godden of Worthing Ltd)

This interesting list of pattern names can be supplemented by reference to an advertisement in the *Pottery Gazette* for 1 February 1888 when A. Wenger said he would 'sell or hire and to match the colours and supply the shapes used with the following patterns'. Then follows a list of 54 patterns, of which the following do not appear in the sale advertisement:

Montilla, Bramble, Garland, Pastoral, Scots, Crosslet, Fan, Old Florida, Nile, Eastern Bird, Rocailles, Citron, Grapes, Whampoa, Danish, Woodland, Park, Ribbon, Birds and Berry, Canton, Tendril, Swallow and Nightshade, Fish, Honeysuckle, Bird and Star, Genoa, Nectarine, French Fan, Flora, Festoon and Bird, Fishermen, Asiatic Pheasants, Squirrel, Marbles.

The last selection of illustrations includes several patterns which feature in one or other of the lists above. They include 'Genoa' which is illustrated on a really unusual cheese dish. The shape, though interesting, hardly does justice to the pattern (Plate 180). The pattern 'Java' is a bright, bold and attractive one, very distinctive and typical of its period (Plate 182). This statement is even more apposite to Plate 184 decorated with the coloured-in print which may be the 'Fan' pattern – it is alas, not so marked. The range of items pictured on the plate serve to remind us very obviously of the 1870s and early 1880s prevalent 'Aesthetic Movement'. This curious design movement – one could hardly call it a style – combined in a remarkable way some of the design characteristics of Japanese art with a curious – perhaps even spurious – mock medievalism. Such flights of

184

185
186

fantasy as were engaged in by the Minton Studio in the early 1870s in pursuit of 'Art for Arts sake', an approximation of the credo of the Aesthetes, was not for the stolid Davenport factory. The plate illustrated is a rare excursion into Japonism. The last two illustrations in this section are much more typical of late Davenport. The potting on the 'Bamboo' shape tureen (Plate 185) leaves much to be desired, but the piece printed with the 'Iolanthe' pattern (Plate 186) has a certain modern, forward look about its shape. It bears the highest pattern recorded on earthenwares, No. 4053.

As far as we are aware, no systematic study has yet been made of the later Davenport earthenware pattern numbers. Certainly, none has been published. It would seem, and one can be no more positive than supposition, that the earthenware patterns formed a continuous range from the very early creamwares right through to the end of production. Thus we recorded earlier the highest number noted on a true creamware as 442 (see Plate 37) and throughout the discussion of the miscellaneous and later wares, the pattern numbers, where known, have been given. One can be fairly positive in stating that pattern numbers were not given to wares which only carried a transfer print. However, there are very many wares which bear a basic print which is then filled in or otherwise enamelled over. Without exception such pieces which bear any trace of on-glaze decoration, be it enamel, gilding, or lustre *normally* have a pattern number assigned

184. Plate with Japanese 'Aesthetic Movement' symbols, probably the 'Fan' pattern. Diameter 10in. Marks E 8A, E 6 (for October 1879), and Design Registration mark 1879. (Ex-Lockett Collection)

185. Tureen and ladle in the 'Bamboo' shape printed with the 'Eton' pattern. Overall length 9in. Tureen marked with the printed name mark. Ladle marked E 5. (Hacking Collection)

186. Sauce tureen, lid and stand in the 'Eldon' shape, printed and coloured in enamels with the 'Iolanthe' pattern. Ht 4½in. Mark: indistinct impression for June 1884. (B. M. & A. C. Walters Collection)

196 · Earthenwares and Stonewares

to them. Doubtless, there will be exceptions, but it was accepted factory practice throughout the Potteries not to give transfer patterns a number, but to give separate numbers to any pattern which involved enamelling or gilding on the glaze. It is not easy to give dates for pattern number introduction when the quantity of patterns noted is so few. From the dated pieces studied it would appear that patterns in the 3000 range belong to the 1870s and in the 4000s to the 1880s. Perhaps some reader would care to make a full and systematic study and publish their findings. The list of patterns sold at the closing sale reminds us of just how long-lived some patterns were. 'Muleteer', for example, was over fifty years old, and many others had lives of twenty, thirty, forty years or more. Thus it is no surprise that after the sale Wengers and others should be advertising that they owned or could produce these old and popular patterns. The firm of Gibson & Sons produced wares marked with the words 'Gibson & Sons' then over a cartouche which contained the pattern name 'Sèvres' was written 'Late' and below it 'Davenport'. A clear indication that they were using the old copper plates for the 'Sèvres' pattern which appears in the sale list. A plate formerly in the Hacking collection now presented to the City Museum, Stoke-on-Trent has an even more impressive mark. This reads: 'Manuf. for A. S. Sneddon & Co. Queen St. Glasgow' in one cartouche, and in another: 'Antique Fruit and [Flowers? not clear] Engraved by W. Brooke in 1878 for Davenports. Reproduced by A. Brooke Successor for Beardmore & Co. England.' After all that the pattern is totally undistinguished and unmemorable. The interest in Davenports' patterns may still have been alive almost twenty years after the closure, for on 1 June 1906 an advertisement in the *Pottery Gazette* announced: 'Davenport engravings. – For Sale, large quantities of Copper plates, including many of Davenport's best patterns. Can be seen by appointment. Thomas Hughes & Son, Longport.'

These later wares of the Davenport factory have as yet not commanded the attention of collectors to the same extent as have either the earlier pots or even the wares of some of their contemporaries. As has been remarked before, there are no magnificent majolica peacocks such as Paul Comolera modelled for Mintons; no colour glaze experiments of the type undertaken by Léon Arnoux, indeed barely a nod is given in the direction of fashion. The last two decades of production are decidedly down-market from some of their more illustrious contemporaries. Yet, as we have tried to show in the illustrations and the text, there is much to admire in the everyday and serviceable wares for which John Shirley and his team of managers and designers were responsible. In particular as the wares of the earlier periods become ever more expensive, and in some cases command even higher prices than the porcelain equivalent, the later earthenwares offer scope both for the acquisition of relatively inexpensive items, and also provide an excellent opportunity for research. It could almost be argued that there is an entirely new factory there waiting to be discovered, researched, written about and published, much as the bone china wares of New Hall, at present, are far less well known than the hard paste. We would like to think that the much fuller treatment given here, compared with my 1972 book, of both the later earthenwares and the later china, will encourage collectors and researchers, and stimulate them to add to our knowledge of the many aspects of Davenports' later production which could still uncover much new information and provide many fascinating pots to add to our collections. We hope this chapter has provided a few signposts pointing in the right direction.

Part Three:
The Porcelains

17 The Early Davenport Porcelains

The important subject of this chapter presents great problems. We have no evidence of the date when John Davenport sought to produce in Staffordshire china or porcelain in addition to his established earthenwares. The earliest examples were apparently unmarked and probably closely emulated other manufacturers' shapes and styles.

In seeking to establish when porcelain was first made by the Davenport firm at Longport we find that the Directories are strangely unhelpful. Certainly *Holden's Triennial Directory* of 1805 described John Davenport as a manufacturer of china and earthenware, and we have firm evidence that Davenport was able to display a reportedly ornate range of highly finished porcelains by September 1806.

The following evidence in the form of a contemporary account was published in the local *Staffordshire Advertiser* on 20 September 1806, and relates to the visit of the then Prince of Wales (destined to become Prince Regent in 1811 and then King George IV in January 1820) and the Duke of Clarence (later to become King William IV). These two Royal visitors were keenly interested in the local pottery manufactories and had visited Spode's works and, of course, Wedgwood's renowned Etruria works before visiting Davenport's factories at Longport. The press account of this Royal visit reads in part:

On Saturday morning the Illustrious Party proceeded to view Messrs. Davenport's Manufactory of Ornamental Pottery and China Wares. . . .

Of the fine Specimens of Porcelain, produced at this Manufactory His Royal Highness observed, that he considered them in texture and execution equal to the old Sèvres, that the colours and Paintings did great credit to the Artists and that he should feel proud in exhibiting them to his Foreign Visitors . . . His Royal Highness ordered Services of several of the finest and most valuable kinds. Of the Ornamental parts of the manufactory His Royal Highness was pleased to say that the vases, urns etc. in point of execution and ornament were unique in their kinds and gave orders for a collection of the most beautiful and highly finished specimens.

There exists still at Windsor Castle part of a well-decorated dinner service which almost certainly represents that ordered during the 1806 Royal visit to the Davenport factory. These pieces bear a painted mark which may well be unique to this early Royal order, the word 'Longport' over a large anchor device. A tureen perhaps originally from this service is shown in Plate 289. The well-painted Chinoiserie-style decoration is typical (but not unique to Davenport) and related designs crop up on many early Davenport porcelains. These Chinoiserie-style patterns, linking we believe with the 1806 Royal purchase, are painted on a rather soft bone china body and covered with a glaze that is rather prone to fine crazing. This body has often discoloured over the years, now having a creamy appearance, which in moderation need not be disfiguring.

Even allowing for a degree of publicity-oriented extravagance in the wording of the press announcement relating to this Royal visit it does seem clear that porcelains were on display and that these comprised not only useful services but more ornate articles such as vases. Furthermore, some at least of these were well painted by hand by one or more trained painters. In short, these 1806 articles were not early experimental essays in porcelain manufacture. In this connection, it is relevant to mention that in the following year Davenport opened a London showroom to display his earthenwares, his chinaware, and the Davenport glass.

The Royal archives include some very interesting accounts for Davenport wares supplied after the Royal visit and probably these articles were ordered at that time, in September 1806.

The complete service was very extensive and included many intricate forms and unusual articles which would not necessarily have been included in standard early Davenport porcelain dinner and dessert services. If all these objects had been available for the Royal visitors to inspect on their visit in September 1806 then the Davenport management must be congratulated on their enterprise.

The very grand combined Dinner, Dessert, and Tea and Coffee service was initially invoiced to The Prince of Wales on 1 August 1807, with a combined invoice for various purchases, including glass, being submitted in December 1807. However, the porcelains had been finished and seemingly delivered by 1 August as the first invoice includes a charge for eight packing cases.

The 1807 bill-head includes an engraved view captioned 'Wholesale Warehouse, Old Dock, Liverpool'. However, this view includes several kilns and therefore it may depict the Longport manufactory. No mention is made of a London showroom but in this year the firm had taken the Shakespeare Gallery to display glass, earthenware, and china, an event recorded by the manager of the Wedgwood rooms.

The Staffordshire address is simply given as 'Longport, near Newcastle, Staffordshire'. John and James Davenport merely described themselves as 'Potters and Glass makers', with no reference to porcelain. No doubt a new, more ornate bill-head was introduced soon after this Royal order was completed.

The original invoice mixed the dinner and dessert service pieces together, but in the following list I have separated the services in, I believe, the correct manner. The original heading read: 'A full Dinner & Dessert Service & Tea & Coffee service to match of fine china. Painted Chinese Temple & rich burnished gold mosaic Border.' The Dinner service comprised the following articles; the prices are per piece, unless stated.

	£	s	d
4 Tureens & covers, oval for Soup	11	0	0
4 stands to ditto.	4	0	0
2 Tureens & covers for soup, round.	11	0	0
2 Stands for ditto.	4	0	0
10 Tureens for Sauce / 10 stands to ditto	11	0	0
24 oval dishes & round ditto, from 23 to 15 inches, in sizes.	£72 the set		
2 Large dishes with Gravy wells	4	10	0
20 ditto less, in sizes from 15 to 12 inches	£40 the set		
44 ditto from 12 to 9 inches	£66 the set		
2 deep Sallad Dishes, square	4	10	0
3 Root Dishes with pans for [hot] water	9	0	0
6 Large Ice Pails for Wine (Sceaux)	3	0	0
4 Smaller ditto.	2	0	0
120 Dinner Table Plates, flat		16	0
40 ditto. soup		16	0

The Dessert wares comprised:

	£	s	d
6 Ice-Cream Pails with linings & covers for confectionary (Glaciers)	8	10	0
48 Large Dessert Dishes open border	1	4	0
144 Dessert Plates, large size		15	0

The tea and coffee porcelains included:

	£	s	d
4 sugar boxes and covers	1	15	0
4 cream jugs		18	0

4 slop Basons	*10*	*0*
48 tea cups and saucers	*18*	*0*
48 Coffee cups and saucers	*18*	*0*
8 chocolate cups with covers and stands	*2 15*	*0*

The total amount charged for these porcelain services in 1807 was £844 12s 0d, a very considerable sum at that period.

Unfortunately I do not believe that the pieces still surviving in the Royal collection bear a pattern number, so we cannot be sure of the pattern numbers reached by September 1806. It is regrettable that the invoice does not give pattern numbers, for if it did we could also have learned if different numbers were then applied to dinner, dessert and tea-wares of the same pattern. This plan seems to have been employed at later periods. Nor do we know if this was a new design first used for this Royal order or if – as may be more likely – it was one of several stock patterns already in production and available for the Prince of Wales to choose from. Almost certainly this Chinese-style design or versions of it remained in production as a standard pattern for some years.

The make-up of the Royal dessert service and of the tea and coffee set is strange, if this surviving account represents the complete order. The dessert service seemingly does not include a centrepiece, nor are fruit baskets and stands listed. It is worthy of note that the 48 large dessert dishes had 'open' borders, by which I assume the edges were pierced. The 144 large dessert plates represent a very great number, especially when compared with the 40 soup plates in the dinner service. The lack of dessert centrepieces may have been rectified by an additional delivery of '39 Compoteers in sizes, Painted to Pattern rec^d. Chinese Figures & gold border' invoiced on 29 May, 1808, at £58 10s 0d.

The tea and coffee services did not include tea or coffee pots although four each of the covered sugar boxes, the cream jugs and slop bowls were invoiced. Perhaps the Prince had a surfeit of silver teapots. It is interesting to see that the teawares included eight chocolate cups with covers and stands. These were apparently decorated to match the other porcelains and were seemingly intended to be used rather than be regarded as cabinet or show-pieces. They were at £2 15s 0d each quite costly articles. An early Davenport bone china coffee cup and saucer which may well relate to the 1806–7 Royal order is shown in Plate 187.

While discussing this important order it is interesting to note that the 'Ice Pails for Wine' supplied in two sizes did not have liners or covers. They were open pail-like objects similar to modern ice pails, but the related pails with liners and covers were listed as 'Ice Cream Pails for confectionery' and these were presumably used with the dessert porcelains. Today we tend to call such objects fruit coolers, see Plates 256–7 for later examples.

The Staffordshire Advertiser's account of the Royal visit in September 1806 includes references not only to the porcelain services but also to ornamental objects such as 'vases, urns etc.' which 'in point of execution and ornament were unique in their kinds and [the Prince of Wales] gave orders for a collection of the most beautiful and highly finished specimens'.

The Royal account does in fact include an interesting long list of such ornamental articles invoiced in December 1807 nearly a year after the Royal visit. Unfortunately the brief descriptions do not indicate if such articles were in porcelain or in one of the several types of earthenware or stoneware produced by Davenports and other firms of the period. On balance I believe that some at least were porcelain vases or 'jarrs' and certainly the styles of decoration were ornate and befitting of porcelain articles. One might also note that with these vases one finds also listed costly Caudle cups and Cabinet cups and stands, which were almost certainly in the porcelain body even though no such description was included in the listing. Certainly, however, the Davenport firm was producing attractive well-painted earthenware vases and other ornamental articles at this period and some of these Royal examples may have been earthenware, see Plate 53.

I will here list the ornamental articles supplied to the Prince as evidence of the types of decoration capable of having been produced by Davenports in 1807. Again no pattern numbers or sizes are quoted, although descriptions of the 'Jarrs' do have numbers from 1 to 15 against them. Perhaps this was merely to enable the invoice to be checked against the contents of the boxes and one cannot now be sure if the 'Jarrs' or vases bore such numbers applied in a permanent manner. The decoration will be found to include flowers, fruit, landscapes, birds, figure subjects with various ground colours including yellow, and with intricate even etched gilding. Several articles are described as being ornamented 'in Lustre' or with bronze effects. The lustre effects were doubtless achieved by the use of platinum, a technique reputedly introduced into the Potteries by John Hancock in about 1805 (see *Staffordshire Porcelain*, ed. Geoffrey Godden, 1983, p. 563).

		£	s	d
2 Antique Shape Jarrs Painted Lustre, Landscapes	(1)	3	3	0
2 ditto ditto Flowers	(2)	3	3	0
1 ditto ditto ditto	(3)	2	0	0
2 ditto ditto Landscapes large	(4)			
2 ditto ditto ditto less	(5)	8	8	0
2 ditto ditto ditto less	(6)			
2 Pot Pourres, Calcedony, painted in Flowers	(7)	2	15	0
3 Jarrs Large, 2 less, Calcedony, ditto	(8)	4	4	0
2 Jarrs Painted Coloured Landscape and Bronze handles	(9)	1	5	0
1 Jarr ditto Grecian Figures & Etch'd in gold	(10)	4	4	0
1 ditto ditto less	(11)	3	3	0
2 Portland Vauses, Etch'd Figures	(12)	2	2	0
1 Jarr, etch'd, Lace border in Lustre	(14)	2	2	0
1 ditto	(14)	2	2	0
1 ditto, Calcedony, Painted Flowers & Black ground	(14)	1	10	0
1 ditto, Calcedony Painted Flowers & Etch'd Lustre Fruit ground color'd & wash'd with yellow ground (or green)	(14)	2	2	0
1 ditto, Lace Border	(14)	1	10	0
1 ditto, Vandyke ditto	(14)	1	5	0
2 ditto, Painted Fruit, Brown ground & yellow Grun [sic] wash'd Rings &c.	(15)	2	2	0
1 Jarr with leaves in green		1	5	0
1 ditto, Painted Landscape &c.		1	5	0

187. Early bone china coffee cup and saucer enamelled with the 'Chinese Temple' pattern as associated with the 1806–7 Royal order. Painted with 'Longport' over an anchor. Diameter of saucer 5½in. *c.*1806–7. (Jill Gosling)

203 · The Porcelains

This section of the December 1807 Royal Account also includes '2 Jugs and covers Lustre Landscapes &c' at £1 5s 0d and also '24 Egyptian porouse Wine Coolers, Emboss'd' at 10s 6d each. The latter are certainly of earthenware as might be these lustre decorated covered jugs, but the following items in the same listing seem to have been in the porcelain body judging from their cost and general description:

	£	s	d
2 Caudle Cups & Stands Painted Landscapes &c.	*2*	*2*	*0*
2 ditto Birds	*2*	*2*	*0*
2 ditto Painted Chinese	*1*	*15*	*0*
1 Cup & Saucer Chinese	*1*	*0*	*0*
1 Caudle Cup Painted Landscape &c.		*15*	*0*
1 Cabinet Cup & Stand Etch'd in Gold &c.	*1*	*1*	*0*
1 ditto Painted Landscape &c.	*1*	*1*	*0*
1 ditto Lustre ditto	*1*	*1*	*0*

These ornamental cups, like the 'Jarrs' or vases, present problems as the invoice does not state whether they were of porcelain or earthenware. In the absence, at the moment, of any evidence, we believe that the cups and stands just described were of porcelain; and on balance we believe that the vases were also made in the bone china body, if only because the styles of decoration suit well such wares and because they were ordered by Royalty. If such pieces should come to light, they may well bear the painted Longport place-name with the anchor device, as this mark occurs on other Royal pieces still at Windsor. The anchor is painted in a large size, see p. 209.

Two pot-pourri and several of the vases were described as 'Calcedony'. This term has now – over 180 years later – proved somewhat troublesome to define, but Terry Lockett has helpfully produced a receipt for a Brameld earthenware body mix dated May 1808 and headed 'Chalcedony or Orange'. This term obviously relates to the very fine orange-tinted earthenware which was so favoured at the Davenport works, although it is by no means unique to that factory. It could be finely engine-turned and decorated with gold trimming, and was often extremely attractively painted with monochrome landscapes. It is a high-grade product normally embellished with care in the porcelain style.

John Davenport was certainly producing good quality china in 1806, but we are not sure what type of porcelain was first produced as two distinct and very different Davenport bodies occur. We have rather soft bone chinas often with a finely crazed glaze, as seen with the designs we associate with the 1806–7 Royal orders. The crazing of the glaze which I have mentioned is not, of course, restricted to this factory and the fine cracks or break-up of the glaze has probably happened over the years, the body and glaze appearing perfect when the pieces were first sold.

However, other early Davenport porcelains are of a very compact body of the type we term a hybrid hard-paste porcelain. These pieces, which are sometimes impressed-marked 'Davenport' over an anchor device, present several problems. One would expect these hybrid hard-paste specimens to predate the softer bone china, as was the case with several other manufactories such as Miles Mason or John Rose (of Coalport), but this was not necessarily the case with Davenports, for this name appears quite frequently on the harder bodies whilst the early 'Longport' written place-name can occur on the bone chinas. It does seem reasonable to assume that Davenport would have used the non-personal 'Longport' place-name mark before adopting the 'Davenport' mark. Most manufacturers of the early 1800s failed to use name-marks. It would, we believe, have been unlikely for Davenport to have employed his name-mark initially and then ceased to use it in favour of the non-personal 'Longport' mark. However, it must be stated that some "Davenport" marked earthenwares appear to predate 1806 and that the above remarks may relate only to the porcelains.

A study of pattern numbers does not help to resolve the problem as the early Davenport porcelains, of both types, do not usually bear such numbers. One must remember that John Davenport operated more than one factory and it could be that different types of porcelain were being manufactured at the same period, perhaps at separate factories.

In the absence of evidence to the contrary we will assume for the time being that the hybrid hard-paste porcelains postdate the first bone chinas. It is possible that the rather superior hard-paste body was introduced to overcome the difficulties experienced with the bone china in its earliest period of manufacture. Whilst, as we have stated, several of the large manufacturers were producing the hybrid hard-paste type of porcelain in and soon after 1800, Davenports would have been by no means alone in making what we now term bone china. The Derby porcelain and glaze was very soft as was the Minton body – seemingly from its earliest period. The Spode porcelain, although more compact than the Davenport, was also of bone china type: indeed, Josiah Spode is generally credited with having perfected the mix. There does not seem to be any reason why the Davenport management should not have commenced porcelain manufacture by producing bone china. It is possible that the management was making both types of porcelain at the same period, maybe at different works, but on balance I do not think that this was the case; and even if it were so, it is difficult to explain the different modes of marking the products. However, my co-author Terry Lockett believes it likely that the bone china was in continuous production and that the harder body was reserved for certain types of article, notably the bulb-pots. It is very difficult, if not impossible now to prove which theory is correct but, if only to underline the point that two totally different bodies were in production and that they are usually marked in different ways, I will retain my opinion (no more) that a policy change leaves us with separate periods. The different periods of Davenport porcelains which I now tentatively suggest are:

Early 'First period' bone china	c.1803–7
Hybrid hard-paste porcelains	c.1807–12
Second period bone china	c.1812 onwards

These dates are not at this stage of our knowledge (when no dated specimens are known) hard and fast and some amendments may later be necessary. It should be noted, however, that the hard-paste period is relatively short and that specimens are decidedly scarce. The hybrid hard-paste Davenport porcelains will be discussed later in this chapter and they are illustrated in Plates 238–42. The post-1812 bone china body seems to have been amended from time to time, there is certainly no one Davenport bone china formula.

Apart from the 1806 Royal order, the early bone chinas in the main comprise, as one would expect, tea and dessert wares. A large percentage of the pieces, especially the earliest, were completely unmarked, but other examples, mainly the dessert forms, may bear the painted mark 'Longport', rarely with an anchor device below. A relatively few pieces bear the impressed 'Davenport' name-mark with the anchor device and some bear both the impressed mark (applied in the forming process before firing) as well as the overglaze 'Longport' mark added during or after the decorating stage.

The earliest bone china seems to be of a type generally used by other manufacturers of the period. I have had a piece from the typical 'Longport' marked dessert service shown in Plates 231–4 tested by British Ceramic Research Ltd, with the following basic result expressed in percentages:

Silica	32.2	Lead Monoxide	2.1
Lime	26.3	Potash	1.7
Phosphorus Pentoxide	19.5	Magnesia	.7
Alumina	15.8	Ferric Oxide	.4

This analysis will not vary greatly from other standard types of the same approximate period, although the percentage of Phosphorus Pentoxide and therefore the amount of calcined bone in the mix is on the high side. An analysis of early Spode bone china of this approximate period has given 16.5%, of Minton bone china 17.5%, and of rather later New Hall 17.7%. These give percentages of bone ash in the original body of about 40%. Today, it is usually 50% or more. The Davenport sample showed about 43%. The point must be made, however, that the mix within a given factory would have altered slightly from time to time or from one batch to the next.

The next teaware shape that we can feature is quite different from the bone china cup and saucer shown in Plate 187. The pieces are also in a totally different body – the hybrid hard-paste porcelain – yet we believe that the pieces now shown in Plate 188 fit into this chronological sequence at this point, in about 1808.

In turning to consider the very rare Davenport essays in the hybrid hard-paste porcelain mix as far as the teawares are concerned, we have the familiar difficulties of a lack of pattern numbers and the fact that not all the pieces bear the impressed Davenport name-mark. At present many early Davenport specimens are probably misattributed to the Coalport factories or to other makers of this popular type of body in the 1800–10 period.

Our remarks on the possible similarity of the early Davenport wares to the Coalport porcelains were prompted by a part tea service in the collection of Miss Diana Darlington. The covered sugar-box and a tea cup and coffee can are shown in Plate 188. The base of the sugar-box bears the impressed Davenport name and anchor device (the potting is rather neater and thinner than most Coalport examples and the oval plan is rather more elongated than the Shropshire specimens) but the cups are unmarked. The knob seen on the sugar-box cover is a later metal replacement: the original knob was most probably of ring form. Miss Darlington also has the oval stand to a teapot, and this stand also bears the impressed name-mark and anchor device. This item shows that an oval-plan teapot was also made. For the purposes of our subsequent reasoning we have assumed that these pieces formed part of a complete service which was originally made at the same factory, Davenports. We must, however, note the very slight possibility that the unmarked cups were later replacements to a Davenport service or that the set was decorated by a non-factory gilder/decorator using a selection of blanks made at different factories. However, many other obviously Davenport cups are likewise unmarked and the items do have the appearance of having been made at the same period and at the same factory.

The trouble we have taken to pose these possiblities is because the cups seem to us in form and body all but indistinguishable from the well-known and quite common Coalport Bute cup shape and the related coffee can. Coalport examples from both the John Rose and the Anstice Horton & Rose factories are illustrated in Geoffrey Godden's *Coalport and Coalbrookdale Porcelains* (1981), Plates 34, 38, 40, 41, 44, 45, and 48. These Coalport cup and coffee can shapes have been recorded in a set dated 1807 (Godden's Plate 44) and the Bute-shape cup was still in use in 1810 when it was depicted in the foreground of Thomas Baxter's workbench as drawn by Baxter in 1810. This drawing is in the Victoria & Albert Museum. However, these cup and coffee can forms were standard shapes in favour over a relatively long period and the fact that some Coalport examples were being decorated in 1810 does not mean that the Davenport examples can not be dated to 1808 or earlier.

The fortunate owner of these rare early Davenport teawares kindly gave me one of the coffee cans which I, in turn, sacrificed in the name of science (there not being any previously published analysis of Davenport's hybrid hard-paste porcelain) by sending a piece to be analysed. I here assumed that this coffee can, matching in its gilt decoration the impressed marked covered sugar bowl and the tea-pot stand, was also of Davenport manufacture. The results in percentages are:

Silica	76.00
Alumina	18.04
Potash	3.04
Soda	1.26
Lime	.68

Iron	.28
Magnesia	.16
Titanic acid	.03
Loss	.19

This, as might be expected, is very similar in the main percentages to other hybrid hard-paste porcelains of the approximate period 1800–10. We give for comparison the basic analysis of four other makes, including the earlier true hard-paste Bristol. In giving these I have limited the results to those in respect of the Silica, Alumina, Potash, Soda, and Magnesia, disregarding the very variable trace elements. These results differ, of course, from the bone china analysis in that no Phosphorus Pentoxide was detected. The earlier so-called soap-rock porcelains such as Worcester or Caughley would also have shown a higher percentage of Magnesia.

		Silica	Alumina	Potash	Soda	Magnesia
Bristol	c.1775	73.20	22.80	2.43	0.29	0.25
New Hall	c.1795	71.90	20.80	3.40	1.71	0.18
Coalport	c.1805	74.50	19.90	2.84	1.61	0.14
M. Mason	c.1805	63.46	26.76	3.25	1.79	1.76

We do not therefore believe that Davenport hybrid hard-paste porcelains can be distinguished from other makes by means of chemical or other forms of analysis. Rather, we must examine closely the shapes, the patterns, and the pattern numbers where these are present. The shape must form our best guide at this stage of research.

The helpful use in some instances of standard shapes for both earthenwares and the Davenport porcelains does not seem to have been carried over to the early

188. Oval covered sugar box (replacement incorrect knob) with Bute-shape cup and coffee can. Hybrid hard-paste porcelain. Sugar 4¾×3¾in. Impressed mark Davenport over anchor (P 3) on sugar bowl, c.1807–10. (Diana Darlington Collection)

teawares, at least not so far as our present knowledge goes. All we have to go on in regard to the harder paste examples is an oval covered sugar box with its later replacement knob, shown in Plate 188 with the matching Bute-shape cup and straight-sided coffee can – articles which do not have any helpful distinctive features. The oval-bodied sugar box is impressed marked as is the related oval teapot stand. We need to find a matching early oval teapot form and the, presumably oval, jug shape. Some rare bone china examples are known but are, I believe, of a slightly later date and have non-ring handles.

We do not know at this stage of our research if only one form of Davenport hybrid hard-paste porcelain tea set was made (probably, as has been suggested, with a straight-sided 'old oval' form teapot) or whether several different, as yet unrecognized, Davenport teaware shapes were produced during the short period that this firm was making the hybrid hard-paste porcelains.

It is almost inconceivable that the even then important Davenport firm was not producing a large quantity of teaware in the 1805-10 period for this was the staple of all English porcelain manufacturers, large and small. In the case of Davenport we are probably seeking unmarked specimens which may not even bear a pattern number. Certainly if pattern numbers do occur on such hybrid hard-paste procelain teawares, they will be quite low – under 100.

John Davenport, like other leading British manufacturers, was well aware of the porcelains being produced by the Continental manufacturers and, in particular, by the French potters many of whom were sending their highly fashionable porcelains for sale in the London shops. An 1811 letter in the Wedgwood archives at Keele University (20843-29), for example, contains the statement: '. . . for the fine goods we are yet much behind our neighbours the French in elegance and taste and the Chinese in price and value.'

At this period the Davenport factory would probably have been producing the glossy-surfaced hard-paste porcelains but very soon afterwards the basic mix seems to have changed back to bone china, that is, if you agree with my proposition that both the hard and the softer bone china were not made at the same period. This later bone china was softer than the hybrid hard-paste but more dense than the first bone china. The new glaze, too, was superior and the wares do not display the discoloration associated with the first Davenport bone china mix as used in our first period, *c*.1803–7.

Several Davenport porcelain forms of the approximate period 1810–20 show French influence, in particular the vases, as shown in Colour Plate XXVII and Plates 300 and 306–10, although similar vase forms were likewise favoured by other English manufacturers. Some Davenport ornamental articles, such as swan-form ink-pots, display a decided French air.

18 Porcelain Marks

P 1

P 2

P 3

P 4

P 5

5A

The P prefix used stands for porcelain. In listing these marks it must not be assumed that all pieces will bear a mark – this was certainly not the case in regard to the earlier specimens made before about 1830 – nor must it be assumed that an unmarked piece must be early!

The bone china pieces, wares associated with the 1806–7 Royal order, bear a painted mark of the place-name LONGPORT over a large anchor device (P 1). Such an early painted mark from the coffee cup and saucer shown in Plate 187 is here shown. The anchor device in its large size and its exact form without the top cross-bar, seems to be unique to this period.

The mark most often found on the early bone china is the painted name 'Longport' without the anchor (P 2). Being hand-painted many variations in style and size occur. Sometimes the place-name is rendered in joined writing letters, on other specimens it is rendered in italics or capital letters. In my opinion this mark is found only within the 1805–10 period.

The impressed anchor and Davenport name-mark (P 3) very rarely occurs on early bone china (Plate 188) but is usually associated with the hybrid hard-paste porcelains which I have tentatively dated to the 1808–12 period. Indeed it seems to be the only class of mark found on this body. Note the upper- and lower-case letters on this early porcelain version of a later earthenware mark in which the name is given in capitals.

It should be noted that although the anchor device (in various forms) occurs as part of most Davenport marks, it must not be assumed that any anchor mark necessarily denotes a Davenport origin. This is far from the case, as the anchor was used by many firms, and not only in the British Isles.

After about 1810 or 1812 a series of printed marks occur, all of which include the personal name DAVENPORT. The rarest and probably the earliest (P 4) comprises a horseshoe shape strap framing the name with a fouled anchor in the centre. This is usually printed in red and was often transferred on to the porcelain on the workman's thumb.

A rather similar, often thumb-transferred DAVENPORT and anchor device (P 5), is usually referred to as the ribbon mark. This standard mark was used over a long period but the early use (in the approximate period 1812–30) is confined to on-glaze red or occasionally brown, not underglaze blue which signifies a later dating from about 1845 onwards. A very rare variation of this mark has the ribbon and name enclosed within a box-like frame (P 5A).

Other marks which were used within the approximate period 1812–40 include the two- or three-line versions of the name and address mark.

DAVENPORT	DAVENPORT
LONGPORT	LONGPORT
	STAFFORDSHIRE

A crown may appear over both these word marks. We designate these P 6 or P 6 crowned and P 7 or P 7 crowned. The uncrowned versions are usually earlier than the crowned device but this is not always the case as, for example, the uncrowned P 7 occurs on the Dover Horticultural Society plates of the 1830s, see p. 271. A quite rare Royal mark (P 8) was used within the period 1830–June 1837. This printed, overglaze, device takes the form of a crowned garter. The garter contains the words 'Longport. Davenport, Staffordshire' while 'Manufacturer to their Majesties' appears in a central position. This, seemingly, marks the fact that the Davenport firm produced porcelains for William IV. Its use would not have extended into the post-June 1837 Victorian period. It is

209 · The Porcelains

unlikely that this special printed mark was the only one employed during the 1830–7 period.

The personal name Davenport often occurs below the printed diamond-shaped shape or design registration mark, on registered shapes produced from 1849 onwards. Likewise the name may occur as part of special pattern marks when the added design was a printed one. Such pattern marks more often occur on earthenwares than on porcelains. These two marks will be referred to simply as the registration mark and printed pattern mark. In the latter case the mark is a special one unique to one design and the name of this pattern is often incorporated in that mark.

A standard mark of the post-1845 period was the ribbon device, our P 5, but printed in blue rather than red. We will simply refer to this as 'P 5 blue'. Being printed in blue the mark does not appear so sharp as the on-glaze red version. Terry Lockett has noted this mark in black, a variety which he dates to approximately 1850–70, but the black version appears to be very uncommon.

The standard post-1870 (all these dates are of necessity approximate) mark was the crowned three-line name and address mark but printed in red rather than pale puce (P 9).

Some post-1870 or later plates, dishes and other flat-wares bear an impressed DAVENPORT mark applied in a straight line (P 10). It should be noted, however, that some stock of such blanks seem to have been sold off after the firm's closure and that consequently not all examples were decorated by Davenports. I have previously noted in my *Encyclopaedia of British Pottery and Porcelain Marks* the impressed mark DAVENPORTS LTD. I am, however, not now sure that this form of mark was employed. The plate shown in Plate 288 which is signed and dated 'R. Eaton. 1887' bears only mark P 10 as does another late example with its original 'Davenports Limited' paper label.

The last standard Davenport porcelain factory mark we have to record is DAVENPORT'S (P 11). This is to be found on flat PATENT slabs or plaques but, as will be noted, many of these were seemingly sold in an undecorated state and this mark should not be regarded as proof that the added decoration was applied in the factory or that the artist was employed by Davenports. Also several examples of Emile Lessore's painting have been recorded on marked Davenport plates but he is not regarded as having been employed by this company. The firm seems, like others, to have been happy to sell blanks for decoration by other firms or persons.

In addition to the standard marks mentioned one rare version of the anchor and name device appears to have been used only on goods sold from the Liverpool premises and in general this device will be found on pieces which postdate 1860. The printed mark comprises a crown with the name DAVENPORT below. Descending from the crown through the name is a large anchor device and the address '30 Canning Place, Liverpool' appears in a ribbon below.

The factory marks enable most Davenport porcelains to be approximately dated but, unfortunately, the impressed Davenport and anchor device (P 3), when applied to porcelains, does not include the year numbers which were applied to the later earthenware versions of this mark (see p. 73). It should be noted that the marks referred to in this chapter relate only to the porcelains, other marks may be unique to the earthenwares or to the stone china body.

Apart from the marks it might be helpful to mention at this stage the pattern numbers and the painters' tally marks. Although we, the joint authors, have both stated previously that the tearwares, the dessert wares, and the dinner wares bear different series of pattern numbers, we now think it unlikely that this was the position in the early days when the porcelain body was first introduced. It seems more reasonable to believe that the numbers were entered in a pattern book or list in consecutive order as the patterns were introduced, irrespective of the type of article the pattern was to embellish.

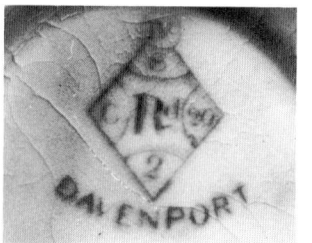

210 · The Porcelains

It could be that later as the number of patterns became unwieldy, the list was split or subdivided. However, this division is now difficult to explain or to see how it would work when no prefix or other distinguishing cypher was used. Could the porcelain works really have, for example, three different pattern 100, one for teawares, one for desserts, and one for dinner services? Some other factories, such as Ridgway, certainly used different series but here there was no direct duplication as the numbers (after 999) were fractional and expressed under different numerators. This was not the case at the Davenport factory where (with minor exceptions) the numbers are all written in a straightforward manner. The exception is in a multicolour printed teapot of *c*.1840 which bears the pattern number 2/1001. This fractional number, it is believed, relates to the novel printing technique, see p. 166, although a matching cup is reported as having only the simple, non-fractional, number 1001.

The Davenport porcelain pattern numbers (which differ from the earthenware, stone china, and ironstone series) commenced at 1 and climbed to the 800s for teawares by the time the Royal mark P 8 was in use in the 1830s. Teawares of the form registered in January 1849 usually bear numbers in excess of 2000. An account of the 1860s includes teawares of patterns 3164 and 3297 and by the 1880s the teaware pattern numbers were in the 6000s. The dessert patterns are discussed on pp. 243 ff.

In general the Davenport pattern numbers, at least on the pre-1850 examples, are painted in a small and neat manner, often in gold. They may easily be overlooked and a glass is often required to read the numbers correctly. Painters' personal tally marks may occur by or under the pattern number and take various forms, a small square, triangle or circle, to cite the simplest. On some, mainly pre-1830 pieces, only the painter's tally mark occurs, the plate shown as Plate 248 being such a specimen. However, such tally marks occur, with pattern numbers, on the products of several nineteenth-century manufacturers and, as yet, our research does not enable a positive identification to be made solely on the existence of such a personal device. However, we do reproduce below a selection of Davenport's painters', or gilders', tally-marks found on porcelains belonging to the joint authors. These usually occur in the period 1815–60 but not on all specimens.

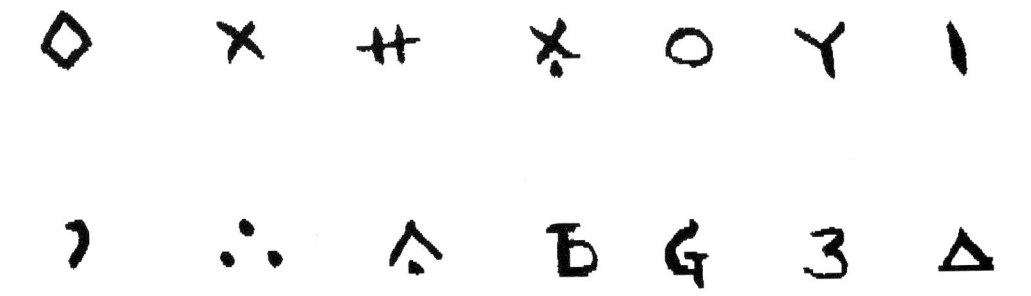

Turning from the review of the marks, the pattern numbers, and the personal tally marks to discuss the porcelains, we find that the early Davenport bone china teawares are extremely difficult to trace, to identify, and to date. They seem to be unmarked (except for the Royal order example) and are usually devoid of a pattern number. The relatively few examples we have traced tend to be of the more expensive type – drawing-room specimens. Terence Lockett has, however, suggested, probably correctly, that the early Davenport porcelains included the inexpensive, rather cottagey, formal floral designs that are associated with the New Hall factory at Shelton. These simple designs that could be painted by cheap semi-skilled hands and which required no gilding were certainly extremely popular and were produced by most (if not all) Staffordshire porcelain manufacturers. Could Davenport have been the odd man out? If our Longport firm did produce such teawares, the shapes would have been simple, low cost, types with teabowls rather than handled teacups.

19 The Teawares

Turning to the up-market designs, the very rare teapot, covered sugar basin and creamer forms featured in Plate 190 are interesting and quite beautifully painted. These and matching cups and saucers (as Plate 189) were sold by Phillips the auctioneers in 1980. A trio of saucer, tea cup, and coffee cup from this service is shown as Plate 224 in *Staffordshire Porcelain*. The inverted bell-shape coffee cup should be especially noted. The interior features of the teapot are shown by Philip Miller and Michael Berthoud in *An Anthology of British Teapots*. I also show in Plate 191 a matching waste bowl. All these forms can be considered key Davenport porcelain forms of the 1805 period, but as yet only one service is known to us. The branch and leaf handles and terminals to the oval sugar bowl and its cover must be very characteristic and these occur also on the circular covered bowl shown in Plate 192. This piece is neatly painted with the Royal Chinese Temple design with an amended gilt border to the cover. It is possible, however, that the Minton factory occasionally used versions of these twig handle forms.

The unmarked early Davenport bone china teawares are trimly potted although they have a strange earthenware-like appearance. The glaze is slightly matt and is now broken up with very fine crazing. The body is slightly discoloured to a creamy tone. The porcelain has average translucency and feels warm and pleasant to the touch.

The saucers to this service do not have added footrims in the conventional manner but rather the Chinese-style dished out centre to the underside. This technique is by no means unique to Davenport, but we suggest that it is the type of foot to be

189. A tea cup and saucer in the bone china body attractively painted with floral studies. Note the cup shape. Diameter of saucer 5¼in. Unmarked, *c*.1810. (Diana Darlington Collection)

190. Oval form bone china teapot, covered sugar box and creamer from the floral painted service as Plate 189, showing very rare but key Davenport shapes. Teapot ht 5¾in. Unmarked, *c*.1810. (Phillips)

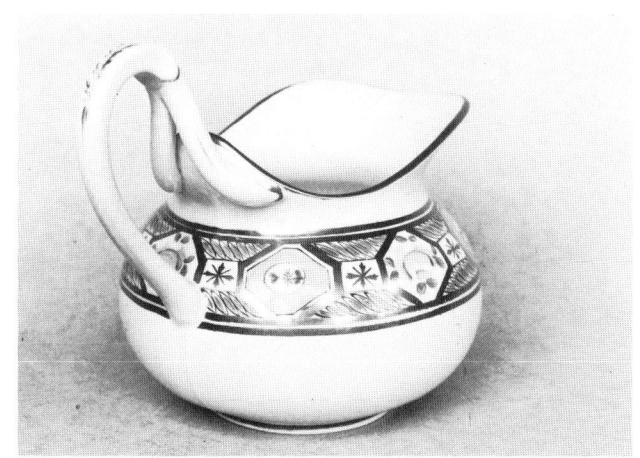

191. The waste-bowl from the floral painted early Davenport bone china tea service shown in Plates 189–90. Diameter 6in. Unmarked, c.1810. (Geoffrey Godden, chinaman)

192. An unmarked bone china circular sugar box and cover decorated with the Royal order 1806–7. 'Chinese Temple' pattern. Note also the twig handles. Ht 5in. c.1810–12. (Geoffrey Godden, chinaman)

193. A well-potted attractive bone china Bute-shape tea cup and saucer painted with figures in landscape and neatly gilt wide borders. Diameter of saucer 5¼in. Unmarked, c.1810–12. (Geoffrey Godden, chinaman)

194. A rare form of bone china milk or cream jug with typical Davenport bifurcated handle form. The pattern is not unique to this factory. Ht 5in. c.1810–12. (Diana Darlington Collection)

expected with early unmarked Davenport saucers. The well-potted landscape-painted cup and saucer shown in Plate 193 has a foot of this type although in this case the tea cup is of a typical and conventional Bute shape and matching coffee vessels would probably have been of the straight-sided can form. It is difficult to point out characteristics in this unmarked Davenport Bute-shape cup but the plain loop handle is rather thicker than one would expect and the loop is a generous one swinging well away from the body. At most English porcelain factories the popular Bute-shape cup remained in production for a long period, from about 1800 to the general introduction of the London-shape in about 1812. This is not to say that the Bute shape (as Plate 193) was the only one available within this period, for the customer would have had a choice of several forms and very many different added patterns, several of which would be variations or direct copies of designs favoured by rival manufacturers.

A rare variation of the inverted bell-shape coffee cup form occurs with an attractive leaf, stem, and flower-head handle. Such an unmarked trio is featured in Plate 195. Another two decorated with the same yellow, gold, and rose panelled, border design are shown in *Staffordshire Porcelain*, Plate 223. The coffee can has an angular handle similar to that on the Royal cup and saucer which I illustrate as Plate 187. It has been stated that other pieces of the original tea service bore the written Longport mark. An oval teapot with a cup and a coffee can are illustrated as Plate 307 in *An Anthology of British Teapots* but no information is there given on the mark. A creamer (Plate 194) with the same pattern has the same divided (bifurcated) handle form as that found on the flower painted oval-plan tearwares shown in Plate 190.

213 · The Porcelains

This so-called (inaccurately) 'Church Gresley' pattern much favoured by several firms was, seemingly, also popular at the Davenport works in the early period for yet another rare form of tea service is featured in *An Anthology of British Teapots*, Plate 715. Some pieces from this service are reported as bearing the impressed Davenport and anchor mark – one more usually associated with the hybrid hard-paste porcelains or with the earthenwares.

We also have a class of low-profiled Davenport bone china teawares embellished with engine-turned ribs, very much in the style of some Davenport earthenwares (see our illustration of the magnificent tea wares in the City of Liverpool Museum, Plate 54). The covered sugar bowl shown in Plate 196 is typical of this tasteful and neatly potted class. This piece shouts its Davenport origin but, alas, it is completely unmarked. However, a similar sugar bowl in the Lockett collection bears the low pattern number 26, see *Transactions of the English Ceramic Circle* 12 Pt 2 (1985), Plate 98b. The oval teapots of this class have a high prow at the front, as shown in Plate 65. All these earthenwares shapes may also occur in early bone china of the period *c*.1805–10. A slightly later variation of these shapes has a higher profile, a heavier knob and outward curving handles to the sugar bowl. A teapot of this form is in the City Museum at Stoke and bears the pattern number 139. This piece is featured as Plate 1242 by Philip Miller and Michael Berthoud in *An Anthology of British Teapots*. A sugar bowl is shown by Terence Lockett in *Transactions of the English Ceramic Circle* 12 Pt 2 (1985), Plate 99A.

The oval covered sugar bowl shown in Plate 197 is also confidently believed to be Davenport although it bears only a pattern number, 297, but here the period under discussion is nearer 1810 than 1800. The shape with its oval mushroom-like knob and inward curling handles matches a blue printed sugar bowl with its matching cream jug and 'new oval type teapot' discussed by Miss Diana Darlington in the *Northern Ceramic*

195. Davenport bone china tea and coffee cup with saucer, showing a rare but seemingly characteristic handle form. Diameter of saucer 5½in. Unmarked, *c*.1810–12. (Geoffrey Godden, chinaman)

196. A neatly potted and engine-turned bone china sugar box and cover of typical Davenport shape, see also Plate 201. Length 6¾in. Unmarked, *c*.1810. (Geoffrey Godden, chinaman)

197. An oval Davenport bone china sugar box and cover of characteristic shape. Grey and gilt border, pattern number 297. Length 8in. *c*.1810. (Geoffrey Godden, chinaman)

Society Newsletter 63 (September 1986), figs 1–2. We show these rare, but unmarked, forms in Plates 198–9. The teacup from this set was of Bute shape with a plain loop handle (as Plate 193). The coffee cups were of straight-sided can form again with a plain loop handle. The saucers are of the early type without an added foot-rim. The teapot shape (Plate 198) matches marked Davenport earthenware examples and the strainer arrangement and the shaped pouring guard within the pot are characteristically Longport. The moulded thickening at the end of the spout is also very characteristic, see the earthenware examples shown in Plates 60 and 65. These pieces which, as the owner stated 'I just knew as I saw each piece appear from the box that they could only be Davenport!', do not bear a pattern number and we expect that in keeping with the practice at several other contemporary factories the blue printed designs were not allocated a number. They did not appear in the pattern book and they were probably ordered and invoiced by means of a reference to a name rather than a number.

Whilst most Staffordshire porcelain manufacturers produced a good range of inexpensive bat-printed teawares, the Davenport essays in this style seem to be distinctly rare. We show in Plate 200 an unusual example printed within hand-applied black line edges. The probable period of such decoration is *c*.1810–15. If it were later, one would expect the prints to have been applied to London shape teawares, see p. 213. Here we have a cup shape which we have not previously featured and it is to be expected that over the years many more examples of on-glaze printed Davenport designs will be identified.

The next forms of Davenport porcelain teawares to be discussed are far more

198. A rare oval unmarked Davenport porcelain teapot decorated with an underglaze blue print. Length 10¾in. *c*.1810–15. (Diana Darlington Collection)

199. The blue printed covered sugar bowl and creamer matching the teapot shown in Plate 198. Sugar bowl 8¼in. long, *c*.1810–5. (Diana Darlington Collection)

commonly found than those previously mentioned but they still, in the probable period 1810–15, do not normally bear a Davenport name-mark. However, the same forms were produced in stone china (see Plate 90) and such non-porcelains do bear standard Davenport marks.

      The teapot and covered sugar bowl featured here as Plate 201 and Colour Plate XVI represent these new forms. These pieces bear the pattern number 310 painted in a small neat manner. Both these pieces bear the painted name and address 'J. Mist, N 82 Fleet Street' on the inside flange of the covers. This relates to the well-known London retailer James Mist, who of course stocked many different makes of ceramics. James Mist's sole occupancy of these Fleet Street premises can be dated to the 1809–15 period. He had been in financial difficulties from at least August 1812 when Minton was paid five shillings in the pound on monies owing, but Mist was included in the *London Gazette* of 29 April, 1815. It is unlikely that Davenports (or any other manufacturer) would have supplied porcelains to Mist after this date, or perhaps even after the 1812 difficulties. Certainly these teawares of pattern 310 predate the spring of 1815. As we

200. A breakfast-size Davenport tea cup and saucer decorated with untitled black bat-printed views. Printed ribbon mark (P 5). Diameter of saucer 6⅜in. (Diana Darlington Collection)

201. The bone china teapot and cover to match the sugar box shown in Colour Plate XVI. Identical markings. This characteristic Davenport shape also occurs in the stone china body. Length 11in. c.1810–12 (Geoffrey Godden, chinaman)

202. Teapot cover showing the characteristic formal floral knob form.

216 · The Porcelains

have earlier stated, Davenports took Mist's former premises in 1818 as their own London showroom.

This teapot and sugar bowl are neatly and painstakingly painted, but the enamels have a rather flat matt appearance which is typical of other Davenport enamelling of this period. The bone china body has again discoloured to a creamy tint.

These shapes are, we believe, unique to the Davenport firm and the knob form (Plate 202) and the handle shapes can be regarded as being very characteristic. The tea-strainer is an applied almost circular grid protruding into the teapot in a convex manner. This too, is characteristic but not unique to our factory. The manner of shaping the pouring-guard is also characteristic and in this case the flange of the cover has been cut back to help retain the cover in place when the teapot is tilted to a pouring position. This undercutting of the flange is a rare refinement found on some Davenport teapot covers. The moulded form of the spout is considered unique to this class of Davenport teaware.

The matching cream or milk jug form is shown in Plate 203, whilst another example is shown as Plate 79 in *Davenport Pottery & Porcelain 1794–1887*. The matching teacup and saucer form is particularly attractive and examples embellished with pattern 293 are illustrated in Plate 204. In our experience these shapes bear very attractive quality porcelain patterns and it would consequently seem that these shapes were reserved for the more expensive, better-class designs. Pattern numbers up to 327 have been noted on these shapes.

The next shape of Davenport teapot to be considered is surprisingly rarer than the leaf-handled form just discussed (Plate 201). It is the 'New Oval' shape, which with minor differences was produced by most English porcelain factories in about 1810. A

203. Davenport bone china creamer of the shape to match the teapot and sugar box shown in Plates 201 and Colour Plate XVI. Note the handle form. Pattern 676. Length 6¼in. (Private Collection)

204. A most attractive Davenport cup and saucer, the chinoiserie decoration in the Meissen style. This cup form relates to the teawares shown in Plates 201–3. Pattern number 293. Diameter of saucer 5¼in. *c.*1810–12. (Geoffrey Godden, chinaman)

205. A 'new oval' shape Davenport teapot and stand decorated with 'Japan' pattern, Davenport's pattern 557. Length 10½in. *c.*1810–15. (Geoffrey Godden, chinaman)

217 · The Porcelains

good, well-decorated Davenport example is shown in Plate 205. This 'Japan'-style design is Davenport's pattern number 557. The convex strainer and the shaped pouring-guard are identical to these features on the previous teapot discussed, and the flange of the cover is similarly cut back. The gilt radiating dashes on the painted oval knob seem to be a favourite Davenport feature. One would expect the teacup accompanying these 'Old Oval' teapots to be of Bute shape and the coffee cup to be of the straight sided 'can' variety (see Plate 188). Some Davenport coffee cans have a Mason-type projection at the top of the handle, or an inward projection near the lower end, see Michael Berthoud, *An Anthology of British Cups*, Plates 237–8. My 'Old Oval' teapot is unmarked, except for the pattern number, and this lack of a name device at this relatively late period *c.*1810–12, may account for the rarity of the pieces known to us. They just have not been correctly attributed to the Davenport works. However, cups of pattern 460, with a teapot of this 'New Oval' shape have been reported with a Davenport printed name-mark. These teapot forms are found embellished with a surprisingly lengthy range of pattern numbers, for as with all Staffordshire firms, the 'New Oval' teaware forms were standard productions. The Davenport version of the creamer form and the simple coffee can are shown in Plate 206. The design on these pieces is number 141.

It should also be noted that this 'New Oval' shape was seemingly reissued some sixty years later, in the 1870s, although it is not now known if the example shown in *An Anthology of British Teapots*, Plate 1308, was merely a specially ordered replacement to a broken earlier teapot, or if it represents a later standard production shape.

I have mentioned the standard Bute-shape cup on several occasions. A very rare Davenport variation on the loop-handled type is shown in *An Anthology of British Cups*, Plate 251. This example has an angular handle and, as such, it may represent a replacement to a non-Davenport service, rather than a Davenport teaware form.

We, the joint authors, had intended to illustrate only clearly marked examples when we set out on this project. It was a good but perhaps too high an ideal and certainly we feel quite sure about our attribution of many unmarked examples. Had we stood by

206. A 'new oval' shape creamer with pale salmon band of pattern 141 and a matching coffee can. Painted pattern number. Creamer ht 4⅜in. *c.*1810–15. (Diana Darlington Collection)

207. A tastefully restrained unmarked coffee can and saucer, perhaps of Davenport manufacture. Diameter of saucer 5¼in. *c.*1815–20. (Geoffrey Godden, chinaman)

this rule we would not have been able to illustrate, for example, the early bone china teawares which are very, very seldom marked. I now wish, even when we have progressed to the 1815–20 period, to illustrate in Plate 207 a delightful French or Welsh-style coffee-can and saucer, I cannot be sure of its Davenport source and it is completely unmarked. Yet it speaks to me as being Davenport at its best and the management certainly employed one or more superb rose painters in the Billingsley manner. The one Davenport feature which I can cite is the gilt trim on the handle which seems to match exactly that on the marked coffee can illustrated in *An Anthology of British Cups*, Plate 237. The Spode-type indented handle on this rose-painted coffee can does rarely occur on Davenport examples but it is not unique to these two factories.

The 'London'-shape Davenport porcelains of the approximate period 1812–20 are well shown in Plate 208 which features the main teaware forms in this universally popular and fashionable basic shape. London-shape teawares were made by all English porcelain manufacturers at this period and many unmarked examples cannot now be identified with any certainty, the cups and saucers being particularly difficult to differentiate. Chapter 15 of *Staffordshire Porcelain* is devoted to a general coverage of this form.

In the case of the teawares here shown of pattern 554 we have the helpful feature of a printed Davenport and anchor mark. This so-called ribbon mark (P 5) was very often transferred on to the porcelain from a charged copper plate by means of the thumb and so shows thumb-print lines. This method of transferring the impression would have been so much more convenient than using transfer paper or a glue bat, but it is only suitable for small devices. A rather rarer and perhaps slightly earlier engraved mark also occurs on London-shape teawares up to at least pattern number 662. This ribbon-like mark (P 4) has an almost complete oval ribbon with the name DAVENPORT, without the cut tails mark P 5, and the fouled anchor device is at a slight angle. These marks are reproduced on p. 209. With this 'London' teapot form the handle shape and the knob form should be noted and the strainer is again of circular convex form.

The London-shape teawares can rarely occur with relief-moulding of the type

208. Representative Davenport 'London-shape' teaware forms of the 1812–20 period. Decorated in underglaze blue and gilt, pattern number 554. Teapot length 10½in. Printed ribbon mark (P 5), c.1812–20. (Godden of Worthing Ltd)

219 · The Porcelains

called by Michael Berthoud 'Palm-leaf and wreath'. This most attractive relief design is by no means unique to the Davenport factory as can be seen from the *Anthology of British Cups*, p. 60, which includes a Davenport teacup, see also that author's Plate 404.

This attractive style of relief-moulding is well shown on the delightful teapot which I feature as Colour Plate XVII. This example shows well the excellence of body and of glaze achieved at the Davenport works by the early 1820s. The body no longer has a tendency to discolour. The glaze has a greater depth and gloss and is less inclined to craze. Indeed this pot will stand comparison with the products of any of the great British china manufacturers.

A rather later version of the London-shape has cups which have twelve facets. An example of this unusual type is shown in *Anthology of British Cups*, Plate 471.

Overlapping with the standard London-shape teawares which were being produced over a long period, we have some rarer shapes which in general bear more expensive styles of decoration and which were consequently more expensive for the buyer. One of these is the so-called Etruscan-shape teacup with its low and wide bowl and angular upward pointed handle, as here shown in Plate 209. The pattern number

209. A so-called Etruscan-shape Davenport trio, well painted with pattern 689. Diameter of saucer 6in. Printed ribbon mark (P 5), c.1820–5. (Geoffrey Godden, chinaman)

210. A typical Davenport covered sugar bowl painted with roses and gilt. 4¾in. Printed ribbon mark and pattern number 730, c.1820–5. (Geoffrey Godden, chinaman)

211. A rare form of Davenport teacup decorated with underglaze blue ground and well gilt. Diameter of cup 3½in. Printed ribbon mark (P 5) and painter's tally mark, c.1820–5. (E. H. Chandler Collection)

212.

range for these shapes is usually in the six or seven hundreds but, of course, an earlier pattern can be added to a newly introduced shape causing abnormalities in the numbering sequence. These Etruscan shaped teawares of the early 1820s usually bear a thumb-transferred ribbon mask (P 5) which includes the DAVENPORT name. We have not as yet located a teapot to match these cup shapes but complete services must have been produced.

The Etruscan-shape teawares can also be found embellished with relief-moulded wreath and floral motifs. Two marked cups of this type are featured in *An Anthology of British Cups*, Plates 313 and 314.

The two circular marked Davenport teapots illustrated as Plates 1803 and 1805 in *An Anthology of British Teapots* are of this approximate period, but the handle form does not match well the Etruscan cup form. The elegant covered sugar shape is shown here in Plate 210, note the ring handles and their attachments which link with the early covered sugar bowl shown in Plate 188. This example bears the thumb-transferred ribbon name-mark (P 5) and the pattern number 730. The small size teapot shown by Mr Berthoud as his Plate 1849 may well also link with this sugar bowl.

The cup shown in Plate 211 bears a thumb-transferred DAVENPORT ribbon mark (P 5) with a painter's tally mark of three dots, but no pattern number. This shape, which Michael Berthoud terms scallop-edge with Old English handle, was a very popular one at the Ridgway factory and at the Rockingham and Coalport factories (to name only the best-known versions) although it seems to be extremely rare in Davenport porcelain. Indeed, it is so rare that I thought my marked example must be a replacement for a set made elsewhere. However, a further example is illustrated as Plate 533 in *An Anthology of British Cups*. It seems probable, therefore, that it represents a further Davenport teaset shape of the 1820s. The existence of matching teapots, covered sugars, and jugs is a certainty!

On the other hand, the marked Davenport coffee cup of Daniel shape shown in the *Anthology* as Plate 558 is probably a replacement to a Daniel service rather than a stock Davenport shape.

212. A tasteful green ground Davenport trio with thick, tooled, gilding and flower painting in the manner of Gould. Diameter of saucer 5¾in. Printed ribbon mark and pattern number 841, c.1825–30. (Godden of Worthing Ltd)

221 · The Porcelains

The green bordered trio of pattern 841 shown in Plate 212, is of superb quality and the gilt border is raised and moulded. In its overall quality one might be excused for terming a single cup and saucer a cabinet piece rather than part of a tea service for everyday use. Yet we have the teacup and the coffee cup with the saucer and as such, we consider this trio must represent part of a very special tea and coffee service. As such, the retail price may have been sixteen or eighteen guineas rather than the average price of two or three pounds for a standard set.

It is also difficult to decide if the splendid cup and saucer from the Victoria & Albert Museum collection, here shown in Plate 213, is a cabinet piece or if it was intended for use. The overall impression is of fine Paris porcelain, the ground colour is a matt green with the birds and foliage resisted out to show the underlying white porcelain, on which the details were added. I have a similar example which bears on both the cup and the saucer the painter's tally mark, a Y-like device but no pattern number. There is also on the pieces the horseshoe-like DAVENPORT name-mark and anchor, P 4.

If we consider, I think correctly, that such a cup and saucer was a show piece, it does not follow that all cups and saucers of this shape were for display only. The same form could well have been embellished in a less expensive manner for table use. In the case of this basic shape there is certainly a slight variation used for the standard teawares. The attractive high loop handle remains but the body of the cup has a graceful curve in place of the rather angular bowl of the Victoria & Albert Museum's cabinet cup. I show the two versions side by side in Plate 214. The form on the right can occur in several sizes, one, seemingly, a breakfast cup of a large size. This point can apply equally to all basic forms.

I have mentioned standard teawares and the richer individual display or cabinet pieces. There are also the rare breakfast services which were made in smaller quantities. I can quote the make-up of such a set as listed on a sales invoice dated 7 August 1827. The pattern number is not given but as the china was described as gold lines we must, I think, assume that it was not painted with flowers or landscapes and did not have a coloured border. This was sold from the London showrooms at 82, Fleet Street and comprised:

6 Breakfast cups and saucers at	2s	6d
6 Coffee cups and saucers at	1s	8d
6 Breakfast plates at	2s	1d
2 Cake plates (of different sizes) one at	2s	11d
one at	2s	6d
1 milk jug and cover	3s	9d
1 slop bowl	2s	1d

213. A graceful marked (P 4) Davenport green ground cup and saucer with resisted birds in landscape pattern and wide gilt borders. Cup ht 2½in. c.1820–5. (Victoria & Albert Museum)

214. Two slightly differently formed Davenport coffee cups. Left, as Plate 212, painter's tally mark 'Y'. Ht 3¼ and 2¾in. Printed ribbon mark (P 5) on each. (Geoffrey Godden, chinaman)

222 · The Porcelains

2 plates at 2s 6d
1 sugar Box and cover 3s 9d

These descriptions need a little clarification. Firstly, breakfast cups are large teacups about double the capacity of the standard cups. I believe that the coffee cups listed at a lesser rate would have been of normal size. The breakfast plates would have had a diameter of seven or eight inches. Such plates were included in the breakfast services but not in teasets at this period. The milk jug was larger than a normal cream or milk jug and would have been of upright form with, as described, a cover. The slop bowl may have been of larger than normal capacity.

In this case the purchaser did not order a teapot. This may have been because these breakfast utensils were required to enlarge an already existing tea service which included a teapot. Alternatively, the buyer may well have owned a silver teapot and wished to use and display this article. Likewise no coffee pot was ordered. They were made by most other firms but are rarely found today. Indeed, we can only recall having seen one marked Davenport porcelain coffee pot.

While remarking on this individual 1827 order we would like to make the point that while all services had a standard make-up for pricing purposes, the buyers could always purchase exactly what they wanted, from a single odd cup to a double service. Some breakfast services might have included covered muffin dishes, egg cups, egg cup stands (for three, four, six or more egg cups), honey pots, butter dishes, even toast-racks. Here we are quoting some of the articles known to have been made by Davenport's contemporaries. It is well worth seeking Longport examples: Jonathan Gray's collection includes two different forms of marked Davenport egg cups. Some two-handled cup-like bowls also occur, which may have been part of breakfast services.

Another surviving account, dated 14 January 1840, does give us some comparisons between the price of the large breakfast cups and saucers and the standard items of the same pattern – an inexpensive gilt Etruscan vase design. The breakfast cups and saucers were 21s a dozen, whereas the standard ones were 14s, a third cheaper. To underline my point regarding the varying make-up of a service, this purchaser required eighteen cups and saucers and four bread and butter plates instead of the usual two.

The same buyer, A. Brooks, Esq., also purchased the colour-printed earthenware dinner service for twelve persons discussed in chapter 15 and illustrated in Colour Plate XII and Plates 139, two drab-ware jugs at 1s 4d each, and a pair of 'richly cut' glass, quart-size decanters and a pair of pint-size decanters. These would also have been made at Davenports as this firm was one of the few china and earthernware manufacturers also to have produced glass ware.

Reverting to the porcelains, Mr Brooks in January 1840 also purchased five individual cups and saucers of differing patterns and perhaps of different shapes. Unfortunately these are not described on the invoice, but two cost 1s 6d each, two 1s 7d, and one 2s. It is possible that these individual specimens could have been of the type illustrated in Plate 215. Several years ago I purchased from a single source twelve or more of these cups and saucers, each bearing a different very decorative design. It seems that these were originally made and bought as single examples, perhaps for use as a harlequin set for afternoon tea or coffee. The cups are of a delightful almost feline form, with little faces at the top of the handle peering into the cup. I show examples from this set in Colour Plate XVIII and in Plate 215. Others are illustrated in *Staffordshire Porcelain*, Plate 231.

Another rare and splendid cup and saucer form occurs and is very much in the Paris-style although it was certainly copied by British manufacturers. These special pieces have a row of mock pearls in relief around the cup just under the lip and a fan-like ornamental device within the handle. Such display cups and stands may be expected to be decorated in the richest style, with raised gilding.

Considering the relatively small number of marked Davenport teawares which seem to be available for inspection today, it is amazing how many different basic shapes were produced by this firm. It is unfortunately impossible for us to illustrate all post-1830 teaware forms, but we will show representative types. However, after about 1860 the number of new shapes seems to have been drastically reduced. Amongst the teapot shapes we are unable to illustrate is the pattern 774 example shown in *An Anthology of British Teapots*, Plate 1855. One of the printed marks is certainly helpful in approximately dating objects on which it appears. This is the crowned garter mark which includes in the centre (under the name DAVENPORT) the words 'Manufacturer to their Majesties'. This mark (P 8) and the Royal association should relate to the fact that the Davenports produced a large and magnificent dessert service for William IV (see pp. 244–7), although this was probably not completed before the middle of 1831 or even 1832. This William IV garter mark should not have been used after the death of William and the accession of Queen Victoria in June 1837.

The strange shell-shape teapot with seaweed relief motifs shown in Terence Lockett's *Davenport Pottery & Porcelain* as Plate 86 bears this royal mark but I regard this piece as a novelty pot, and do not believe that it was intended to form part of an everyday tea set.

We are fortunate to be able to include here illustrations of a gilt porcelain tea set of pattern 851. Each piece bears the strap mark (P 4) printed in brown but the hitherto unrecorded Davenport shapes are a strange mixture. The coffee pot form (Plate 219) and especially the handle is similar to some Coalport examples of *c*.1810–15. The attractive cream or milk jug (Plate 218) is typically Davenport and in its general shape and handle shape links with the sprigged example illustrated in Plate 295. However, the teapot and sugar bowl shapes appear rather later in style, for example, similar to

215. A yellow ground, shell painted, French-style coffee cup and saucer. Cup ht 3½in. Ribbon mark (P 5), *c*.1825–30. (Godden of Worthing Ltd)

216. A rare form of footed teapot decorated with gilt pattern 851. Ht 6½in. Printed mark (P 4), *c*.1830–35. (Hacking Collection)

217. The covered sugar bowl matching the teapot shown in Plate 216. Ht 5½in. Printed mark (P 4) and pattern number 851, *c*.1830–35. (Hacking Collection)

224 · The Porcelains

218. The elegant porcelain milk jug accompanying the teapot and sugar bowl shown in Plates 216–17. This basic form with its typical Davenport handle is also featured in Plate 295. Ht 3¾in. Printed mark (P 4) and pattern number 851, c.1830–5. (Hacking Collection)

219. The very rare form of marked Davenport coffee-pot which accompanied the teawares shown in Plates 216–18. This shape is reminiscent of a Coalport shape of 1810–15. Ht 10½in. Printed mark (P 4) and pattern number 851, c.1830–5. (Hacking Collection)

Copeland & Garrett forms of the post-1833 period. This strange grouping of very rare and seemingly unrelated Davenport tea and coffee service shapes is important and may well lead to the discovery of unmarked examples. They certainly show, yet again, that almost anything can turn up in Davenport pottery or porcelain. Of course, in dating such sets one must consider the latest feature, not the earliest. The teapot suggests a date in the 1830s, rather than the 1810–15 period of the coffee pot shape. The pattern number 851 also confirms this later date. We are indebted to Mr Jack Hacking for having reported this service.

The light green and gilt teawares shown in Plate 220 bear this pre-1838 Royal mark (P 8) and the pattern number 869. We make no apologies for re-illustrating this service, because photographs featuring all the related shapes of a tea service are now so rare. Not only do complete services seldom come on the market but when they do the tendency is for dealers to split them up, selling the teapot to one customer, the creamer to another collector, and so on. It may suit the sellers and indeed the individual buyers but the opportunity to record the various forms is usually lost.

It might be thought that these rococo shapes of the 1830s were the only ones produced by Davenports at this period but this is clearly not so and at least two near variations are known. The cup and saucer of pattern 981, shown in Plate 221 represented a very near match to those depicted in the group photograph. The marked Davenport teapot shown in Plate 222 is in detail quite different from the Royal marked example. This bird-painted teapot might perhaps be dated c.1837–40.

The cream or milk jug shown in Plate 223 is a rather later example of this general early Victorian rococo style. The pattern number is 1299 and the new mark comprises the crown above the words DAVENPORT LONGPORT STAFFORDSHIRE, arranged in three lines (P 7). This mark is printed over the glaze, normally in a pale puce colour. This was a standard mark within the approximate period 1835–45. When printed in red the piece can be considered to be of a later period – c.1870 onwards. The teacup to match this jug is probably the wide and low one shown by Terence Lockett in this 1972 book, Plate 84, iii, which is of pattern 1225, or Plate 783 in *An Anthology of British Cups*. This latter work underlines the point that various manufacturers produced similar shapes and that very careful comparison should always be made.

The teapot shown in Plate 224 is a very much simplified version of the rococo

225 · The Porcelains

220. Representative shapes from a marked Davenport teaset of pattern 869, decorated in pale green and gilt. The top object is the teapot stand. Teapot ht 7¾in. Printed Royal mark (P 8) and pattern number, c.1830–7. (Geoffrey Godden, chinaman)

221. A green and gilt Davenport coffee cup and saucer with bird and floral centre. Note the handle form. Diameter of saucer 6¼in. Ribbon mark (P 5) and pattern number 981, c.1830–40. (E. H. Chandler Collection)

type featured in Plates 220 and 222. This example bears the crowned overglaze P 7 mark in puce and the pattern number 1266. It can reasonably be dated to c.1840. A rather more simplified version of this basic shape occurs and an example is shown in *An Anthology of British Teapots*, Plate 2044: another pot of the same approximate period is shown there as Plate 1951.

    The covered sugar bowl illustrated in Plate 225 also seems to be of the 1840–50 period and is very close in general style to the teapot shown in Plate 224. The sugar bowl bears the crowned P 7 mark and the pattern number 1468. The pattern is a neat but inexpensive one: the flower sprays and the festoon borders are printed in outline and then coloured-in by hand, usually by women. This technique is by no means unique to

222. An ornately-moulded Davenport rococo teapot of different form to that shown in Plate 220. Ht 9in. Printed ribbon mark and pattern number 916, c.1837–40. (Private Collection)

223. A light green and gilt bordered floral painted creamer. Ht 4¾in. Printed in three-line name mark (P 7) and pattern number 1299, c.1840–5. (Private Collection)

224. An unusual form of Davenport teapot decorated in buff and gold. Ht 7½in. Printed crowned three-line mark (P 7) with pattern number 1266, c.1840–45. (Private Collection)

225. A moulded sugar bowl form embellished with a relatively inexpensive form of decoration Printed outline design coloured-in by women painters. Ht 6¾in. Printed three-line mark (P 7) and pattern number 1468, c.1840–50. (L. Richmond Collection)

the Davenport factory. It should be mentioned that at this period, in the early 1840s, there was depression in the trade and the wages, such as they were, had been reduced.

On 20 January 1849, W. Davenport & Co. registered a new set of teaware shapes. The shapes depicted in the official files are for the teapot, the covered sugar bowl, the jug, and a cup and saucer. A very attractive good quality teaset of pattern 2427 in these 1849 registered forms (which we could term 'Stanley') is in the City of Stoke-on-Trent Museum at Hanley. Pattern numbers found on these 1849 registered shapes range from about 1900 to approximately 2500. On many of the registered pieces one finds the diamond-shape registration device (see Appendix) with the name DAVENPORT added below. Some later (post-1852) issues of these shapes correctly do not bear the registration as the cover was for a three-year period only. These popular Davenport teaware shapes were chosen for the colourful teawares supplied to the City of Liverpool. These examples bear pattern 1946, a very colourful red and gilt design, with the addition of the City Arms in gold, and also bear the special marks of the Davenport warehouse at 30 Canning Place, Liverpool (see p. 210).

A jug and cup and saucer of pattern 2130 is shown in *Staffordshire Porcelain*, Plate 663 and a blue and gold trio of teacup, coffee cup, and saucer is here shown in Plate 226. This pattern is numbered 2440, the flowers and butterfly on the blue ground are in raised gold and the whole appearance is superb quality. Had the company taken a stand at the Great Exhibition in 1851, this is the type of porcelain which they might well have displayed. Alas, they did not compete and we lost the opportunity to read about or see engravings of their products in the 1850–1 period.

It could well be that the firm was suffering difficulties at this time. The output of, at least, porcelain teawares – the staple of the industry – seems to have been at a low ebb. One now experiences great difficulties in tracing marked Davenport examples of the post-1850 period. One must remember, however, that in the case of the Davenport factories they were concerned with the manufacture of earthenware of all types, also with glass. If trading difficulties were experienced the porcelain side of the company would have been the first to suffer a cut-back.

Three documented specimens of the early 1850s are still preserved, we hope, but they may not be readily accessible for, on 24 May 1854, on the occasion of Queen Victoria's 34th birthday, the following 'local articles of art and industry' were deposited under the foundation stone of the new Burslem Town Hall: 'Flint glass goblet by W. Davenport, Porcelain centrepiece by W. Davenport, Dinner plate by W. Davenport', plus an Alcock figure of the Duke of Wellington, a mosaic jug by Boote, and colour-printed earthenwares from T. J. & J. Mayer's Dale Hall works.

Several post-1855 Davenport cup shapes are illustrated in Terence Lockett's 1972 book and in *An Anthology of British Cups* and we must resist the temptation to retread this ground. An undated William Davenport & Co. (Liverpool) account of the 1860s includes an interesting array of Davenport glasswares and earthenwares, including a dinner service for 18 persons in earthenware, coloured and gilt pattern 2376 at £14 18s 0d, earthenware chamber services, green glazed dessert wares, as well as drab-ware jugs. The relatively small quantity of china includes a breakfast service of pattern 3164 charged at £3 16s 0d and various items of 'gilt' teaware of pattern 3297. The last additional item was '24 tea plates gold lines', £1 10s 0d. As is generally known the early tea sets did not have the small tea plates, only two large plates which are variously described as bread and butter or as cake plates. The Davenport firm was obviously producing such additional 'tea plates' in the 1860s.

Terence Lockett in his 1972 book correctly remarked upon the dearth of Davenport teawares to be found dating about 1865 onwards. However, an interesting document has been reported to us by Robert Copeland, the Historical Consultant to Spode Ltd and formerly Director of the preceding firm of W. T. Copeland & Sons Ltd. This is the Price List for China, Earthenware, and Glass as manufactured by Davenports Ltd in its closing years. The list is not dated but it clearly relates to the period subsequent to the formation of the new Limited Company in August 1881 (for which see our account on p. 65).

We can usefully quote here the section relating to the teawares as this information had not hitherto been published and the facts, no doubt, also relate to the porcelain produced in the 1870s, if not in the 1860s. We are greatly indebted to Mr Copeland for reporting this document and for placing it at our disposal.

The standard tea services were of 39 and of 40 pieces each, costing from £7 16s 9d (£9 13s 5d) to £11 2s 0d (£13 19s 6d). The higher prices for the forty-piece set

226. A finely-decorated trio in blue and tooled gold of the shape registered on 20 January 1849 but popular into at least the mid 1850s. Diameter of saucer 5¾in. Registration mark with Davenport name under and pattern number 2440, *c*.1849–52. (Geoffrey Godden, chinaman)

227. A red and gold teacup and saucer, the centre bearing the arms of the City of Liverpool in gold on a salmon ground. Diameter of saucer 5½in. Pattern number 1946. Special Canning Place Davenport supplier's name-mark on cup, *c*.1855. (Godden of Worthing Ltd)

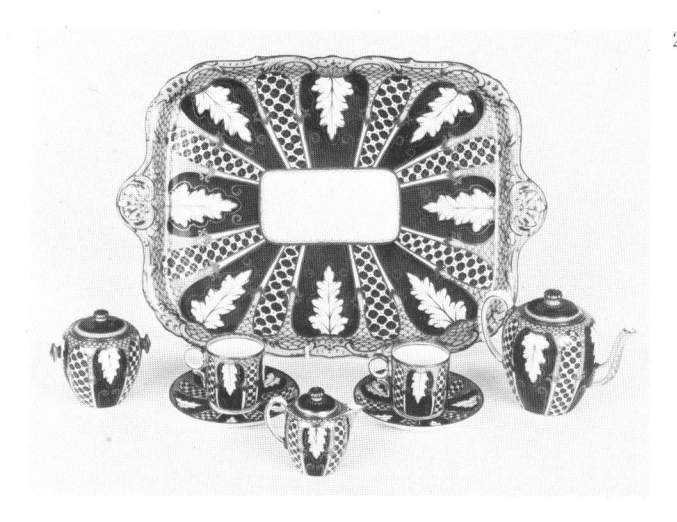

probably is accounted for by the inclusion of a teapot. This vital unit is not, however, listed in the separte listing of the different items which are given as:

12 tea cups and saucers,
12 coffee cups,
1 cream ewer,
1 slop bowl,
2 B and B [Bread and Butter] *plates.*

In addition the Davenport list included Breakfast services for six persons and for twelve. Items tabulated separately include: plates in four sizes (8, 7, 6 and 5in. diameter); dishes in two sizes (12 and 10in.); two sizes of broth bowl and stand; butter-tub and stand; toast-rack; muffin plate and cover; honey pot and stand; milk jug; sugar bowl; egg cup and 4in. plate; egg stand – 4 cups; egg stand – 6 cups; roll tray; and two sizes of coffee pot.

Separately listed one finds déjeuner tea sets in forty-two different price bands. These sets, which were very popular in the Victorian period, comprised a large china tray with smaller than usual teapot, covered sugar bowl, creamer (often with a cover), bowl, and two teacups and saucers. One model Davenport déjeuner tea set is shown in Plate 228. Some rare larger déjeuner services included four cups and saucers. The articles listed separately but still in forty-two price bands were:

oval teapots [large 18s size],
oval teapots [smaller 24s size],
sugar bowls in two sizes,
Watcombe teapots in three sizes,
croquet cup and saucer,
moustache cup and saucer,
round jug stands in three sizes,
oval jug stand,
sardine box and stand,
'Chelsea' marmalade,
round water kettle [pint size],
oval water kettle [quart size],
Oxford breakfast cruet set.

228. A well-decorated and colourful blue, orange, and gold Davenport déjeuner teaset complete with its tray. Tray 18×13in. Printed crowned three-line name-mark (P 7), pattern 3959, c.1865–75. (John Leslie Antiques)

The larger oval teapots were available at prices ranging between 2s 3d for those with very sparse decoration to 25s for those of the same form and size but with the richest style of decoration. Such variations of prices applied to all articles, a déjeuner slop bowl ranging, for example, in forty different prices upwards from 1s to 9s 6d. It follows that the styles of decoration were large and the patterns available even at this late difficult period in the firm's history were extremely varied. The difference in the price depended solely on the cost of decorating the porcelain blanks.

Apart from the déjeuner services Davenports also produced 'Café Noir' sets on trays. Type 1 comprised a 10in. tray, a coffee pot, and 9 small coffee cans and stands. These ranged in price from 9s 6d to 18s 6d. Set number 2 comprised an 11in. tray, a coffee pot, a covered sugar bowl, a covered cream jug, but only six coffee cans and saucers. For these the price ranged between 11s and 21s 6d. A further set with octagonal wares on a square tray were also available but at higher prices, between 17s and 29s 5d. As with other services all these units were available separately.

While this list gives no indication of the patterns on these late tewares, some of the most popular were the colourful so-called Japan patterns in the style so much favoured at the Derby factory. The Davenport factory specialized in such colourful porcelains in the 1870s and 1880s especially. Such pieces normally bear the red printed DAVENPORT, LONGPORT, STAFFORDSHIRE devices with a crown above (P 7, crowned). The pattern numbers tend to be in excess of 3000 and run up into the 6000s. The small set shown in Plate 229 possibly represents part of an afternoon teaset or even a 'Café Noir' set of the second type complete with the covered cream jug. The Japan-type pattern with its areas of deep, underglaze blue with overglaze enamels and gilding is typical of this popular type. The Davenport esays in this style are well painted and are superior to most other makes. The range of articles decorated with the late Japan pattern numbered 6060 is very varied and large. All types of Davenport porcelain may be found decorated in this style, ranging from vases to a host of small objects, pin-trays, etc.

The post-1881 Davenports price list also includes a selection of very much more utilitarian nature. These were priced only in an undecorated state and with gold edging, the later being approximately fifty per cent higher than the plain examples. The objects comprised mugs, in three sizes; two-handled mugs; sickfeeders, in three sizes; mugs with funnels, in three sizes; oval potting dishes, in four sizes; and broth bowls and stands, in three sizes.

The page of engraved teacup and saucer shapes as printed in this late price list is interesting (Plate 230). Apart from those which are obviously of such a late period (such as the two on the top line), the Bute shape of the early 1800s still appears, as does the low Etruscan form associated with the 1820s (see Plate 209). The moulded form registered in January 1849 (see Plate 226) appears bottom right in a slightly amended form, titled 'New Stanley', hence my designation 'Stanley' for the original shape.

229. A colourful Davenport Japan pattern, small-sized teaset. Printed crowned three-line namemark (P 7), c.1870–80. (Royal Ontario Museum)

[Illustration: A page from the Davenports Limited price list of the 1880s showing cup and saucer shapes labelled S-P, MANCHESTER, N-G, REGENT, DEVON, PLAIN SEVRES, BUTE, LIVERPOOL, H-L, NEW STANLEY.]

Unfortunately the teapot shapes are not shown, only the cups and saucers.

The late Davenport bone chinas should be clearly marked. On most flat-wares, plates, saucers, etc. the impressed mark DAVENPORT should appear, although this was often lightly impressed or has been partly obliterated by the glaze. The standard printed mark is the crowned three-line device P 7, in red. Various retailers' marks may occur on specimens especially ordered by these firms. The globe-mark of John Mortlock is reasonably common.

These ten basic shapes were seemingly all in production in the 1880s and forty-piece tea services were available in, at least, four price brackets ranging from £9 13s 5d to £13 19s 6d, yet such late Davenport teawares are, in our experience, extremely scarce. Several reasons for this could be suggested. Possibly it is simply that most collectors have, as yet, concentrated on the earlier periods and have not troubled themselves to seek out and purchase the later specimens. If this is the case as seems most likely, there is a golden opportunity for new collectors to turn their attention to this neglected period.

However, one must also remember that the factory was in a steady decline from the 1870s, and had rather lost its way in the industry. At the same time many new porcelain manufacturers had entered the race. The new firms introduced novel shapes and styles and had, in general, more drive than the seemingly staid Davenport management. In the difficult last years the separate factories had been sold off to other firms and in the 1880s at a period of general depression in the trade only the Unicorn Works and the glass works remained in the name of Davenports Limited.

230. A page from the Davenports Limited price list of the 1880s showing in basic outline form the cup and saucer shapes then available. (Courtesy Spode Museum Collection Trust)

231 · The Porcelains

Nevertheless, the range of Davenport porcelain teawares produced in the more than eighty years from c.1805 to 1887 is immense. Particularly in the 1830–50 period specimens are reasonably plentiful and cups and saucers at least should not be too expensive. These teawares, of course, form only part of the firm's productions and we must now turn our attention to another important article – the dessert services.

It must be remembered, however, concerning teawares, dessert services, and all other products that when Davenports Limited finally ceased late in 1887 all the engraved copper plates, moulds, and other working materials were offered for sale. These were acquired by other firms, if only to match old Davenport designs. For example, in October 1888 John Hughes of Cobridge advertised in the *Pottery Gazette* that he had purchased the Davenport pattern books. At the same period Thomas Hughes took over Davenports' Unicorn Works. Several Staffordshire firms from 1888 had access to former Davenport designs and some may well have used the Davenport name which formed part of the original engraved design on the copper plate. Some Davenport tea service shapes and patterns were used by Hammersley and several such Davenport shapes and designs occur in the Hammersley pattern books, with that firm's fractional lettered pattern numbers. For example, Hammersley's pattern T/9038 relates to a pattern on Davenport new oval shape teapots, cream jugs, etc.

20 Dessert Wares

In my experience, one finds more Davenport dessert wares than tea sets. Such dessert services can be considered a speciality of the company. A complete service of the approximate period 1805–25 would have comprised: centrepiece (comport) and stand; pair pierced baskets and stands; six or more side dishes comprising a pair (or more) of each of three basic shapes; twelve plates. Of course, smaller or larger sets were also sold according to the demand of the buyer. Some, but probably not all sets had also a pair of covered tureens and ladles for sugar and cream. Some dessert services may have included eighteen or even twenty-four plates. These early Davenport dessert plates are somewhat larger in diameter than most other makes, over rather than under nine inches. Special or very costly sets would have included a pair of wine, or fruit, coolers.

Several early dessert services were well painted with landscape designs, such compositions sometimes including figures and buildings. They are rather boldly painted but by a good practised hand. On porcelain these landscapes (Plates 231–4) tended to be

231. A very rare and early form of Davenport bone china dessert tureen from the part service shown in Plates 233-4. Ht 8¼in. *c*.1805–10. (Godden of Worthing Ltd)

232. An early Davenport bone china dessert dish, with gilt border. Rare combination of impressed and painted marks P 3 and P 2. 10×7½in. *c*.1805–10. (Private Collection)

233. The centrepiece to the landscape painted bone china dessert service shown in Plates 231 and 234. 8¾×7in. *c*.1805–10. (Godden of Worthing Ltd)

233 · The Porcelains

painted in natural colours but on some of the fine earthenwares, especially the tinted bodies, the scenes are charmingly depicted in monochrome, see Plate 34.

Other early bone china dessert services were painted with Chinese figure compositions with wandering flowered and leafy branches forming the border. The basic pattern shows three figures in a garden standing by a table. Shall we call it the 'Table Pattern' to distinguish it from the Royal 'Chinese Temple' design? Typical examples are shown in Colour Plate XIX and in Plates 235–6. I have seen a dessert plate of this pattern with 'No. 9' painted in red. This may well represent the pattern number for this design which was apparently produced for ten or more years. This pattern was also applied to the rare early Davenport dinner services and a version occurs on Davenport earthenware services.

Some rare, seemingly early Davenport dessert services were also painted with large studies of birds. Such an example is shown as Plate 220 in *Staffordshire Porcelain*. This form of decoration may also occur on rare, early vases, see Colour Plate XXVI. A superb early Davenport bone china dessert service painted with named birds is preserved in the McCord Museum of Canadian History, Montreal. Specimens from this set are illustrated in Mrs Elizabeth Collard's article 'Davenport and the Comte de Buffon', *Collectors Guide*, February 1989. This article and Mrs Collard's researches are interesting on two counts. Firstly the bird studies are attributed to the Comte de Buffon Georges Louis Leclerc's part work *Histoire Naturelle des Oiseaux* (Paris, 1770–86) and it is interesting to note that most of the names of the birds depicted on this service are rendered in French – as are the studies painted on the vase shown here in Colour Plate XXVI which is painted in the same style and almost certainly by the same hand as the

234. A Davenport bone china dessert basket and stand from the service featured in Plates 231 and 233. Basket, length 9¾in. Painted 'Longport' marks P 2, c.1805–10. (Godden of Worthing Ltd)

235. An early form of Davenport bone china pierced fruit basket from a dessert service, handle form as Plate 234. Length 10in. Painted 'Longport' mark, c.1805–10. (Private Collection)

236. A oval Davenport dessert basket and stand painted with the 'Table' pattern. A slightly later shape than that shown in Plate 235. Length 10¾in. c.1810. (Courtesy Phillips)

237. Representative shapes from a rare 'Japan'-style Davenport bone china dessert service, decorated mainly in green. Centrepiece ht 6¼in. Most pieces from this set were unmarked, a few pieces bore the impressed name-mark over the anchor device, c.1805–10. (L. Richmond Collection)

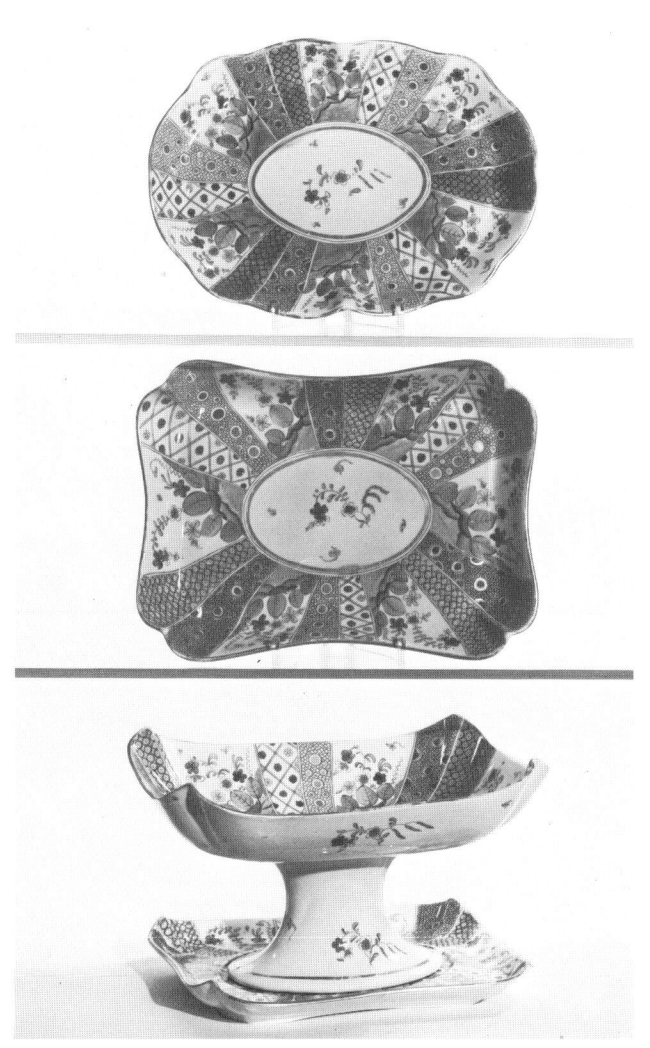

service displayed in Montreal. The second point of interest is that while most of the shapes shown in Mrs Collard's article are known forms, the cream (or sugar) tureen is an intriguing variation on that shown in Plate 231, the main point being that the large rose-form knob is similar to that associated with the 1806 Royal order, as here shown in Plates 289–90. There cannot be very much difference in period between this bird-painted dessert service with the rose knob and the acorn-knobbed version used in the service shown in Plates 231, 233–4. Both sets have the painted Longport name-mark, but in the Montreal set one piece also has the early impressed Davenport and anchor device, as my Plate 232. Other early Davenport sets were, no doubt, painted with floral designs, as were some tea services and certainly the slightly later dessert services such as those featured in Plates 238–41. Other early bone china dessert sets would have been decorated with formal Oriental style designs, of which that shown in Plate 237 is a good example.

I show in Plates 231–7 the characteristic Davenport bone china dessert service shapes. Each of the pieces illustrated bears the painted location mark 'Longport' (P 2). This is sometimes in script, at other times in capitals. Unlike the pieces associated with the Royal order, the painted anchor device does not occur. However, the centrepiece stand for another dessert service (Plate 232) has the standard 'Longport' painted mark as well as the impressed 'Davenport' name over the anchor (P 3). This may be considered to be a rare transitional example linking the two early methods of marking the Davenport porcelains. In most cases the bone china is slightly discoloured with age and has a creamy tint. The glaze is usually slighty crazed, but not in a disfiguring manner.

235 · The Porcelains

238
239

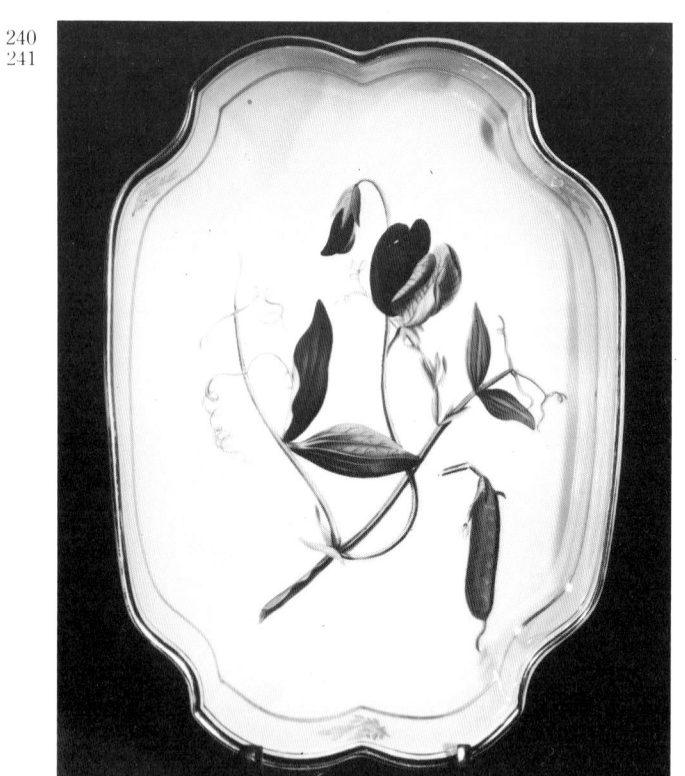

240
241

In contrast to these often 'Longport' (P 2) marked dessert wares, we have some rare but superb examples produced in the hybrid hard-paste porcelain and which I have tentatively attributed to $c.$1807–12. Our knowledge of these dessert wares is really based on one service which is well-painted with named botanical specimens, see Plates 238–41 and Colour Plate XX. I purchased this set some thirty years ago and then had the foresight to have examples photographed and I also retained one damaged dish for inclusion in the Godden Reference collection. Each piece bore the impressed Davenport and anchor mark (P 3) but no pattern number. The quality of the flower painting was really superb.

The various shapes differed from those found in the bone china services as shown in Plates 243–7, suggesting that the hybrid hard-paste mix was used at a slightly different and, I believe, later period. But the main difference lies in the body and its covering glaze. Here we find a distinct improvement over the first bone china with its finely-crazed glaze and general tendency for the body to discolour.

The Davenport hybrid hard-paste body has proved remarkably sound over the

236 · The Porcelains

238. Davenport hybrid hard-paste porcelain oval dessert centrepiece and stand, part of the set featured in Colour Plate XX and Plates 239–41. Stand 10¼ × 7⅛in. c.1807–12. (Godden of Worthing Ltd)

239. The fruit basket and stand from the hybrid hard-paste porcelain botanical dessert service featured in Plates 238, 240–1. Note the rope-like handle form. Basket length 10in, ht 3in. Impressed mark P 3, c.1807–12. (Godden of Worthing Ltd)

240. One of the side-dish shapes from the impressed-marked (P 3) hybrid hard-paste porcelain dessert service. 10 × 7¼in. c.1807–12. (Godden of Worthing Ltd)

241. A further dessert dish shape in the hybrid hard-paste porcelain body. 10½ × 7½in. Impressed mark P 3. c..1807–12. (Godden of Worthing Ltd)

242. An attractive hybrid hard-paste porcelain dessert tureen, with rope-like side handles. This shape would have accompanied services of the forms shown in Plates 238–41. Ht 6¾in. Impressed mark P 3, c.1807–12. (Geoffrey Godden, chinaman)

243. The centrepiece from an unmarked bone china dessert service painted with studies of butterflies and insects. Further pieces from this set are shown in subsequent illustrations. Ht 6in. c.1810–10. (Godden of Worthing Ltd)

244. The matching dessert basket and stand, of a form linking with marked Davenport specimens, see Plate 236. Stand 10¼ × 7¾in. c.1810–15. (Godden of Worthing Ltd)

years. The compact, high-fired body and its related hard glaze has not crazed or otherwise deteriorated, nor have the pieces been disfigured by staining. The glaze has retained its original high gloss and the pieces generally appear as if they had just left the factory. The passage of almost two hundred years has not left its mark as is so often the case with the Davenport bone chinas with their softer body and glaze, although, of course, gilding can become worn with use over the years.

It is now difficult to understand why the Davenport management, and indeed other makers of this type of hard body and glaze, discontinued it in favour of the bone china. The main reason must surely have been the cost of the raw materials and of firing the harder body. One must always remember that potters were in a very competitive business and that their costs had to be very carefully monitored if they were to remain solvent. The hybrid hard-paste porcelain was remarkably stable but perhaps too costly.

The oval and footed centrepiece to this botanical service is shown in Plate 238 with its stand. This centrepiece shape also occurs in marked Davenport creamware, see Plate 48, and this duplication of shapes in the porcelain and the earthenware bodies

237 · The Porcelains

245

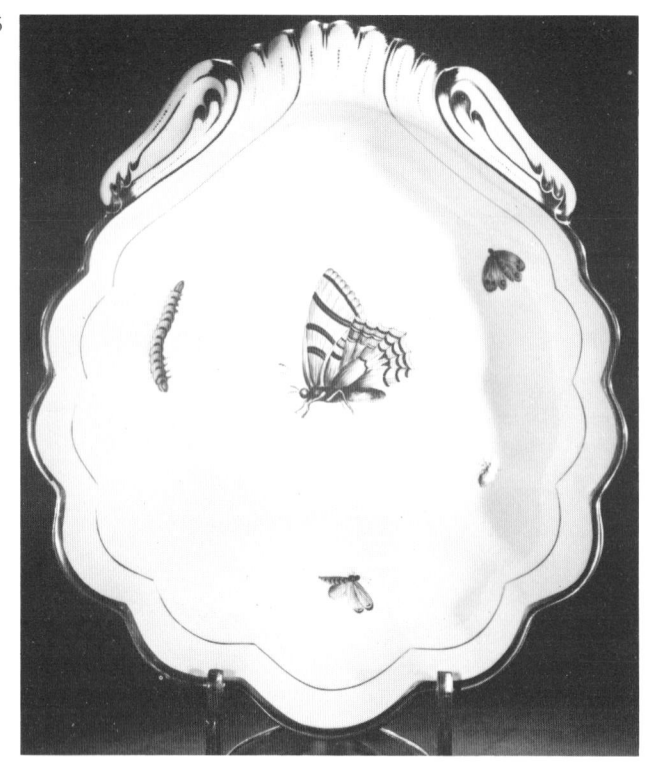

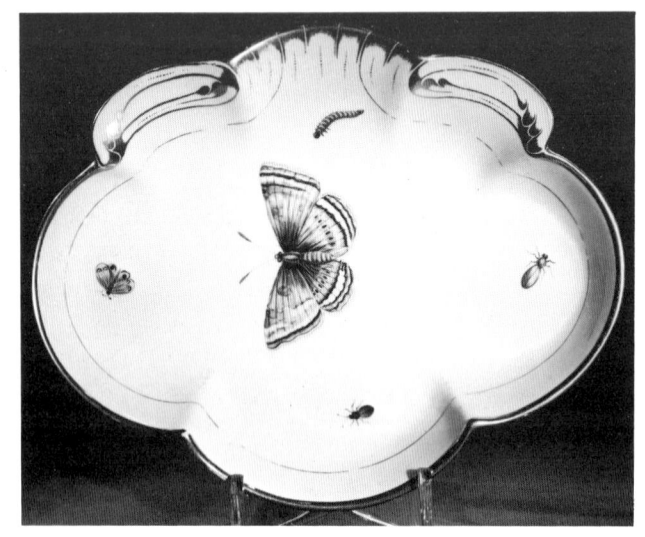

246
247

should be helpful in identifying unmarked porcelains. Likewise the handled dishes shown in Colour Plate XX are of a form found in Davenport creamware and other earthenwares.

Other hybrid hard-paste side dish forms from this one service are shown in Plates 240–1. One of the two fruit baskets and stands is shown in Plate 239. Once again the shape varies from that found on the 'Longport' marked bone china baskets (as Plate 234). Note, for example, the mock twisted rope handles in place of the ear-like handles on the bone china basket.

My botanical service was lacking the pair of tureens which were usually part of early dessert services. One was for cream and the other for sugar, to dress the fruit, for these were truly dessert (fruit) services. If this hybrid hard-paste service originally had such tureens they would almost certainly have been of the form shown in Plate 242 which illustrates yet another very decorative Davenport dessert (unnumbered) pattern. This

238 · The Porcelains

245. One of the handled dishes from the butterfly painted dessert service. The moulded handle form links with marked Davenport wares. 9½×8in. *c.*1810–15. (Godden of Worthing Ltd)

246. A further dessert dish shape from the graceful butterfly and insect painted service. Note the restrained gilding. 10×7½in. *c.*1810–15. (Godden of Worthing Ltd)

247. A plate from the unmarked butterfly decorated service, identified by the linkage of shapes with marked specimens. Diameter 8¼in. *c.*1810–15. (Godden of Worthing Ltd)

248. A marked bone china dessert dish well painted with fruit on a table with shaded background. Painted two-line mark 'Davenport Longport'. Diameter 8¼in. *c.*1810–15. (Victoria & Albert Museum 2250-1901)

249. An unmarked dessert plate, the central panel of which is similar in style and composition to the marked dish shown in Plate 248. Painted pattern number 116. Diameter 8¾in. *c.*1810–15. (Geoffrey Godden, chinaman)

tureen, like the basket, has mock twisted rope handles, and again the form was also produced in earthenware. We believe all these hybrid-paste dessert service shapes to be unique to the Davenport factory.

As previously explained, this hybrid hard-paste body was used over a relatively short period, perhaps because it was too costly or it needed to be fired at a higher temperature than the other products and was therefore inconvenient to produce. The next identified class of Davenport dessert service is therefore in a bone china body. However, this is now of an improved mix, the related glaze is not prone to crazing, and the more compact body does not tend to discolour. The quality of the porcelain, as well as the tasteful decoration, is well evidenced by the completely unmarked, butterfly and insect painted part service shown in Plates 243–7. The centrepiece is certainly of the same form as the earlier bone china examples (as Plate 237) but the basket and side dish shapes are newly introduced. The oval basket shape is related to a later marked example (P 4) with relief moulding (Plate 252). The shell-shape handled dish (Plate 245) is of a standard French shape copied by most English dessert service makers, but this precise version links with marked Davenport specimens, including those in the stone china body which we can approximately date to 1815–20 onwards. It is worthy of note that the diameter of the plates in this service is 8½in., that is smaller than the earlier bone china examples which average 9¼in.

The dessert plate shown in Plate 249 bears only the pattern number 116, yet we are sure that it is from a Davenport dessert service of the approximate 1810 period. In general style of the fruit painting it links well with the square dessert dish in the Victoria & Albert Museum (Plate 248). This museum example bears the DAVENPORT, LONGPORT mark, on two lines. The drawing of the table is exactly the same as that on the 116 plate, as is the black single line edge within the gilt line. The fruit painting on the dish is traditionally attributed to the ceramic painter Thomas Steel, who is better known for his later work on Derby and Minton porcelain (if he worked at the Davenport factory it would have been prior to 1815). It is just possible that both the unmarked plate and the marked dish came from similar dessert services of a harlequin nature – a fashionable practice wherein the gilt borders (or the central motifs) would vary from piece to piece within the same set. Both the V & A dish and the plate have a finely-crazed glaze and they could be rather earlier than the date I suggest.

The printed name mark (P 6) occurs on the relief-moulded plate shown in Plate 251. This moulded form was a very popular one at several factories – Coalport, Derby, Nantgarw, Swansea, etc. This plate, although it may be from a dinner service, suggests

239 · The Porcelains

that the Davenport factory also produced such dessert services, indeed a well-painted example is in the Victoria & Albert Museum collection. Perhaps the service sold by Christie's on 7 August 1835, as Lot 17 was of this type: 'A dessert service of Davenport porcelain painted and embossed with flowers, consisting of two ice pails, covers and liners, one centre, 12 dishes and 24 plates.'

The dessert basket shown in Plate 252 has this style of relief moulding. It must be remembered, however, that Davenport specimens are scarce and are outnumbered by other makes. A Coalport example, with the date 1819, is illustrated by Geoffrey Godden in his book *Coalport and Coalbrookdale Porcelains* (Antique Collectors' Club 1981, revised edn).

Other types of moulded floral border designs were employed on Davenport services. Christie's sale of the Duke of York's property on 23 February 1827 included, for example: 'Part of a table service of Longport china, consisting of four ice-pails, covers and liners, four fruit baskets and stands, 14 fruit dishes of different sizes and 67 table plates, white with embossed borders and coronet with gold cyphers.'

This set then sold for £10. While described as a table service – the old term for a dinner service – it appears to be more in the nature of a dessert service; but even if it were a dinner service, dessert services would have been made to match the floral embossed border. This moulded border was obviously in production before the death of Frederick Augustus, Duke of York (1763–1827), the second son of George III, on 5 January 1827. A plate from the Duke of York service is here shown (Plate 259), hardly over-decorated, but the relief-moulded border is interesting. Other similar services were made for other members of the royal family.

250. A moulded-edged dinner plate from the service made for the Duke of York and sold at Christie's in February 1827. Diameter 9¼in. Red printed two-line Davenport Longport mark, c.1820–5. (D. Sherborn Collection)

251. A rare marked Davenport bone china moulded bordered plate of a type more commonly made by other firms. Diameter 9¾in. Painted Davenport Longport mark, c.1815–20. (E. H. Chandler Collection)

252. An oval Davenport dessert basket of the same basic form as Plate 262 but with relief moulding as Plate 251. Length 10½in. Printed mark P 4, c.1815–20. (Private Collection)

240 · The Porcelains

A class of Davenport porcelain dessert service shapes which link with the colourful stone china wares is here represented by the porcelain pieces of pattern 700 shown in Plates 253–5. The footed centrepiece and the tureens have near matches in Coalport and some other porcelains of the approximate period 1815–20, but these examples all bear the printed Davenport so-called ribbon mark (P 5). Rather earlier Coalport examples, particularly of the four-footed low centrepiece, are shown in Godden's *Coalport and Coalbrookdale Porcelains*, Plate 30.

The high pattern number found on this service seems to us to be too high for the period of the dessert ware shapes and for the style of the added pattern, both of which are attributed to the 1815–20 period. As all these Davenport pieces bear the same number it seems unlikely that an error in numbering was made by the painter, but dessert ware pattern number 200 seems nearer the mark than 700, if the numbers of this period were subdivided into separate teaware and dessert ware numbers. It could be that this 700 number represents the initial series of combined numbers and that the system was amended soon after this point. Certainly some dessert wares of obviously later date bear lower pattern numbers, see for example Plates 260, 262.

From about 1820 the use of the earlier fruit baskets and stands seems to have been generally discontinued. However, some of the more expensive services, both dessert and dinner sets, had pairs of wine coolers or ice pails. It is not known if the very earliest porcelain services had such luxury items. The earliest type known to us is represented by the magnificent base shown in Colour Plate XXI. The quality of the flower painting and the gilding is superb and we must assume that the decoration represents a dessert service pattern of the approximate period 1810–15. Unfortunately this piece does not bear a pattern number, only the red printed early mark 'Davenport' in a scroll over an

253. A Davenport footed dessert centrepiece of a form also produced by other firms. Pattern number 700 with painter's tally mark. 10¼×8¼in. ht 4in. *c.*1815–20. (Godden of Worthing Ltd)

254. A marked Davenport oval dessert tureen and cover from the service featured in Plates 253 and 255. Length 7¼in. Printed mark P 5 and pattern number 700, *c.*1815–20. (Godden of Worthing Ltd)

255. A marked Davenport dessert dish from the service shown in Plates 253-4. 10×7in. Printed mark P 5 and pattern number 700, *c.*1815–20. (Godden of Worthing Ltd)

241 · The Porcelains

256

257

anchor (P 4). This surviving piece lacks its original liner and cover and the cover might have been similar to the stone china ice pail shown in Plate 92 as the base shape is extremely similar in both examples. We have turned the base slightly to show better the moulded animal-head handles but it must be noted that similar handle forms can occur on Coalport, Herculaneum, and Spode porcelains of the approximate period 1805–15. They are not unique to Davenport.

Two rather later forms of Davenport ice pails are shown in Plates 256–7. The first was probably also originally equipped with a liner and cover, for use with ice and fruit, but they were sometimes sold (in pairs) as open ice pails to cool wine. The complete example, with its Warwick-type handles, is a large and magnificent specimen with marvellous quality matt and burnished gilding.

Writing of quality, we cannot resist republishing the illustration of the matt green border flower-painted dessert set of the early 1820s (Plate 258). The set as sold by Sotheby's in 1969 comprised forty-four pieces and represented a magnificent spectacle. The Latin name of each flower was written on the back of each piece, although surprisingly there was no pattern number. The mark was the ribbon device (P 5).

The oval dish shown in Plate 259 is of the same approximate period 1820–5 and is of the same shape as that just illustrated as Plate 258 left. Like that example it bears mark P 5 but not a pattern number. The basic border design of full-blown back-to-back roses was used on Davenport tea and dessert services but was, of course, also favoured by many other rival factories, including Daniel and Spode.

The plate shown in Colour Plate XXII also has the ribbon mark (P 5) with, in

256. A marked Davenport ice pail base or wine cooler. Such pieces normally included a liner and cover. Ht 7¼in. *c.*1820–5. Printed mark P 5. (Courtesy Phillips)

257. A superb and imposing Warwick vase style ice pail, liner, and cover, for fruit. Ht 12½in. Such objects were made in pairs. Printed mark P 5. (Godden of Worthing Ltd)

242 · The Porcelains

this case, the pattern number 170 with a painter's tally mark. We regard this pattern number as one of the new subdivided class, issued after rather than before the pattern 700 service shown in Plates 253–5. The rose painting and the gilding is of superb quality as is the porcelain and the glaze. This plate has the overall appeal of a Swansea specimen.

The green and gilt dessert service illustrated in Plate 260 bears the ribbon mark (P 5), printed in blue, and the pattern number 276 with painter's tally marks. The value of this illustration is that it shows together various standard shapes of the approximate period 1830–40. Other examples of this shape bear pattern numbers ranging from the mid 200s into the 400s. These were obviously popular forms over a considerable period and at least one variation occurs where raised flower-heads were added, see Plates 267–8. The dessert service of pattern 276 with its fine quality raised and modelled gilding shows that we should not be too dogmatic in attributing the underglaze blue version of the ribbon mark to a post-1850 period.

258. Representative pieces from a matt green bordered Davenport botanical dessert service of fine quality. Centrepiece ht 6½in. Names of specimens painted on reverse. Printed ribbon mark P 5, c.1820–5. (Courtesy Sotheby's)

259. A rose-painted and well-gilt dessert dish of the same form as shown in Plate 258. 11½×8½in. Printed ribbon mark P 5, c.1820–5. (Geoffrey Godden, chinaman)

243 · The Porcelains

A handled and footed dish of this class bears a simple leaf design and the pattern number 302 (with a painter's tally mark), but the same design on a teacup and saucer is numbered 901. Obviously by this period in the 1830s two (or more) pattern numbering systems were in use, although this was not the case when the dessert set of pattern 700 was made in the 1815–20 period.

Unfortunately the special service made for William IV in or about 1830 does not bear a pattern number so we cannot tie in a number to this datable set. Also the shapes, some of which are shown in *Davenport Pottery & Porcelain 1794–1887*, Plates 72–3, seem unique to this one service. I show a tureen from this service in Plate 263. If other items of these Royal service forms should be discovered they should be of the 1830–5 period. This service and its documentation does, however, enable us to record the name of a Davenport flower painter, Gould, who was, one may assume, the leading flower painter of this period, for an undated letter quoted by Mr Lockett states: 'The centre Groups or Bouquet should be *well done* and all by Gould if possible'. The spelling is open to some question, it could be 'Goold' but, alas, we have been unable to find any other information on this ceramic artist, who may well have died before the Census returns of 1841. We

260. Representative pieces from a dark green and gilt bordered dessert service showing typical shapes. Centrepiece ht 6½in. Printed ribbon mark P 5 and pattern number 276, new series, c.1830–40. (Godden of Worthing Ltd)

261. A moulded-edged dessert plate decorated with simple vine and grape border design. Diameter 9¼in. Printed three-line mark (P 7) with pattern number 776, c.1830–40. (F. Cherry Collection)

244 · The Porcelains

have not noted his hand on Davenport porcelains of the post-1840 period. It does occur on dessert pattern 298 on pieces which bear the royal mark P 8, see p. 273.

During the reign of William IV (1830–7) the special printed mark (P 8) incorporating the words 'Manufacturers to their Majesties' should have been used. This is, however, very scarce on dessert porcelains and it could be that it was not the sole mark employed within this period. The other standard name-marks could well also have been employed. The finely-decorated plate shown in Colour Plate XXIII with its ornate and deeply-moulded edge bears the royal mark showing that this dessert service shape was in production in the 1830s. An oval dish from a similar bordered dessert service is shown in Plate 264. Mr Lockett's 1972 book includes an illustration of an oblong dish of this type, also with the royal mark and the pattern number 356.

Referring to the royal marked plate, this does not bear a pattern number, but the well-painted fruit is named. By 1830 Thomas Steel, the well-known fruit painter, had probably left Staffordshire for the Rockingham factory in Yorkshire and the raspberry panel as well as the surrounding flowers were possibly painted by Gould. The Sèvres-style panels of colourful birds in landscape are common on Coalport and Daniel porcelains

262. A marked dessert dish of the same class as Plate 260. Dark green with thick gilding, flower painting possibly by Gould. Length 11in. Printed three-line mark P 7 with pattern number 294, new series, *c*.1830–40. (Mrs W. S. Manor Collection)

263. A damaged dessert tureen probably from the service made for William IV in or about 1830. Ht 11in. Replacement metal finial. Printed three-line mark P 7, *c*.1830. (Sotheby's Sussex)

245 · The Porcelains

264. A moulded-edged dessert dish well painted with an apple-green ground and named view, 'The Bridge over the Peneus, at Larissa'. Length 10¼in. Printed mark of type not recorded. Pattern number 360, c.1830–7. (Henry Spencer & Sons)

265. A superbly potted and decorated dessert tureen and cover from a special armorial service. Green ground with raised and tooled gilding. Ht 9in. Crowned three-line mark P 7, c.1830–7. (Godden of Worthing Ltd)

266. An attractive yellow-bordered moulded-edged dessert plate of characteristic form, see also Plates 267–8. Printed three-line mark P 7. Pattern number 274, c.1835–40. (F. Cherry Collection)

267. A grey-bordered and crested four-footed dessert dish of the same moulded border design as featured in Plates 266 and 268. 10½ × 8¼in. Printed in blue ribbon mark P 5, c.1835–40. (Geoffrey Godden, chinaman)

246 · The Porcelains

268. A buff and gold-bordered dessert dish with the same basic handle form as shown in Plate 260. 10½ × 7½in. Crowned three-line mark P 7. Pattern 727, c.1835–40. (W. A. Davenport Collection)

269. A Davenport grey and gilt-bordered dessert service comport with moulded flower-head border motifs, to match Plates 266–8. The centre well painted with floral sprays. Diameter 11¾in. Printed three-line name-mark P 7 under crown, c.1835–40. (Sotheby's Sussex)

270. A grey and gold-bordered Davenport dessert comport, the centres painted with different flowers. Ht 8½in. Crowned three-line mark P 7 and pattern number 388, c.1835–40. (Godden of Worthing Ltd)

and represent typical ceramic decoration of the period. They are certainly not unique to Davenport's productions. The thick but rather matt gilding with its raised dot-work should be noted.

The yellow-bordered dessert plate shown in Plate 266 is of a quite rare shape of the approximate period 1830–5. It bears the uncrowned three-line name-mark (P 7) and the dessert pattern number 274. The four-footed crested dessert dish shown in Plate 267 bears the ribbon mark (P 5) but no pattern number. The dish of pattern 727 shown in Plate 268 also relates to these two-flower bordered dessert wares.

The centrepiece or fruit comport to these services takes the form shown in Plate 269. This in its general form is very close to contemporary Coalport, Grainger-Worcester, and Ridgway examples. The Davenport examples will bear non-fractional pattern numbers almost certainly in the 200 to 400 range but most examples will bear one of the standard Davenport printed marks.

Moving from a simple crest motif to a piece bearing the full Arms of a family, we have the truly superb quality dessert tureen shown in Plate 265. The gilding on a green ground is particularly fine, the various details being worked in raised gold. This is obviously from an extremely expensive, one-off service that does not bear a pattern number. The moulded top border links this shape with the plate shown in Colour Plate XXII and in Plate 264.

The marked flower-painted dessert wares shown in Plates 270–3 illustrate further Davenport dessert service shapes popular from the mid 1830s onwards. The pattern number is 388, the mark P 7, crowned. Dinner services also had a very similar moulded edge and intertwined handles, see Plate 293. A service made for Queen Victoria has this moulded edge (see Colour Plate II).

247 · The Porcelains

271
272

273

The attractive open-work bordered plate shown in Plate 274 is of pattern 513, marked with the crowned three-line name and address device. This piece represents yet another Davenport dessert shape of the 1830s. The simpler pierced bordered plate (Plate 275) of pattern 540 bears the same mark and is again of this approximate period. Both shapes are uncommon but the latter occurs in unpierced versions, see Plate 279.

Further standard dessert service shapes, probably of the 1840s, are shown in Plate 276. These green bordered pieces bear the crowned three-line DAVENPORT, LONGPORT, STAFFORDSHIRE mark with the pattern number 841. Other patterns on the same basic shapes can be far lower, for example, 572. On the other hand, patterns in excess of 1380 have also been noted and serve to underline the popularity of these dessert shapes. The variety of added patterns may be gauged by comparing the

248 · The Porcelains

271. A dessert dish from the service featured in Plates 270 and 272–3. 9¼×7¼in. c.1835–40. (Godden of Worthing Ltd)

272. A further form of Davenport dessert dish from the service shown in Plates 270–1 and 273. 11×8in. c.1835–40. (Godden of Worthing Ltd)

273. The moulded-edged plate from the dessert service shown in Plates 270–2. Diameter 9½in. Crowned three-line mark P 7. Pattern number 388, c.1835–40. (Godden of Worthing Ltd)

274. A rare and attractive form of moulded and pierced-edged buff and gilt dessert plate. The painted bird crest is unique to one order. Diameter 9¼in. Crowned three-line mark P 7. Pattern number 513, c.1838–40. (Private Collection)

275. A maroon and gilt moulded and pierced-edged dessert plate, well painted with floral centre. Diameter 9¼in. Crowned three-line mark P 7. Pattern number 540, c.1840–5. (Godden of Worthing Ltd)

276. Representative pieces from a green and gilt-bordered dessert service, painted with various landscapes in the manner of Jesse Mountford. Comport ht 8½in. Crowned three-line mark P 7, c.1845–50. (Godden of Worthing Ltd)

magnificent dessert plate shown in Colour Plate XXIV with the more restrained floral pattern featured in Plate 278. It is not only a question of taste as to which was chosen but also of price. The richly-decorated service might well have been three times the price of the simpler design. Various marks (P 5 and P 6 or P 7) may occur on these forms.

The pale green and gold bordered dessert wares shown in Plate 279 bear well-painted (named) views in the style of Jesse Mountford. The moulded design and the whole appearance of this service is reminiscent of the rather earlier Copeland & Garrett porcelains. This set bears the blue-printed ribbon mark (P 5).

At this period the Davenport bone china body was remarkably pure and compact, giving with its covering glaze remarkably little difficulty in the firing. William Evans in his *Art and History of the Potting Business* (1846), quoted one receipe for 'Davenport's china body'. This he stated comprised 12 lbs bone, 8 lbs 13 oz. (China) Stone, 5 lbs 9½ oz. China Clay, 2 lbs 7 oz. blue clay, 1 lb 9½ oz. flint, ¼ oz. blue clax.

The attractive landscape painted plate shown in Plate 280 illustrates a further

249 · The Porcelains

277
278

279

Davenport border design of the 1850 period. This pattern is 949. This form was seemingly known as 'Vine Edge' and was also used for dinner wares, see Plate 294. Another simple moulded edge form of the 1850–60 period is shown in *An Illustrated Encyclopaedia of British Pottery and Porcelain*, Plate 199.

The footed centre comport featured in Plate 281 together with the plate shown in Colour Plate XXV represent a registered form taken out on 11 March 1856. As these two examples show, this, and any other form, can be decorated in several different styles. The marks are the diamond-shape registration device for this entry with L for 1856 in the top inner angle. The name Davenport appears below this device which is printed in blue. The pattern number on the floral dessert plate is 1174 with a painter's tally mark. Matching side dishes are shown in Plate 282.

The well-painted scenic-centred part dessert service shown in Plate 283 illustrates yet another shape of the 1855–65 period. In this case the pattern number is

277. A green ground dessert dish, with small scenic panels, within gilt borders. 11×8¼in. Blue printed ribbon mark. Pattern number 877, c.1845–50. (E. H. Chandler Collection)

278. A tastefully simple moulded and gilt-edged Davenport dessert plate. Diameter 9¼in. Blue printed ribbon mark. Pattern number 1383, c.1850–5. (C. Rhead Collection)

279. Representative pieces from a moulded-edged green and gilt dessert service, painted in the manner of Jesse Mountford. Comport ht 7¾in. See Plate 275 for pierced version of this shape. Blue printed ribbon mark. Pattern number not recorded, c.1850. (Godden of Worthing Ltd)

280. A green bordered Davenport dessert plate with moulded edge, perhaps 'Vine edge', see Plate 294. Diameter 9⅛in. Blue printed ribbon mark. Pattern number 949, c.1850–5. (Mrs J. Magness Collection)

281. A dessert comport of the moulded form registered on 11 March 1856, and found decorated with various patterns. Ht 8¼in. Registration device with 'Davenport' below, c.1856–9. (Sotheby's)

282. Three dessert dishes in the form registered on 11 March 1856, painted with floral pattern 1174. Registration device with 'Davenport' below. Centre dish length 11¼in. c.1856–9. (Sotheby's, Sussex)

283. A richly-gilt Davenport dessert service painted with various named views. Diameter of plates 8¾in. Pattern number 1462. Blue printed ribbon mark, c.1860–5. (Courtesy Phillips)

250 · The Porcelains

251 · The Porcelains

284.

285A.

WINGED DOLPHIN FOOT

TWISTED DOLPHIN FOOT

REGINA

DEVON

284. A well-painted Davenport dessert plate of a characteristic late form. Diameter 9¼in. Blue printed crowned P 7 mark. Pattern number 1775, *c.*1870–80. (Godden of Worthing Ltd)

285A. A pink and gold-bordered dessert comport with 'Twisted dolphin foot'. The centre painted with named view of Loch Katrine. Ht 5in. Pattern 1756. Blue printed crowned P 7 mark, *c.*1870–80. (W. Broad Collection)

285B. Dessert comport and plate shapes reproduced from the firm's price list of the 1880s. (Courtesy Spode Museum Collection Trust)

252 · The Porcelains

285B

OCTAGON

DEVON

EMPRESS

DAISY

1462 and the names of the scenes are written on the reverse of the pieces. These views are not only British but also Italian, Greek and from the Near and Middle East.

The floral painted plate shown in Plate 284 illustrates a popular dessert edge, with twelve indents, form of the 1870s into the 1880s. This example is of pattern 1775 with printed mark P 7 crowned. The dolphin-supported dessert comport of pattern 1756 shown in Plate 285A represents one of the comport forms associated with the indented plate shape. This form is featured in the Davenports catalogue of the 1880s as 'Twisted Dolphin Foot'. However, by this period the top is circular, not indented as in my example. I reproduce the engraving by kind permission of The Spode Museum Collection Trust (Plate 285B).

A similar ornate comport base is also engraved and described as 'Winged Dolphin Foot' and the top is lobed in a shamrock-like form. Less elaborate late comport forms are shown in the engraving, and were given the names Octagon, Devon, Empress, and Daisy.

Although we tend now to regard the later Davenport bone china dessert services of the 1870s and 1880s as being distinctly scarce, the Davenports price list includes such services in forty-eight price bands. These prices are based on the cost of a

286. A moulded and pierced-edge plate painted with 'Duchess'. Diameter 9¼in. Impressed 'Davenport' mark. No pattern number, c.1880–7. (W. Broad Collection)

287. A pink-bordered pierced-edged late Davenport plate with very well-painted landscape centre. Diameter 9¼in. No pattern number, probably a display plate rather than from a service. Impressed 'Davenport' mark. (Godden of Worthing Ltd)

288. A moulded-edged plate of an earlier form (see Colour Plate XXIII) with well-painted floral design. Diameter 9¼in. Signed on reverse 'R. Eaton. 1887'. Impressed 'Davenport' mark, c.1887. (Godden Reference Collection)

254 · The Porcelains

single plate and range from 1s to £1. The difference in unit price depended on the added decoration although the fancy comports such as the dolphin-footed examples were priced an extra 1s 6d, 6s 6d, 7s 6d, or 8s depending on their size.

The standard late services were sold in two basic sizes, the eighteen and the twenty-six piece service. The first comprised 12 plates, 4 low comports, and 2 higher comports standing 6 in. high. Such short services ranged in price from £1 9s 0d to £25 4s 0d. The twenty-six piece dessert service comprised 18 plates, 4 low comports, and 4 higher (6in.) comports. These services cost from £2 3s 0d upwards in forty-eight steps to £37 8s 0d. In reading these and other prices one should bear in mind that a working man's wage probably ranged between one and two pounds per week.

In addition to these basic services the separate price-listing included dessert centrepieces approximately fifty per cent more than the 6in. high comports. In addition cream bowls and stands were included. However, in practice very few dessert services of the 1870s and 1880s included such tureens, which were standard features of the pre-1850 services. The standard late footed comports were made in three sizes, low or 4½ and 6in. high. It would appear, however, that the 4½in. comports were withdrawn in the mid 1880s as these are crossed through on the price list.

Many of the late services would have been decorated with the colourful blue, red, and gold so-called Japan patterns. All post-1880 dessert services or parts thereof bear the impressed name-mark DAVENPORT. Although the firm had lost its way at this period there seems to be no evidence of standards being lowered. The later dessert services are as good quality: difficulties may have arisen from the fact that the Davenport porcelains were too costly in comparison with the wares being produced by the many competitors in the market.

The pierced-edged plate illustrated in Plate 286 bears the late impressed name-mark but no pattern number. It was, however, decorated at the factory, not sold off as a blank, for it bears the remains of a Davenport Limited, Longport, paper label. Another finely decorated and also unnumbered plate of this shape is shown in Plate 287. Two other impressed-marked ornately moulded plates are shown in Terence Lockett's 1972 book, Plate 103. We are, however, not sure if these plates were part of complete dessert services or if they are purely decorative examples.

We end this dessert service section with yet another problem. The moulded-edged plate shown in Plate 288 bears the impressed DAVENPORT name-mark which occurs on other late plates and it is signed on the reverse 'R. Eaton' and dated 1887. As such it represents probably the latest datable specimen of this factory's production. Yet the style of decoration is more reminiscent of the 1830s and this ornate bordered design is usually found on pieces of that period, see Colour Plate XXIII and Plate 264. Can this be simply a throwback to earlier days or a plate made to match an earlier service, or a single specimen plate? This plate has every appearance of being factory decorated, and yet signed work is almost unheard of and Robert Eaton (see p. 275) has not previously been listed as a Davenport artist. A puzzling plate indeed, but a characteristically attractive specimen.

21 Dinner Services

Porcelain dinner services were certainly made throughout the history of this factory, but they are today quite rare and they would always have been made in small quantities when compared with the tea and dessert services. Porcelain dinner services have always been extremely expensive and too costly for all but the most wealthy end of the market. The various earthenware examples, the many blue printed, and later the sets printed in other colours and even the multicoloured services were extremely good value and were very fashionable and decorative. From about 1815 the introduction of the durable Stone China, which could be very neatly potted and decorated with colourful and often richly gilt patterns, also affected the market for the more expensive porcelain dinner services.

The 1806–7 Royal order does, however, show that the factory was capable of producing such porcelain services. This admittedly special order included both round and oval soup tureens of large size, dishes up to nearly two feet long, ornate ice pails, hot water dishes, etc. These pieces would have been in the early, rather soft, bone china. One early tureen form is shown in Plate 289. This is similar in design to the royal service and bears the painted Longport and anchor device associated with the royal commission. A similar odd cover decorated with the rather similar 'Table' pattern is shown in Plate 291, illustrating the splendid floral knob to greater effect.

We have not, as yet, noted any Davenport dinner services in the hybrid hard-paste body used for some rare tea and dessert services c.1808–12 but other manufacturers, notably John Rose of Coalport, were producing dinner services in a similar type of compact, durable china.

In the 1820s Davenport produced a dinner service for King George IV. A covered vegetable dish from this blue-bordered service is shown in *Staffordshire Porcelain*, Plate 226. The knob takes the form of a crown but, of course, not all crown finials are of Davenport origin. The pattern number on this service is 242.

The high-quality dinner plate shown in Plate 291 should also date from the 1820s but it does not bear a pattern number. This lapse may perhaps be accounted for by the fact that it is a one-off special order with crested and armorial centre. If we are correct in assuming that this large dinner plate represents but part of a complete service, the cost of the set must have been very high – well over £200. The skill in laying the deep green ground is considerable but the time spent in applying and tooling-up the thick gold ornamentation was all important – not that the almost pure gold was ever given away. Picture the large platters, the tureens, and the sixty or more plates, all of which had to be

289. A large oval soup tureen and cover, painted with the 'Chinese Temple' design as chosen by the Prince of Wales in 1806. Length 18in. Marked with the painted 'Longport' name over an anchor device, c.1806–10. (City Museum & Art Gallery, Stoke-on-Trent)

290. A large dinner service tureen cover with similar floral knob to that shown in Plate 289 but this cover would be from a different shape tureen. Painted with the related Chinoiserie-style 'Table' design. Length 7¾in. c.1806–10. (Godden Reference Collection)

289
290

291. A Davenport bone china dinner plate with green border and raised and tooled gold inner border of foliage and birds. The centre decorated with crest and armorial bearings (Britten? family). Diameter 10in. Printed 'Davenport' and anchor strap P 4, c.1820–5. (Godden Worthing Ltd)

292. An elaborate sauce tureen from a Davenport armorial dinner service, painted with floral sprays. Length 8¾in. Printed Royal mark P 8 and pattern number 379, c.1835–7. (Godden of Worthing Ltd)

293. An oval dinner service tureen and stand with a large meat-platter. Characteristic moulded edge. Platter length 16½in. Blue printed ribbon mark. Pattern number not recorded, c.1845–55. (Sotheby's)

hand-gilt in this slow painstaking technique. This raised gilding appears on many other Davenport porcelains of the 1820s and 1830s (see Colour Plate XXIII and Plate 69) but it is by no means unique to Davenports.

The sauce tureen (Plate 292) from another special armorial dinner service bears the William IV royal mark (P 8) of the 1830s. The dinner service pattern number is 379. Elaborate as the moulded shape undoubtedly is, the porcelain body has not stood up to its intended use. There are many body cracks and the base is discoloured: perhaps it has been misused even although it must have been a costly purchase. The oval salad bowl is shown in *An Encyclopaedia of British Porcelain Manufacturers*, Plate 134.

The most commonly found Davenport bone china dinner service is represented by Plate 293 which shows the general lobed oval tureen shape and the moulded edge. These dinner service shapes of the approximate period 1837–60 are prone to body faults and pieces are very often cracked. The same edge design also occurs on dessert services, see Plates 270–3. This form of moulded-edged plate was certainly in use by the end of 1837, for it was the shape on the specimens at the banquet given in the Guildhall in November 1837 in honour of the young Queen Victoria. An example of the twenty-four dress plates, valued at the time at ten guineas each, is shown in Colour Plate II. The simplified version of the service comprised five thousand plates of various sizes (see p. 53) and twelve hundred dishes, three hundred tureens, etc., all supplied in a matter of a few weeks by Davenports.

257 · The Porcelains

Although Davenport porcelain dinner services are very seldom seen the firm's price list of the 1880s does include services for twelve and eighteen persons. The first set comprised: 'Soup tureen and stand, 4 sauce tureens and stands, 4 covered dishes, 1 Gravy dish, 18 inches, 11 platters ranging from 18 to 10 inches, 1 salad bowl, 48 dinner plates, 12 soup plates'. The larger set comprised: '2 soup Tureens and stands, 4 sauce Tureens and stands, 4 covered dishes, 1 Gravy dish, 20 inches, 16 platters, ranging from 20 to 10 inches, 1 salad Bowl, 72 Dinner plates, 18 soup plates'. These sets were each listed in twenty-three different price scales, from £38 to £91 and from £56 to £133 respectively. In the 1880s one could probably purchase a house for this higher sum and most workers would not earn such a sum in a year!

Surprisingly, sixteen basic shapes of dinner ware are engraved in this late list, and three of these shapes were available with either round or oval tureens, giving the customer a choice of nineteen shapes. However, it is not clear if all these shapes (Plate 294) were made in the porcelain body.

294. Sixteen late Davenport soup tureen forms reproduced from the catalogue of the 1880s. (Courtesy Spode Museum Collection Trust)

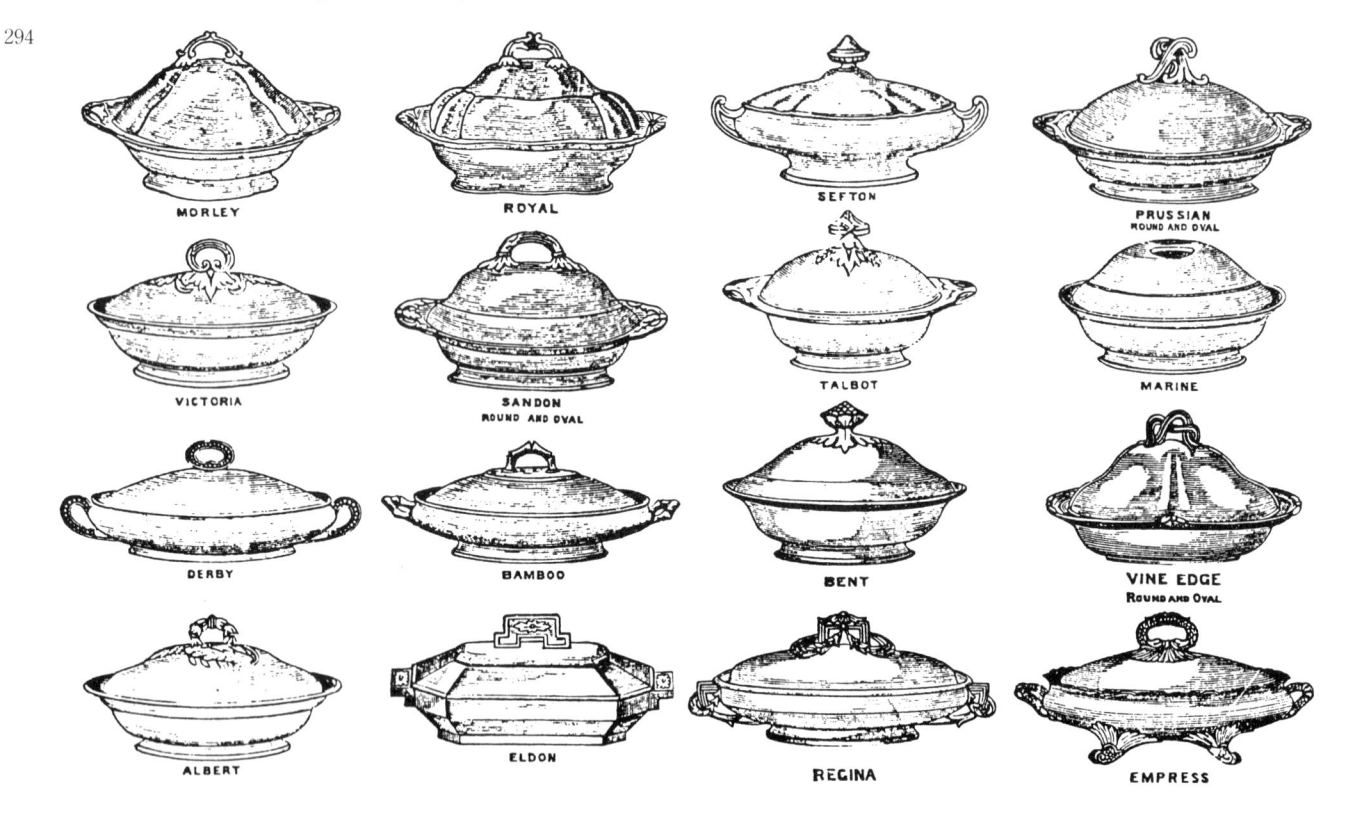

258 · The Porcelains

22 Useful Wares

Apart from the porcelain tea, dessert, and dinner wares previously discussed many other objects were made. However, the varied utilitarian articles tended to be made in earthenware or in ironstone or stone china, if only to keep the price down. In October 1825 Henry Pontigny (the manager of the London showrooms) wrote to John Davenport at Longport: 'I had yesterday one of his [Spode's] Paris folks and am going to sell him Ewers, Basins, Chambers, Soap & Brush boxes in china . . . I presume you make or can make in china all the Patterns of Ironstone . . . I wish you would let me into the secret of the difference of value between the same articles in Ironstone & China . . .' Henry Pontigny then makes the important point, 'Ironstone is not admitted in France, China is'. The earlier point about ironstone patterns being used on china may explain the existence of stone china pattern numbers on some porcelains, whereas normally the stone chinas had their own pattern number system.

Whereas the articles mentioned in this 1823 letter may be regarded as toilet or bedroom wares, many articles were intended for use on the table or to fulfil other household functions. We have yet to identify many of the porcelain jugs and mugs, many of which must have been produced. One popular form of decoration for such articles was white sprigged figure motifs applied to a lilac ground. I show in Plate 295 a marked Davenport example. I have two New Hall pieces of this type which are both dated 1818, but this type of decoration was in favour at Spode, Ridgways, and several other factories in the approximate period of 1815–25. This Davenport example is neatly produced and is a little joy. The same sprigged technique was used in the jardinière shown as Plate 316. Both jugs and mugs would have been so embellished and made in several different sizes. The basic shape and handle form was probably also used for Davenport jugs and mugs painted in the normal manner with, for example, flowers or landscape designs.

The rather plain jug featured as Plate 296 is very well potted and neatly decorated. It represents another early Davenport jug shape. The period is difficult to judge but this form should have been in production c.1805–15. This unmarked example, in

295. An attractive lilac ground Davenport porcelain jug with sprigged, white reliefs. Ht 4in. Impressed Davenport and anchor mark P 3, c.1815– 25. (Diana Darlington Collection)

296. A simple but attractive and well-potted Davenport porcelain jug, painted with landscape in sepia. The handle is typical of Davenport products. Ht 6¼in. c.1805–15. (Diana Darlington Collection)

295
296

259 · The Porcelains

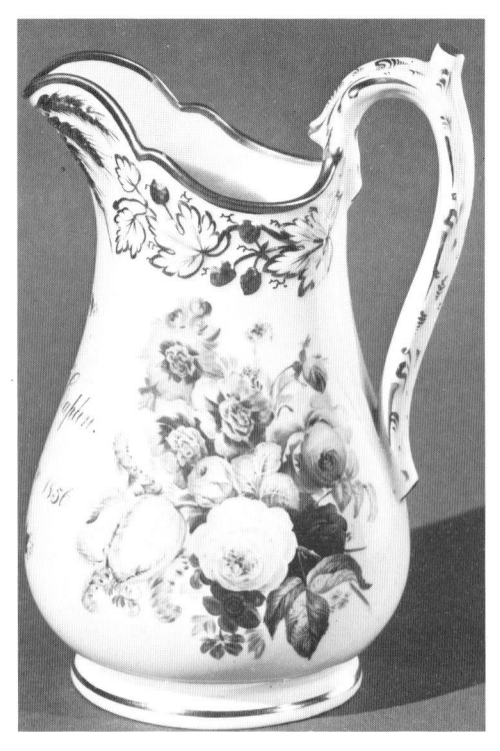

a private collection, bears a typical well-painted monochrome landscape design in sepia but other specimens of this shape were, no doubt, decorated with flowers, multicoloured landscapes or even colourful Japan patterns. Examples with this precise form of moulded handle are well worth seeking out.

The jug form shown in Plate 297 is of the period c.1830–40. It was one of three presentation jugs with the owner's initials added under the lip. Many such sets were made rather than single specimens. The heights of these were 5½, 6½, and 7¼in. The printed mark was the three-line P 7, crowned. An earthernware version of this basic shape occurs, see Terence Lockett's 1972 book, Plate 31.

By at least the mid 1850s the fashionable jug shape had become taller. A good inscribed and dated example with the blue ribbon mark (P5) is shown in Plate 298. The wheat-ear and leaf-and-hop motif around the top is moulded in relief and this may be regarded as a characteristic Davenport jug shape of 1850–60. Thousands of moulded jugs were made by other firms in the popular Parian body but as far as our present knowledge is concerned Davenports do not seem to have entered the Parian market.

Other decorative but useful porcelains include candlesticks, both the tall, pillar-type and the dainty small so-called chambersticks with their carrying handle and projection for the separate extinguisher. A ribbon marked example is shown in Plate 299. Inkstands and inkpots were, no doubt, also made in several different shapes. A delightful French-style swan form inkpot is shown in Plate 300. Another French-style inkwell, a boy with a barrel on a wheelbarrow illustrated in *Staffordshire Porcelain* (Plate 237), perhaps represents Davenport's only essay in figure modelling. Other inkpots and pen or quill holders can be likened to little bowls mounted on square plinths. We would not be surprised if Davenports had produced more than a dozen different shapes of inkpots between 1810 and 1830, but we have as yet only met with four such delights. One newly-found example decorated with a blue-scale ground and bearing the rather rare printed mark P 4 is shown in Plate 301.

Well-painted gilt baskets would also have been made in porcelain. These would have been moulded in various forms and would have been made in different sizes and shapes. An example is shown in Plate 301, the flower painting may well have been by

297. One of a set of three initialled jugs, simply gilt and painted with floral groups. Ht 5½, 6½ and 7¼in. Crowned three-line mark P 7, c.1830–40. (Sotheby's, Sussex)

298. An inscribed and dated 1856 moulded-bordered Davenport jug of a characteristic form. Ht 7¾in. Blue printed ribbon mark P 5. Dated 1856. (Godden of Worthing Ltd)

260 · The Porcelains

299. A tastefully restrained Davenport chamber-candlestick, the separate extinguisher missing from its conical housing. Ht 2in. Printed ribbon mark P 5, c.1825-35. (Private Collection)

300. A crisply-moulded French-style swan inkpot/pen-holder, the body with very slight (smear) glaze and tastefully gilt. Length 3½in. Printed ribbon mark P 5, c.1815-20. (Private Collection)

301. A rare Worcester-style blue-ground Davenport inkpot/pen-holder now missing the cover. Floral painted panels and gilding. Printed scroll mark P 4, c.1810-15. (Geoffrey Godden, chinaman)

Gould, see p. 272. The moulded form of this basket matches the dessert shapes illustrated in Plates 260–2 and should be of the same period, c.1830–40, which also suits the mark P 7, uncrowned. Moulded-edged trays of various sizes would also have been made and decorated in rich styles.

Other porcelain objects are very difficult to classify or to differentiate between useful and decorative articles. The 1806 Royal order included Cabinate [sic] Cups and stands at one guinea and Caudle cups and stands at the same price. The rare early covered cup and stand from the Victoria & Albert Museum collection is here shown as Plate 303. This bears the early painted Longport mark and could well be of the same form as those supplied to the Prince of Wales in 1807, '2 Caudle cups and stands, Painted Landscapes, &c. £2-2-0'. A really superb caudle or cabinet cup and stand is in the delightful Russell-Cotes Museum at Bournemouth and it is well worth a trip to this south coast resort just to view this single specimen.

The richly-gilt blue ground Sèvres-style coffee can and saucer in the City Museum at Stoke-on-Trent as shown in Terence Lockett's 1972 book, Plate 82, must surely be a cabinet cup and saucer, not one to be used as part of a service. We have also noted small tulip-form cups and their saucers: such pieces were made at several French and English factories and can be classed as cabinet wares.

I have also seen quite early porcelain punch-bowls some with an attractive turned foot. These were not marked but I am sure of their Longport origin, c.1805–20. It would be strange indeed if such conventional large bowls were not made during the whole porcelain period.

302. A decorative Davenport basket with well-gilt wide border and floral centre in the manner of Gould. 1×8½in. Printed three-line name-mark P 7, c.1830–5. (Godden of Worthing Ltd)

303. A rare and early Davenport covered cup and stand, well painted with landscapes within gilt frames. Diameter of stand 6in. Painted 'Longport' mark P 2, c.1805–10. (Victoria & Albert Museum)

The various Davenport partnerships catered for the memento market by producing reasonably low-priced porcelains for local markets. These usually small objects such as trays, baskets, and mugs often bear prints of local buildings or views. Sometimes these prints are coloured by hand and are enriched with gilt edges or borders, but the cheaper range were merely printed in a single colour. Such a small mug with a named print of Lichfield Cathedral is shown by Terence Lockett (1972) Plate 98. Similar examples are known with prints of Rotherham, Lincoln, Carlisle, and elsewhere.

23 Ornamental Objects

Once again the 1806 Royal order and report of the Prince of Wales's visit to the Davenport works indicate that at an early period John Davenport was producing ornamental, as well as useful wares. We read that: 'Of the ornamental parts of the manufactory His Royal Highness was pleased to say that the vases, urns etc. in point of execution and ornament were unique'.

Of the articles he ordered in September 1806 were 'Antique shape Jarrs', 'Pot Pourres', 'Portland vauses', as well as vases described merely as Jarrs. The 1807 invoice does not state if these ornamental vases and 'jarrs' were of porcelain or of earthenware. In my opinion the decoration (as listed on p. 203) suggests that they were of china, but my co-author is not convinced that all were.

It is worth noting that the decoration included etched gilding, bronzed-effect handles, and lustre. The last most probably referred to the bright silver-like trimming that had been newly introduced by the use of non-tarnishing platinum. As I write this paragraph there is in a London shop a delightful set of porcelain vases painted with Davenport-style monochrome landscapes, with platinum borders and ring-handles and attachments, similar to those found on marked Davenport bulb pots of the type shown in Plates 314–15. This set of vases are unmarked and are described by the dealer as probably Herculaneum (Liverpool). There is a very good chance that these specimens are Davenport, but, of course, monochrome landscapes and lustre decoration is not unique to our factory.

Assuming that the Royal order vases were of porcelain, in the early bone china body, as were the tea, dessert, and dinner services, then the vase shown in Colour Plate XXVI may well be of this early period, *c*.1806–10. The matt brown handles may represent the bronze handles found included in the 1806–7 Royal order. Handles seemingly from the same moulds were used on marked Davenport bulb pots. The bird painting is superb and the full names of the breeds are painted under the base. It is not suggested that this vase exactly matches the Royal order but bird painting of this type occurs on early Longport-marked dessert plates.

The open Davenport-marked vase shown in Plate 304 is of an early period, approximately 1810 and this form may be similar to some of the Royal pieces two, at least, of which had ring handles. I noted at the time this vase (one of a set of three) was sold by Sotheby's in May 1974 that it was of the hybrid hard-paste body and that it bore the impressed Davenport and anchor mark (P 2). If my dating of this body (see p. 205) is correct this vase would postdate the Royal order.

Another large and magnificently-decorated Chinese-form covered vase in the hybrid hard-paste body is illustrated in Terence Lockett's 1972 book, Plate 92. This vase, in the Castle Museum at Nottingham, bears the impressed Davenport and anchor mark and is earlier (*c*.1810) than originally described.

The small covered vase shown in Plate 305 is marked on two lines DAVENPORT LONGPORT and may be dated *c*.1815–20. The strange head-handles may enable other, unmarked, Davenport pieces to be identified. A pair of these vases is on display at the Victoria & Albert Museum.

The Davenport firm, like other porcelain manufacturers, produced some very decorative slender vases in the French Empire style. These were often made in sets of three, the central vases being taller than the pair of side vases. These Empire-style Davenport vases occur in two distinct shapes, with an additional slight variant and in various sizes and are decorated in many different styles.

Probably the earliest of the French Empire vases is that shown in Plate 306.

The flower and fruit painting is of superb quality, perhaps by Thomas Steel (see pp. 278–9) or by Gould (p. 272). The gilding too is of the finest, equalling the French. Purists might, however, claim that the reverse side of a similar French vase would be more restrained than this Davenport example, see Plate 307. This shape of Davenport vase c.1815–20 is very rare.

This vase and all these French Empire examples were made in two units and were subsequently bolted together. I make this basic point because it is sometimes believed that such bolted vases have been repaired. The bolts can give trouble over the years: they sometimes become loose and the two units rattle together, or the screw can be overtightened and so break the vase. An expanding rusty bolt may also cause damage. While I have justly praised the magnificent Davenport vase shown in Plate 306 it must be stated that some firing faults are evident. These show as slight cracks in the body, a fault in much Davenport porcelain, especially with the large specimens, though hard-paste examples would not have this problem.

A rather more common form of Davenport vase is here illustrated in Colour Plate XXVII and in Plates 308–9. They are, one should remember, only more common because more were originally made, since they were popular with the buying public.

The example shown in Colour Plate XXVII is particularly charming on account of the white biscuit (unglazed) porcelain winged female figures, in the French taste which John Davenport respected (see p. 26). These features are more usually fully gilt. Here we have a pleasing contrast. The blue ground colour is again in the French taste, being matt rather than glossy. The gilding, especially on the reverse side, is again very much in the French manner and taste. This vase, like the larger specimen shown in Plate 309, has a well-painted panel depicting a basket of flowers and fruit – a typical decoration of the period. Interestingly, this specimen has under the base a clearly painted capital G. This could be the painter's personal tally or identification mark as used by Gould. It also bears the printed ribbon mark P 5.

The dark (underglaze) blue ground vase shown in Plate 309 is of the same general form as that just discussed, but it is both a size larger at 11¾in. high and not of

304. One of a set of three early Davenport urn shape vases with ring handles, in the hybrid hard-paste body. Ht 8in. Impressed Davenport and anchor mark P 2, c.1807–12. (Sotheby's)

305. A floral panelled Davenport covered vase of unusual form. Ht 5⅜in. Painted 'Davenport, Longport' mark. (Victoria & Albert Museum)

264 · The Porcelains

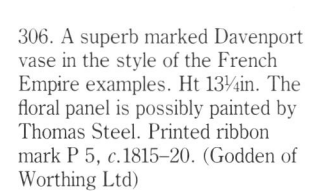

306. A superb marked Davenport vase in the style of the French Empire examples. Ht 13¼in. The floral panel is possibly painted by Thomas Steel. Printed ribbon mark P 5, c.1815–20. (Godden of Worthing Ltd)

307. The intricately gilt reverse side of the French-style vase featured in Plate 306. Some of this gold is matt with tooled and polished designs. Size and date as given in previous caption. (Godden of Worthing Ltd)

308. A blue-ground Davenport French Empire-style vase with floral panel. Handle form as Colour Plate XXVII but treated in a different manner. Ht 11¾in. Printed ribbon mark P 5, c.1820–5. (Geoffrey Godden, chinaman)

265 · The Porcelains

such good overall quality. The gilt band around the central panel is not tooled in a decorative manner as were the other vases and the flower painting is not of such minute quality. The handles are also gilt all over in a standard manner. This ribbon-marked vase is, of course, a desirable object, but all basic shapes were decorated not only in different styles but also in varying qualities which would have affected the original cost. A common denominator with all three vases discussed is the gilt treatment of the square bases. This may help to identify other, unmarked, specimens.

The slight variant on this basic shape is shown in Plate 310. The body form is more like an ice-cream cone and the handles join the top of the female heads. This shape is probably slightly later (c.1820–30) than those shown in Plates 308–9, although all bear the printed ribbon mark P 5. This form of handle occurs on a splendid pair of vases shown in Geoffrey Godden's *Encyclopaedia of British Porcelain Manufacturers*, Plate 133.

We should mention the existence of a large and imposing impressed-marked Flight Barr & Barr Worcester urn-shaped vase or ice pail of c.1820–5, painted with views of Buildwas Abbey in Shropshire. This fine piece was illustrated by Terence Lockett in *Transactions of the English Ceramic Circle* 12 Pt 2, 1985, Plate 100b. This specimen also bears a Davenport printed mark. It is difficult to explain this double marking. The piece in body, shape, and decoration appears to be entirely Worcester and it could be that Davenports purchased this piece for a special order, perhaps as a replacement to a damaged Worcester original, and added their own mark before delivering the article. Commercially speaking it would have been far cheaper to have ordered such a large non-Davenport shape from Worcester than to have endeavoured to produce such a piece at Longport. It is the only Davenport mark on Worcester porcelain known to us.

The large green ground covered vase shown in Plate 311 bears the two-line printed LONGPORT DAVENPORT mark. The reverse side is painted with birds. It is a most unusual form but, no doubt, this model was made in various sizes. Other vase shapes are shown in Terence Lockett's 1972 book, Plates 91 and 93. Other ornate Davenport vases of the period c.1830–40 are illustrated in *Staffordshire Porcelain*, Plates 236 and 238, with rather later examples shown in Plates 239–40.

309. The reverse side of the vase shown in Colour Plate XXVII. Note the French-style matt gold design on the matt blue ground. Ht 9¼in. Printed ribbon mark P 5, c.1820–5. (Geoffrey Godden, chinaman)

310. A matt blue-ground Davenport vase in the French style but differing in detail from the shapes previously illustrated. Note the handle joining the top of the female heads. Ht 11½in. Printed ribbon P 5, c.1820–30. (J. & E. Vandekar)

311. A large and unusual green-ground covered vase. The reverse side painted with birds. Ht 14½in. Printed mark 'Davenport Longport', c.1825–35. (Private Collection)

312. A marked Davenport pot-pourri vase with green ground richly gilt. The reverse side painted with flower panel 15¾in. high. Printed mark Davenport Longport under a crown, c.1835-45. (Sotheby's, Sussex)

313. A set of three Davenport bulb-pots (missing the pierced tops) in the hybrid hard-paste porcelain body, well painted with fruit in the manner of Thomas Steel. Ht 6 and 4¾in. Impressed 'Davenport' and anchor mark P 2, c.1807–12. (Christie's)

266 · The Porcelains

311
312

313

We cannot resist illustrating as Plate 312 another of the large and superb Davenport covered vases which closely rival Coalport, Worcester, or Minton essays in the same general style. These vases have moulded and pierced covers and were probably used for pot-pourri to scent a room. The well-painted landscape side is shown here: the reverse side is of equal quality, with a large group of flowers. The gilding is superb and in general these magnificent vases show Davenport's competence in the 1830s at its best.

Seemingly one of the most popular of the early Davenport objects were flat-backed bulb-pots to dress a mantel. These occur in both pottery and in porcelain, normally in the hybrid hard-paste porcelain body. Several complete sets of three have survived but not always with their pierced covers. The most usual form is that shown in Colour Plate XXVIII and in Plates 313–14. Three others of this type are shown in *Staffordshire Porcelain*, Plate 216, and by Terence Lockett, 1972, Plate 96. The manner

267 · The Porcelains

314
315

in which the ring handles curved outwards from the body should be noted: the mock riveted attachment is seen in Plate 314, an illustration which shows well the attractive monochrome landscape painting which is such a feature of the Davenport wares. All these examples bear the impressed Davenport and anchor mark (P 2) rather than the later upper case version that has been erroneously quoted elsewhere. These slightly flared bulb pots all appear to be in the hybrid hard-paste body and to predate 1815. The flat, pierced covers are usually missing but when present the openings are of a quatrefoil shape. A very much rarer Davenport bulb pot shape is shown in Plate 315. This is nearer to the conventional D-shape pots as made by contemporary firms such as John Rose of Coalport or the Chamberlains at Worcester, but it is unique to Davenport in this exact form. The high standing bulb holders(?) rising from the loose top are more prominent than those of other makes and perhaps make this shape a little ungainly, but the superbly painted monochrome views make up for any faults! This piece too is in the hybrid hard-paste body and bears the impressed name and anchor mark P 2. These half-round flat-back bulb pots were usually made in pairs or in sets of three, the central one being larger than the side-pieces. They were extremely popular up to about 1820 after which they seem to have gone out of favour.

Very much rarer are the circular jardinières with their under-dishes. A good example is here shown in Plate 316 but the photographer has reversed the stand, perhaps to make a more pleasing picture. The top section (which has a drainage hole in the base) should stand within the saucer-shaped stand. The decoration of 1815–25 is the popular white sprigging on a pale blue ground, similar in style to the jug shown in Plate 295. The style is not by any means unique to Davenport. A later square-form jardinière – a cross between Paris porcelain and the Royal Pavilion at Brighton – is shown by Terence Lockett, 1972, Plate 99. This piece is in the City of Stoke-on-Trent Museum at Hanley. I am very happy to let it remain there! Two such shapes are illustrated here as Colour Plate X. More to my taste are the selection of ornamental miniature baskets and the cabinet cup and stand illustrated in Plate 317. Each piece bears a printed ribbon mark (P 5) and each is beautifully painted with the ever-popular full-blown roses. We do not know the name of the painter but it was certainly not William Billingsley. These rose-painted pieces have a Derby or a Swansea scent about them and are delightful representatives of a whole host of cabinet or miniature pieces made by the Davenport works in the period *c*.1815–40.

The covered box – perhaps a small pot-pourri basket with its pierced cover –

314. One of a set of three Davenport bulb pots (missing the pierced tops) in the hybrid hard-paste porcelain body, attractively painted with landscapes in monochrome. Ht 6in. Note the ring handle and mock-rivet attachment. Impressed 'Davenport' and anchor mark P 2, *c*.1807-12. (Godden of Worthing Ltd)

315. A very rare form of Davenport flat-backed bulb pot and cover painted in monochrome. Length 7½in. Ht 6½in. *c*.1807–12. (Godden of Worthing Ltd)

268 · The Porcelains

serves to remind me that the Davenport management also issued floral encrusted porcelains in the Dresden style. Most of our leading firms embellished standard shapes with such encrusted porcelain flowers in the so-called Coalbrookdale manner. I am reminded of this because I have owned this shape of covered basket with such added flower-work, which was hand-made and applied by lady 'flowerers'. A ewer decorated in this style is shown by Terence Lockett, Plate 91, and a very colourful pair are on view in the Victoria & Albert Museum. John Davenport writing from London mentioned such floral encrusted porcelain as new in a letter dated 23 October 1831, although the fashion surely predates this letter by several years:

> *I have been thinking of recommending to you the sending over for your Xmas sales a quantity of these new things in raised flowers – as baskets, boxes, cups and stands etc. in imitation of Dresden & which are now selling very cheap – in addition to any of our own make we could buy from Rose & Co. & others to form a complete variety . . .*

At the top of this 1831 letter there is also a list of suitable items '6 Baskets, 12 Eau de Cologne Bottles, 12 Toilets, 12 Inkstands'. Such items were probably later made at the Davenport factory – the Toilets, in this context will be small ewers or bottles for sweet-

316. A pale blue-ground Davenport small size cache pot or jardinière and stand (here shown in an incorrect upside-down manner). Typical but not unique, white relief decoration. Printed ribbon mark P 5. 3¼in. high, c.1815–25. (David Golding)

317. A most attractive group of Davenport miniature pieces, all painted with the full-blown rose pattern, neatly gilt. Printed ribbon mark P 5. Covered pot-pourri basket 8in. long, c.1820–30. (Phillips)

269 · The Porcelains

smelling toilet water. In addition to requesting that Dresden-style floral encrusted porcelains be produced at the Longport works this letter does show that the Davenports were not averse to buying articles from other manufacturers to broaden their stock. The showroom still made its profit without the many risks and costs of manufacturing new lines. Details of John Rose & Co.'s Coalbrookdale wares in this style are given by Geoffrey Godden in *Coalport and Coalbrookdale Porcelains*. Interesting costings for this type of work are quoted in his *Minton Pottery and Porcelain of the First Period 1793–1850*.

Other niceties of the period included at least the pyramidal (or conical) incense or pastille burners. A marked Davenport example was shown by Terence Lockett, 1972, Plate 97, right. The records of Messrs Chamberlain show that in the early 1820s these were being made in Worcester and priced between one and two pounds, according to the type of added decoration, see Geoffrey Godden's *Chamberlain-Worcester Porcelain*.

Turning from shapes to pure decoration, the Davenport works, like other leading nineteenth-century porcelain manufacturers, produced plaques or white slabs for the porcelain painters to decorate as an oil painter would embellish a blank canvas. Mr Lockett has noted circular plaques, but the most plentiful are oblong and measure about eight by six inches. These often have the words DAVENPORT'S PATENT impressed into the porcelain near one edge. The impression is quite small and the words are often missed – even by the artist who may have painted on the marked side! Many of these Davenport plaques were probably sold in an undecorated state to professional ceramic artists. They are thinner in gauge than most other porcelain slabs but I have been unable to trace the Patent under which they were made. It seems certain that no such Patent was taken out by Davenport. Examples have been noted with dates in the late 1840s: one dated 1854 is in the Victoria & Albert Museum. A rather surprisingly late reference to Davenport plaques occurs in *British Pottery Marks* by G. Wooliscroft Rhead (London, 1910): 'We know today of Davenport slabs in white china, between thirty and forty years old, which are being painted and fired without the least risk of "spitting" in the glaze; a test which we believe no other china glaze could sustain . . .'

Could these white Davenport slabs have been old stock finding their way on the market after the closure of Davenports in the late 1880s or did the porcelain painters still have available stocks of these plaques which seemingly were the best obtainable? As previously indicated, not all signed painting on these Davenport slabs (or indeed on plates or dishes) was carried out by painters employed at the Davenport factories. However, there is a possibility that some Davenport painters decorated and signed such pieces when working in their own time – a common practise in the whole industry, where the sale of a good ceramic painting could be a very welcome addition to the family's income.

Just as these plaques were made as a base for finely enamelled ceramic pictures, so too were some plates. Some very richly decorated plates could have been dress plates put on a table at an important function purely to be marvelled at and to be taken away and replaced by the dinner or dessert service plates, which would have been decorated in a less rich manner. Other very ornately painted plates could have been dressing for display cabinets, if indeed there was any distinction.

Perhaps the richest Davenport dress or cabinet plates are those with royal portrait centres. We shown in Colour Plate XXIX and in Plate 319 three of these magnificent display plates. Others in the Yorkshire Museum bear portraits of Princess Charlotte and King George IV. These are quite outstanding and different from any other Davenport porcelain. One would love to learn their history, and who decorated such splendid pieces. They seem to bear the indistinct initials of the artist, perhaps J.B. or T.B. However, these initials do not fit any known Davenport artist and the style of decoration and quality of the miniature portrait painting is unlike any on other Davenport porcelains. It could well be that these plates were decorated by a non-factory artist, as a special commission. It could even be that the artist was Thomas Baxter, the London, Swansea, and Worcester ceramic painter. These pieces are certainly in his style. These superb and unique plates are to be discussed by Miss Diana Darlington in the Northern Ceramic Society's *Journal*, vol. 7 (1989).

A delightful figure-painted Davenport plate in the Victoria & Albert Museum must certainly be an example of a purely display plate, not made as part of a service. As a general rule such special one-off designs will not have a pattern number but this does not mean that any specimen lacking a number was a special, unique, specimen!

An interesting example of display plates are those made by Davenports in the 1830s as prizes for class winners in the Dover Horticultural and Floral Society annual shows. Such large usually matt green bordered plates are painted with tasteful floral specimens and they bear a special circular mark relating to this society, which was founded in 1833. Apart from the special 'Prize' mark these plates bear the three-line DAVENPORT. LONGPORT. STAFFORDSHIRE mark (P 6, uncrowned). What attractive awards these plates represent, and no silver to keep clean! The Faversham Horticultural Society also gave as prizes such Davenport plates: these are dated 1836. Perhaps other Societies also joined in the fashion.

318. Detail of the Royal portrait plate of George III shown in Plate 319. (Private collection)

319. Two plates from the set of display plates finely painted with portraits of Prince Adolphus Frederick and George III (right). Diameter 10in. Printed scroll mark P 4, *c*.1825. (Phillips)

24 Painters and Gilders

We unfortunately know very little about the many talented painters and gilders who practised their art, or craft, upon the Davenport porcelains. It is obvious that, as such wares were being produced in large quantities over more than eighty years, a considerable number of hands must have been employed. Alas, no signed factory work is recorded nor do the original factory pattern books, wage books, or other helpful archives seem to have been preserved. Little or nothing is known about those persons whose names have been recorded by earlier writers while, in most cases, we have no supporting evidence to prove their association with the Davenport firm.

The only painter's name to be recorded in the few documents that have been preserved is that of Gould. As recorded by Terence Lockett in his 1972 book, William Davenport in writing to his brother Henry about the 1831 Royal Service, noted that the floral bouquets on this very important commission 'should be well done and all by Gould if possible'. Even this hand-written name is not all that clear and the name could well be 'Goold'. One can safely assume that this artist was the best flower painter available to the management at this period, but there is no record in ceramic literature of an artist of this name. I have, however, traced a Job Gould described as a china painter in the Hanley 1851 Census Returns. I cannot guarantee that this person was the Davenport painter as his age in 1851 was given as forty, which would make him about twenty in 1831. It may well be thought that so young an artist could not have been the foremost flower painter then available to Davenports. It could be that Job's father was also a flower painter at Davenports and that he had died before the 1841 Census or that of 1851. It is worthy of note that Gould's hand can be recognized (by the similarity to the flower painting on the Royal Service) on various examples of Davenport porcelain (Plate 320), and that all such pieces seem to predate 1850 – unless, of course, he changed his style at some period. Here we have a clear mention of a Davenport artist but no further references to his existence. I now list the few known Davenport decorators in alphabetical order.

Richard Ablott

Richard Ablott has often been cited as a Davenport artist and certainly 'Davenport Patent' plaques occur with signed examples of his landscape painting. On the evidence of these he was a first-rate ceramic painter and many of the fine landscape views found on Davenport dessert services could well be his work.

Most accounts of Ablott's ceramic career are based on John Haslem's classic work *The Old Derby China Factory: the Workmen and their Productions* (London, 1876). Haslem, himself a Derby artist, noted:

Among the last batch of apprentices at the Derby factory were Richard Ablott and Edward Prince, both of whom were landscape painters. After leaving Derby, Ablott was employed by different manufacturers, chiefly in the Staffordshire Potteries, and for a time at Coalport: he is now working for Messrs Davenport. In the Derby Exhibition of 1870, Mr. Carter of Derby, shewed a dessert-service which was made at Coalport, and painted with views in Derbyshire by Ablott, and he has since had services, numerous plates, and other pieces painted with rich and highly finished landscapes by the same artist . . .

We do not know know when Richard Ablott was taken on at Derby as an apprentice in his early teens. Perhaps it was in the 1830s or the 1840s, but clearly it was prior to the closure in 1848. Strangely, I cannot trace any record of Ablott having been employed at the Coalport works although he could have been there at some period. He is not included in the very full wage list dated 29 January 1859, nor is he included in the less complete records of 1834 and of the early 1840s. I have not noted his name in the available Coalport pattern books.

If Haslem was correct, it seems likely that Richard Ablott was at Coalport between the closure of the old Derby works in 1848 and the time of the 1859 wage list. Consequently he could well have been in the Staffordshire Potteries by 1859 and possibly employed by Davenports from then until at least 1876, at which approximate period Haslem noted his employment at the Davenport factory. If he was born in about 1816 he would have been around sixty years of age in 1876.

It is worthy of note that I have not come across Ablott's name associated with any of the other major factories – Minton, Ridgway, etc. – so he could well have been employed only (or mainly) at the Davenport works after leaving Derby and Coalport, although Haslem did state that Ablott was employed by 'different manufacturers', by which I assume he meant several.

Just as John Haslem, a nineteenth-century Derby historian, recorded some key facts about this artist, it has fallen to a present-day Derby historian and Curator of the Works collection, John Twitchett FRSA, to record further facts. Mr Twitchett, with Betty Bailey, record in a joint work *Royal Crown Derby* (Antique Collectors' Club, 3rd edn, 1988) that Richard Ablott was born in Canada, the son of an English soldier serving in Manitoba. Members of the family in Canada have specimens of his work including not only landscapes but also floral studies. Unfortunately, the family do not seem to have a record of Richard's date of birth or death or at least none is quoted by John Twitchett. As previously stated, Richard Ablott was still painting at the Davenport factory in the mid 1870s. A signed example of this artist's work on an impressed marked 'Davenports Patent' plaque is shown in Plate 321.

Jesse Austin

This designer and engraver was reputedly apprenticed at the Davenport works, but his work was most probably confined to engraving the copper plates mainly for the decoration of the earthenwares rather than the porcelains – the concern of this section. Details of Austin's career are given in chapter 15.

William Brookes

Although Brookes's name is sometimes associated with the Davenport firm, he was basically a free-lance engraver and his work would have embellished the earthenwares rather than the porcelains.

R. Capey

Mr Lockett in his 1972 book records two signed circular plaques of the 1875–85 period by

320. Detail of Gould-style flower painting on a dessert dish of pattern 298. Painted Royal mark P 8. The ribbon device will not appear on all Gould floral bouquets, *c.*1830–7. (Godden of Worthing Ltd)

321. An impressed-marked Davenport Patent porcelain plaque, the landscape painting signed R. Ablott. Plaque 9½×6¾in. *c.*1850. (Martin Hutton Collection)

273 · The Porcelains

this artist. These pierced plaques were of Little Moreton Hall and of Coniston Lake. Mr Lockett noted that these plaques had the appearance of being factory decorated, a point he no doubt made as many such late plaques and plates were sold in the white and were then decorated by free-lance painters or by amateurs. I have, however, been unable to trace any other records of this artist.

Stephen Chesters

Stephen Chesters was a very talented independent ceramic artist, a professional rather than an amateur. His signed work – mainly landscapes – can be found on impressed-marked 'Davenport's Patent' slabs but he was not a factory artist.

He exhibited paintings on porcelain at the annual Royal Academy Exhibition, 1849–57. A further painting submitted from a Scarborough address in 1885 was not necessarily by this artist. Various signed examples of his work bear dates in the 1850s and he exhibited at the 1851 Exhibition, at which period he was residing in London. The Jury awarded Chesters 'Honourable Mention' and in their report stated: 'The picture by Murillo (The Holy Family) in the National Gallery has been admirably copied by this artist on porcelain. Every trait in the original is rendered with the utmost delicacy, this work reflects the highest credit on its author.'

It is possible that Chesters later moved to Staffordshire. He certainly showed work at Stoke in 1866 – see the *Art Journal* 1866, p. 212 – and the *Pottery Gazette* in 1884 referred to Chesters 'of Staffordshire' as being 'another good landscape painter'. It is possible, but by no means certain, that at some time in the 1860–88 period he carried out some work for the Davenport factory either on a free-lance basis or as an employed hand. His ceramic painting, when he was not working on a piece-rate basis, would be far superior to the normal run of factory decoration.

William Clowes

Mr Lockett included William Clowes in his list of Davenport decorators, citing Jewitt as his authority. This nineteenth-century chronicler, however, only states that Clowes was 'one of Mr Davenport's workmen' and I am not aware of any evidence to show that he was a painter.

Joshua Cristall

This well-known water-colour artist was reputedly apprenticed at the Davenport works, but this seems improbable as he was born in about 1767. He would therefore have been nearly thirty years of age when this firm was established. He was certainly connected with the Caughley porcelain works near Broseley during Thomas Turner's ownership of the factory prior to 1799 as various undated letters are addressed to 'Mr Cristall at Mr Turner's China Manufactory'. Joshua Cristall had apparently earlier been placed (apprenticed?) to Hewson, the London china and glass dealer.

It is however possible that some of the landscape painting on early Davenport bone china was carried out by Cristall. The painting on such examples as we show in Plates 231–4 has a professional freedom of style and is almost water-colour on porcelain. This, however, is just a faint possibility, not a probability, especially as his association with the fine arts seems to have commenced by at least 1805.

Joshua Cristall should certainly be regarded as a fine art painter rather than as a china decorator. He was a founder member and later President of the Royal Society of Painters in Water Colours. He died in London on 18 October 1847, aged eighty.

James Cutts

This celebrated designer and engraver has been associated with the Davenports, but he was mainly an independent engraver selling his copperplates and designs to various potters. Some of his work is signed: it will occur on earthenware rather than porcelain.

Robert Eaton

Robert Eaton's association with the Davenport factory is based only on the signed and dated 1887 plate shown in Plate 288. The plate bears the late impressed mark DAVENPORT but in its style of decoration and moulded edge, it relates rather to the 1830s (see Colour Plate XXIII and Plate 264 for shapes).

Robert Eaton's name appears in the Coalport wage list of the 1859 period when he received a low remuneration, pointing perhaps to his being quite young and inexperienced at that time.

Two signed 'R. Eaton' plates are in the Allen collection at the Victoria & Albert Museum. These are included in the catalogue (nos. 403–4) as Coalport. One is a fruit study, the other floral. This artist could well have painted some of the later Davenport porcelains, but on the other hand, the one signed plate may be leading us on a false scent.

W. Fletcher

This artist has been ascribed to Davenport in the past but purely, we believe, on the strength of two plates in the Allen collection (nos. 515–16) in the Victoria & Albert Museum. These plates are not marked and were attributed to Davenport only because of the similarity of gilding. A Coalport origin for the blanks is likely.

These figure subject plates are both signed 'W. Fletcher Junr. Del. et Pinx.', a form of signature unlikely to be found on factory-decorated porcelains. Fletcher may have been a gifted amateur ceramic painter but we do not believe he had any direct connection with the Davenport factory. These unmarked Coalport-type lobed-edged plates are shown in the catalogue of the Herbert Allen Collection, Plate 89 and in W. Mankowitz and R. G. Haggar, *The Concise Encyclopaedia of English Pottery and Porcelain* (London, 1957), Plate 37, bottom row.

Gould

See pp. 244 and 272 for comment on this Davenport flower painter.

James Holland

This water-colour painter was reputedly apprenticed to the Davenports. He was born in 1799 so any apprenticeship should have been in the period *c*.1813–18. It is not known if he continued to work at Longport or if he decorated porcelains. Examples of his non-ceramic painting are in the City Museum & Art Gallery at Stoke-on-Trent.

Emile Lessore

This former Sèvres figure and landscape artist came to the Staffordshire Potteries in 1857 or 1858. He initially worked for Mintons but soon moved to Wedgwood where he decorated both creamwares and majolica-type earthenwares in his individual free style. He returned to his native France in 1868 but continued to decorate blanks for Wedgwood. Lessore died in 1876.

At least one signed example of his work is known on a printed ribbon marked Davenport porcelain plate, see Terence Lockett's 1972 book, Plate 100. However, we cannot accept Lessore as a Davenport painter and this or other examples only serve to show the reputation of the Davenport blanks with ceramic painters, and that the management were happy to sell such undecorated porcelains. The Lessore examples are helpful in proving a pre-1876 dating for this trade.

Daniel Lucas

Dan Lucas senior was reputedly employed in early life as a painter at the Davenport factory 'at glass and china painting'. Our authority for this statement is the usually correct John Haslem in his book *The Old Derby China Factory* (London, 1876).

Haslem, who had worked with many of these pre-1848 Derby painters, also noted 'for a quarter of a century prior to the closing of the Derby factory[Lucas] was the principal landscape painter employed at Derby . . . His colouring lacked variety, and his style was heavier than that of the painters before his time . . . On the close of the works Lucas left Derby, and, for some years, was employed in painting japan (tinned metal) ware in Birmingham, where he resided until his death about 1867, only a few days before completing his 80th year.'

It would therefore seem that Dan Lucas was born at Derby in or about 1787. He would have been eighteen or so by 1805 when the Davenports began producing porcelain, but John Haslem suggests that he was at Derby from about 1823 onwards. However, the Census returns help to indicate when the Lucas family were in Derby. William Lucas, Daniel's second son (a good gilder) was born in Shelton in about 1812 (he gave his age in 1851 as 39), but the third son, Daniel junior, was born in Derby in about 1818 (giving his age in 1851 as 33). It would therefore appear that Daniel Lucas senior (or rather his wife!) was in the Staffordshire Potteries in 1812 but that the family had returned to his native Derby by 1818.

Daniel Lucas is well known as a landscape painter but the early water-colour-like rather broadly-painted landscapes found on the early Davenport dessert services of the type featured in Plates 231–4 are unlike the rather heavy, oil-painting-style landscapes associated with Lucas's post-1818 work on Derby porcelain. John Twitchett in his *Derby Porcelain* (London, 1980) noted: 'His painting has an opaque, oily nature and a somewhat dull and monotonous palette'. This authority also stated that Daniel Lucas came to Derby from the 'Davenport Factory about 1820'. As I have stated, he was back in Derby by at least 1818 and it should be noted that John Haslem originally mentioned that Lucas painted Davenport glass and porcelain. It should be remembered that some of this glass was highly decorated. The Royal Order included for example '6 Fan Lights, Trophies of War and stained borders. 1 Centre Fan Light. His Royal Highness's Arms in stain'.

Jesse Mountford

Again John Haslem, the former Derby painter, gives us the basic details of his contemporary's movements. Haslem relates that Jesse Mountford was one of the Derby landscape painters discharged by Robert Bloor about 1821 and that this painter subsequently worked at Coalport for about fifteen years. Haslem continued:

On leaving [Coalport], *he was employed as a landscape painter for twenty five years at Messrs Davenport's, Longport dying there in 1861 . . . On the day he died he had been at his usual employment at Messrs Davenport's, and in the evening was preparing his (fishing) tackle . . . when the summons came which for ever put an end to both his artistic and piscatorial pursuits . . .*

The 1841 and 1851 Census returns fill in some of the details and help to tie down the period when he left Coalport for Staffordshire. They show that Jesse Mountford was born at Hanley in the Potteries in about 1799 – he gave his age in 1851 as 52. Children were born in Shropshire in 1826 and in 1831, presumbably whilst Jesse was still at the Coalport factory. Two other children were born in Shelton in the Staffordshire Potteries in 1835 and 1836. It would therefore seem that Jesse Mountford transferred to Davenports between 1831 and 1835. As stated by Haslem he worked there literally up to his death in 1861. He was obviously a competent landscape painter and much, if not most, of the scenic painting on Davenport porcelain between about 1835 and 1861 would have been his work. The porcelain plaque shown in Plate 322 is a rare signed and dated example of his painting. This could well be a Davenport plaque. His factory work on dessert services, etc. is, of course, not signed but the pieces shown in Plates 276 and 279 may be considered as possibly painted by this former Derby and Coalport landscape painter.

William Pitts

Terence Lockett stated in his 1972 book that this London sculptor, designer, and painter 'worked on designs for the Royal Service' made for William IV in 1830 or 1831. However, the only mention of this designer seems to be in the negative 'we can't get anything from Pitts'. It could be that William Pitts (1790–1840) was merely slow to deliver promised designs. Certainly, it seems unlikely that he worked on day-to-day designs or models for Davenports and he should not be regarded as a factory employee.

Shaw

It is believed that the anonymous author of the 1903 book *When I was a Child* was C. Shaw. Writing of the early 1840s this author stated: 'My father, as I have stated, was a painter and gilder. He worked at Davenport's. A new manager there introduced new methods of conducting the business. For one thing he introduced female labour in a department which had hitherto belonged almost exclusively to the men'. The first part of this statement directly concerns us in this section but, alas, no mention is made of the father's Christian name.

The 1841 census returns provide three possible Davenport painters and gilders with the surname Shaw: Enoch Shaw, described as a painter then aged 48, who was born in Burslem (Tunstall census); James Shaw, a gilder in his early twenties in 1841 (Longton census); Richard Shaw, porcelain painter, aged sixty and born outside Staffordshire (Shelton census).

Enoch Shaw, who was still living in Tunstall in 1851, then gave his occupation as Earthenware painter, but young Shaw did not state that his father was a porcelain painter. On balance I am inclined to suggest that it was James Shaw, the young gilder, who was referred to in 1903 as a former Davenport painter and gilder. Although the elderly porcelain painter, Richard Shaw, lived closer to the Davenport factory, it seems unlikely on account of his age in 1841 that he could have fathered a son who was to publish a book sixty-two years later.

William Slater, Senior

The Derby painter and historian, John Haslem, is again the source of our information on the Slaters. Haslem stated:

William Slater . . . was apprenticed at the Pinxton China Works. He . . . removed to Derby in 1813 . . . In early life he worked a short time for Robinson & Randall in London, but he was employed at the Derby factory, with little intermission, from the time he left Pinxton until its close in 1848.

He was a good general hand, painting fruit, insects and armorial bearings well,

322. A Davenport porcelain plaque signed on the reverse 'J. Mountford, 1851'. About 12×9in. (Ex-Godden Collection)

but excelling more particularly as a gilder and gold chaser. Shortly after the close of the [Derby factory in 1848] he went into the Staffordshire Potteries, and was employed at Messrs Davenport's of Longport, until is death in 1867 aged 73 years.

William Slater may have moved from Pinxton to Derby prior to the date (1813) given by Haslem (his son having been born in Derby in 1812), but otherwise Haslem's account seems very authoritative. However, the 1841 Burslem census returns show a Derby-born William Slater, then aged 49, as an 'Earthenware manufacturer's manager'. I am not certain whether this relates to the Derby painter of this name as there is a possible discrepancy of a year in the ages; but on balance it seems that William Slater, the Derby painter, may have worked for Davenports in the early 1840s in a managerial capacity, although he may well have painted special commissions. As stated by Haslem, William Slater senior was employed by the Davenports up to the time of his death at the then ripe old age of 73.

William Slater, Junior

John Haslem is again our source for the basic information on this Derby-trained ceramic painter and gilder. He states that William was the eldest son of William Slater, that he was an excellent gilder and that he was apprenticed at the Derby works, and further that he 'left Derby before the close of the works and was for many years foreman of the painters and pattern designer, at Messrs Davenport's. He died at Longport in 1865, at the age of 58.'

William Slater junior was, according to Haslem, born at Derby in about 1807. However, the 1851 census return shows that he was then aged 39, giving a date of birth of about 1812. William Slater seemingly left Derby before his father in 1848 and a daughter was born in Burslem in about 1840, Eliza being aged eleven in 1851.

William Slater junior was apparently at Davenports from about 1840 to his death in 1865. According to Haslem, Slater was, at least in the later years, foreman of the painters and pattern designer. Could we call him the Art Director? Certainly he must have been a key figure in the decorating department. He was also one of a large family of ceramic decorators. His younger brother, Joseph, was likewise a key figure at Mintons and before then at Alcock's Hill Pottery at Burslem.

Edwin Steel(e)

Terence Lockett has stated that Edwin Steel(e), the first son of Thomas Steel, is 'traditionally alleged to have worked at Davenports'. I, that is Geoffrey Godden, have not been able to find evidence to substantiate this belief. John Haslem does not state that Edwin was employed at Davenports. He does state that Edwin was apprenticed at the Derby works and that he later worked at the Rockingham factory. Haslem continued: 'Both Edwin and Horatio Steel were chiefly employed in the Staffordshire Potteries after leaving Derby, Edwin at Messrs Minton's and at some of the best manufactories. He died in 1871 in his 68th year . . .

The 1851 Census returns show that Edwin was born at Burslem in about 1805, at a time when his father Thomas was probably employed at the Davenport factory. His wife Charlotte gave birth to daughters at Derby in about 1827 and 1833, even though Edwin Steel(e)'s name appears on the Rockingham Militia lists in 1827 and 1828. Their two sons, Thomas and Edwin, were born in Shelton in 1836 and 1839 respectively, showing that the family was in the Staffordshire Potteries by this period. Edwin Steel(e)'s name appears in the 1861 Hanley Census returns but, as I have stated, there seems no firm evidence that he was, or was not, employed by Davenports.

Thomas Steel

Thomas Steel (*c*.1771–1850) is one of the most famous of our nineteenth-century ceramic painters. His speciality was fruit and flowers although, no doubt, he could, if required, turn his attention to other forms of decoration. His work is well known on Derby porcelain, on Rockingham examples, and then on Minton wares. John Haslem wrote: 'Thomas Steele [sic], whose first painting on china has never been surpassed, was a native of the Staffordshire Potteries where he first learned his art. He worked at the Derby factory from 1815 . . .'

If Haslem was correct in his firm dating for Thomas Steel's arrival at the Derby factory our artist would then have been approximately forty-four years of age. He should therefore have been working in the Staffordshire Potteries for twenty years or more before this. Tradition has it that Thomas Steel was apprenticed, or worked at, the Davenport factory. He can hardly have been apprenticed there for he was about 23 when the Davenport pottery was established. He could certainly have decorated Davenport porcelains in the early years of the nineteenth century up to his leaving for Derby c.1815.

The 1841 Census Returns, basic as they are, show that Thomas Steel was born in Staffordshire as were his sons Edwin (c.1803), Thomas (c.1805) and Horatio (c.1808). The 1861 Census Returns helpfully show that Horatio, then aged 53, had been born in Longport, in or about 1808.

The plate of pattern 116 and the square dessert dish in the Victoria & Albert Museum (Plates 248–9) are certainly painted in the style associated with Thomas Steel's later work at Derby, Rockingham, and for Minton when he returned to the Potteries. Some of the bulb pots too are painted in his style, see *Staffordshire Porcelain*, Plate 216.

The main questions are for how long did Steel work at the Davenport factory (he may have worked for a period for Minton or at some other factory) and what other style of painting did he practise? The fruit painting would hardly have kept him in full employment. He may well have been responsible for some of the fine flower painting, single, botanical type, specimens, or conventional groups found on pre-1815 Davenport porcelain. Haslem noted that later at Derby Steel painted 'both flowers and insects well'.

Part Four:
Davenport Glass

The contents of this section are largely based on the research of Ronald B. Brown published in the *Journal of the Glass Association* (1, 1985, 30–40). Mr Brown has also generously allowed me access to his original research notes. Additional contemporary references have been supplied by Rodney Hampson.

The combination of an earthenware factory, the production of porcelain and the manufacture of glass is unique in English industrial history. No documents have so far been discovered which can inform us why John Davenport embarked upon the making of glass at Longport. We can only surmise that his experience as a merchant in Liverpool led him to believe he could prosper in the venture. The glass works was established in 1801 on land adjacent to the Longport Pottery site. Looking at the area today, the Glass Works lay between the factory now occupied by Arthur Wood & Sons and Price's Teapot manufactory (see Plate 1). It is just possible that some of the small buildings in this area are remnants of the former glass works, but very careful survey work using the surviving 1881 factory plan would be necessary to establish this. To all intents and purposes the Glass Works seems to have been totally demolished. Unfortunately, it is not possible to see any glass cones on the 1888 panorama photograph of the factory (Plate 7), nor do we know of any illustration of the Works either in its heyday or subsequently, prior to demolition.

As was his normal practice at this period Davenport bought the expertise he lacked. The firm in 1801 was separate from the Pottery concern and traded as Davenport, Kinnersley and Grafton. Kinnersley was the banker, and one suspects merely the sleeping partner providing some risk capital. Edward Grafton, a Stourbridge glass-maker from Brettell Lane, Brierley Hill, provided the practical working experience. As there was no indigenous trained labour in North Staffordshire it is more than likely that Grafton would engage glass blowers and other skilled craftsmen known to him from the Stourbridge area to provide a competent work force. It is recorded that advertisments were placed in the *Birmingham Gazette* for glass blowers, wages of 12 to 18 shillings a week being offered.

In whatever manner the new Works was staffed it seems to have been remarkably successful from the very first. We have already noted on p. 16 the purchase by John Davenport of a 'Looking Glass' from Grafton in 1802, and commented upon the engagement of Thomas Lakin whose activities spanned both the pottery and glass sides of the enterprise (p. 14). Grafton and Lakin, with others whose names have not come down to us, must have formed an excellent and innovative team. They seem to have been able to produce glass of the highest quality and of most unusual types very early on.

Of all the glass manufactured at Longport that made under the Patent of 1806 is the most readily remembered. This was more than an experimental method of decoration. The surviving specimens testify to the attractiveness of the finished product, though reading the Patent specification one can realize that the process must have been difficult, time-consuming and labour-intensive.

The Patent was taken out on 1 August 1806 (No. 2946) and details of it are fully given in Ronald Brown's article. Suffice to say that the principle behind the process was to take a carefully prepared mixture of two glass batches, which was then ground and levigated. 'When the glass is sufficiently levigated it may be mixed with a menstruum . . . to prepare the menstruum . . . I take one part double refined loaf sugar dissolved in two parts of pure water, to which is added . . . about one third part of common writing ink.' This curious mixture of ground glass, sugar, water, and ink is then coated on the glass to be decorated using a hair brush, with the designs being drawn into it with a pointed metal or bone tool. When the pattern has been completely drawn, the vessel is then heated to the point of 'semivitrification.' If the piece were overfired and vitrified it lost the effect of a slightly rough granular surface which was what was aimed at in emulation of a pattern which had been wheel ground. This process just described has a superficial resemblance to that of an engraved glass, but it is in fact a unique process. Occasionally writers have mistaken the surface textural finish for that of etching and described it as such. Indeed it is just possible that the factory themselves referred to glasses so decorated as 'etched' for the sake of convenience (see the Royal order printed below). But it is clear from the description that this is a hand finished 'painting' and tooled method of decoration and that acid as used in the conventional form of etching is not part of the process – always assuming that the Patent specification is an accurate description of the process performed. In the specification John Davenport claimed that his invention could be used for flat glass as well as vessels and that it would not attract dirt on the rough unpolished parts of the design as did wheel engraved decoration.

Looking at the three splendid examples of Patent glass illustrated in Plates 323–5, two aspects strike one immediately. Firstly, the delicacy, almost fragility of the pattern. This is perhaps not so evident in the fine photographs which have been specially lit to make the most of the design, but holding an actual glass the pattern, like that of the finest stipple engraving, seems merely to have brushed the surface of the glass leaving a barely perceptible imprint. Despite this the pattern has stood the test of time remarkably well and remains a permanent and fixed delight. One also cannot help noticing, on reading the full list of 18 Patent glasses that Mr Brown was able to locate and describe, how many are decorated with 'picturesque' country scenes so closely akin to the monochrome landscapes which adorned the ceramic wares from Longport. It is only supposition, but one feels that the influence if not the direct hand of Thomas Lakin is present in the choice of subject. Such charming country scenes were also features of the decoration of Lakin's own earthenwares when he left Davenport in 1810.

It is not known for how long the factory produced these Patent glasses. Almost all are drinking vessels, and I understand that more have been reported since 1985 when Ronald Brown listed and described 18 of them. Again uniquely of Davenport glass these pieces are marked on the base with the word Patent. They are thus the only examples which we can say with absolute certainty were made by Davenport, though the provenance of other later items is strong, and the documentary evidence in some cases is conclusive.

Within a few weeks from the enrolling of the Patent, the Glass Works was included in the itinerary of the Royal party of the Prince Regent and the Duke of Clarence (see p. 16). Though the two Princes expressed their gratification at the progress of the China and Earthenware departments, the future George IV went even further with regard to the glass. He admired the effect of the new Patent glass discussed above and, as well as ordering glass, as he had done ceramic articles, he also appointed Davenports as 'Glass Makers to His Royal Highness', an honour whose ceramic equivalent he had bestowed upon Spode during the same tour of the leading factories. The visit is fully reported in the *Staffordshire Advertiser* of 20 September 1806.

The Royal order for glass which was kindly provided to Mr Brown from the Royal Archives by Sir Geoffrey de Bellaigue, Surveyor of the Queen's Works of Art, is in two parts. The first, dated 18 April 1807, has not been published in full before, and reads as follows:

A Service of Glass Etch'd Grecian Border as under

48 Monteiths	4/6	£10: 16: 0
72 Wine & Water Glass's	5/-ea.	18: 0: 0
24 Ale Glass's	2/6	3: 0: 0
60 Wine Glass's	2/-	6: 0: 0
24 Liquor Glass's	2/-	2: 0: 0

323. Large cylindrical rummer on a stem with two ball knops, decorated with a rural scene using the Patent process. Ht 6in. Mark 'Patent', c.1810. (Courtesy Asprey)

324. Rummer decorated with rustic picturesque landscape by the Patent process. Ht 6in. Mark 'Patent', c.1806–10. (Private Collection: photo Courtesy Jeanette Hayhurst)

325. Rummer decorated with a cottage in a rural setting by the Patent process (the reverse of Plate 324). Ht 6in. Mark 'Patent', c.1806–10. (Private Collection: photo Courtesy Jeanette Hayhurst)

323

324
325

6 Quart Decanters & Stoppers Etch'd Feathers	22/-	6: 12: 0
6 Three pint Water Caroffs	22/-	6: 12: 0
6 Quart double ring'd Decanters, Etch'd His Royal Highness's Arms in full	55/-	16: 10: 0
6 Water Caroffs Ditto	55/-	16: 10: 0
6 Quart Decanters richly Cutt & Etch'd His Royal Highness's Arms in full	95/-	28: 10: 0
		114: 18: 0
	4 Cases	1: 3: 0
		116: 1: 0

283 · Davenport Glass

It is fascinating to speculate on the whereabouts of these glasses. They appear not to be traceable in the present Royal collections, but one cannot imagine this considerable quantity of glass, a goodly part of it decorated with the Prince of Wales's Arms or 'Feathers', having completely disappeared from the face of the earth. Some examples must be somewhere waiting to be recognized. The invoice uses the word 'Etch'd' and as discussed above it is not certain whether these glasses were decorated by conventional etching or whether the Patent method was used. The discovery of just one glass with the 'Grecian border' (Greek key as we term it) and either the Prince of Wales's feathers or the full Royal Arms would solve the problem. As he had expressed his admiration for the Patent it would seem most likely that it was this that he would purchase.

As it has become better known this Patent glass has been much sought after. But even so, there must still exist many glasses in collections which are unrecognized, either because they lack the Patent mark or because it has been removed at some time, as has been noted on a number of specimens. They will simply be regarded as examples of engraved or etched Regency glasses. I know of no evidence to suggest when the manufacture of Patent glass ceased. Ronald Brown gives a date span of 1806–10 for the pieces he illustrates. This may well be accurate, if we assume that Lakin had much to do with the process. Certainly, both on stylistic grounds and the sheer effort involved in the process, which would have had less appeal to John Davenport after Lakin's departure, one cannot imagine a date beyond 1815 for such pieces to continue in production.

A second portion of the Royal order for glass was invoiced on 24 June 1808. It reads as follows:

4 Panes 17×12 Inches Mosaic & Stain'd Border . . .	30/-	6:	0:	0
8 ditto " Etch'd Figures from Flaxman with Staind Imboss Border	30/-	12:	0:	0
6 Fan Lights Trophies of War, & Staind Borders	25/-	7:	10:	0
1 Centre Fan Light His Royal Highness's Arms in Stain . . .		2:	0:	0
	2 Cases	0:	7:	6
		27:	17:	6

This order too is of considerable interest, and no further information is forthcoming as to where the fan lights and decorated panes of glass were to be placed. Brighton Pavilion as we know it today was not completed until 1821, though the Prince was living in Brighton for part of the time and was actively planning the Pavilion at this date. Perhaps the glass was to be stored until his seaside extravaganza was built. Otherwise one assumes the glass would have been used at Carlton House, the Prince's London residence in 1808. If this were so it would now almost certainly be lost, unless it had been removed to either Buckingham Palace or Brighton. As far as can be ascertained it is in neither place.

Within a year after the Royal order and visit, the original partnership was dissolved. This was reported in both the *Staffordshire Advertiser* of 26 September 1807 and the *London Gazette* for the same year p. 1289. Both Kinnersley and Grafton left the partnership. The Glass Works now came under the same partnership as the Pottery, that is of John & James Davenport.

After this flurry of information about the early years of the Glass Works, evidence for almost the whole of the next eighty years is very patchy. For the sake of completeness we will note what references we have, but in no sense can this chapter be regarded as a definitive history of Davenport glass. The usual source of material, the Foxley papers, are not very helpful on glass matters. The few references I have found help to fill in the picture a little. Other sources such as the *Staffordshire Advertiser* and the *Pottery Gazette* contain far fewer references to the Glass Works than to the Pottery, though in some cases the two enterprises are regarded as one. Nor have any detailed accounts been found such as we have for the Pottery at various dates in its history. Thus what follows is in no sense a consecutive history, rather an indication of the general development of the Glass Works.

Shortly after the 1806 Royal visit (according to the *Pottery Gazette* of 1893 in a retrospective article) the firm received orders from the Cities of Liverpool and London for glass and from the Emperor of Russia for a composite order for China, Earthenware, and Glass, each piece to bear the Imperial Arms. No date is given in the 1893 article and no further references to the Russian order have been noted, though the earthenware plate of *c.*1845 illustrated on Plate 128 carries the Romanoff double-headed eagle. Could this be part of the Imperial order?

There is good evidence, however, of a commission in 1811 from Earl Grosvenor for a set of coloured windows in the Saloon in Old Eaton Hall. Illustrations of drawings for these windows, which, on balance, are more likely to have been painted than stained glass, appeared in *Country Life*, 18 February 1971.

Nor is there any ambiguity about the orders for Liverpool. Ronald Brown has found many interesting references to Davenports supplying glass for the City's use principally in the Town Hall. For example on 1 March 1811 J. & J. Davenport were paid £55 0s 0d for Sky Lights, and in March 1818 they were paid £36 12s 4d for 'Glass for the Mayor's Table'. The ledgers of Liverpool Select Committee, Finance (352/MIN/FIN/1–5) from which these excerpts are taken recorded on 7 March 1818 that:

The Surveyor having produced a variety of designs and estimates from several persons for furnishing three chandeliers for the Saloon and Drawing Room in the Town Hall. Resolved: That the designs now marked by the Chairman be adopted, and that the Surveyor be authorised to order same from Messrs. Davenports at a sum not exceeding One Hundred Guineas each.

On 30 September payment was made to John & James Davenport for three glass chandeliers of £317 5s 0d. On 8 April 1820 Davenports were paid a further £264 6s 5d 'For Glass Chandeliers for Town Hall', and on 7 October 1820 a further £185 0s 0d was paid for chandeliers. Just how many this involved is not easy to calculate, as earlier in the year there were accounts for upgrading the chandeliers from twelve to eighteen lights each and in April it was minuted that 'the three chandeliers be introduced into the Great Ballroom to be lighted with gas'. Some of these splendid examples of Davenports' glassmaking abilities may still be seen in Liverpool Town Hall, and one is illustrated in Plate 4 in Mr Brown's article noted above. Further details of the Town Hall may be found in an article by Prof. Reilly in *Country Life* of 23 July 1927.

It is highly likely that this connection between the Davenport Glass Works, the Canning Place showroom in Liverpool, and the City was maintained over many years, and as further items of glassware were required Davenports would be the obvious first choice in making any order. Indeed Mr Brown found additional evidence of this association, again in the Minute Books, when items of glassware for the Town Hall were purchased in the 1830s: 'Davenport, Fynney & Co. [the style of the Liverpool enterprise at this date, see p. 42] for Glass for use at the Mayor's Table £164 16s 8d', 24 February 1832. On 14 March 1834 'For Glass and Earthenware for use at Mayor's table £62 10s 2d', and on 27 March 1835 to H. & W. Davenport (a rare use of this title) 'for Glass for the Mayor's Table £55 9s 10d'. There were records of 'Sundries' at various dates for the churches of St Luke's and St Michael's. We have already recorded on p. 32–3 the transactions relating to the enlargement of the Canning Place warehouse and showrooms. All in all, the Liverpool connection would appear to have been just as strong in the glass trade as it was in the china and earthenware.

The first item of note in the Foxley papers (Pottery Corespondence) as it happens concerns Liverpool. This letter and those which follow have mostly not been published previously. On 13 November 1812 James Davenport wrote to his partner John from Liverpool. He comments:

As to the General business here, the En'ware department is done as well as it can be by Fynney, the Glass business appears to have suffered and Carpenter appears to have but little knowledge but he's attentive and will no doubt improve he appears to have no knowledge of the export business, but they have never had a price to go by and I perceive from what we have been doing lately that we have been charging 15 & 20 pc't more than Holts. Fynney has never taken much notice of this glass business owing to J. D. Junr having taken him up sharp when he has said anything & told him to mind his own business . . . I have been with several firms who have ships on and have promised to give us their favours, we had an order yesterday from W. Brown for 7 Hhds Glass we got him to take part of those made up for Carruthers, our Stock of Glass here and at Runcorn is very heavy. I almost agreed with Mr Brown to take the Green Gooseberry bottles, we must have the new duty . . . (Foxley 1)

An interesting letter giving the first documentary indication that an export trade in glass was also conducted from Liverpool, though apart from the mention of the gooseberry bottles there is no indication of what is being exported or where to. The letter also sheds a little more light on the animosity which existed between James Davenport Jun. and Mountford Fynney (see p. 36).

The note at the end refers to the duty on glass which was payable on the quantity of raw materials (not the finished product) and was enforced by Excise officers who made periodic on-site inspections. John Davenport's attitude to the inspectors is made plain in two very long letters which he wrote in May 1817 (Foxley 26–7). The first is to E. J. Littleton, MP. In it Davenport complains of the malevolence and victimization he has experienced at the hands of the Excise officers and asks him to intervene with the Board of Trade to put a stop to the oppressive behaviour of the local excise officials towards the Davenport Glass Works. He writes:

Such have been my feelings that for months back, since it happened, I have not entered the Glass House – and but from compassion to the workmen and their families who must have been ruined in these times of [pressure ?] *we should have shut up the Works.*

Even allowing for John Davenport's well-known hyperbole he does seem to have suffered somewhat. He expands his feelings in a letter to his son Henry Davenport, a copy of which is sent to Mr Littleton who has apparently intervened with the Board of Excise on his behalf, but most of the grievances he complained of earlier are still in evidence. He writes:

For more than Twenty Years I have at considerable expense of time and Money been with the foremost in support of Government, for the truth of which assertion I could appeal to many of those at the Head of it, and surely I may not be taxed with vanity if I have estimated my services above the value of a reprimand or even the removal of some of its lowest officers who had personally insulted me, and who had declared a predetermined hostility to my concerns [he again threatens to leave the glass trade] *. . . We have at considerable expense brought the manufacture to a greater degree of perfection than has been before accomplished, and were hoping for a return of profit, yet we are not willing to sacrifice our feeling for profit alone, nor to continue a trade wherein our character is to be aspersed by such men as we complain of . . .*

Davenport must have received some satisfaction, or simply his anger cooled. The glass works remained open, and I have not recorded any further correspondence on this subject. The glass tax remained in force until finally repealed in 1845.

The next glass reference of which we have note is a letter from Henry Davenport to his father written on 30 April 1822 from Longport to Salisbury Square: 'I found most things here as I left them, the Cutting shop is a noble edifice but I wish it was a storey lower, we must however, be content now it will not quite ruin us I hope.' Apparently the affair of the Excise men had been forgotten and rather than close the business new premises had been built for the Cutting shop. Perhaps an indication that trade in cut glass items was thriving.

In 1826 we have another reference to glass this time from the notorious Henry Pontigny. In a letter to Henry Davenport, a substantial quotation from which was published in *Davenport Pottery & Porcelain*, p. 14. Pontigny writes:

As for Glass, it is your own fault if you have no orders from us for Common Cut Goods. – I get button flint wines fluted or fingered weight 3 oz at 8/- per doz. 5% discount without any risk of cutting – Best Tumblers ½ pt fluted or fingered 6½ at 10/6 - 5% disct, without any risk. If you like to get up 5 or 600 dozs of each at these prices we shall sell them . . . I believe we want more fingered than fluted.

The Breakage account you sent by last [post] *is beyond belief, and we must have a strict inquiry on foot about it. £80 worth during a period we had hardly any glass from you is beyond belief and beyond bearing . . .'*

This is one of the rare documents to give us some impression of the types of glass being manufactured at Longport. It will not help us to identify Davenport cut glass, fluted or fingered wine glasses, but it is an insight into the nature of their trade, which as we have already seen encompassed stained and painted window glass, Patent glass, chandeliers, and most types of drinking vessel.

That they were also capable of *tours de force* is indicated by an account of the Banquet held on Thursday 8 September 1831 at the 'Legs of Man' in Burslem to celebrate the Coronation of William IV. The event was reported the following day in *The Staffordshire Advertiser*. Mr Spencer Rogers acted as President and upon the orders of the Vice-President Henry Davenport, 'a beautiful cut glass Coronation cup was set upon the table, manufactured by Mr Davenport of Longport, capable of holding 4 gallons, which was filled with punch by order of the Vice-President.' Surely such an impressive vessel has not disappeared for ever? Unless, that is, it was broken in the revelry of toasting the new King, who had after all placed a very substantial order for Davenport china which was at that very time being used at the King's Coronation Banquet (for which see p. 43).

Even more impressive was the glass which was made especially for the Banquet given at the Guildhall by the City of London for Queen Victoria. Extensive quotations from the *Staffordshire Advertiser* for 11 November 1837 have already been given on p. 53 concerning the china service. The account recorded:

The China and cut glass were provided by Messrs Davenport of Fleet Street. Owing to their incredible exertions [it will be recalled that the order was only given on 13 October] *it was completed on Monday last and forwarded to Town from their factory in Staffordshire.* [Then follows the description of the china given on p. 53, followed by] *The decanters, claret jugs, Champagne, Hock, and other glasses, are all richly cut, and ornamented with a vine border, varied with the rose, thistle, and shamrock, and the Royal Arms.*

The supply for her Majesty's table consisted of three dozen wine glasses, three dozen small claret glasses, three dozen large ditto, three dozen Champagne ditto, two dozen liqueur ditto, two dozen goblets, two dozen carafes and tumblers, two dozen hexagon massive decanters, one dozen claret ditto, eighteen wine glass coolers, two dozen topaz coloured hock glasses, six water jugs, one dozen topaz coloured finger glasses, two dozen ice plates, and four earthenware antique jugs, with the Royal and City Arms in relief.

For the entertainment generally, there were furnished by the Messrs Davenport 1,600 wine glasses, 800 claret ditto, 800 Champagne ditto, 800 hock ditto (emerald green), 800 tumblers, 400 hundred decanters, 300 water bottles and tumblers, 350 wine glass coolers, &c.

Though the bulk of the glasses provided for 'the entertainment generally' appear to have had no distinguishing features, the glasses for the Royal table are surely described in sufficient detail for collectors and curators to be able to recognize them. If specimens were identified it would add considerably to the corpus of known Davenport glass.

As was remarked in Part One, this splendid occasion must surely have given great satisfaction to John Davenport, though alas there is no correspondence to record it. At the time of the Banquet, the firm was trading in his son's name as William Davenport & Co. There remains a slight element of doubt as to whether all the glass for the Royal Banquet was actually made in Staffordshire. Ronald Brown has found references to Powells, the Whitefriars Glass Works, supplying Davenports with glass in the period 1835–7. It is just possible that through the London showroom some of the many thousands of pieces supplied to the Guildhall were actually made in London. Even if this were the case it would not apply to the decorated wares used at the Royal tables. These, and surely some still exist, would be that truly rare item, a documented example of Davenport glass.

Davenport glass is mentioned in certain documents, but not always as helpfully as one would wish. In the Account dated 14 January 1840 relating to the supply to 'A. Brook Esq.' of 'A Dinner Set for 12 persons Colored Muleteer', which Geoffrey Godden discusses on p. 166 and of which the bill-head is shown in Plate 138, glass items are also included. Apparently the showroom at 82 Fleet Street also supplied: '2 Quart Decanters, richly cut, £1 15 0 and 2 Pint ditto £1 4 0.'

The order book of Thomas Goode for 1829–30 also contained the following items noted by Geoffrey Godden some time ago:

Davenports
The Marquess of Tavistock
May 17th 1830 3 coloured ink stands (Davenports)   9/-
Mr Thomas Gibbs
Dec. 29th 1829 4 Square glass dishes (moulded) (Davenports)   £1 16 0
John Watson Walmsley
Oct 7 1828 4 Cut salt cellars (Davenports)   £1 8 0
The Prince Esterhazy
19 Dec 1829 1 White & gold bath bowl & stand (Davenports)   8/-
His Excellency Col Cockburn, Belize, Honduras
Sept 30th 1829 6 oval cut salt cellars (Davenports) 7/3 ea.   £2 3 6
           2 Quart Glass Jugs (Davenports) 31/6   £3 3 0
The Rev'd John Dalton
Nov 12th 1829 1 Pair Quart Decanters (Davenport)   £2 2 0
           2 do. Pint do. (do)   £2 16 0

Clearly, Messrs Goode were happy to supply the aristocracy and gentry with Davenport glass, which must have met their high standards.

We have already recorded on pp. 55–7 the evidence provided to the Royal Commissioner Samuel Scriven for his report on Children's Employment published in 1843. The Commissioner also visited 'Messrs W'm DAVENPORTS Glass Manufactory, Longport', and the evidence of just two witnesses was published in the Report:
No. 263. Thomas Wiltshire, *aged 12.*
I am employed by Mr. Davenport to sweep the cutting shop, run on errands, break pumice stone – nothing else. I can read and write. I went to day-school before I came to work. I go to Sunday-school now, at New Methodists. They teach me to read the Bible and that. I come to work at half-past six, sometimes a little before, and go into the hovel until the cutting-shop is open, to warm myself. I go home to breakfast at nine o'clock, and always take my half hour. I go in the other bank to dinner with my sister; she is a transferrer; father is a printer; mother is dead; another sister cuts paper; a young brother stops at neighbour Knowles's between school-times. I get plenty to eat and drink. I get holidays at wakes, and races, and at Christmas.

A simple statement which vividly recreates the life of a Longport family in 1842. Father a printer, his daughters working in the Pottery with him, the twelve-year-old son at the Glass Works, the mother dead. The whole life of the family revolved round that tiny area of land bounded by the canal and the road in front of the factories. The second testimony is given by:

No. 262. Aaron Maintford, *aged 32.*

I am the foreman of the Messrs Davenport's glass-works; have been so employed 16 years; altogether with them 24 years. We have 64 persons employed; out of this number there are not more than six children under the age of 13, and chiefly to run on errands and sweep and clean the premises; they are not occupied in any department of the manufactory; they are engaged with the view of taking them ultimately as apprentices, beginning at the age of 14. There are 11 apprentices regularly bound by stamped indenture for a period of seven years to the glass-blowing and cutting. They come (the cutters) at six in the summer, and leave at six. In the winter they come at seven in the morning, and leave at six, being 11 hours per day, deducting an hour and a half for meals. The blowers work 48 hours per week, seldom ever more, and work in sets of 16 each, for six hours together, and change every six hours, night and day, excepting Saturday nights, Sundays, and Sunday nights. There is one man employed to supply coal to the oven or furnace, who is changed every 12 hours. We are obliged to keep the furnace up on Sundays. We have no females on the premises, except three women who clean the glass after it comes from the cutting-shop. I do not believe that there is any process in glass-blowing unhealthy either to the boys or men.

A fascinating glimpse into the Glass Works and its organization. We know of no other document which gives the precise size of the Works at any period. It does not seem to be too charitable to suggest that on this evidence Davenports Glass Works was a well-run and orderly medium-sized enterprise.

Whether Maintford was the Manager of the Works is not made clear by his title 'foreman'. In 1836 the 'Manager' was a Mr Walker whose death that year at the age of 49 was reported in the *North Staffordshire Mercury* of 2 March. It is noteworthy that Maintford must have started at Davenports at the age of eight.

As has already been indicated there is very little documentary evidence for long periods. But in the light of the two statements above one can visualize the Glass Works as a smaller, more intimate, and possibly more friendly workplace than the huge Potteries of Davenports with the overall total of 1200–1500 men, women, and children. Given the nature of glass-making one could almost imagine that this was a place where craftsmanship and skill sometimes took precedence over profits. Something of this atmosphere is conveyed by a description of the manner in which the citizens of Burslem celebrated the end of the Crimean War. This lengthy description is printed in full in Ronald Brown's previously noted article. Suffice to say here, that in the grand procession *Mr William Davenport's employees carried an enormous globe with the word 'PEACE' engraved in large letters upon it. It was manufactured at the Glass Works there, measured nearly ten feet in circumference and the 'glory hole' had to be specially enlarged to admit it being finished off . . . it was preserved in Messrs Davenports showrooms until a few years ago. It was carried by twelve glass blowers who wore glass hats . . . there was also carried by two glass blowers, an enormous ship entirely made of glass . . . the object of the greatest interest was an enormous glass goblet capable of holding nine quarts . . . the goblet was both filled and emptied many times at the subsequent festivities . . .* (Pottery Gazette, 1 May 1893)

This retrospective description must be recounting an episode still fresh in the folklore of the area.

A more immediately personal occasion is noted two years later in the *Staffordshire Advertiser* (26 June 1858) which records the celebration of the Jubilee of eight men, all of whom had completed at least fifty years in the service of the Glass

Works. One veteran had served fifty-eight years, which by a simple process of subtraction would imply that he had been employed from the very first, in 1800, a truly astonishing record. A celebratory dinner was held at the Glass Works, cannons were fired and balloons let off. Some 120 folk dined, presided over by Mr Shirley. One of the elderly employees recounting tales of the bad old days spoke of his experience as an engine turner when all he received for a full week's labour was 3/-. Amongst the toasts drunk was one to the health of Mr Behrens of the Lübeck establishment, yet one more indication of the importance to Davenports of their export trade. The names of four of the worthies are recorded, Thomas Bridgens and Thomas Bloor, glass blowers, William Lear and William Mee (or Meigh), cutters.

It is perhaps worth adding at this point that Appendix 2 of Ronald Brown's article contains the names of at least three of the above in a list of workpeople compiled from the Census Returns of 1851 for Longport. Also on the list is the name of Cyrus Hill who is noted as a glass cutter. Mr Brown has researched this man, and it appears from the testimony of his descendants that he was 'the chief designer for Davenports in the period 1850–65'. Very recently Cyrus Hill's recipe notebook and certain glass and ceramic items have been presented to the Victoria and Albert Museum. These include prototypes of glassware said to have been designed specially for a state banquet given by Queen Victoria. We hope that Mr Brown will soon publish the results of his work on Cyrus Hill.

We have no means of knowing if the malaise which affected the Pottery in the period *c.*1865–80 also infected the Glass Works. This period is certainly in need of detailed research. The first direct documentary hint of difficulties so far recorded comes from the *Pottery Gazette and Glass Trade Review* in 1878. In the July issue it was announced that Davenports had suspended all their glass hands *sine die*. The September issue said that work had still not been resumed, but in October it was announced that a restart had been made in September. It will be recalled that this was a period of the gravest difficulty for Henry Davenport (see p. 63, and *Davenport Pottery & Porcelain*, pp. 25–31). Work may have resumed, but stock continued to pile up in the showrooms and warehouses. One of the many expedients tried to improve the 'cash flow' was a sale of Goods at the Canning Place showroom in Liverpool which took place over 24–30 January 1881. In all some 1200 lots were disposed of, many of course china and earthenware, but many hundreds of lots of glassware were also sold. I have a copy of the sale catalogue before me, and whereas it is certain that not all the ceramic items are of Davenport manufacture, it is not quite so clear cut with reference to the glass. If the vast majority of items for sale are of Davenport manufacture then the range is truly impressive. For the record just half a dozen lots chosen almost at random are quoted:

310. Pair table water bottles, eight frosted glass vases, butter cooler, celery case, two tazzi bases, celery glass, and pair of decanters.
853. Cruet stand, with six cut bottles, twelve coloured hyacinth glasses, and twelve puce hock glasses.
901. Twenty-four ports, twenty-four sherries, eighteen clarets, twenty-four champagnes, and twelve liqueurs, fine made glasses with hollow cut stems and Grecian key border.
977. Centre fruit tazza, two cut marmalades, with covers, sugar basin and cream jug, cheese dish, cut butter cooler, two salts, and water jug.
1198. A Noble Crystal BOHEMIAN VASE, on pedestal, pencilled in white enamelled foliage, and richly gilt, 28 inches high.
1199. A fine specimen Massively Cut Glass Cover TAZZA, of the finest quality.
1200. Parian statuette, 'STORM', shade and gilt stand.

The last three lots in the sale cannot help but remind us that Davenports were merchants who sold the wares of many makers, and thus any attempt to use this and other sale catalogues as totally reliable sources for the identification of their products is a highly tendentious undertaking. We assume that Bohemian means 'Made In Bohemia' and to the best of our present knowledge Davenport did not manufacture parian.

With this warning in mind, what glasses can be attributed to Davenport? One answer is that with absolute certainty only those marked Patent. But we do have a good knowledge of the range of their products from the information published here, from the list which Ronald Brown drew up from his analysis of the 1881 sale, and from an invoice for Monte Video which he illustrates. There seem to have been few types of table glass which were not in their repertoire and, as we have noted, at various times, mirrors, stained and painted window glass, and massive chandeliers: a very extensive range. To make any further progress in attribution with a product like glass which bears no maker's mark, we have to turn to provenance. The City Museum at Stoke-on-Trent has over the years received gifts of glass from members of the public whose forebears had worked at the Glass Works. Some of these Mr Brown illustrates. The items donated include glass of the so-called 'Nailsea' type, and bells made of ruby glass, as well as the more conventional items. The Museum was also given glass by Major J. L. Davenport, and these examples have surely the best provenance of all. Furthermore, there are still private collections in the Stoke area which contain glass handed down from former factory employees. Again Mr Brown illustrated several of these. It is only by a careful sifting and checking of the reliability of this type of provenance that one can be sure of the origin of the many specimens of unmarked glass that might just be Davenport.

Neither my fellow author Geoffrey Godden nor myself have done the necessary research on the surviving attributed glass, we thus felt unable to publish illustrations of pieces about which we had insufficient knowledge. There have been reports of a catalogue of Davenport glass, but neither of us has seen such a document. Nor, unfortunately, did Davenport register any of their glass designs which would have provided another starting point. Nevertheless, the historical facts set out in this chapter can be verified and, we very much hope, built upon. As to the wares, we have confined our illustrations to the marked Patent examples, and to giving a detailed description of some of the glass made to special and Royal order. We would not wish to leave any possible false trails by going any further in illustrating pieces at this stage.

It is also worth mentioning, though by now it should be common knowledge, that certain pressed glass pieces, such as the paper-weight modelled as a Landseer lion, Punch and Judy, Britannia, and many vases and useful glasses, carry a mark of an anchor with the initials J on one side of the shaft and D on the other. This mark has nothing to do with the glass made by John Davenport. It is the mark of John & James Derbyshire of Manchester. (Full details and illustrations of Derbyshire's glass may be found in the specialist books on English Press-Moulded Glass by C. R. Lattimore and Raymond Slack).

The formation of Davenports Limited in 1881 temporarily arrested the decline of the firm. In 1887 as already noted (p. 67) the factory premises were sold. The advertisements for the glass works have no revealing lists of wares as did the Pottery. The notice in the *Staffordshire Advertiser* of 26 November 1887 was brief and to the point:
DAVENPORTS (Limited) – Highly Important and Unreserved SALE – GLASS WORKS, LONGPORT, BURSLEM.
Mr HENRY STEELE has been instructed to SELL by AUCTION, at the GLASS WORKS as above, On Monday and TUESDAY, November 28 and 29 (and Following Day, if necessary) the whole of the Valuable WORKING PLANT of GLASS-CUTTERS' MACHINERY, Valuable GLASS-MAKERS MOULDS, LATHES, MATERIALS, ENGINE, BOILER, SHAFTING, &c. particulars of which are contained in Catalogues, which can be obtained (Price 2d each, to admit two Persons) at the Offices of the AUCTIONEER, Queen's Chambers, Burslem. Sale Each Day at One o'Clock. The Glass Works are situate within Five Minutes' Walk of the Longport Station on the North Staffordshire Railway.

And so a once-great concern whose life spanned the reigns of four Sovereigns and whose glass had graced the tables of Monarchs and Princes, was finally broken up and sold without reserve or compunction.

Appendix: The Registered Shapes and Patterns 1849–1886

Compared with other leading manufacturers the Davenport firm registered very few of their shapes or added designs, a mere thirty basic entries spread over more than thirty years. Yet, as many registrations related to standard shapes, this number can be multiplied by many hundreds as the same shape might be decorated with one of the very many then fashionable patterns, ranging from the cheapest style, without gilding, to the most ornate and costly designs. This is particularly true of the porcelain teaware forms bearing the device for 20 January 1849.

Without exception, the registered shapes relate to useful wares, tea service shapes (Plate 226), a few dessert service forms (as Colour Plate XXV and Plate 282), rather more dinner service forms, and a variety of toilet service shapes – the bedroom sets were quite comprehensive and formed a very important part of any pottery's output before piped hot water became almost universally available. A middle-class home might have only one tea or dinner service, but every bedroom would need its toilet wares (see Plates 171 and 176), if only the basic jug and basin and the chamber-pot. Most of these Davenport registrations relate to earthenware rather than to porcelain objects.

The shapes or added printed designs which were officially registered at the Design Registry Office in London under the Design Copyright Act 5 & 6 Victoria c. 100 bore a diamond-shape device with various letters or numerals in the inner angles. This system applied within the period 1843–83. The arrangement of such coding was unique to each entry in the Design Registry files and from these numerals and letters the day, month, and year of the original entry can be ascertained. The registration, in effect a form of copyright, lasted for three years.

The key for decoding the system, or rather systems as the arrangement was amended in 1868, is here explained in Table form. By reference to this, you can discover the date of the entry and the 'parcel number' or entry number for that one day. There would have been a slight delay, a week or so, before the allotted mark was received back at the factory and worked into the moulds or engraved copper plates for the design or for the new special marks, but always remember that the date of registration is only the earliest possible date of manufacture and not an exact date of production.

The Davenport registration entries are here listed together with the various trade styles used at that period. The number added after the year is the parcel number, a useful help in checking the accuracy of your decoding, especially when the mark is indistinct. The original files are preserved at the Public Record Office at Kew under the references BT 43 for the 'Representations' or drawings etc. and BT 44 for the 'Registers' containing the dates and the makers' names.

Table of Registration Marks 1843–1883

Above are the two patterns of Design Registration Marks that were in current use between the years 1842 and 1883. Keys to 'year' and 'month' code-letters are given below. The left-hand diamond was used 1842–67, the right-hand 1868–83.

Year and Month Letters

1842–67
Year Letter at Top

A	=	1845	N =	1864
B	=	1858	O =	1862
C	=	1844	P =	1851
D	=	1852	Q =	1866
E	=	1855	R =	1861
F	=	1847	S =	1849
G	=	1863	T =	1867
H	=	1843	U =	1848
I	=	1846	V =	1850
J	=	1854	W =	1865
K	=	1857	X =	1842
L	=	1856	Y =	1853
M	=	1859	Z =	1860

1868–83
Year Letter at Right

A	=	1871	L =	1882
C	=	1870	P =	1877
D	=	1878	S =	1875
E	=	1881	U =	1874
F	=	1873	V =	1876
H	=	1869	W =	(Mar. 1–6) 1878
I	=	1872	X =	1868
J	=	1880	Y =	1879
K	=	1883		

Months (both periods)
A = December
B = October
C or O = January
D = September
E = May
G = February
H = April
I = July
K = November (and December 1860)
M = June
R = August (and September 1–19 1857)
W = March

Davenport Registered Shapes and Patterns 1849–1886

W. Davenport & Co.	20 January 1849	2	Moulded teaware shapes (see Plate 226) This is the first registration in Davenport's name, the 1845 date given against Plate 801 in *An Anthology of British Cups* seems to be an error.
	3 January 1850	1	Designs for dinner ware forms.
Davenport & Co	23 October 1852	4	Design for dinner ware forms (see Plate 326).
Davenports & Co.	14 January 1853	3	Printed designs 'Niagara'.
	18 January 1853	2	Design for toilet and teaware shapes – 'Plain French'.
	6 October 1854	4	Moulded tea and breakfast ware forms – 'Cambridge' shape.
	11 March 1856	1	Moulded dessert ware forms (see Plate 327).
	14 November 1856	9	Moulded designs for dinner wares – 'Union' shapes.
	27 November 1856	3	Moulded teaware and toilet ware forms.
	3 February 1859	2	Moulded teaware forms.
	3 February 1859	2	Moulded ewer and basin forms.
	28 October 1859	1	Moulded dinner ware forms.
	12 April 1861	3	Moulded tea, dinner and toilet ware forms, 'Erie' shapes.
	9 October 1868	5	Tea, dinner and toilet ware forms, 'Parisian' shapes.
	27 May 1869	8	Tea, dinner and toilet ware forms, grape vine motifs.
	10 January 1874	15	Two forms of menu tablets for table use.
	21 November 1877	8	Jug and ewer forms.
William Davenport & Co.	13 March 1879	1	Toilet ware forms, 'Berlin' shape.
	13 March 1879	1	Dinner ware forms, 'Empress'.
	13 March 1879	1	Dinner ware forms, 'Regina'.
	13 March 1879	1	Toilet ware forms, 'Cyprus'.
	14 August 1880	12	Toilet ware forms, 'Regent' shape.
Davenports Ltd.	30 September 1881	3	Toilet ware forms, 'Grecian' shape.
	8 May 1882	18	Tureen form and toilet ware shapes.
	9 January 1883	11	Dinner ware forms, 'Clifton' shape.
	20 February 1883	13	Printed design, 'Delaware'.
	19 July 1883	4	Toilet ware forms, 'Antique' shape.
	2 August 1883	3	Toilet ware forms.
	1 November 1883	27	Toilet ware forms, 'Hanley' shape.

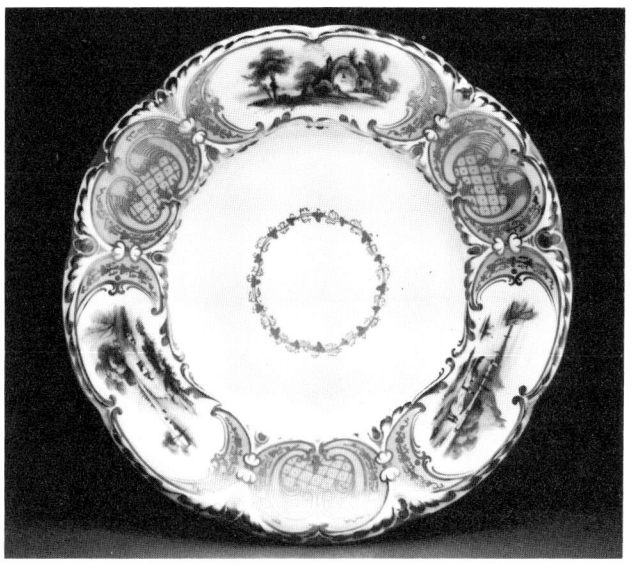

326. A marked 'Davenport & Co.' earthenware or 'Ironstone' plate of a form registered on 23 October 1852. Diameter 7in. Pattern 'Canton', potting numerals for 1860 by anchor device. (Geoffrey Godden, chinaman)

327. A moulded-edged Davenport porcelain plate of a form registered on 11 March 1856. Diameter 9½in. c.1856–9. (Victoria & Albert Museum)

328. A later Davenport Ltd earthenware dinner plate printed with the 'Mersey' design, a strange mixture of Oriental and Lancashire motifs, registered on 29 March 1884. Diameter 10¼in. Impressed Wm Davenport & Co. mark with date of potting 3.82. Special Davenport Ltd printed mark as reproduced on p. 75, c.1884–7. (Victoria & Albert Museum)

From 1 January 1884, the system of marking registered designs was changed. The old (1842–83) diamond-shaped device was discontinued and each entry was given a simple number commencing at 1. On the objects such reference numbers were usually prefixed 'R^D No' as an abbreviation for Registered Number. A few Davenport entries occur under the following references:

4310	29 March 1884	Jug form.
4311	29 March 1884	Tureen form.
4312	29 March 1884	Printed design, 'Mersey' (see Plate 328)
24402	23 March 1885	Tea urn.
30422	25 July 1885	Covered dish shape.
34191	22 September 1885	Toilet ewer shape.
46849	9 April 1886	Printed design.
56252	15 September 1886	Printed design for earthenwares.

Further information on the Design Registration systems as used in the British Isles is given in *Staffordshire Porcelain*, Appendix III. The Stoke-on-Trent City Museum at Hanley contains a good selection of ceramics of registered forms or bearing registered printed designs.

Sources and Bibliography

Unpublished Sources

There are four main collections of primary source material from which we have drawn heavily throughout the book. These are:

1. *The Foxley Papers*
These were deposited in the Hereford County Record Office by the late Major J. L. Davenport of Mansel Lacy. There are two basic collections. The first is titled 'Pottery Correspondence' and has a general reference number B 47 followed by the number of the relevant letter. Throughout the book we have used only the letter number for items from this file. Extensive quotations were made from these letters in Terence Lockett's book, *Davenport Pottery & Porcelain 1794–1887*. Some have been reproduced again where we felt that this was warranted, others have been omitted or briefly summarized. The period covered is 1812–35.

There are many other papers in this archive which relate to more general family and financial matters. These have been studied and used for the first time in this book. They carry different reference numbers which have been quoted in full. These cover the entire nineteenth century and beyond.

2. *The Rigby, Rowley and Cooper Papers*
The records of this firm of solicitors of Newcastle under Lyme deposited in the Staffordshire County Record Office (Stafford), contain a considerable number of legal papers, such as details of mortgages, title deeds, marriage settlements, and trusteeships relating to various members of the Davenport family. They are classified under a basic grouping D3272/1/4 with additional numbers for individual items. These papers could well repay further study by anyone who wished to compile a full business or family history of the Davenports. They cover the entire period of the factory's life.

3. *The Wedgwood Papers*
Housed at the University of Keele, these contain a small section of letters between Josiah Wedgwood II and John Davenport in the period *c.*1797–1817 (Ref. Nos 12805–75 to 12821–75).

4. *The Wood Papers*
A large collection of letters deposited in the City Museum, Stoke-on-Trent. They cover the period 1875–87 and were quoted extensively in the 1972 book, but less so here to avoid unnecessary repetition.

The other major primary sources used have been the files of the *Staffordshire Advertiser* and the *Pottery Gazette*. Specific references have been made to these publications throughout the text. We have also quoted from the *London Gazette* and a number of other primary sources such as the Fire Insurance records which are all individually noted when they occur.

Early Historical Works

A number of early books have been particularly helpful in the historical section:
Jewitt, Llewellynn, *The Ceramic Art of Great Britain* (2 Vols, Virtue, 1878)

Shaw, C. (An Old Potter), *When I Was a Child* (1903; Caliban, 1969)
Sleigh, J., *A History of the Ancient Parish of Leek in Staffordshire* (1883)
Ward, John, *A History of the Borough of Stoke-upon-Trent* (1843; 1969; Wibberley, Hanley reprint, 1984)

Articles since 1972

Brown, Ronald B., 'The Davenports and their Glass 1801–1887', *Journal of the Glass Association* 1, 1985

Godden, G. A., 'Davenport: There's None That Can Compare', *Collectors Guide*, February, 1975

Gray, Cherry (ed.), *Catalogue of an Exhibition of Davenport Pottery and Porcelain* (Blackburn Recreation Department, 1978)

Lockett, T. A., 'John Davenport and his Wares', *Transactions of the English Ceramic Circle* 9 Pt 1, 1973

Lockett, T. A., 'Early Davenport Porcelain – A Note of Revision', *Journal of the Northern Ceramic Society* 3, 1979

Lockett, T. A., 'Davenport Porcelain', in G. A. Godden (ed.), *Staffordshire Porcelain* (Granada, 1983)

Lockett, T. A., 'Early Davenport Wares – Recent Discoveries', *Transactions of the English Ceramic Circle* 12 Pt 2, 1985

Lockett, T. A., 'Early Davenport – Discoveries and Difficulties', *The Ceramics Index* 2 No. 1, January 1988

General Bibliography

In this list we have only included those books which are referred to a number of times in the text, or which have a reasonable amount of accurate text or illustrations of Davenport wares. Where we have made just the occasional or single reference to another book or article, this is printed in full at the appropriate point in the text.

Adams, P. L. W., *John Henry Clive* (Newcastle, 1947)
Bemrose, G. V., *Nineteenth Century English Pottery and Porcelain* (Faber, 1952)
Berthoud, M., *An Anthology of British Cups* (Micawber, 1982)
Burchill, F. and Ross, R., *A History of the Potters' Union* (Ceramic & Allied Trades Union, Hanley, 1977)
Camehl, A. W., *The Blue-China Book* (1916, Dover reprint, ed. G. A. Godden, 1971)
Collard, E., *Nineteenth Century Pottery and Porcelain in Canada* (McGill, 1976)
Collard, E., *The Potters' View of Canada* (McGill-Queen's Univ. Press, 1983)
Coysh, A. W., *Blue and White Transfer Ware 1780–1840* (David & Charles, 1970)
Coysh, A. W., *Blue Printed Earthenware 1800–1850* (David & Charles, 1980)
Coysh, A. W. and Henrywood, R. K., *The Dictionary of Blue and White Printed Pottery 1780–1880* (Antique Collectors' Club, 1982)
Crellin, J. K., *Medical Ceramics in the Wellcome Institute* (Wellcome Institute, 1969)
Cushion, J. P., *Pottery and Porcelain Tablewares* (Studio Vista, 1976)
Evans, W., *The Art and History of the Potting Business* (1846, reprinted in *Journal of Ceramic History* 3, 1970)
Godden, G. A., *British Porcelain. An Illustrated Guide* (Barrie & Jenkins, rev. edn, 1986)
Godden, G. A., *British Pottery. An Illustrated Guide* (Barrie & Jenkins, 1974)
Godden, G. A., *An Illustrated Encyclopaedia of British Pottery and Porcelain* (Barrie & Jenkins, 1980)
Godden, G. A., *An Illustrated Encyclopaedia of British Pottery and Porcelain Marks* (Barrie & Jenkins, reprint 1986)

Godden, G. A., *Encyclopaedia of British Porcelain Manufacturers* (Barrie & Jenkins, 1988)

Godden, G. A., *Godden's Guide to Mason's China and The Ironstone Wares* (Antique Collectors' Club, 1980)

Halfpenny, P. A. and Lockett, T. A. (eds), *Staffordshire Porcelain 1740–1851* (Catalogue of the Third Exhibition from the Northern Ceramic Society, City Museum, Stoke-on-Trent, 1979)

Haggar, R. G., *The Masons of Lane Delph* (G. L. Ashworth & Bros Ltd, 1952)

Larsen, E. B., *American Historical Views on Staffordshire China* (3rd edn, Dover reprint 1975)

Little, W. L., *Staffordshire Blue* (Batsford, 1969 and 1987)

Lockett, T. A., *Davenport Pottery & Porcelain 1794–1887* (David & Charles, 1972)

Lockett, T. A. and Halfpenny P. A. (eds), *Stonewares & Stone Chinas of Northern England to 1851* (Catalogue of the Fourth Exhibition from the Northern Ceramic Society, City Museum, Stoke-on-Trent, 1982)

Lockett, T. A. and Halfpenny P. A. (eds), *Creamware & Pearlware* (Catalogue of the Fifth Exhibition from the Northern Ceramic Society, City Museum, Stoke-on-Trent, 1986)

May, J., *Victoria Remembered. A Royal History 1817–1861, entirely illustrated with commemoratives* (Heinemann, 1983)

Milbourn, M. and E., *Understanding Miniature British Pottery and Porcelain 1730-Present Day* (Antique Collectors' Club, 1983)

Miller, P. and Berthoud M., *An Anthology of British Teapots* (Micawber, 1985)

Owen, H., *The Staffordshire Potter* (1901, Kingsmead reprint 1970)

Scarrett, W., *Old Times in the Potteries* (1906, reprint 1969)

Schuler, V., *British Toby Jugs* (Kevin Francis, 1986)

Shaw, S., *A History of the Staffordshire Potteries* (1829, reprint 1970)

Thomas, J., *The Rise of the Staffordshire Potteries* (Adams & Dart, 1971)

Thornhills, G., *John Davenport the Politician* (Unpublished dissertation in the Library of the University of Keele, 1984)

Victoria County History of Staffordshire (M. W. Greenlade *et al.*) II and VIII (University of London, 1967, 1963: relevant sections reprinted by Staffordshire County Library, 1981, 1983)

Warburton, W. H., *A History of Trade Union Organisation in the North Staffordshire Potteries* (Allen & Unwin, 1931)

Wedgwood, J. C., *Staffordshire Pottery and its History* (Sampson Low, 1913)

Index

This is a working index. We have not included references to current collectors, auction houses, Museums, Societies, authors or publications in the index. These are fully recorded with the objects or in the appropriate bibliographies. The index concentrates upon potters, places, and types of wares. Pattern names are dealt with alphabetically in the appropriate sections. Numbers always refer to pages.

Ablott, R., 272–3
Absolon (of Yarmouth), 89
Ackerman prints, 93–4
Adams, William, 16
Adolphus Frederick, Prince, 271
Aesthetic Movement, 195–6
Alcock, Joseph, 61
Alcock, S. & Co., 228
Allen, Robert (of Lowestoft), 96
Amsterdam, 48
Analysis of porcelain, 205–8
Arnoux, Leon, 58, 197
Artists and their work, 87–9, 272–9
Austin, Jesse, 170–2, 273

Baskets, porcelain, 260–1
Bat printing, 126, 128
Baxter, Thomas, 206, 270
Beardmore & Co, 197
Behrens (of Lübeck), 290
Bennett, Luke, 51
Bent, Sir John, 19, 59
Billingsley, William, 219
Binns, C. F. (*The Story of the Potter*, 1898) for printing processes, 126–8
Black basalt, 17, 97–100
Black-ground wares, 182–3
Bloor, Thomas, 290
Blue printed wares, 29–30, 39, 48–9, 134–5. For pattern list 1794–c.1845, 136–165. See also Transfer printed wares for further entries
Bourne, Edward, 52
Boyle, Messrs, 174
Brameld, Thomas, 92
Brameld wares, 179–80. See also Rockingham Pottery
Bridgens, Thomas, 290
Bridgewater, Duke of, Inn, 51–2, 63
Brighton Pavilion, 284
Brindley, James, 11
Brindley, John, 11–12
Bristol porcelain, 207
Brook(s), A., 223, 288
Brooke(s), W., 197, 273
Brussels warehouse, 24, 37
Buckingham Palace, 44, 284
Bulb pots, 83–5, 93, 105–6, 113, 138, 263, 267–8
Burslem Town Hall, 228

Cabinet cups, 261
Cabinet plates, 270–1
Caldwell, James, 26–7
Canada, trade with, 37–9
Canals (Trent & Mersey, etc.), 51, 61. See also John Davenport, property purchases
Caneware and terra-cotta, 101–9, 189, 204
Canning Place, see Liverpool
Capey, R., 273–4
Carlton House, 284
Castleford wares, 110, 113, 138
Caudle cups, 261
Caughley porcelain, 274
Ceylon, trade with, 187–8
Chadwick, David, MP, 63–4
Chalcedony coloured wares, 92–6, 140, 204
Chalk body wares, 179–80
Charlotte, Princess, 270

Chesters, S., 274
Child & Co. (Edinburgh), 114–7
Childrens' Employment, Parliamentary Papers, 55–7
Childrens' wares, see Miniature wares
China-glaze wares, 76–91
Clarence, Duke of, see William IV
Clarke, Edward, 53
Clews, M., 56
Cliff Bank Pottery, Stoke, 16
Cliff, Clarice, 17
Clive, John Henry, 44
Clowes, William, 274
Coalbrookdale style, 269–70, 272–3, 275–6
Coalport porcelain (and John Rose & Co.), 204, 206–7, 221, 239–42, 245, 247, 256, 267, 269–70
Coloured-body earthenware, 92–6, 183–4. See also Chalcedony
Commemorative wares, 186–7, 262
Cooper, S. Herbert, 63–7; (papers) 296
Comolera, Paul, 197
Copeland & Garrett and Copelands, 53, 58, 156, 225
Copeland, W.T. and Copeland wares, 44, 58, 188, 228, 249
Creamware, 79–91, 188
Crimean War, celebration of peace (Glass Works), 289; (diary of) 20
Cristall, Joshua, 274
Cutts, James, 274

Daniel porcelain, 221, 242, 245
Daniel, Walter, Sen. & Jun. (Newport factory), 17, 46
Dashwood, Alfred H., 65, 67
Davenport, Charlotte Lucy, 20, 50
Davenport, Christopher (Liverpool), 31
Davenport, Maj. David J. C., 19–20
Davenport, Diana Eliza, 20, 50
Davenport, Diana Elizabeth, 22, 65
Davenport, Diana S. (née Diana Smart Ward, Mrs John Davenport), 14, 19, 26, 35, 62
Davenport, Elizabeth, 10, 19, 46, 59
Davenport, Revd G. H., 19, 65
Davenport, Hannah, 46
Davenport, Harry T., MP, 20, 65
Davenport, Henry (son of John), 18, 20–2, 28, 32–4, 36–8, 42–3, 45, 48–9, 51–2, 57, 134, 179, 272, 286–7
Davenport, Henry (son of William), 21–2, 60–70, 290
Davenport, James, Sen., 14–15, 18, 23–4, 31–3, 35, 42, 284–5
Davenport, James Jun., 24, 32, 35–7, 286
Davenport, John, 10–53, 57, 60–1, 69, 76, 134–5, 259; (character) 48–50; (wares) see separate types of ware; (glass) 281–8; (property purchases) 16, 45–6
Davenport, John II, 19–21, 24, 35, 59
Davenport, John Coltman, 20
Davenport, Maj. John L., 19, 291, 296
Davenport, Jonathon, 10, 46
Davenport, Joseph, 20, 24, 35–6
Davenport, Marianne, 21
Davenport, Marianne Henrietta, 22, 65
Davenport, Mary, 21
Davenport, Mary Ward, 20, 50

Davenport, Richard, 10
Davenport, Richard (Liverpool), 31
Davenport, Sarah E., 65
Davenport, Uriah, 24–5, 32, 35–6
Davenport, William, and William Davenport & Co., 20–2, 35–6, 38, 43, 45–6, 51–65, 228, 272, 288–90
Davenport, William (Liverpool), 31
Davenports Ltd, 65–70, 210, 294–5
Davenports Patent, (Glass) 281–4, 291; (Porcelain) 270, 273–4
Demcile, John, 55
Derby porcelain, factory, and Crown Derby, 28, 191, 205, 230, 239, 272–3, 276–9
Derbyshire, John & James, 291
Dimmock, Messrs, 174
Don Pottery, 180
Donovan, James, 103, 137–8
Dover Horticultural Society, 209, 271
Downs, Alfred, 56
Drabwares, 182–3
Dresden style, 269–70
Dublin, 10

Eaton, Robert, 255, 275
Ebbetts & Gale (New York), 37
Evans, William (*Art & History of the Potting Business*), 106, 109, 174, 249
Excise duty, glass, 286–7
Exports, (general) 31–40, 59, 183, 187–8; (to Spain) 34, 37; (to Italy) 34, 37; (to Canada) 37; (to Holland and Belgium) 48; (to India) 187–8; (to USA) 37–40

Factory conditions, 54–8
Factory, sale of 193–7
Faversham Horticultural Society, 272
Felspathic stoneware, see Stoneware
Ferguson & Day (New York), 37
Figures, porcelain, 260
Fletcher, W., 275
Flown blue, 172–4, 188
Ford, Charles, 69
Foreign trade, see Exports and individual countries
Foxley estate, 19, 22
Foxley Papers, 10, 14, 19–21, 23, 28, 33, 37, 45, 50–1, 61, 285–6, 296
France, 10–11, 14
Franklin, B., 49, 159–60
Fynney, Mountford, 23–4, 32, 36, 38, 42, 286

George III, 160, 271
George IV (or Prince Regent or Prince of Wales), 16, 41, 43, 92, 200–1, 256, 263, 270–1, 282–4
Gibson & Sons, 197
Gilders, 272–9
Glass Works, and its products, 14, 16, 18, 23, 30, 46, 53, 65, 276, 281–92; (sale of) 67–70, 290–2
Good from Oven, 58
Goode, Thomas, 288
Goodwin & Harris, 141
Gould, 244, 261, 264, 272
Grafton, Edward, 15–16, 28, 281, 284
Grand Junction canal, 15–16
Great Exhibition (1851), 58–9, 227
Green-glazed wares, 180–2

Greyhound Inn, 63
Grosvenor, Earl (of Eaton Hall), 285
Guildhall Banquet (1837), 53–4, 287–8. See also Victoria

Hamburg, 20, 24–5, 35–7, 63
Hammersleys Ltd, 232
Hancock, John, 203
Hard paste, see Porcelain
Harrison, John (Stoke Works), 18
Haslem, John (*The Old Derby China Factory*), 272–3, 275–9
Heathcote, R. E., 44
Henderson & Gaines (New Orleans), 38–9
Henshall, Hugh, 51–2
Herculaneum Pottery, Liverpool, 138, 242, 263
Hereford County Record Office, 14, 19, 25
Hill, Cyrus, 290
Hicks & Meigh, 117–18
Holland, James, 275
Hughes, John, 69, 232
Hughes, Thomas, 52, 64, 69, 232
'Hyphen' painter, 87–8

India, trade with, 187–8
Inkpots and inkstands, 260
Insurance policies, 17–18, 296
Ireland, 10–11
Ironstone china, 188–9. See also Stone china
Islington China Works, 10

'Japan' patterns, 230, 260
Jardinière, 268
Jasper ware, 64
Jelly moulds
Jones, Capt. of the *Macedonian*, 160

Keele, University of, 12, 40, 45, 69, 208
Kinnersley, Thomas, 10, 16, 21, 42, 281, 284

Lakin, Thomas, 15–16, 28, 93, 281–2
Leek and Leek Parish Church, 10, 46–8
Lees, Moses, 56–8
Lessore, Emile, 210, 275
Lidstone (*The Londoniad*), 59–60
Littleton, E. J., MP, 286
Liverpool, City, and Warehouse (also Canning Place), 10–11, 18, 23, 25, 31–3, 36, 42, 61, 63–6, 188, 201, 210, 227–8, 285–6, 290
Lockett, John (Longton), 187–8
Lockett, Thomas, 51
London Gazette, 11, 17, 42, 284, 296
London and the Showroom (also 82, Fleet Street), 16, 23, 33–5, 37, 42, 53, 63, 65, 67, 124, 201, 222, 285, 287–8
Longport Hall, 22, 63
Longport House, 12, 60, 63, 67
Longport Volunteers, 14–15
Longport Wharf, 51–2
Longport Works (including sale of and Royal visit), 11, 16–17, 23, 42, 46, 49, 65–70, 193–7, 200–4, 263
Lower Bridge Works, 63
Lübeck, 35, 37, 63, 290
Lucas, Daniel, Sen., 87, 275–6
Lustre decoration, 92–3, 95, 176–9, 191, 203

Maer Hall and estate, 22, 54, 57, 64, 66
Maintford, Aaron, 289
Majolica, 58, 197
Marks, (on earthenwares and stonewares) 71–5, 85, 90–1, 94–5, 100, 120, 176, 179–80, 189, 196–7, 293–5; (on porcelain) 168, 185, 200–2, 204–5, 209–11, 219, 231, 235, 293–5
Mason, C. J., 114
Mason, George Miles, 44
Mason, Miles, and Masons wares, 114–15, 117, 119, 204, 207
Massey, Thomas, 55–6
Mawdsley, James, 30, 54
Mayer, T. J. & J., 170, 228
Meigh, Messrs, 174
Meigh, William, 57
Messina, trade with, 37
Miniature wares, 190–1
Minton works and wares, 11, 17, 27, 48, 58–9, 67, 76, 119, 134–5, 137, 157, 188, 197, 205–6, 216, 239, 267, 275, 278–9
Mist, James (and Abbot & Mist), 23, 216–17
Montreal, 160–1, 234–5
Mortlocks, 231
Mountford, Jesse, 249, 276

Nantgarw, 239
Napoleon (and Egypt), 106
Nelson, 95, 106
Newport factory, 17–18, 61
Newport House, 18, 46, 61
New Hall porcelain, 206–7, 211, 259
New York (trade with, and agencies), 33, 37, 40, 63, 66, 192

Opaque china, 188–9 (see also Stone china)
Orange body wares. See Chalcedony and Coloured-body earthenware

Painters, see Artists
Parian, 58
Pastille burners, 270
Pâte–sur–pâte, 63
Patent, (glass) 281–4; (porcelain) 270
Pattern books, 69
Pattern numbers, see Marks
Pearlware, 79–91
Peasant enamel decoration, 183
Pennington, Mrs Jane, 10
Perry, Commodore and the *Niagara*, 161
Peterloo Massacre (1819), 41
Picturesque style decoration, 88–9, 93–4
Pike, Zebulon Montgomery, 162
Pinxton porcelain, 277–8
Pitts, William, 277
Politics, (John Davenport's views) 41–2; (John Davenport's elections) 44–5, 49
Pomerania, the SS, 187
Pontigny, Henry, 20, 33–5, 42, 259, 287
Pontigny, Victor, 33–4, 38, 42, 179
Porcelain, (early wares) 17, 200–8; (hard paste) 204–8, 236–9, 256; (analysis of bodies) 205–8; (Marks) 209–11; (Teawares) 212–32; (Dessert wares) 233–55; (Dinner wares) 256–8; (Useful wares) 259–62; (Ornamental wares) 263–71

Portland vase, 83, 92–3
Pottery Gazette (& *Glass Trade Review*), 37, 41, 63, 65–7, 69, 191, 232, 284–5, 289, 290, 296
Powells of Whitefriars, 288
Pownall, William, 11
Pratt, F. & R., 170–2
Price, Uvedale, 19
Price fixing, 29
Price's teapot factory, 51–2, 281
Prince of Wales, see George IV
Prince's Square, Longport, 17
Printed patterns (and copper plates for), 39, 69, 74–5, 94, 188, 193–7. See also Transfer printed wares
Punch bowls, 118–19, 261

Railways, 49
Registered shapes and patterns, 293–5
Ridgways, 48, 58, 134, 138, 165, 174, 180, 211, 221, 247, 259
Rigby, Rowley & Cooper papers, 296
Riley, J. & R., 16
Rio de Janeiro, trade with, 37
Robinson & Randall, 277
Rockingham porcelain and factory, 43, 221, 245, 278
Rogers, J. & R., 138
Rose, John, see Coalport
Royal Orders, services etc., 41, 43–4, 53–4, 62, 92–3, 95, 106, 176, 200–4, 209, 235, 244–5, 256, 263, 276, 282
Russia, trade with, and services for the Emperor, 37, 157, 285

St Paul's Church, Longport, 20, 60
St Petersburg, 20, 35, 37
Sanderman, A. E., (*Notes on the Manufacture of Earthenware*, 1901), printing processes, 128–34
Scott, Sir Walter ('*Illustrations*'), 162–3
Scrivens, Samuel (*Children's Employment*, Royal Commission Report), 55–8, 288–9
Sèvres, 173, 197
Shapes, earthenware, 194
Shaw, Revd Charles (*An Old Potter*), 54–5, 57, 277
Shaw, Enoch, James and Richard, 277
Shaw, Simeon, 101, 122
Sherwin, James, 20
Shirley, John, 60–1, 65, 197, 290
Shirley, Joseph, 59–61
Slater, William, Sen., 277–8
Slater, William, Jun., 278
Smith, William & Co., 171
Sneddon, A. S. & Co., 197
Spode factory and wares, 11, 16–17, 26–7, 29–30, 33, 43, 76, 110, 114, 134, 138, 143, 166, 200, 205–6, 209, 242, 259, 282
Staffordshire Advertiser, 10, 16, 20, 22–3, 27, 43, 47, 57, 62, 67–8, 200, 202, 284, 287–90, 296
Staffordshire County Record Office, 25, 35, 61, 65
Staffordshire Sentinel, 60
Stained glass, 284
Steel, Thomas, 239, 245, 264–5, 278–9
Steel(e), Edwin, 278–9
Steele, Henry, 68–9, 291

Steele, Horatio, 278–9
Stone china, 114–21, 188–9, 256, 259
Stone colour, see Coloured-body earthenware or Chalcedony
Stoneware, white felspathic, 110–13, 189–90
Stourbridge, 281
Strikes and labour unrest, 54–5, 57–8
Swann E. (Globe Pottery, Tunstall), 69
Swansea, Cambrian Pottery, porcelain, 140–1, 239, 243

Tally marks (painters'), see Marks
Tax on porcelain and earthenware (1811), 26–7
Terra-cotta, 106–9, 204
Thomason, James, 28–9
Toby jugs, 184
Toft, Adolphus, 171–2
Toilet services, 192–4
Top Bridge Pottery, 20, 51, 69. See also Longport Works
Transfer printed wares, 122–75. See also Blue printed wares and Printed patterns. Blue printed pattern list (1794–c.1845) 135–65; (in sections alphabetically): (Chinoiseries) 137–40; (English Country Scenes) 140–54; (Foreign Scenes) 154–7; (Floral patterns) 157–9; (Literary and Commemorative) 159–65; (Multi-coloured printed wares) 165–72; (Flown blue) 172–5. Later printed patterns, 193–7
Trentham Park, 16
Trubshaw Cross, 12, 67
Turner, John, and *The Turners of Lane End*, 23, 101, 110, 113–15

Unicorn Bank, Longport, 11–14, 65
United States, trade with, 37–40

Vases, porcelain, 263–9
Victoria, Queen, 53, 58, 186, 224, 228, 247, 257, 287–8, 290. See also Royal Orders

Wardle, John, 187–8
Warley, Maj., 65
Warranted mark, 94, 101–2
Wedgwood, Josiah I (and his wares), 76, 97, 101, 104, 165
Wedgwood, Josiah II (and his wares), 16, 26–7, 29, 42, 44
Wedgwood, wares and papers, 11, 16–17, 41, 43, 53, 59, 61, 67, 77, 82, 103, 179–80, 200, 208, 275, 296
Wellington, Duke of, 43, 228
Wenger, A. Ltd, 69, 191, 195, 197
Westwood, 10, 18–19, 27–8, 45, 48
Whiteware, 77
When I was a Child, see Shaw, Revd Charles
William IV (and Duke of Clarence), 16, 43–4, 53, 200, 224, 244–5, 257, 282, 287
Williamson, Hugh Henshall, 21, 46, 51–3
Williamson, Robert & Co., 20, 45–6, 52
Windsor Castle, 200
Wiltshire, Thomas, 288–9
Wolfe, Thomas, 10–11, 31–2
Wood, Arthur & Sons, 13–14, 69, 281
Wood, Enoch & Sons, 165, 171
Wood, E. T. W., 21, 63–4
Wood, George, W., 65
Wood, John, 64
Wood, Mountford, 64–5
Wood papers, 61, 63–6, 296
Worcester, (Flight & Barr), 43, 266–7; (Graingers) 247; (Chamberlains) 270
Working conditions, 54–9

York, Duke of, 240